An Introduction to Systolic Algorithm Design

An Introduction to Systolic Algorithm Design

G. M. MEGSON

Lecturer in Computer Science,
University of Newcastle upon Tyne

CLARENDON PRESS · OXFORD
1992

Oxford University Press, Walton Street, Oxford OX2 6DP
Oxford New York Toronto
Delhi Bombay Calcutta Madras Karachi
Petaling Jaya Singapore Hong Kong Tokyo
Nairobi Dar es Salaam Cape Town
Melbourne Auckland
and associated companies in
Berlin Ibadan

Oxford is a trade mark of Oxford University Press

Published in the United States
by Oxford University Press, New York

A catalogue record for this book is available from the British Library

Library of Congress Cataloging in Publication Data
Megson, G. M.
An introduction to systolic algorithm design / G. M. Megson.
Includes bibliographical references and index.
1. Computer algorithms. 2. Systolic array circuits. I. Title.
QA76.9.A43M44 1992 004'.35—dc20 91-45002
ISBN 0 19 853813 8

Set by Integral Typesetting, Gorleston, Norfolk
Printed by Great Britain by
Bookcraft (Bath) Ltd
Midsomer Norton, Avon

PREFACE

This book introduces the basic principles of systolic design. It is motivated by and attempts to answer the following questions: 'What is a systolic algorithm?', 'How do I start designing a systolic array?', and 'How do I improve an existing systolic design?'. These questions are answered by distinguishing between a systolic algorithm and a systolic array, the former being constrained by basic 'axioms' of systolic design and the latter being dependent upon 'heuristics' defining the limitations of manufacturing technology. The text is based around my own experiences of designing systolic algorithms and presenting lectures to audiences with little or no background in parallel processing. I do not claim that the examples selected are exhaustive, but they can be used to build up a working set of common topologies and data flows which allow more complex examples to be developed.

Before starting to write the body of the text it was clear to me that there were two ways to present the material. The first was a mathematical and formal description of each algorithm and the corresponding array development. The second was less formal but more intuitive. One of my intentions in developing the text was to provide intuitive insight into the 'art' of designing systolic algorithms. I use the term art in the sense that it is a skill acquired through knowledge and practice which leads to that spark of innovation that allows a designer to go beyond existing theory and break new ground in a subject. Virtually all good designers exhibit this attribute; it is what separates them from the rest. My experience, which is obviously subjective, has shown that this insight is difficult to teach and is often a necessary precursor to developing the more formal aspects of the subject such as algorithm synthesis. Indeed, many people never acquire the ability. The more mathematically minded reader who baulks at the prospect of descriptions in a less than mathematically tight and rigorous way must remember that the development of any practical subject requires the establishment of technique by example and experimentation, the fleshy details of a satisfying formal specification being fitted to particular problems retrospectively. Systolic design is no exception and I have opted for the second approach, delaying a formal description of the design process until the last chapter.

Finally, the pace of publication in systolic computation, and in parallel processing in general, continues to grow. At some stage the text had to be frozen, which inevitably means that some new material has been omitted. I have sought to provide references which in turn provide good references themselves allowing the development of understanding to cascade from paper to paper. I cannot claim to have caught all the significant works and apologize for any omissions.

Readership

This text is aimed at senior undergraduates, postgraduates beginning research, and their equivalents in the computer science and electrical engineering industries. The method and style of presentation has been kept at a simple level to allow new readers to enter the subject and to provide a suitable background for more advanced studies.

About the text

There are three basic themes in the book—theory, applications, and performance. The latter two are emphasized and occupy approximately two-thirds of the text. The former is present largely as an undercurrent in the form of an intuitive design methodology and is not formalized until the last chapter. As the text progresses, a working set of examples that can be used to develop more complex designs and concepts is developed. The basic design principles are summarized at the end of each chapter and are complemented by sets of exercises which extend the work and improve on the examples. In most cases solutions to the problems can be found in the literature. Chapter 1 motivates the reader for the subsequent chapters and establishes the basic axioms and heuristics for systolic design. Chapter 2 introduces a basic design methodology which can be used to focus thoughts and ideas about design objectives. Chapters 3, 4, and 5 develop specific examples from the areas of linear algebra, table generation, and non-numerical problems. Chapters 6 and 7 discuss some of the more practical issues relating to the implementation of systolic devices and the improvement of existing designs. Chapter 8 formalizes the design process and considers the principle of systolic synthesis.

Course organization

In preparing the text, the overriding goal was a course that could be taught in a single term and which was geared towards students with at least one year of computing experience with exposure to basic algorithms and linear algebra courses. The flowchart below indicates possible course organizations based on chapters. There is no need to present all the material in a chapter, so a range of examples can be selected to suit individual tastes. The choice is whether to present the material in Chapter 8 before or after the examples, and this depends upon the ability and background of the class.

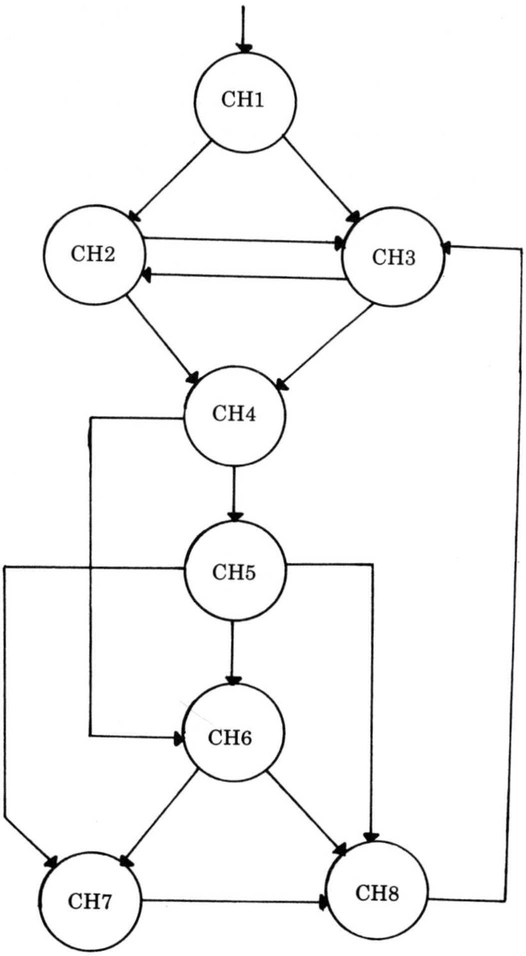
CH1
CH2
CH3
CH4
CH5
CH6
CH7
CH8

ACKNOWLEDGEMENTS

During the preparation of this book, I have read many papers and talked with many people who have influenced the work directly and indirectly. Particular people who require special mention are Rajka and Predrag Popovic, Dan McCue, and David Comish, who read drafts of the manuscript; and Professors David Evans and George Irwin, who acted as useful sounding boards for some ideas; and finally my wife Helena who, I am sure, at times thought that I would never finish the text, but remained patient throughout.

Newcastle upon Tyne
August, 1991 G.M.M.

CONTENTS

GENERAL NOTATION

$\mathscr{A}$ number of cells in a design (associated with a bound on area).

$\mathscr{T}$ total number of time steps (a single step is the cost of the most complex cell function).

e efficiency (i.e. total number of steps an average cell is active during algorithm execution).

The symbols $\gg$ and $\ll$ mean much greater and much less than, respectively.

$|\cdot|$ denotes the absolute values of the number $\cdot$, and $\|\cdot\|_p$ is the p-norm of a vector.

$i = 1(1)n$ or $i = 1, 2, 3, \ldots, n$ the value i takes values from 1 to n in steps of one.

$S = \{s_1, s_2, \ldots, s_n\}$ a set of size n with elements s_i (the order of the elements is not significant).

$P = \langle s_1, s_2, \ldots, s_n \rangle$ a sequence of length n with elements s_i where the order is significant (i.e. s_i precedes s_{i+1}).

$x = (x_1, x_2, \ldots, x_n)$ is a vector of size $n \times 1$ and x^t is the transpose of x.

$A = [a_{ij}]$ a matrix; when the matrix has n rows and m columns it is called $n \times m$. A^T is the transpose of A.

A linear combination of n vectors has the form $\alpha_1 x_1 + \alpha_2 x_2 + \cdots + \alpha_n x_n$ where the x_i are vectors and the α_i are scalars.

$f(e)$: $E \to Z$ is a mapping of elements from the set E to elements of the set Z; if e is in E then $f(e)$ is in Z.

A polynomial of degree n is a function of the form $p(x) = a_0 + a_1 x + \cdots + a_n x^n$; the values a_i are scalars (called coefficients) and $a_n \neq 0$.

$\lim_{e \to \infty} f(e)$ is the value of $f(e)$ as e tends to infinity.

A Euclidean space of dimension n is the space formed from the Cartesian product of the set of real numbers (e.g. $R \times R \times R$ is a 3-D space).

A graph is defined as $G(V, E)$ where V is a set of vertices and E is a set of ordered pairs of the form (x, y) (for vertices in V). When $(x, y) \neq (y, x)$ a directed or digraph is defined.

Note 1: Where confusion could arise upper-case letters denote matrices, lower-case letters are vectors, and Greek lower-case letters are scalars.

Note 2: Subscripts and superscripts are used to distinguish different instances of the same variable.

1
INTRODUCTION

1.1 Overview

What is systolic design? A rather taciturn reply to this question could be that it is the art of defining and manipulating systolic algorithms to achieve certain constraints. This definition is unsatisfactory for a number of reasons: it gives no indication of what systolic algorithms are, how they are defined, what constitutes manipulation, or the kind of constraints that need to be satisfied. A concise definition of a systolic algorithm (Leiserson 1981) is the combination of the concepts of pipelining, regular interconnection structures, and the rhythmic recurrent pumping of data to solve computationally intensive tasks. Unfortunately this statement is also uninformative because it assumes prior knowledge of parallel processing and does not adequately explain the meaning of the term 'systolic' in this context.

To give an intuitive feel for systolic processing let us embark on a rather fanciful, but nevertheless useful, analogy. The term systolic is in fact derived from physiology, where it is used to describe the rhythmic contraction of the heart as blood is pumped around the body. Now the body itself is composed of approximately 1000 million million cells. Cells of the same kind are grouped into tissues which have special tasks to perform. One of the many tasks of the blood is to deliver oxygen to all the body tissues. The cells need oxygen to live and use it to perform chemical reactions which produce energy and maintain bodily functions. The reactions also produce waste matter which the blood carries away from the cells to organs that dispose of it. Blood returning from tissues to the heart passes through the lungs where it exchanges carbon dioxide and waste gas accumulated from the cells for more oxygen. Full of oxygen, the blood returns to the heart and is pumped out to the tissues again. This simple description tells us everything we need to know about systolic processing. In systolic computation body cells and tissues are replaced by simple processing elements grouped into arrays which have specialized tasks (or algorithms) to perform. The circulating blood is replaced by the concept of data flow and individual blood cells carrying oxygen are replaced by discrete pieces of data. The processing elements perform simple computations on the data when it arrives and generate results. These results are passed on from processing element to processing element as data flows around the system. New data is entered and old data removed as the data flow passes through some external device (called the host) made up from a more conventional computer architecture. The emphasis is on the exploitation of parallelism on a massive scale (all the cells work simultaneously) and the cooperation of a number of simple cells (processors) to achieve a particular task. As with all analogies the reader is warned at this point not to take the correspondence too far—for one thing the use of the pumping action and data circulation in computation abstracts away the overwhelming details of physiology. In addition, we do not envisage (with current technology at least) using millions and millions of processors. However, by considering the human body to be a vast and complicated machine we can still learn a great deal from nature about building reliable and robust computer systems. We will consider this statement again in Chapter 6 when fault tolerance is discussed, but for now let us return to our definition. The task of systolic design may be defined more precisely as the investigation of the cell types required, the way they are connected, and how to circulate the data through them in order to compute the solution to specific problems.

The study of systolic algorithms encompasses four distinct areas.

1. *Recurrence relations.* These are mathematical statements describing the relationship between items of data and embodying a loose order in which calculations should be performed. For example, the relation

$$y_{k+2} = y_{k+1} + y_k \tag{1.1}$$

generates the Fibonacci numbers (when $y_1 = y_0 = 1$ and $k \geq 0$). In contrast, the recurrence

$$y_{ij} = y_{i-1,j-1} + y_{i-1,j} + y_{i,j-1} \tag{1.2}$$

for $i = 1, \ldots, n$ and $j = 1, \ldots, m$ defines a rectangle rule (the values can be interpreted as the corners of a rectangle). In (1.1) the recurrence defines a total order on the instructions, which demands that the computation proceeds by evaluating terms in the order $k = 1, 2, \ldots$, while the recurrence (1.2) defines a partial order allowing elements such as y_{42}, y_{33}, and y_{24} to be computed in parallel. Systolic design is about finding partial orderings for the computation of an algorithm so that parallelism can be exploited.

2. *Interconnection structures.* Here one looks at ways in which processors or cells might be connected (e.g. lattice or crystalline structures) so that they can evaluate partial orders of instructions efficiently and effectively. For example, communicating with your immediate (nearest) neighbours is allowed but non-local communication is avoided, because it is more practical to construct these types of arrays. Formally, a systolic algorithm can be represented by a directed graph in which the nodes of the graph represent cells and the arcs between them communication links. The direction of the arcs indicate the direction of communication, and labels can be added to show the flow of data or the contents of nodes. When the design is represented pictorially it is usually called an array.

3. *Analysis.* Once a number of systolic designs exist for the same problem it is natural to ask questions about their performance and to decide in what sense one is better than another. For example, one might ask questions like—'How many cells does design X require?', 'What is the minimum number of cells for problem Y?'. In fact we are usually interested in the area ($\mathscr{A}$, number of cells) and the time ($\mathscr{T}$, computation time) of a design. Different solutions to a problem can be graded according to the values $\mathscr{A}\mathscr{T}$ or $\mathscr{A}\mathscr{T}^2$ with the design minimizing the measure often considered the best. Historically, these metrics have their origins in mathematical models of VLSI circuits (Thompson 1979; Brent and Kung 1979). The early systolic designs were aimed at VLSI implementation and such measures seemed appropriate. Indeed, tight bounds on circuit complexity using such measures can be established for a range of problems (Savage 1981). The more recent moves towards so-called programmable systolic devices brings into question the applicability of such measures in general—however, they are quite simple and for our purposes perfectly adequate.

4. *Synthesis.* To produce algorithms we need to combine sets of recurrences with connection structures. Performing this task in a systematic way (possibly with the aid of a computer) is called synthesis. The methods of synthesis can be *ad hoc* heuristic rules based on experience, or more formally derived manipulations. Some examples include retiming (of the data flow) and space–time transformations (such as projection and array unrollings). In all cases the aim is to try to reduce the area–time trade-off of a problem until it meets some external engineering constraints or reaches a theoretical minimum. In the former case we accept the design when it becomes practically useful for the desired application, in the latter we stop because the design is in some sense optimal.

These informal definitions help to develop the basic concepts of systolic computation but do little to indicate why it is becoming increasingly popular. There are essentially two reasons for accepting the systolic approach to algorithm design: the first is pragmatic, the second more philosophical.

Consider the pragmatic problem first. In a sequential (one-processor) machine a program executes an instruction by fetching the operands (the data) from a global memory, performs the operation, and then stores the result. For long and computationally intensive tasks retrieving and storing data form a bottleneck and limit computation speed. The problem is often termed Von Neumann's bottleneck because sequential computer architectures are based on the organization of the original sequential machine built by Von Neumann. In systolic algorithms the bottleneck is avoided by reusing data and intermediate results many times while they circulate around the cells. The effect is to reduce the number of retrieve and store operations to the global memory, open up the memory bottleneck and speed up the program by using additional processors. The cost is that a completely new architecture has to be designed for each problem that we want to solve—that is, the systolic machine becomes algorithmically specialized. Now, the concept of parallelism is by no means new. Indeed parallel processing paradigms such as SIMD (Single Instruction Multiple Data), MIMD (Multiple Instruction Multiple Data), data flow, vector processing, and so on have been available for many years (Flynn 1972, Handler 1977, Feng 1972). The point is that systolic algorithms challenge an established doctrine in computer science; the idea of general-purpose computation.

Sequential computing is based on the premise that we have only a single processor; under this constraint algorithm design is largely about minimizing memory space and the number of program instructions. In contrast parallel computing allows many processors and places emphasis not only on the number of instructions, but the cost of communicating data between processors. The number of processors and how busy they are kept throughout the computation is also important. How many processors we need and how many we can keep busy determine the design efficiency, but this in turn is dependent upon the partial orders of instructions that are available for a particular problem. It follows that a general-purpose parallel machine must trade off efficiency against the flexibility of being able to compute solutions to a wide range of problems. Problems whose partial orders map onto the architecture in a natural way will be very efficient, but most problems will have to settle for some inefficiency. Of course this does not mean that the algorithms will not be fast, because it is possible for an inefficient parallel algorithm to outperform an efficient sequential version. Consequently the actual performance of the general-purpose parallel machine may be acceptable in the majority of cases. Indeed, substantial and acceptable gains in performance can often be achieved by brute-force parallelism—that is, just by adding processors without any real analysis of the problem. Where a problem does not have a natural mapping we can always force it to fit the architecture by mapping to the available connection topology and then fine-tuning the program code to improve performance.

The design of computer systems is Cartesian—separating programs and machine, and programs into algorithms and data structures is natural. On the face of it this separation is a good idea because it permits software portability (i.e. easy movement of programs from one machine to another) and allows a single architecture capable of executing all programs to be constructed (which is cost effective). In contrast systolic design is holistic (or at least non-Cartesian) in approach. It should be clear that in parallel processing the algorithm, data structure, and machine architecture are all intimately intertwined. Indeed, it is this fact that makes the design of parallel algorithms difficult. In the systolic paradigm, this fact is recognized and no attempt is made to separate algorithms from architectures. We allow the recurrence relations to determine the connection topology and cell definitions, which in turn define the machine architecture. It follows that the final design is inherently special purpose. The advantage is that the basic cells are optimized and data pipelined so that a design can be operated at much greater speeds than a general-purpose equivalent. In addition the communication between processors is an inherent feature of the design process, as is the number of cells, so the final architecture is tuned specifically to the given problem. Such properties are highly desirable when one considers so-called embedded systems where only a specific function must be computed rapidly and repeatedly. In fact we are surrounded in everyday life by simple and repetitive tasks which do not require the full computing power of general-purpose machines. An important feature of embedded systems is that they are integrated into a much larger environment which can restrict the shape and form of the input and output data for algorithms. A holistic approach to design allows the final solution to remain sensitive to these needs and hence the overall system objectives.

Finally, the choice of whether one adopts a general-purpose or special-purpose architecture is largely dependent upon circumstance. If you need flexibility, general-purpose computing would appear the best way to proceed; if your problem is restricted and repetitive perhaps a special-purpose device is better. Consequently one might dismiss systolic design as merely another design technique geared towards special-purpose machines—this would be a mistake. It is true that systolic designs are algorithmically specialized, but in a sense so are algorithms tuned for specific parallel machines. In the latter case the tuning is specific to a particular target architecture, in the former the architecture is a free parameter. It follows that a systolic algorithm is more portable than tuned code for particular machines. A systolic design provides an architecture suitable for the given recurrences. It is up to the implementor whether this architecture is physically realized in hardware or interpreted as a virtual topology (or graph) which can be mapped onto an existing (and possibly general-purpose) architecture. I am not implying here that the mapped systolic algorithm will be faster or more efficient than a finely tuned version on the same machine, simply that systolic design is a philosophy which supports parallel algorithm development in a general sense. In the past, parallel algorithm design has been largely an *ad hoc* subject. Although some automatic methods for generating parallel programs from sequential versions (most notably FORTRAN vectorizing compilers) have been devised, they have had limited success because they are geared towards specific architectures and ultimately a limited set of partial orders on instructions. The recent advances in formal manipulation methods for systolic algorithms promise a more rigorous base from which to develop general methods for manipulating and designing parallel algorithms.

1.2 The convolution problem

To illustrate the components of a systolic design outlined above we shall, in this section, consider the so-called convolution problem. As pointed out by Kung (1982*b*) this problem has a particularly simple structure which recurs in many useful applications but also results in a number of informative systolic algorithms that illustrate many features of systolic designs. The problem may be stated simply as follows: compute the recurrence

$$y_i = w_1 x_i + w_2 x_{i+1} + \cdots + w_k x_{i+k-1} \tag{1.3}$$

for $i = 1(1)n + 1 - k$ given the sequences $w_1, w_2, \ldots, w_k$ and $x_1, x_2, \ldots, x_n$, where n and k are positive integers. The w_i values are sometimes called weights. In the above paper Kung considers seven different systolic solutions to this problem and even then does not exhaust all the possibilities. We shall consider just three designs, two of which have become standard formats for this type of problem.

Figure 1.1(a) shows the first design. It consists of four cells each with two inputs and two outputs, the x values move left to right, the y values right to left, and the weights (w values) are stored one per cell. The cell definition is given below the array showing the input and output format with a statement of the calculation to be performed alongside. The diagram is actually a labelled digraph representing the interconnection structure which we call the *array*. The algorithm computation occurs in a series of *steps* or *cycles*. In a single cycle we move the output data from each cell to the cells indicated by tracing along the arcs and then perform the operation associated with the cell definitions. It is assumed that all the cells operate in parallel and a synchronous method of timing is adopted (although asynchronous methods can be used in a final implementation). To verify the array operation the reader is encouraged to trace out the data flow for several cycles by drawing a number of copies of the array with the correct data movements. You should find that the array does in fact compute the recurrence (1.3). The trace shows a series of *snapshots* which evolve the computation in space–time and graphically illustrate the partial ordering of instructions for the given recurrence. Because the w values never move in space they will be termed *stationary*, while the x and y values are *non-stationary*. By using the tracing method it is easy to show that all the y_i values of (1.3) are computed in $\mathscr{T} = 2n + k$ steps and with k weights we also require $\mathscr{A} = k$ cells. The timing can be derived directly from the array (without snapshots) as follows. We have n values for x each of which is followed by a zero to force the correct synchronization of data thus making the total input length of the x sequence $2n$. Elements are input one per cycle and the x_1 must be in the rightmost cell before computation starts (see figure) which requires an additional k steps because we have k cells. Thus $\mathscr{T} = 2n + k$ and $\mathscr{A} = k$, as

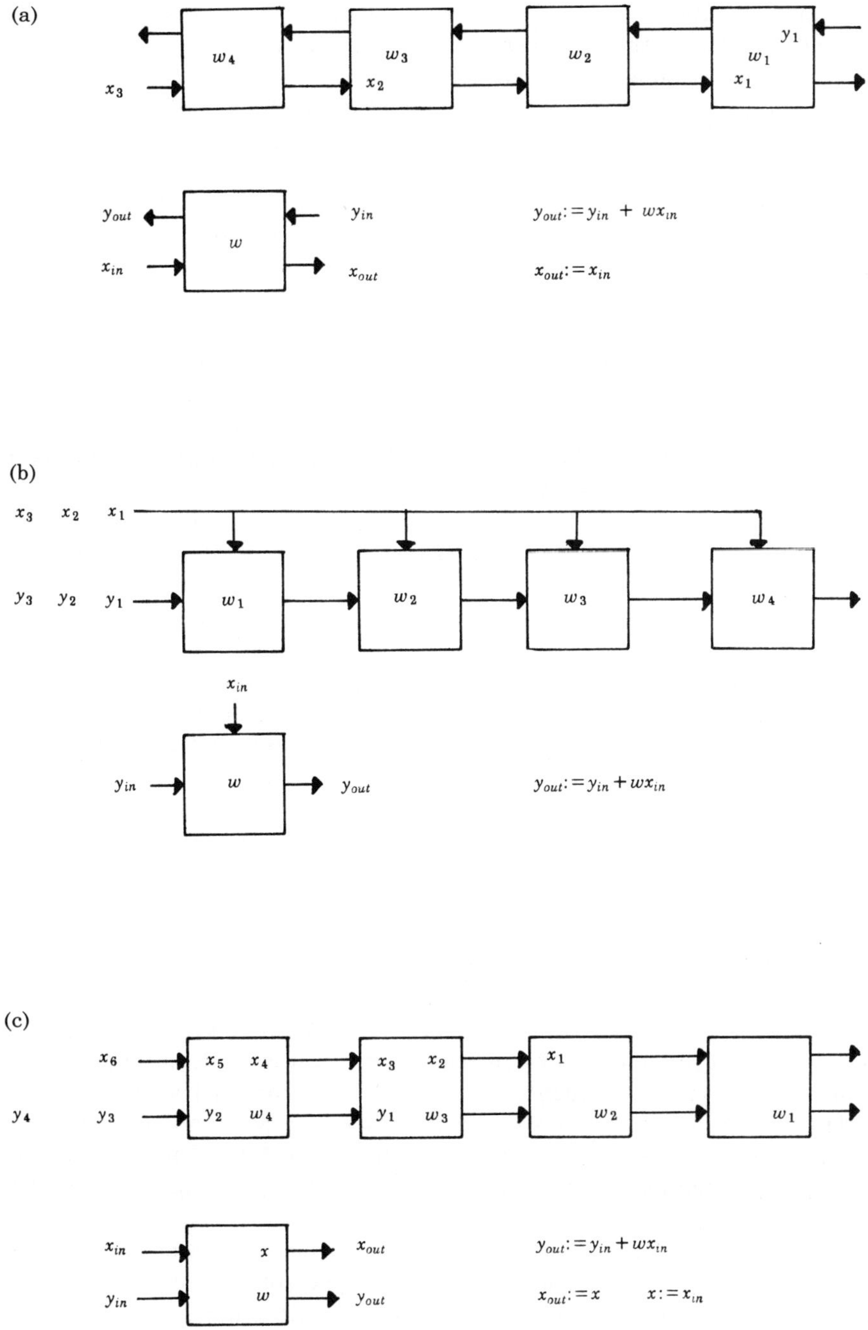

Fig. 1.1 Systolic arrays for convolution: a) bidirectional array; b) array with broadcast; c) unidirectional array

demonstrated by the trace. If you have drawn the snapshots correctly you will also find that the cells perform useful calculations only on alternate steps, so the design is 50 per cent efficient.

Next consider Fig. 1.1(b), which is another design for convolution but uses a different partial order for computing (1.3). Again the cell definition is given below the array. The x and y sequences are non-stationary with the weights stationary, but no synchronizing spaces are required. Instead the x values are *broadcast* to all the cells simultaneously—this assumes that the propagation (or communication) time of a value along the longest connection is negligible. In practice all connections have a communication time proportional to their length, but we consider this later; for the moment simply distinguish this array by calling it *semi-systolic* in comparison with the previous and the next design whose nearest-neighbour connections make them *purely systolic*. Drawing out snapshots of the new design illustrates that the y_i accumulate a single term of the recurrence (1.3) from each cell before leaving the array. We need $\mathscr{A} = k$ cells to gather k terms. The value y_1 is output after k steps (the *array latency*) and y_{n-k+1} after $\mathscr{T} = (n - k + 1) + k = n + 1$ steps. If we neglect the period when the array is filling or emptying, all the cells work on every cycle so the design is 100 per cent efficient, a fact that is reflected in the improved computation time.

Finally consider the design in Fig. 1.1(c), which is yet another solution to (1.3) with another partial order. This new array differs from the previous designs in three important ways. First, the x and y values move in the same direction—an attribute that is highly desirable in fault-tolerant designs (see Chapter 6). Second, the x and y move at different speeds, the x requiring two cycles to pass through a cell and the y only one. Third, the terms in a particular y_i are accumulated in reverse order to the previous two schemes. Again trace out the computation using a series of snapshots to test the design. You should find that the array requires $\mathscr{T} = (n - k + 1) + k = n + 1$ steps. The time follows because we have $n - k + 1$ values for y and an array latency of k cycles for k cells, consequently $\mathscr{A} = k$. Once the array is full all the cells perform computations on every cycle so the design is 100 per cent efficient.

Having seen how to map the recurrence (1.3) onto several connection topologies with different cell definitions we can now perform some simple analysis and attempt to identify the best design. Table 1.1 summarizes the area and times for the designs above and shows the $\mathscr{A}\mathscr{T}$ and $\mathscr{A}\mathscr{T}^2$ bounds, where in the latter we have retained only the major term. The efficiency has been represented as a fraction of unity, so that $e = 1$ is equivalent to 100 per cent efficiency. Using $\mathscr{A}\mathscr{T}$, $\mathscr{A}\mathscr{T}^2$, or efficiency, design 1 loses to the others which in turn appear equally good. In fact design 3 should be preferred because it is *purely* systolic not *semi*-systolic. The analysis here is superficial because it does not take into account the magnitude of the x, y, and w values nor the way they are represented or used by the cell definitions (bit serial or bit parallel). For the record, the basic computation in all the designs is

Table 1.1 Area–time trade-offs for convolution

Array	$\mathscr{A}$	$\mathscr{T}$	$\mathscr{A}\mathscr{T}$	$\mathscr{A}\mathscr{T}^2$	e
Design 1	k	$2n + k$	$2nk + k^2$	$4n^2k$	0.5
Design 2	k	$n + 1$	$nk + k$	n^2k	1
Design 3	k	$n + 1$	$nk + k$	n^2k	1

called the *inner product step* and recurs in many systolic designs involving matrix computations. One can see in this example that the inner product is an atomic action for gathering a single term of the recurrence and so offers the simplest basic cell. One would expect the definition to produce a minimal hardware requirement for implementation. We will address these issues later when bit serial versus bit parallel design is considered in Chapter 6, but for most of the examples such details will be ignored and attention will remain focused on mapping recurrences to connection structures.

1.3 A brief history

More than a decade has passed since the first systolic principles were introduced (*circa* 1978) and in hindsight a number of important events have shaped the field. For simplicity we will divide these main developments into three loose categories—*demand, practicality*, and *theory*—which illustrate the social as well as scientific motivations for a new direction in parallel computing.

The development of parallel systems in general has been motivated by difficulties encountered in implementing so-called natural problems from the real world on sequential (Von Neumann) machines. A typical example is the problem of signal and image processing which deals with the important applications of communication using mediums such as sound and vision (and their extensions outside the human range of perception, e.g. radar/sonar). Complications with implementation arise for two main reasons

1. The world is an inherently parallel environment and produces problems to solve which are parallel in nature.

2. The more accurate the mathematical model of the problem is, the more complex and computationally intensive the algorithm for solving it becomes.

The algorithms that result can be divided into two categories depending upon the amount of sequential computing time they require. In the first case we have algorithms whose execution time is an exponential function of the problem input length while in the second the computing time is a polynomial function. In the exponential case parallel processing is motivated by the fact that small increases in the problem size produce large increases in the computation time; it follows that the time for even relatively small and useful problem sizes can be enormous (i.e. greater than a human lifespan). Parallelism offers to make these previously impractical solution techniques feasible. In the polynomial case small changes to problem size normally result in small changes in the computation time and as a consequence reasonably sized problems can be solved in an acceptable time limit. Parallelism has two roles in this case. First we will often want to solve a series of problem instances in succession (e.g. simulating some process over a number of time steps) so the motivation is to accelerate a solution of a single problem and thus reduce the time for a sequence of solutions to a reasonable limit. What constitutes a reasonable time depends upon the application. For example, we might want a solution to a problem within a fixed (or hard) time constraint. This leads to the second role of parallelism in achieving real-time computation speeds. The concept of systolic computation evolved to produce practical and low-cost parallel processing for the latter problem but as time has progressed its sphere of influence has widened to encompass the other areas mentioned above.

In the early days the driving force behind systolic processing was the idea of using VLSI (Very Large Scale Integration) for computationally intensive tasks (such as signal processing). Indeed it was the major focus of attention in governmental, industrial, and university research establishments as a means of bridging the gap between theory, algorithms, and their implementations. The constantly increasing demands for high-performance real-time signal processing illustrated the need for vast computation capabilities in terms of both volumes of data and computation speed (S. Y. Kung 1984). Fast, low-cost, high-density VLSI devices promised practical cost-effective, high-speed parallel processing for large volumes of data in applications which demanded real-time operations. Fortunately these algorithms relied upon the solution of linear equations, and as Leiserson (1981) demonstrates such computations are well suited to systolic arrays. The insight of H. T. Kung was to realize that the rapidly developing silicon chip industry coupled with automata theory could satisfy this demand. Until the development of VLSI techniques the construction of parallel computers with large numbers of processors had been limited by the prohibitively high costs of manufacture. Existing machines had been improved by tinkering with the traditional Von Neumann architecture, for instance by cycle stealing, direct memory access (DMA), and pipelining of the fetch and execute operations in instructions. Parallel machines were left mainly as special one-off productions primarily of research interest. The development of new manufacturing techniques for the fabrication of small, dense, and inexpensive semi-conductor chips created a revolution in the computer industry. With the use of VLSI for circuit manufacture the size and cost of processing elements and memory was reduced, and it became feasible to combine the principles of automata theory with the pipeline ideas of the traditional architectures. The combination was especially attractive because the cost of device manufacture remained constant relative to the circuit complexity.

Now, VLSI technology combines circuit design with high-resolution photographic techniques (Mead and Conway 1979), where it is convenient to place wires on rectangular grids and limit the layers of semiconductor material containing wires and circuit elements to a small number. The task of mapping an interconnection structure onto a chip is simplified if the starting graph representing the network is planar. A circuit is also easier to manufacture if it is modular, that is composed of many replicable components (like cells), because only a few cells must be designed. However, implementation problems still arise when the size of wires and transistors approaches the limits of photographic resolution because it becomes impossible to achieve further miniaturization and the actual circuit area becomes a key issue. In addition the chip area is limited in order to maintain high chip yields (and hence cost effectiveness) which in turn limits the number of connections to the outside world (pins) due to the limited (or finite) chip perimeter. We conclude that a highly restrictive set of constraints is imposed on systolic algorithms. These restrictions form the basis of the systolic design paradigm and limit the large number of possible algorithms to a select few for implementation. We shall list some of these constraints as design heuristics in the next section. For now the interested reader is referred to material on VLSI models and area considerations which can be found in Savage (1981), Ullman (1984), and Kung (1982*a*). Very few systolic designs have been implemented in silicon. The first attempts were the pattern matcher of Foster and Kung (1980), and the 2-D convolution chip (Kung and Song 1982), the pipelined lattice processor (PLP) (Kung and Hu 1983) for the solution of Toeplitz systems, and the more general programmable systolic chip (PSC) (Fisher *et al.* 1983). Commercial companies have taken up the challenge only recently with NCR's geometric arithmetic parallel processor (GAPP), a 6×12 arrangement of single-bit processing cells (each with ALU), and Marconi's SOS systolic array (a CMOS radiation hard bit slice correlator) with applications in radar/sonar, beam forming, finite impulse response (FIR) filtering, and medical electronics. Working designs are limited because of additional problems associated with the limits of photographic resolution, for example difficulties arise such as heat dispersion when the chip is densely packed with components, and mistiming due to propagation delays down wires (particularly as chip feature size diminishes). Systolic arrays themselves reduce the effectiveness of cheap implementation because they are only applicable to a narrow set of problems. Consequently design costs cannot be spread over large numbers of devices (Fisher 1984). Often effective parallelism is only available by expanding the host array interface demanding a high number of pins. Pin count can be controlled to some extent by serializing some computation (see McCanny and McWhirter 1982*a*, *b*, 1983 and references therein, and Chapter 6).

Because of implementation problems the development of the systolic paradigm has witnessed a growing gap between abstract specifications of algorithms and their implementation. For this reason emphasis has recently shifted towards theory and programmability. The theoretical aspects of systolic design can be traced back to the cellular automata of Von Neumann, the Mealy machine (G. F. Mealy 1955), and the Moore machine (Moore 1956). Independently the recent work of Legendi and his associates (e.g. Legendi and Katona 1988; Katona 1982; Umeo *et al.* 1982) has produced the related concept of cellular automatons or arrays. Indeed automata theory itself has been applied to the design of electrical circuits with digital (discrete) hardware, the logic of the nervous systems in man and animals, and the underlying logic of protein synthesis in human cells. The breakthrough in design has resulted from work on mapping recurrence relations directly into space–time where the work of Quinton (1984), Cappello and Steiglitz (1984), Moldovan and Fortes (1986), Li and Wah (1985), and Miranker and Winkler (1984) has been most influential. The essential concept of this approach is to represent the algorithm as a graph structure in space–time, perform geometrical transformations on this graph, and then derive interconnection structures by projections onto the space dimensions. A number of designs (including the convolution problem) have been analysed using these techniques for linear and affine transformations. Current work is aimed at extending the method to non-linear transformations of space–time. Work has also progressed on the formal verification of systolic algorithms. Given an array structure and appropriate inputs and outputs we attempt to prove that the array transforms the inputs to the correct outputs. A number of approaches are possible, two notable ones being Melhem and Rheinboldt (1984) and Chandy and Misra (1986). In the former a set of difference equations is used to represent the array topology—solving the equations verifies the algorithm. In the latter a systolic algorithm is written as a program and the standard approach to verifying programs using invariant arguments is adopted. Another approach which is gaining popularity is to simulate the design using an appropriate parallel language—the correctness is tested for particular problem instances but is not verified in a general sense. Finally some remarks about programmability. The wealth of designs for different applications has illustrated that a number of simple interconnection structures occur repeatedly. This is the same as saying that certain problems map onto generic recurrence formulations for which standard interconnection structures have been developed. The only difference between one design and another is the operations applied to data by cells. For example, the convolution designs can be used as templates for matrix–vector multiplication, polynomial multiplication, and pattern matching problems.

In the latter case we can interpret multiplication as comparison and addition as logical AND (Kung 1982*b*). In a mathematical sense the recurrences represent similar problems in different semi-rings. This feature has been used to create so-called generic arrays which allow a control program in each cell to select the appropriate operations given simple control information (or tags) circulated with the data. Clearly the processing elements used for cells must be more complex and less special purpose than dedicated arrays. The principle is readily extended to the idea of programmable systolic arrays geared towards economic general-purpose processing elements which are entering the market place (e.g. the Inmos transputer™). Designs and implementations using this 'soft-systolic' approach are a subject of current research.

1.4 Applications and axioms

Systolic principles have been applied to a variety of subject areas, some of which are listed in Table 1.2. Many of these designs have contributed to the classification and establishment of rules for systolic design. For example, it was quickly found that the systolic approach generally works well for so-called *compute-bound* problems, but is less effective for *I/O-bound* problems. A problem is compute bound when it requires more sequential computations

Table 1.2 Application of systolic arrays

Signal processing	Signal processor for recursive filtering, implementation of Kalman filters, discrete Fourier transform (DFT), convolution (multi-dimensional), linear algebra machines in digital processing
Numerical problems	Finite element analysis, singular value decomposition, linear time solution of Toeplitz systems, orthogonal equivalence transformations, least-squares (adaptive beam beam forming), eigenvalues and generalized inverses, (symmetric matrices), iterative algorithms
Shapes and patterns	Pattern matching, feature extraction and pattern classification, stereo matching, algorithms for rectilinear polygons
Words and relations	Largest common subsequence problem, dictionary machines, relational database operations, connected work recognition
Automata	Tree acceptors, trellis automata, binary tree automata, design rule checker
General	Shortest path problem, algebraic path problem (including matrix inverse), fundamental sorting problems, linear time greatest common divisor (GCD) computation, priority queues

than sequential input and outputs of data, otherwise it is I/O bound. For instance, the recurrence in (1.3) requires k multiplications and $k-1$ additions per y_i and there are $n-k+1$ values for y, n possible x and k values for the w. It follows that we require $O(nk)$ sequential arithmetic operations and $O(n)$ inputs–outputs of data. Clearly as k increases the number of arithmetic operations dominate the total cost of the computation. If the situation had been reversed with $O(n)$ arithmetic and $O(nk)$ data items the computational cost would have depended on the amount of I/O and the problem would be I/O bound. Of course in this simple example we have assumed that the cost of an arithmetic operation is approximately the same as reading or writing a data item—usually the latter costs much less and the trade-off is more complex. Compute-bound problems clearly have some potential for exploiting parallelism because we can effectively reduce the computation time by performing several operations simultaneously. The same argument applies to I/O-bound problems but the gain in computation speed is not usually as dramatic.

The division of problems into the categories of compute or I/O bound is based on the ratio of communication to computation, which is clearly related to the structure of the recurrence relation describing the task. But the number, speed, direction of the data flows, and the interconnection structure can also be used to define systolic algorithms. For example, in the convolution arrays we distinguished between designs by defining which data flows were stationary or non-stationary. In principle any sequence of data can be made stationary or non-stationary but in practice a designer experiments with various draft data flows to bring out the characteristics of the problem. Normally a result sequence is present whose only purpose is to collect partial and complete results as it moves through the array—it is often this data flow that determines the efficiency and area of the design. As a result initial draft designs consist of experimenting with non-stationary and stationary flow with respect to the result sequence (see exercises). Where designs consist of a number of data sequences flowing in different directions the array is characterized by phrases such as *unidirectional*, *bidirectional*, and generally *k-directional* for k data sequences. In the convolution example we remarked that unidirectional flows are more amenable to fault tolerance—this might be an additional design constraint. The structure of data sequences is also important in determining efficiency and producing estimates of computation time. For instance, in Fig. 1.1(a) each x and y value was separated by a spacing (or *identity*) element which allowed proper synchronization of data elements but did not affect the computation. In Fig. 1.1(b) and (c) the spacing elements were removed. We used the data structure to work out the efficiency of the designs and decide which one was the best.

An interconnection topology (or processor geometry) implicitly defines the number of data sequences and their directions by the position of input/output connections on the array boundary and the directions of cell communication. Figure 1.2 shows some cell geometries that appear frequently in systolic design, the most famous being the hexagonal array of Kung and Leiserson (Mead and Conway 1979). These structures assume a regular two-dimensional connection topology (the basis of early systolic designs) and lead to three types of array (Dew *et al.* 1986).

1. *Two-dimensional (2-D) geometries.* A selection is given in Fig. 1.2.
2. *Collapsed (or degenerate) 2-D geometries.* These can be obtained from 2-D forms like Fig. 1.2(b) and (c) by collapsing the array onto a single row or column (and generally by taking a linear section through the array).
3. *Linear (1-D) geometries.* These are produced from collapsed geometries by restricting input–output to the leftmost and rightmost cells of the array. The convolution designs in Fig. 1.1(a) and (c) are linear arrays.

Figure 1.2(c) illustrates the use of *multiple* cell types and *boundary* cells in particular. There is no reason why the cells have to be all of the same type and often different cells are added to an otherwise homogeneous design to perform more complex tasks than the other processors (see next chapter). Restricting the number of cell types is useful because only a few processors need to be considered thus minimizing the total design time—this becomes important when one is concerned with implementing and debugging practical designs. Indeed modularity is an important feature of systolic design. Confining the complex cells to the boundary of a design also has certain layout advantages for VLSI implementations. A practical criterion for determining if arrays can be constructed is the amount of communication that occurs on the array boundaries between the external environment and the array. For example, suppose that Fig. 1.2(b) has n cells; then there are $n^{1/2}$ connections on each of the four boundaries. It follows that on any particular cycle there can be at most $4n^{1/2}$ input–outputs and n computations giving a ratio of $O(n^{1/2})$. For a collapsed version of Fig. 1.2(b) there are $O(n^{1/2})$ communications and $O(n^{1/2})$ computations giving a ratio of $O(1)$. On the other hand, a linear array has $O(1)$ communications and $O(n^{1/2})$ computations, also giving a ratio of $O(n^{1/2})$. In systolic design we want to minimize the I/O and maximize the computation subject to area–time constraints—higher ratios often signify better designs.

Having seen a simple example of systolic computation in Section 1.2 and briefly considered some of the historical reasons for the development of systolic processing we are ready to state some simple axioms or 'rules' that systolic designs obey. It should be clear that we are not using the term *axiom* in the strict sense adopted by mathematicians but the dictionary definition, meaning a well-established principle that commends itself to general acceptance. We can define our axioms as follows:

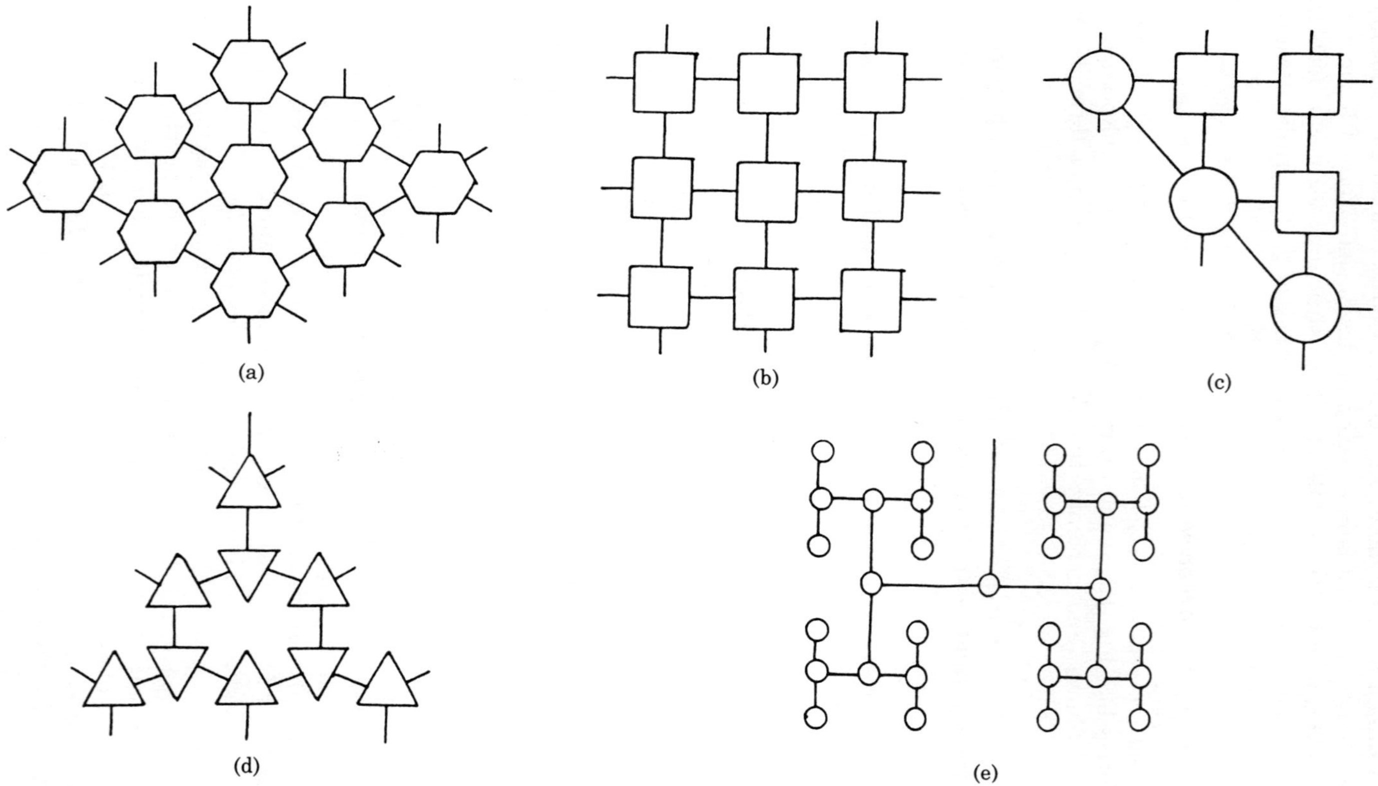

Fig. 1.2 Common connection topologies: (a) hexagonal; (b) orthogonal; (c) orthogonal triangular; (d) triangular; (e) binary H-tree

A[1]: There must be an underlying structure of cells with connections, that is a set of tessellating polygons (defining cells) and a connection topology formed from the implied data flow.

A[2]: Data and instructions must flow through the structure in a rhythmic and recurrent manner.

A[3]: Cells perform only single primitive operations.

A[4]: The flow of data is simple and regular.

A[5]: Connections should be nearest neighbour.

A[6]: The cell structure should consist of only a few types of simple cells.

It is important to note that these axioms are quite abstract and make no assumptions regarding the final implementation of the systolic algorithm. To express what we consider to be practical from an implementation point of view we shall define an additional set of technology-based heuristics. A sample set may be given as

H[1]: The interconnection structure is planar or almost planar (i.e. a graph in which arcs cross only at nodes).

H[2]: The number of inputs and outputs entering a cell is limited (to ensure fixed-size processing elements).

H[3]: Broadcasting to several cells simultaneously is avoided (i.e. no semi-systolic arrays).

H[4]: Long connections are prohibited (to avoid data or clock skew, and prevent erroneous computation).

Systolic axioms establish a framework for adopting a systolic philosophy to algorithm design while heuristics enforce the current practicalities of manufacturing skill and technology. Most of this book explores the limitations and types of designs that can be developed using systolic axioms at a fairly high level of abstraction, but technology determines what gets built and when. The crucial point is that the principles of systolic design are significant in their own right and should be separated from technological difficulties so that the final implementation can be decided at the last possible moment. This view is gaining support in the literature on systolic algorithms, especially since programmable processors suited to parallel processing have started to appear. One might in fact add a new heuristic to cope with the trend

H[5]: Degree of programmability.

and define the following classes of systolic algorithms.

1. *Hard-systolic algorithms.* These are characterized by a very low degree of programmability implied by the control and switching logic built into circuits of actual designs. Such designs are highly desirable from a VLSI viewpoint but make the design inherently special purpose because of limited flexibility. This group contains virtually all systolic algorithms implemented directly in silicon to date.

2. *Hybrid-systolic algorithms.* These permit a medium degree of flexibility perhaps implemented by microprogramming or simple control tags (added to the data). The idea here is to allow a number of cell types to be implemented by the same processor, thereby allowing generic systolic arrays. However, the connection topology is still essentially systolic so this class of algorithms attempts a limited movement away from special-purpose devices in exchange for greater flexibility (and hence cost effectiveness). For example, one might include the Warp architecture developed by H. T. Kung at Carnegie Mellon University.

3. *Soft-systolic algorithms.* These provide a high degree of programmability. The interconnection structure is used as a 'harness' or data structure expressing the amount of parallelism to be exploited rather than a machine architecture. The emphasis is on retaining systolic computation as a design principle, and the mapping of the algorithm onto an available parallel architecture. The algorithm is forced onto an architecture with resulting trade-offs in speed and efficiency due to communication and processor time sharing overheads incurred by simulating the array structure.

It is important to recognize that class 1 is a subset of 2 and class 2 is a subset of 3. Originally systolic design was restricted to problems of class 1, but problems with VLSI manufacturing forced a movement to class 2 with 3 following as a result of commercially viable general-purpose parallel processors. Evidence to support this informal classification can be easily found. Since the concept of systolic computation has become widely accepted the publication of new algorithms has far outweighed the actual number of implementations. Soft-systolic algorithms are becoming more important as the need to simulate the data flow of complicated and higher-dimensional systolic designs increases.

1.5 Systolic systems

The main driving force behind systolic design is the idea that VLSI techniques allow us to use relatively complex and large amounts of hardware at low cost, but as Moldovan (1983) points out 'VLSI is a raw technological environment which requires new ideas in computer organization, theory of computing and other related fields'. Indeed, the use of processor arrays is application driven and leads to two approaches in incorporating them into computer systems.

1. *General-purpose systems.* These are systems where the systolic arrays are fast add-on devices to existing sequential (or parallel) computing architectures (see Fig. 1.3(a)). For example, we could define separate systolic

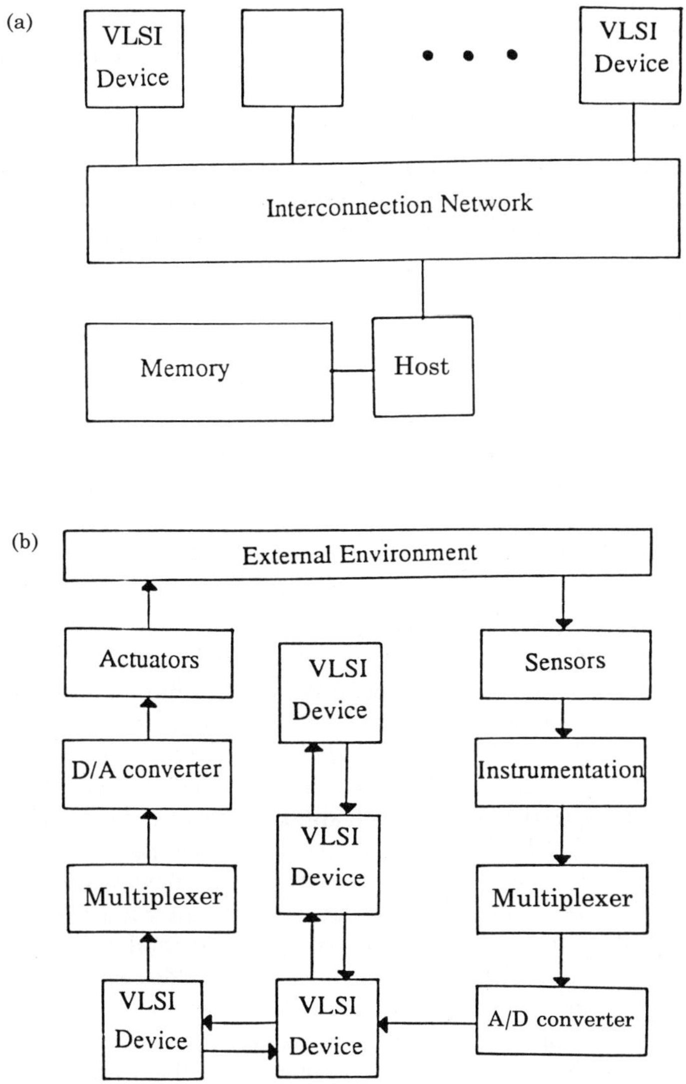

Fig. 1.3 Systolic systems: (a) general-purpose system; (b) embedded system (Courtesy D. I. Moldovan, © 1983 *Proceedings of the IEEE*, Vol. 71)

arrays for the basic linear algebra routines in common use and connect them to the system bus where they become system resources. A solution to a problem is then implemented by calls to the hardware, downloading of data to the device, and then collection of the result; this frees the host machine to perform other work and gives the user access to a fast parallel device if required. The main concept is that existing architectures can be upgraded and orientated towards different problem domains easily, the obvious benefits being in research and development environments where the types of projects will be broadly similar but have changing requirements over relatively short time periods. Devices of this kind are often termed *hardware accelerators*, because the device is used as a resource that improves computation and throughput by specialist hardware.

2. *Embedded systems.* For some applications the need for parallelism is motivated by the time constraints of a problem (see Fig. 1.3(b)). For example, a target tracking system must be able to pick up, identify, and plan an interception trajectory before the target penetrates defences sufficiently to become a dangerous threat. The computation must be performed within a given real-time constraint imposed by the target (its velocity). For such systems the circuits and algorithms must be very fast, and the device itself must be embedded into the rest of the controlling system and integrated with sensors for data collection and actuators for controlled response. In addition there will also be constraints on the size and weight of the design (e.g. in aircraft radar systems) which restrict the trade-offs of speed, efficiency, and cost that are acceptable. If the final design is too slow or fast enough but too bulky, it will be useless.

In a general-purpose system the way that the array is interfaced to the host machine is of key importance. The performance of the array will be dictated by the ability of the host to keep the device full of data. Clearly as the bandwidth of the array increases this task becomes more difficult. To avoid this problem we assume that the VLSI device contains enough temporary storage for a single problem to be loaded from the host before the array is started up. Likewise, the output of the array is collected in the device before being passed back to the host. The advantage of this scheme is that the array can work at full speed. The disadvantage is that one must waste some time to download and collect answers from the VLSI device. Clearly when a problem is compute bound these overheads are minimized because the setup phase of a problem is only a small percentage of the total computation time. In contrast the input–output interface of an embedded system is designed specifically for the application so that the reception, computation, and collection of data can be pipelined and throughput maximized. As implied by Fig. 1.3(b) a number of arrays for different problems can be pipelined together with the output of one forming the input for another. Of course we assume that the input and output formats for the arrays are compatible.

Exercises

1. Find a textbook on physiology and (a) look up the word *systole*, (b) familiarize yourself with the circulatory system.
2. Compare systolic computation with other parallel processing paradigms such as SIMD, MIMD, data flow, and vector processing, taking care to consider the general-purpose versus special-purpose trade-off of implementations.
3. What is the Cartesian philosophy? Explain how it has affected (a) scientific research in general, (b) the design of computer systems and software.
4. Consider possible systolic implementations of the recurrence equation (1.2).
5. Develop systolic arrays for the convolution recurrence (1.3) which have the following characteristics:
   (a) the x and w values are non-stationary and the y values are stationary;
   (b) the y and w values are non-stationary and the x values are stationary;
   (c) the x, y, w values are all non-stationary.
   Work out the area, time, and efficiencies and compare them with Table 1.1 commenting on their advantages and disadvantages.
6. The product operation is defined as

   $$a_1 0 a_2 0 \cdots 0 a_n$$

   where 0 is an associative operator. Develop systolic algorithms for the prefix operation

   $$a_1 0 a_2 0 \cdots a_i$$

   where $i = 1, 2, \ldots, n$.
7. Explain the role of advances in VLSI technology in the establishment of systolic computation.
8. What are the 'axioms' of systolic design and why are they necessary? What is the difference between an axiom and a heuristic?
9. Distinguish between the use of systolic algorithms in a general-purpose setting compared with an embedded application.
10. Briefly explain what is meant by hard-, hybrid-, and soft-systolic algorithms.

2

SPACE–TIME AND RETIMING

A fundamental concept in systolic algorithm design is that algorithms can be represented and manipulated by specifying their data dependencies as graphs in space and time. In this chapter we will define more precisely what we mean by the *space–time* representation of an algorithm, consider some simple methods for manipulating this representation, and show how it can be used to derive different systolic algorithms. However, before proceeding we must take some time to clarify our rather cavalier references (Chapter 1) to the representation of interconnection structures and systolic arrays by graphs.

2.1 Graphs and sequences

To describe systolic algorithms we shall adopt a graph model built up from three basic elements: *cells* (for evaluating simple computations), *links* (for communicating data), and *delay* (for synchronizing data). The communication pattern of channels and cells will be defined by a directed graph (McKevoy 1986). Formally, a graph is defined as $G = (V, E)$ where V is a finite non-empty set of nodes or vertices, and E is a finite set of pairs of vertices representing arcs or edges. In an undirected graph, the ordering of the pair of nodes representing an edge is unimportant, but in a directed or *digraph* the ordering implies direction which is denoted by arrows and can be defined by two functions.

Definition 2.1 A digraph $D = (V, E, \varphi_-, \varphi_+)$ where V is a non-empty finite set of cells and E is a finite non-empty set of links; $\varphi_-: E \to V$ and $\varphi_+: E \to V$ are functions determining the source and destination cells of a link respectively.

Figure 2.1 depicts some examples. Figure 2.1(a) is an undirected graph with $V = \{v_1, v_2, v_3, v_4\}$ and $E = \{(v_1, v_2), (v_1, v_3), (v_1, v_4), (v_2, v_3), (v_2, v_4), (v_3, v_4)\}$ and is non-planar. Figure 2.1(b) is a directed (or digraph) where $V = \{v_1, v_2, v_3\}$ and $E = \{(v_1, v_2), (v_2, v_1), (v_2, v_3), (v_3, v_1)\}$ and is planar. The head and tail functions for edge $e = (v_1, v_2)$ are $\varphi_+(e) = v_2$ and $\varphi_-(e) = v_1$ while for $e = (v_2, v_1)$ they yield $\varphi_+(e) = v_1$ and $\varphi_-(e) = v_2$. It should be immediately obvious that digraphs can be used to represent interconnection structures with unidirectional communication pathways. In Chapter 1, we used digraphs in a loose sense to describe the array structure for different convolution problems where the nodes represented cells and arcs communication links. Note that under our current definition the arrays in Fig. 1.1 are not graphs,

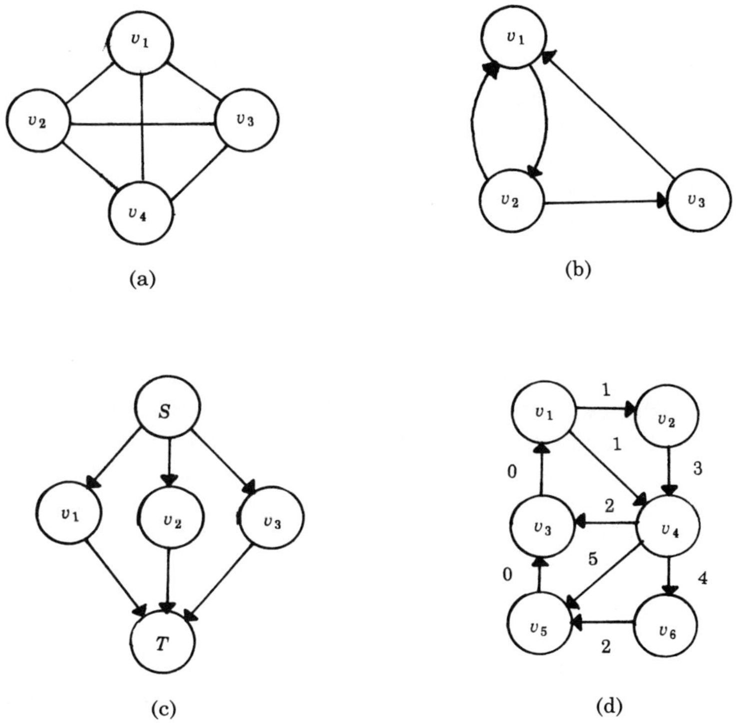

Fig. 2.1 Example graphs: (a) undirected (non-planar); (b) directed (planar); (c) source (S) and sink (T) cells; (d) labelled

because the tail and head functions φ_- and φ_+ are not well defined. To avoid this problem we introduce two additional cells S and T which represent the array interface and act as global sources and sinks of data (see Fig. 2.1(c)). Cell S can only have links directed out of it and represents array input, while T represents array output and only incoming links are permitted. Normally S and T will be omitted from diagrams but they will play an important part in the proofs of Section 2.5 on retiming.

The links in a systolic array will be used to pass data between cells. The history of the data seen on the link will form a data sequence. Sequences will be defined as input, internal, or output sequences. Input sequences will describe the input supplied by the host and output sequences will show the data returned by the array. Both input and output sequences will be shown explicitly on array diagrams. In contrast, internal sequences represent the activity between cells in the array and will normally be implicit. For more complex designs we will also find it useful to augment data sequences with control tags to switch the cell function over time. Tags can be considered as extensions to the data supplied in a data sequence (possibly by bit extension in simple cases) or, where no data are supplied, as pure instruction sequences. Finally, in addition to data sequences we will also identify a weight function delay: $E \rightarrow Z$ with edges (where Z is the set of positive and negative integers). For a given edge e, delay(e) will be the time in cell cycles that a data item takes to propagate down the link. For example, in Fig. 2.1(d) the link (v_3, v_1) has a zero weight and hence zero delay. Alternatively, link (v_4, v_5) has a weight of 5 and represents a five-step delay for data to move from v_4 to v_5. A unit delay will be the cost of the most complex computation of a cell in the graph.

In this chapter we will encounter various interpretations of graphs. In particular we will see how systolic arrays can be produced from finite and semi-infinite graphs in space–time, and how graphs for arrays can be retimed. In the former case we will associate various geometric properties such as position and distance with graphs, in the latter we shall use weight functions as a model of propagation delay. In the text generally it is safe to assume that links have no delay unless otherwise specified and that data sequences move in straight lines. Cells are considered to latch results propagating down a link so that their values are not overwritten accidentally.

2.2 Space–time and projection

In a recurrence equation the data are related using sets of indices. If there are $p > 1$ indices they can be used as a coordinate system to represent the necessary computation in a p-dimensional space. Every point in the space is uniquely defined by a p component vector, and can be mapped onto integer coordinates defined by the axes of the system. If a coordinate identifies a data item that occurs on the left-hand side of a recurrence equation it represents a *potential computation site* where some value (the result of the right side of the recurrence) must be evaluated. The order in which these sites are active defines a partial order on the recurrence computation with respect to time. Now, in order to evaluate the recurrences sequentially at least one of the indices can be interpreted as time, so our p-dimensional space is a representation of space–time with $p - 1$ space dimensions and one time dimension. Observe that when $p = 1$ zero space dimensions are implied; such a situation is clearly impossible because any computation (even a sequential one) requires some space in which to be evaluated. Cappello and Steiglitz (1984) avoid this problem by using a $p + 1$ coordinate system for $p > 0$ indices—but $p + 1$ dimensions are only necessary when $p = 1$. A *data dependency graph* in space–time is constructed by interpreting computational sites as vertices and connecting them together with directed edges to reflect which sites have to produce results required by others. Coordinates associated with terms occurring only on the right side of a recurrence equation are inputs and represent input *data sequences*. The sites visited by the input terms during the computation define a path through space–time which can in general be represented by a $p \times 1$ vector whose direction changes (i.e. the vector elements are parametric functions of time). For simplicity we consider only sequences whose direction is a straight line determined by a linear combination of the direction vectors associated with the coordinate axes. Finally, terms which appear both on the right and left side of the recurrence equations are interpreted as items of data sequences which are modified as they move through space–time.

The process of representing recurrence equations in space–time reduces to specifying lines and defining points. Consequently manipulations of an algorithm implementation can be reduced to considering what happens to lines and points when we change the coordinate system of space–time. To pursue this idea it is necessary to distinguish between the so-called *observer* (where you, the observer, are positioned at the origin) and the *space–time* coordinate systems. The easiest situation to imagine is that the observer and space–time coordinate systems are identical so that only a single perspective of the data dependency graph is possible. If the observer changes position relative to the origin of space–time the perspective on a data dependency graph will also change and reveal different schedules for the computation. It follows that the data dependency graph in space–time gives the designer a global view of a computation. Furthermore, transformations of space–time can be used to design systolic algorithms. Now clearly any implementation of a systolic array is physically confined to space dimensions. It follows that a physical representation of a data dependency graph is produced by considering ways to project space–time (or the data dependency and data sequences) into images in space. Computational sites mapping to the same projected point must define mutually exclusive computations which use the same processor at different times. The graph formed from the projected computation sites and the edges of the dependency graph define an array for the required computation.

In the following paragraphs we will develop some simple systolic designs using this idea. For space–time systems with $p > 3$ a geometric interpretation of the data dependencies cannot easily be visualized, but for $p \leq 3$ space–time can be represented graphically using simple geometric manipulations (see exercises). Fortunately, a wide range of interesting algorithms require three or less indices in their recurrence formulation (see Chapters 3, 4, and 5).

As a first example consider the inner product computation which forms the basic part of many numerical problems. Sequentially this can be written simply using a for-loop program

```
Y[0] := 0;
For j = 1 to n do
  Y[j] := Y[j-1] + A[j]*B[j];
```

where the Y, A, and B are suitable variables. A single variable is sufficient for accumulating the product but we use a vector to make the space–time representation more explicit. In recurrence notation the sequential program can be written as

$$y_j = y_{j-1} + a_j \times b_j, \quad j = 1(1)n \tag{2.1}$$

where $n > 0$ and $y_0 = 0$. In this case there is only one loop (i.e. $p = 1$) so a space with $(p + 1) = 2$ dimensions is necessary if we are to map the calculation into space–time. Equation (2.1) has only one index but two are required so that every potential computation can be assigned to a unique position in 2-D space. A *fully indexed* form of (2.1) is given as

$$y_{1,j} = y_{1,j-1} + a_{1,j}b_{1,j}, \quad j = 1(1)n \tag{2.2}$$

where an arbitary but constant index has been added. Plotting the points $(1, j)$ in the plane and connecting them together according to the left and right sides of (2.2) produces the data dependency graph in Fig. 2.2(a) ($n = 4$). The values $a_{1,j}$ and $b_{1,j}$ are mapped to the coordinates $(1, j)$, and the value of y is said to be *pipelined* because we start with $y_{1,0} = 0$ which is input to the graph at $(1, 1)$ and pipe it from node to node in the j direction until it emerges at $(1, n)$ with $y_{1,n}$ the result of the computation. The j direction represents time and demands that $y_{1,1}$ is computed before $y_{1,2}$ and $y_{1,2}$ before $y_{1,3}$ and so on. Thus, Fig. 2.2(a) can be interpreted as a *loop unrolling* of the sequential program for computing (2.1) in space–time. Indeed the graph and the program are equivalent representations.

Once we have a dependency graph representation the associated algorithm can be manipulated by performing various transformations on the points in space–time. The computation embodied in the original graph will be the same provided the data dependencies between nodes in the graph are preserved. Below we consider three linear transformations—*translate, rotate,* and *scale*—which preserve computation. More complex transformations can be constructed from these basic types or their inverses. Figure 2.2(b) shows a translation, an operation which simply moves the whole graph to a different position in space–time. In matrix notation the points of the graph are modified as

$$\begin{bmatrix} 1 & 0 & \alpha \\ 0 & 1 & \beta \\ 0 & 0 & 1 \end{bmatrix} \begin{bmatrix} i \\ j \\ 1 \end{bmatrix} = \begin{bmatrix} i + \alpha \\ j + \beta \\ 1 \end{bmatrix} \tag{2.3a}$$

which shifts the graph α steps in the i direction and β steps in the j direction. The computation is the same except that it is delayed and does not start until time $\beta + 1$. Figure 2.2(c) illustrates a rotation which is represented

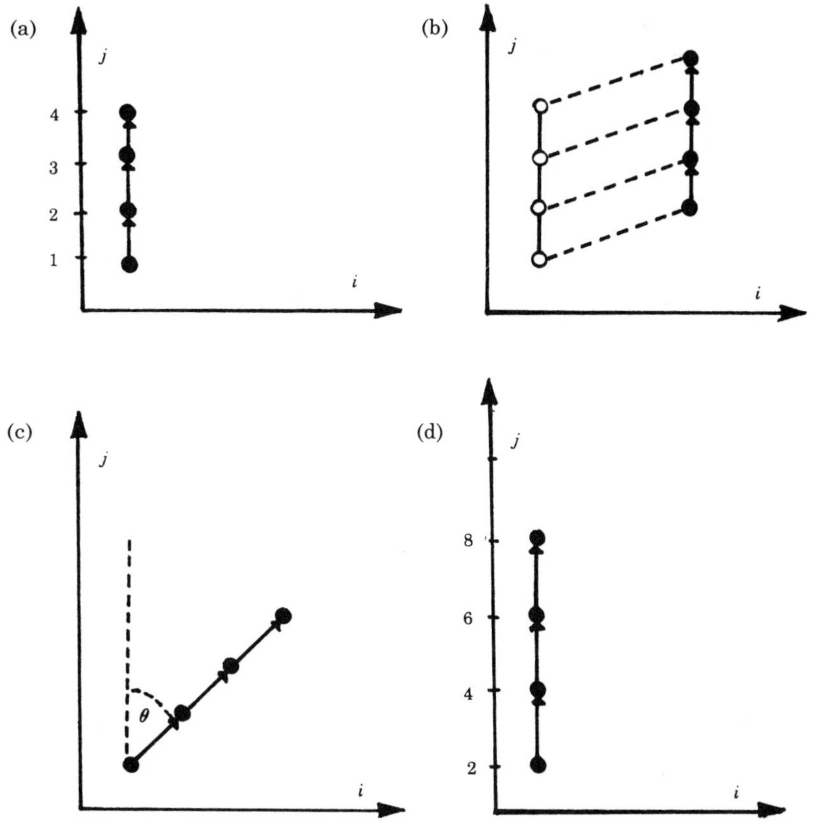

Fig. 2.2 Space–time representation of inner product: (a) dependency graph; (b) translation; (c) rotation; (d) scaling

formally as

$$\begin{bmatrix} c & s & 0 \\ -s & c & 0 \\ 0 & 0 & 1 \end{bmatrix} \begin{bmatrix} i \\ j \\ 1 \end{bmatrix} = \begin{bmatrix} ci + sj \\ cj - si \\ 1 \end{bmatrix} \tag{2.3b}$$

where $c = \cos\theta$ and $s = \sin\theta$ and $-\theta$ is the angle of rotation. Again it is obvious that the computation is preserved and starts at the same time, but the $y_{1,j}$ values are now pipelined in the space as well as time direction. As we will see later, changes in space imply movement from one processing element to another. Finally, Fig. 2.2(d) shows a scaling transformation which can be written as

$$\begin{bmatrix} \alpha & 0 & 0 \\ 0 & \beta & 0 \\ 0 & 0 & 1 \end{bmatrix}\begin{bmatrix} i \\ j \\ 1 \end{bmatrix} = \begin{bmatrix} \alpha i \\ \beta j \\ 1 \end{bmatrix}. \tag{2.3c}$$

In the diagram $\alpha = 1$ amd $\beta = 2$ so that points in the transformed graph are two steps apart. Clearly computation is preserved but now each calculation is assumed to take two steps of time instead of one. In general it is usual to define the cost of the most complicated instruction mapped to a node in the dependency graph as taking unit time. Scaling can be used to normalize graphs so that this assumption is always valid. In particular whole sequences of instructions (or the loop body) can be interpreted as a single computation. It follows that scaling is one way of changing the granularity of a computation.

The next task in designing an array is to construct some projections of the data dependency graph into $p - 1$ dimensions when $p > 1$ and one dimension otherwise. More formally we require a mapping

$$Mv = \bar{v} \tag{2.4}$$

where M is a $p \times p$ matrix and $v, \bar{v}$ are $p \times 1$ vectors. The aim is to reduce one of the components in v to a zero value in $\bar{v}$. For example, when $p = 2$ space–time is two dimensional, but we are interested in projections into one dimension so that the following matrices can be substituted for M:

$$M_1 = \begin{bmatrix} 1 & 0 \\ 0 & 0 \end{bmatrix}, \quad M_2 = \begin{bmatrix} 0 & 0 \\ 0 & 1 \end{bmatrix}, \quad M_1 = \begin{bmatrix} 1 & -1 \\ 0 & 0 \end{bmatrix}. \tag{2.5}$$

Figure 2.3 shows the effect of (2.4) on our example graph in Fig. 2.2(a) for each of the matrices in (2.5). M_1 performs the mapping $(i, j) \rightarrow (i, 0)$ shown in Fig. 2.3(a) which is equivalent to projecting out the j axis. M_2 produces the mapping $(i, j) \rightarrow (0, j)$ corresponding to a projection in the $(-1, 0)^t$ direction to remove the i axis as illustrated by Fig. 2.3(b). Finally, M_2 yields the mapping $(i, j) \rightarrow (i - j, 0)$ corresponding to the direction of projection shown in Fig. 2.3(c). If we interpret the direction of projection as time the projected graph is confined to purely space dimensions and represents an array. Figure 2.4 illustrates the arrays resulting from the above mappings. In the first case, Fig. 2.4(a), the array is a single cell that accumulates the n partial products required sequentially. It follows that $\mathscr{A} = 1$ cells and $\mathscr{T} = n$ steps are required and that the array is 100 per cent ($e = 1$) efficient. The required input and output sequences are obtained by projecting out the data elements assigned to nodes in the original dependency graph. In the second case the array in Fig. 2.4(b) results. The a and b values are skewed in time so that they synchronize correctly with the y values moving along the array. This design requires $\mathscr{A} = n$ cells and $\mathscr{T} = n$ steps but each cell only works

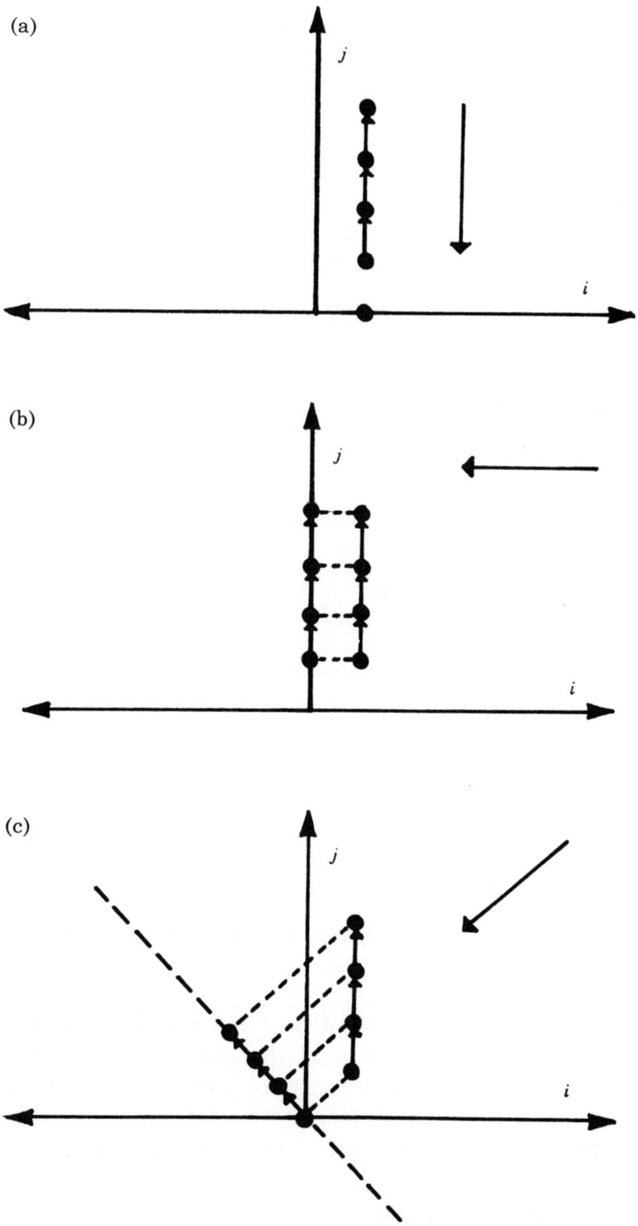

Fig. 2.3 Inner product projection: (a) along j axis; (b) along i axis; (c) along line $(-1, -1)^t$

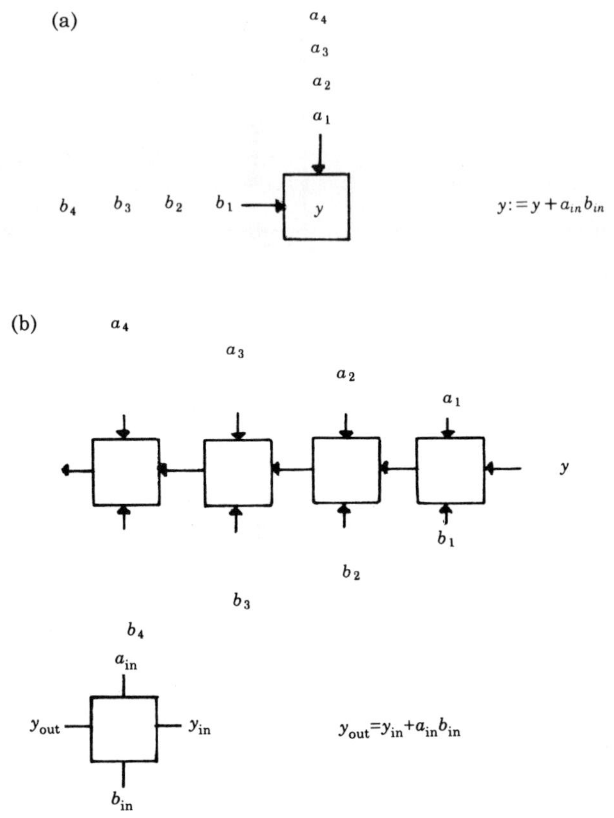

Fig. 2.4 Arrays for inner product computation: (a) sequential array; (b) pipelined array

once in n steps so the efficiency is only $e = 1/n$. Finally, consideration of the mapping in Fig. 2.3(c) also produces the array in Fig. 2.4(b) (which is coincidental and not generally true as we will see later). Comparing the designs shows that the first array has $\mathscr{A}\mathscr{T}^2 = n^2$ and the latter $\mathscr{A}\mathscr{T}^2 = n^3$; thus on the basis of area, time, and efficiency the first design should be preferred.

The use of parallelism in this case appears not to be justified—we will develop better examples shortly. However, before proceeding we point out that the process is quite general and may generate non-systolic as well as systolic designs. We must ensure that the final projected array not only represents a feasible computation but also satisfies the axioms stated in Chapter 1. The projections described in (2.5) will work for any 2-D graph and being linear transformations will always preserve the computation. Unfortunately we cannot guarantee that every projection will produce a feasible array. In our example we have assumed that projections are made in a direction parallel to the direction of a line representing time. Such projections guarantee that computations performed at the same time are mapped onto different array cells (and often introduce the greatest degree of parallelism). If the projection direction is perpendicular to the time line some computations which are to be evaluated simultaneously will be mapped to the same processor making the design impractical.

In general an arbitrary projection matrix can be derived from any direction vector using a two-stage process. First rotate space until the line of projection is coincident with one of the axes, and then project out the axis. In matrix notation

$$M = M_t R \tag{2.6}$$

where M_t is one of the matrices in (2.5) and R is the rotate transform (2.3b). For example, an arbitrary direction $(\alpha, \beta)^t$ maps to the i axis when $c = \alpha/d$, $s = \beta/d$, and $d = (\alpha^2 + \beta^2)^{1/2}$. Consequently a matrix for projecting in the direction $(-1, -1)^t$ is determined by the product

$$M = \frac{1}{\sqrt{2}} \begin{bmatrix} 0 & 0 \\ 0 & 1 \end{bmatrix} \begin{bmatrix} -1 & -1 \\ 1 & -1 \end{bmatrix}.$$

The $1/\sqrt{2}$ results from the fact that rotations do not guarantee to map integer coordinates to integer coordinates. Scaling by a factor of $\sqrt{2}$ will *renormalize* the space so that the properties of unit time and unit area for nodes and arcs in the graph are preserved. In addition the transformed graph can be translated to restore the nodes to integer coordinate positions.

2.3 Loop unrolling and pipelining

The previous example illustrates the basic concepts of projections in space–time but is not very stimulating. To make the problem more difficult suppose we want to compute $m > 0$ copies of (2.1). A two-loop sequential program can be given as

```
For i := 1 to m do
  {
    Y[i] := 0;
    For j := 1 to n do
      Y[i] := Y[i] + a[i,j]*b[i,j];
  }
```

where the inner loop is simply the previous example modified to allow the vector Y to store m different inner products. An equivalent recurrence is

$$y_{i,j} = y_{i,j-1} + a_{ij} \times b_{ij} \tag{2.7}$$

where $y_{i,0} = 0$ and $i = 1(1)m$ for $n > 0$. We add the index j so that y_{ij} represents the value of $y[i]$ at step j of the inner loop. The pipelining of the variable y then follows immediately. The program uses two loops (i.e. $p = 2$) so an unrolling into 2-D space–time is straightforward. Figure 2.5(a) shows the required data dependency graph. Notice that the independent nature of the m different computations is made explicit in the diagram by the lack of connections between nodes in adjacent columns. This follows because each iteration of the i loop corresponds to a copy of the graph for computing (2.1). Values $a_{i,j}$, $b_{i,j}$, and $y_{i,j}$ are mapped to the nodes (i, j) in the usual way.

Now, things start to get interesting when we consider projections of the graph into 1-D space. In Fig. 2.5(a) the j axis is selected as time, the subsequent projection mapping instance i of the m inner products onto a single processor. Thus one way to compute (2.7) is to use m copies of the single cell design of Fig. 2.4(a) independently. Such a design requires $\mathscr{A} = m$, $\mathscr{T} = n$, and efficiency $e = 1$ but clearly misses the design objectives because the host machine requires $2m$ input connections (Fig. 2.6(a) shows the projected data sequences). When $m \gg n$ the design is not very attractive. To overcome this problem we would like to make the designs independent of m, and one way to do this is to project out the i axis as shown in Fig. 2.5(b). This design pipelines the different y_i values through an array of n cells so that problem i starts at time i (i.e. the i axis represents time). The final array is shown in Fig. 2.6(b). This array uses $\mathscr{A} = n$ cells (independent of m), and each problem requires n steps to be evaluated and $2(n + 1)$ host connections. There are m problems pipelined behind one another so $\mathscr{T} = n + m$ steps are required altogether. Notice how the a and b data are skewed to synchronize with the y_i values. These input and output formats can be recovered by noting the order of computation in the unprojected graph and projecting out the data sequences from the values attached to each node. The efficiency is determined from the fact that each cell computes m scalar inner product operations, one for each problem instance, so $e = m/(n + m)$. Finally consider the projection in Fig. 2.5(c); this time we interpret the direction $(1, 1)^t$ as time. The projection produces a unidirectional array of $\mathscr{A} = m + n - 1$ cells as shown in Fig. 2.6(c) which requires $2(m + n)$ input–output connections. The y values are shifted into the array separated by synchronizing dummy elements (zeros in this case). It takes m steps to get the first value y_1 to its correct starting position (the nth cell from the left) before computation begins and n steps to accumulate all the necessary partial products, so the array latency is $m + n - 1$. The input data are of length $2m$ allowing for the synchronizing elements, so the total computing time is $\mathscr{T} = 2m + (m + n - 1) = 3m + n - 1$ steps. Once the array is full of data

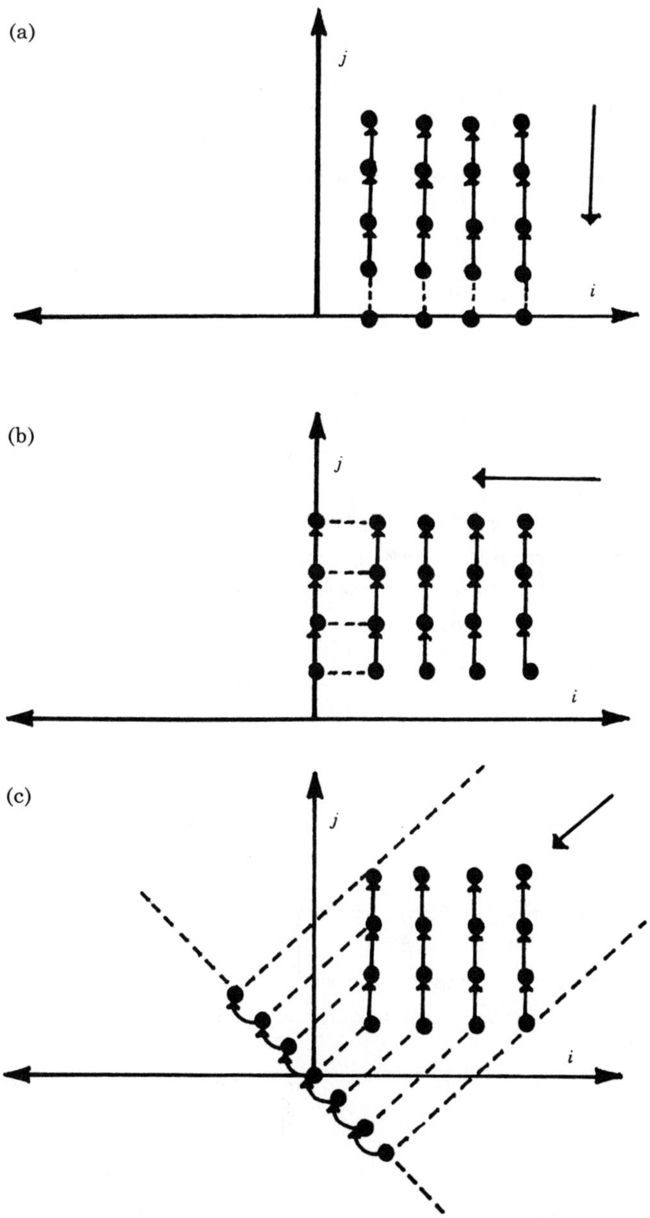

Fig. 2.5 Space–time diagrams for multiple inner products: (a) along j axis; (b) along i axis; (c) along line $(-1, -1)^t$

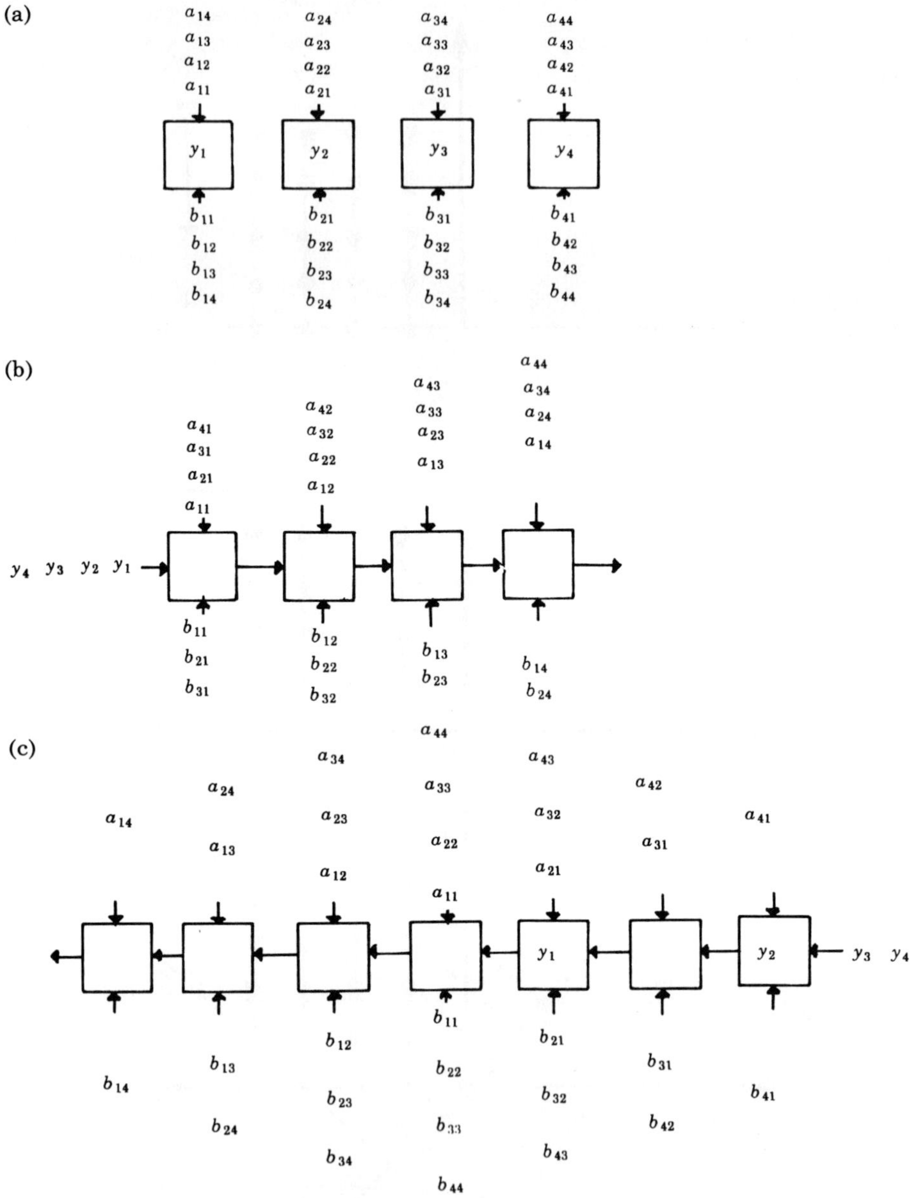

Fig. 2.6 Projected multiple inner product arrays: (a) independent cells; (b) pipelined; (c) alternative pipeline

the array computes with 50 per cent ($e = 0.5$) efficiency. Comparing the designs on efficiency favours the first design, with the second method close behind, especially when $m \gg n$. But the second method requires only n host connections compared with $2m$ and $2(m + n)$ respectively. Next the $\mathcal{AT}^2$ measure yields m^3, $n(n + m - 1)^2$, and $(m + n - 1)(3m + n - 1)^2$ for each of the designs respectively. The choice is clearly between designs 1 and 2 with design 2 more favourable because of the reduced number of input–output connections and leading $\mathcal{AT}^2$ terms of $n^3 + n^2m$ rather than m^3 which exploits the difference between n and m. On the other hand, if $n \gg m$ the first design would be more attractive.

A special case of multiple inner product computation is the matrix–vector product which can be expressed in recurrence form as

$$y_i = \sum_{j=1}^{n} a_{ij}x_j, \quad i = 1(1)n \tag{2.8}$$

where the a_{ij} are elements of an $n \times n$ matrix A, the x_j are elements of an $n \times 1$ vector, and the y_i form an $n \times 1$ resulting vector. From our earlier statements it is simple to verify that the matrix–vector product can be computed using n cells and $n + n$ steps by simply setting $b_{ij} = x_j$, and using Fig. 2.6(b) with $m = n$. Unfortunately this approach requires x_i to be brought repeatedly from the host machine, and it would be better if we could find a way to reuse each of the x_i several times inside the array. To explore this possibility let us develop a more explicit space–time representation for (2.8).

First write eqn (2.8) as a two-loop sequential program with the form

```
For i := 1 to m do
  {
    y[i] := 0
    For j := 1 to n do
      y[i] := y[i] + A[i,j]*X[j]
  }
```

which yields the recurrence

$$y_{i,j} = y_{i,j-1} + a_{ij} \times x_j, \quad i = 1(1)n, j = 1(1)n \tag{2.9}$$

where the variable y is pipelined in the usual way and $y_{i,0} = 0$. Two loops require 2-D space and a second index must be added to the x_j values to create a completely consistent space–time represention. How do we choose the extra index for x? In the case of the y variable it is clear that updates to each y_i are dependent on successive iterations of the j loop, making the pipelining obvious. For the x_j the same assumption is not valid. We could force the x values to be dependent on both loops by replacing x_j with x_{ij} which fully indexes the recurrence but this is just another form of (2.7) with $b_{ij} = x_{ij}$. Besides, why not allow x_{0j} or x_{j0} or any other strategy that produces two indices? For now we just accept that virtually any choice can be made, but the simplest (in terms of retiming and further manipulation) is to add zero components which preserve the ordering of the indices. In the current example this means replacing x_j by $x_{0,j}$ to get

$$y_{i,j} = y_{i,j-1} + a_{i,j}x_{0,j}, \quad i, j = 1(1)n \tag{2.10}$$

where $y_{i,0} = 0$. Now we can unroll the program loops and map the recurrence in 2-D space to get the dependency graph shown in Fig. 2.7(a). The x_{0j} values are broadcast to all the nodes on row j contradicting axiom A[5] in Chapter 1, so the design is at best semi-systolic. For the matrix–vector example we can exploit the correspondence between (2.7) and (2.10) to note that

$$b_{nj} = b_{n-1,j} = \cdots = b_{1j} = x_{0j} = x_j$$

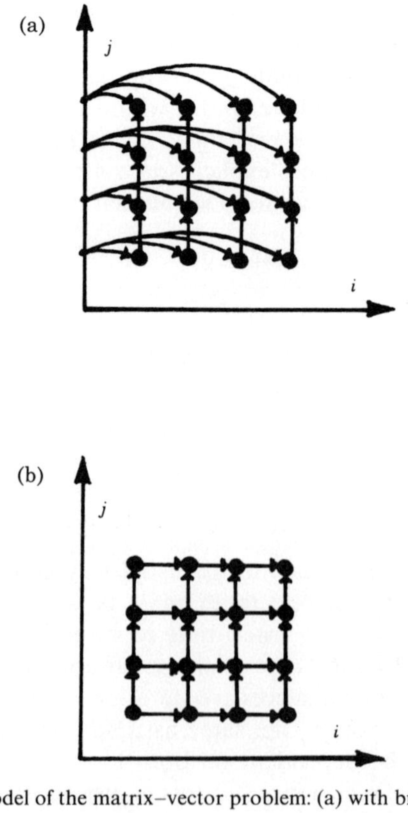

Fig. 2.7 Space–time model of the matrix–vector problem: (a) with broadcasting; (b) with local data movement

from which it is clear that $b_{ij} = b_{i-1,j}$ and as $b_{ij} = x_{0j}$ we can write (2.10) as

$$y_{i,j} = y_{i,j-1} + a_{i,j}x_{i,j}, \quad i, j = 1(1)n \tag{2.11a}$$

$$x_{i,j} = \begin{cases} x_{i-1,j} & i > 1 \\ x_{0j} & i = 1. \end{cases} \tag{2.11b}$$

Unrolling this recurrence in space–time produces Fig. 2.7(b) in which all the communications are nearest neighbour. A simple method for checking whether variables require retiming is to subtract the indices for the variable on the right-hand side of a recurrence from indices on the left-hand side of the recurrence. For example, in (2.10)

$$\begin{bmatrix} i \\ j \end{bmatrix} - \begin{bmatrix} i \\ j-1 \end{bmatrix} = \begin{bmatrix} 0 \\ 1 \end{bmatrix} \tag{2.12a}$$

$$\begin{bmatrix} i \\ j \end{bmatrix} - \begin{bmatrix} 0 \\ j \end{bmatrix} = \begin{bmatrix} i \\ 0 \end{bmatrix} \tag{2.12b}$$

for the y and x variables respectively. In the former the resulting vector is constant so no pipelining is required, but in the latter the vector is dependent on i which implies connections with length proportional to i. Of course we can still produce constant vectors with non-local connections but these are easy to resolve by constructing a routing path through intermediate nodes. The systematic removal of broadcast and non-local connections is called *pipelining* and amounts to retiming the dependency graph. A more formal discussion requires the development of the retiming principle discussed in Section 2.5 and the pipelining and routing method presented in Chapter 8 (the interested reader may like to consider this material now before continuing but it is not essential just yet).

Using Fig. 2.7(b) we can now proceed to project out various arrays for the matrix–vector problem. Projections in the $(0, -1)^t$, $(-1, 0)^t$, and $(-1, -1)^t$ directions are shown in Fig. 2.8 for $n = 4$. In Fig. 2.8(a) the y values are preloaded into the array cells and remain stationary while the x and A values are input as shown. $\mathscr{A} = n$ cells are required and the total length of the x data sequence is also n. The delay through the array implies that y_n starts computation on step n and requires accumulation of n terms to give a total of $\mathscr{T} = 2n$ steps. Each cell performs real computations for n steps so the efficiency is $e = n/2n = 0.5$. Figure 2.8(b) reverses the role of the x and y with the x stationary and y non-stationary. Each y_i value accumulates one term for each cell as it filters through the array so that y_n is output after $\mathscr{T} = 2n$ steps. The area and efficiency are the same as the previous case. Next, Fig. 2.8(c) describes an array in which all the data are non-stationary. The matrix A is input in a diagonal format compared with the column and row orders in the previous two arrays. As a dense $n \times n$ matrix has a bandwidth $2n - 1$, $\mathscr{A} = 2n - 1$ cells are required. The x and y

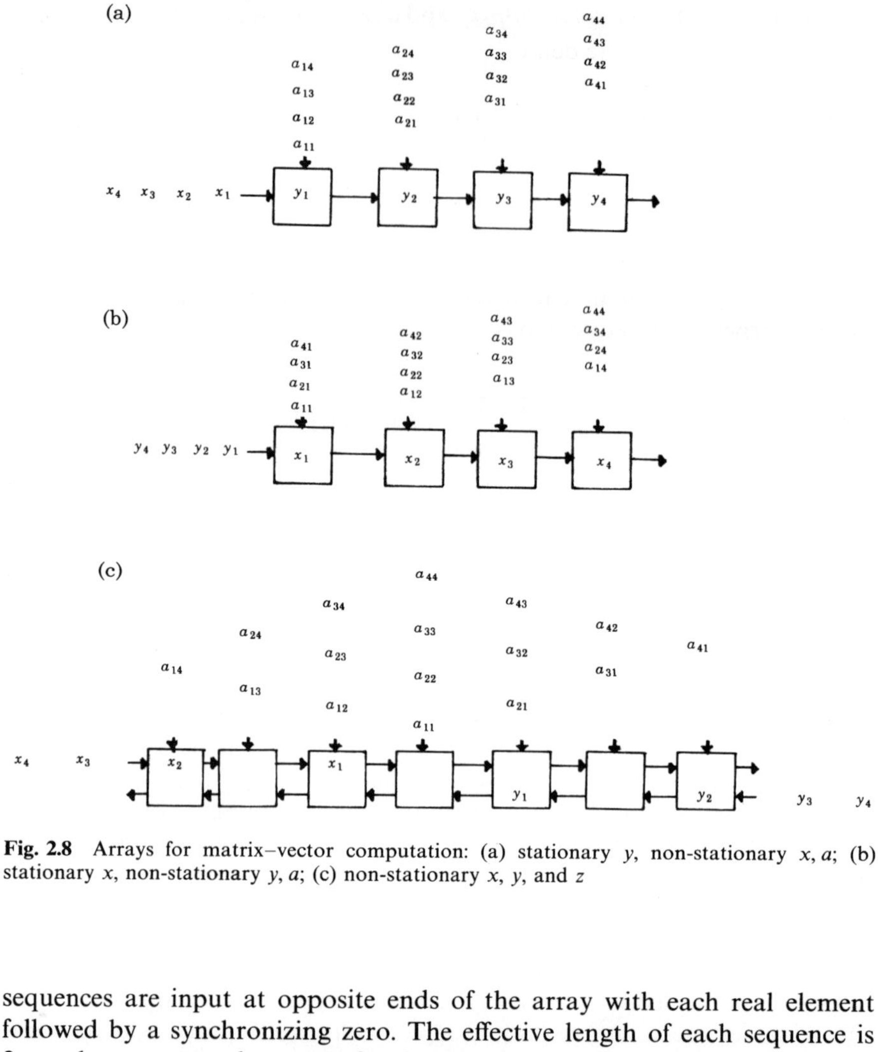

Fig. 2.8 Arrays for matrix–vector computation: (a) stationary y, non-stationary x, a; (b) stationary x, non-stationary y, a; (c) non-stationary x, y, and z

sequences are input at opposite ends of the array with each real element followed by a synchronizing zero. The effective length of each sequence is $2n$ so that y_n enters the array after $2n$ steps and leaves after a further $2n - 1$ steps giving $\mathcal{T} = 4n - 1$ steps altogether. Once the array is full cells work once every two cycles so the efficiency is approximately $e = 0.5$. Draw out some snapshots to clarify the data movement and array operation. The next step is to analyse the designs to indicate which is best. It is clear that all the arrays have roughly the same efficiency so this is not a good measure. The number of input–output connections is $n + 2$ in the first two cases and $2n + 3$ in the latter which favours the first two. However, in both cases some data must be preloaded, which requires extra time and complicates the cell definitions. Linear arrays of n cells can be preloaded in $O(n)$ steps by shuffling data from left to right or in a single step using the matrix connections.

The analysis above favours one of the first two designs—this is true provided the matrices are dense. A special case of the matrix–vector product problem that arises frequently is the $n \times n$ band matrix problem. This is the same as the dense product described above except that for two integers $1 < p, q < n$

$$a_{ij} = 0$$

when $i + p \leq j$ or $j + q \leq i$. The bandwidth of the matrix is $w = p + q - 1$. It is interesting to review the arrays using this new constraint. Figure 2.8(a) and (b) cannot exploit redundant computations introduced by the zeros outside the band of the matrix and always requires $O(n)$ cells. However, the diagonal input format of Fig. 2.8(c) means that cells associated with null diagonals of the matrix receive only zeros and perform no useful computations. Thus the bidirectional array can be reduced to $\mathscr{A} = w$ cells and $O(w)$ input–output connections. The reduced array latency modifies the time to $\mathscr{T} = 2n + w$ steps making the area–time trade-off of the design highly attractive because it is often the case that $w \ll n$. In addition because the data is completely non-stationary there is no need for preloading steps, which simplifies the cell implementation. The array also requires $w + 2$ input–output connections, which is independent of n.

Next, consider the more complex example of computing the product of two matrices. For $n \times n$ matrices A, B, and C this problem can be written as a three-loop sequential program

```
For i := 1 to n do
  For j := 1 to n do
    {
      C[i,j] := 0;
      For k := 1 to n do
        C[i,j] := C[i,j] + A[i,k]*B[k,j]
    }
```

which can be formulated as the following recurrence

$$c_{ijk} = c_{i,j,k-1} + a_{ik}b_{kj}, \quad i, j, k = 1(1)n \tag{2.13}$$

where $c_{i,j,0} = 0$ and the c variable has been pipelined in the k direction. Three-loop programs demand 3-D space–time so the a and b variables must be fully indexed to yield

$$c_{ijk} = c_{i,j,k-1} + a_{i,0,k}b_{0,k,j}, \quad i, j, k = 1(1)n \tag{2.14}$$

from which it is simple to establish (using the subtraction method) that the a and b values require pipelining. Localizing connections in a similar manner to the matrix–vector case we produce the recurrences

$$c_{ijk} = c_{i,j,k-1} + a_{ijk}b_{ijk}, \quad i, j, k = 1(1)n \tag{2.15a}$$

$$a_{ijk} = \begin{cases} a_{i,j-1,k} & j > 1 \\ a_{ik} & j = 1 \end{cases} \tag{2.15b}$$

$$b_{ijk} = \begin{cases} b_{i-1,j,k} & i > 1 \\ b_{kj} & i = 1. \end{cases} \tag{2.15c}$$

Equation (2.15) can be unrolled in 3-D space–time but is much harder to visualize. For simplicity a representation of a 2 × 2 matrix product illustrating the pipelining of individual variables is shown in Fig. 2.9. The diagram can be easily extended to larger matrices.

Two-dimensional systolic arrays for computing the matrix product can be generated by performing different projections of the data dependency from three dimensions into two. Indeed 3 × 3 matrices analogous to those in (2.5) for projecting out the i, j, and k matrices can be given as

$$M_1 = \begin{bmatrix} 0 & 0 & 0 \\ 0 & 1 & 0 \\ 0 & 0 & 1 \end{bmatrix}, \quad M_2 = \begin{bmatrix} 1 & 0 & 0 \\ 0 & 0 & 0 \\ 0 & 0 & 1 \end{bmatrix}, \quad M_3 = \begin{bmatrix} 1 & 0 & 0 \\ 0 & 1 & 0 \\ 0 & 0 & 0 \end{bmatrix} \tag{2.16}$$

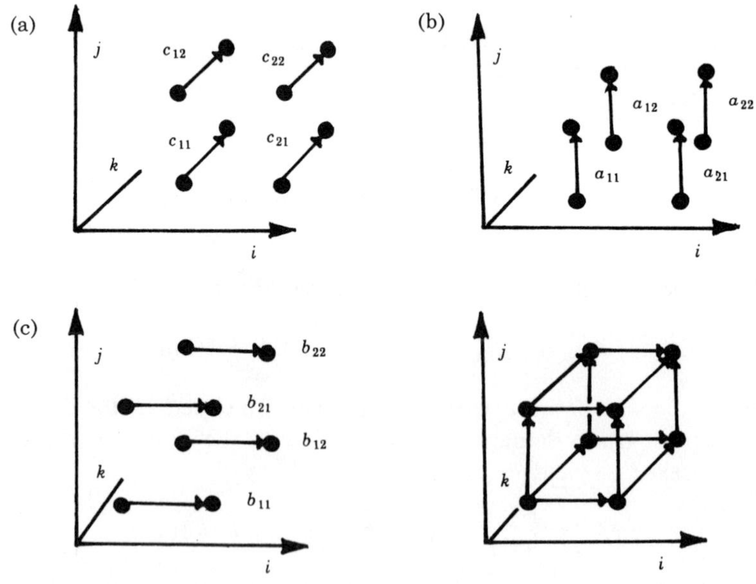

Fig. 2.9 Matrix product data dependencies: (a) c_{ij} values; (b) a_{ik} values; (c) b_{kj} values

and an extension to (2.6) with the form

$$M = M_1 R_1 R_2 \tag{2.17}$$

can be used to provide projections along arbitrary directions by mapping a given direction vector (α, β, γ) onto the i axis and then projecting in the direction $(-1, 0, 0)^t$ (similar formulae exist for the j and k axes). It should be appreciated that mappings such as (2.6) and (2.17) can be generalized in a straightforward way to higher dimensions. Indeed, it is worth pointing out that the number of possible projections for feasible arrays increases as the space–time representation increases in dimension. It follows that many more designs can be generated for n-loop programs than for m-loop programs when $m < n$.

Figure 2.10 shows three possible arrays for the matrix product problem. Figure 2.10(a) is an orthogonally connected array derived using a projection in the direction $(0, 0, -1)^t$ (i.e. along the k axis). The c_{ij} values are stationary while the a_{ij} move from left to right and the b_{ij} move from top to bottom. Tracing a number of snapshots clarifies the array operation and exhibits the principle of *wavefront* data flow. Successive computations are pipelined behind each other in waves which move from the top left to the bottom right corner of the array. For a dense matrix $\mathscr{A} = n^2$ cells are required and $4n$ input–output connections (add $2n$ outputs for unloading the matrix C). Each of the data sequences is of length n and the skewing of data for synchronization purposes means that a_{nn} and b_{nn} are input after $2n$ steps and arrive at the c_{nn} cell after another $n - 1$ steps. We conclude that the total computation time is $\mathscr{T} = 3n - 1$ steps (neglecting the time for unloading the matrix which requires a further n steps). Each of the cells must collect n partial products so the efficiency is $e = 1/3$. Figure 2.10(b) shows the famous hexagonal array of Kung and Leiserson; this array can be produced by projecting the dependency graph along the $(-1, -1, -1)^t$ direction. For A and B matrices with bandwidth w_1 and w_2 respectively $\mathscr{A} = w_1 w_2$ cells and at most $4(w_1 + w_2)$ input–output connections are required. The data sequences can be derived by projecting the data elements mapped onto the nodes of the dependency graph from which it is clear that two synchronizing spaces are required between each real data item. Tracing out some snapshots and moving the data as indicated in the diagram will clarify the array operation. In fact the total delay through the array is $\min(w_1, w_2)$ and the total length of the c data sequences is $3n$ including delays. Consequently the total computation time is $\mathscr{T} = 3n + \min(w_1, w_2)$ steps. Each cell computes real partial products once every three steps so the efficiency is $e = 1/3$ once the array is full of data. Finally, Fig. 2.10(c) illustrates an array derived from a projection in the $(-1, 0, -1)^t$ direction. This array requires $n \times w_1$ cells when w_1 is the bandwidth of the matrix A. Each tier of the array is identical to the array in Fig. 2.8(c) demonstrating that an $n \times n$ matrix product can be interpreted as n independent matrix–vector computations. The matrix A

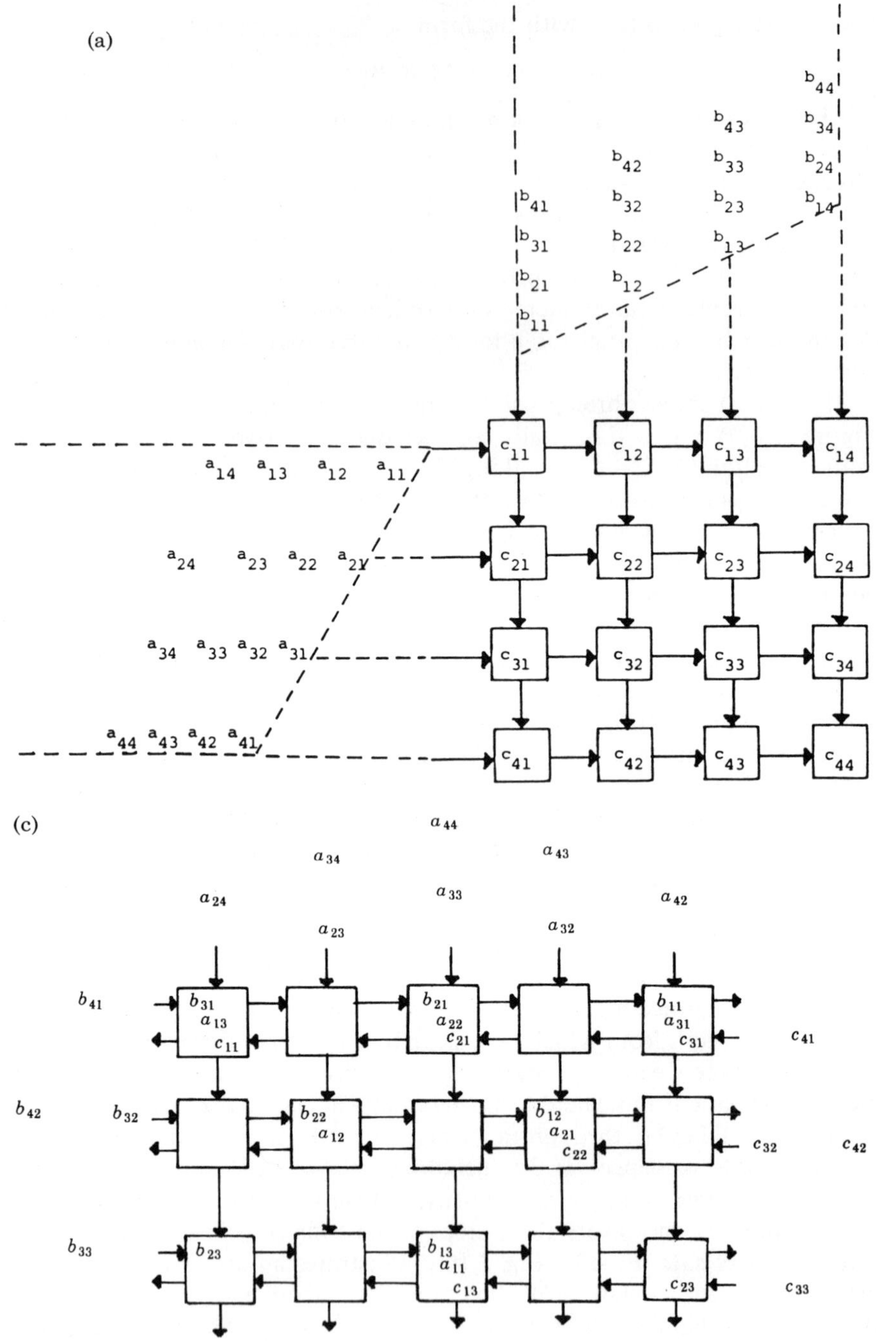

Fig. 2.10 Arrays for matrix product computation: (a) orthogonal (along k direction); (c) pipelined (along line $(-1, 0, -1)^t$)

(b)

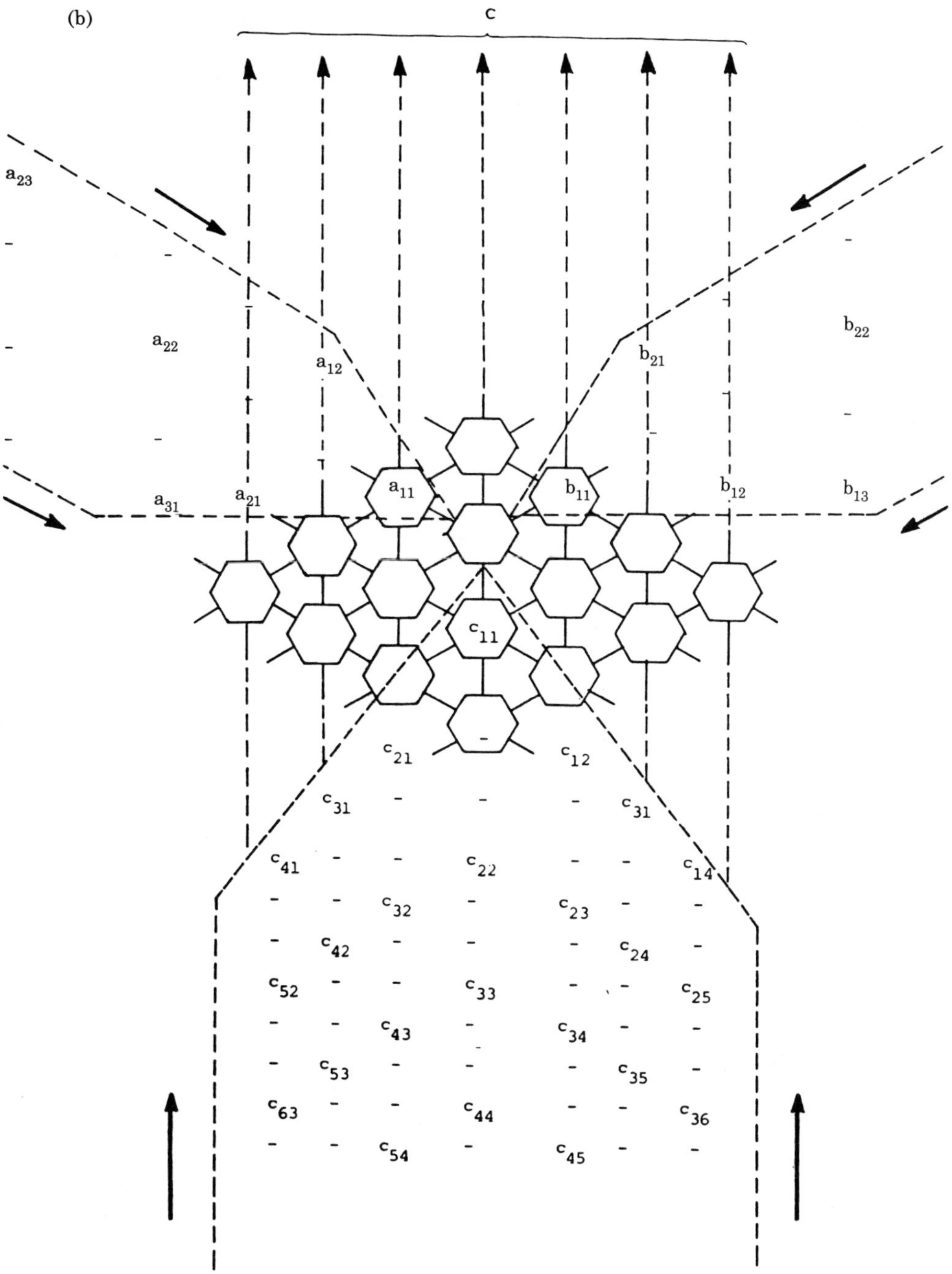

Fig. 2.10 (*cont.*) (b) Hexagonal (along line $(-1, -1, -1)^t$) (C. Mead and L. Conway, *Introduction to VLSI systems*, © 1980, Addison-Wesley Publishing Co. Inc., Reading, Massachusetts, reprinted with permission)

is pipelined from one row of the array to another so that each tier computes a single column of the final matrix C. Synchronization is achieved by adding a dummy value between each real matrix element so that the last c_{ij} value enters the array after $3n$ steps and the array computes with 50 per cent efficiency. The array has a latency of w_1 so that $\mathcal{T} = 3n + w_1$ steps are required in total. Comparing the designs we can see that the orthogonally connected array is most attractive when the matrix is dense because it requires only $3n$ steps and n^2 cells even though its efficiency is not very good. However, when banded matrices are assumed Fig. 2.10(b) is better because it requires only $w_1 w_2$ cells, which is independent of n. In fact most band matrix problems have very narrow bands so that w_1 and w_2 will be significantly less than n. In this latter case the hexagonal product array and the orthogonal array require approximately the same time so the design with the least hardware is preferable. Figure 2.10(c) provides an intermediate alternative when only one of the matrices is banded.

The main point of all these examples is that from a single sequential algorithm we were able to produce, through simple transformations, a sequence of array designs which traded area, time, and efficiency as well as input–output requirements and stationary versus non-stationary data flow. Representing an algorithm with p loops as a data dependency graph in a p-dimensional coordinate system (or two dimensions when $p = 1$) allows a global view of the problem and identifies directions in which computational sites appear bunched together. The choice of which axis in the system represents time is fairly arbitrary so we can interchange axes and apply transformations to manipulate clusters of nodes into orientations where projections into physical space or into time produce attractive area and time trade-offs. The art in systolic design is choosing appropriate transformations to minimize the $\mathcal{A}\mathcal{T}^2$ criterion (or other suitable constraints). Intuitively we can design software packages to enumerate all the possible rotations, translations, etc. and form the projected arrays (see Chapter 8) but for complex algorithms this is a time-consuming task. An experienced designer will often be able to make quick and incisive decisions to prune the design space and rapidly improve a design before employing a software tool.

2.4 Array unrolling and envelopes

The previous sections focused on producing arrays from a given *seed* algorithm. The technique, although useful, is limited by the constraint that data sequences have to travel in straight lines and at the same unit step speed. In addition only simple transformations of the coordinate axes or space–time were considered because they were easy to explain. If we want to define data sequences that change direction in space–time or require non-linear transformations to move computational sites into more favourable locations more sophisticated methods are required. A theoretical treatment of these additional methods would, at this stage, be premature, but to provide a useful stop gap until adequate discussion is possible we will use a technique called *array unrolling* (Culik 1983).

Array unrolling is analogous to the idea of loop unrolling but is applied to an existing systolic array rather than the loop of a program. Recall that a systolic array is the image of a projection of space–time into physical space. An array unrolling reconstructs the data dependency graph and computational sites in space–time. This construction proceeds as follows.

Let $G_1 = (V_1, E_1, \varphi_+, \varphi_-)$ be the graph representing the systolic array. Then:

1. Draw out the snapshots of the systolic array for a number of consecutive time steps. Each snapshot is a copy of G_1 with a different allocation of data items across the nodes. Denote each snapshot as $G_1^{(t)}$ to distinguish the time step.

2. Reconstruct the space–time data dependency graph by connecting each snapshot together. For example, if v_i^t and v_j^t are two nodes in snapshot t and an edge (v_i^t, v_j^t) directed from v_i^t to v_j^t has delay k then replace it by an edge (v_i^t, v_j^{t+k}) connecting node v_i to $G_1^{(t)}$ to node v_j in $G_1^{(t+k)}$.

3. Denote the final graph by $G_2 = (V_2, E_2, \varphi_+^{(2)}, \varphi_-^{(2)})$; this is a space–time graph for the array computation.

Intuitively we have extended (unrolled) the array graph back into space–time, re-creating computational sites projected onto each array cell. Likewise the edges of G_2 are regenerated from the image of projected edges in G_1. Clearly the size of G_2 is bounded in the space direction by the number of nodes in G_1 but can be extended to infinity in the time direction so that G_2 is semi-infinite. Normally we will only be interested in a small subset of the large number of potential computational sites generated which define a computation of a particular length.

One of the main uses of array unrolling is to change existing designs with multiway data flow into equivalent arrays with unidirectional flow so that fault-tolerant techniques can be used for implementation. Figure 2.11 demonstrates the method for a bidirectional array. First we apply the above algorithm to produce the semi-infinite graph with diagonal data movement. It should be clear that the horizontal direction represents space while the vertical direction is time. The unrolled graph shows us that the data flow in the array was completely non-stationary. Next we observe that the unrolled graph is isomorphic to the one shown below it—this can be seen by the nodes labelled ABCD. The two graphs are equivalent, so reversing the unrolling procedure on the second graph will produce an array for the same computation. This rolled-up array is illustrated at the bottom of the diagram and is unidirectional. It is important to note that this mapping can be made without recourse to the original recurrence equations so that knowing one

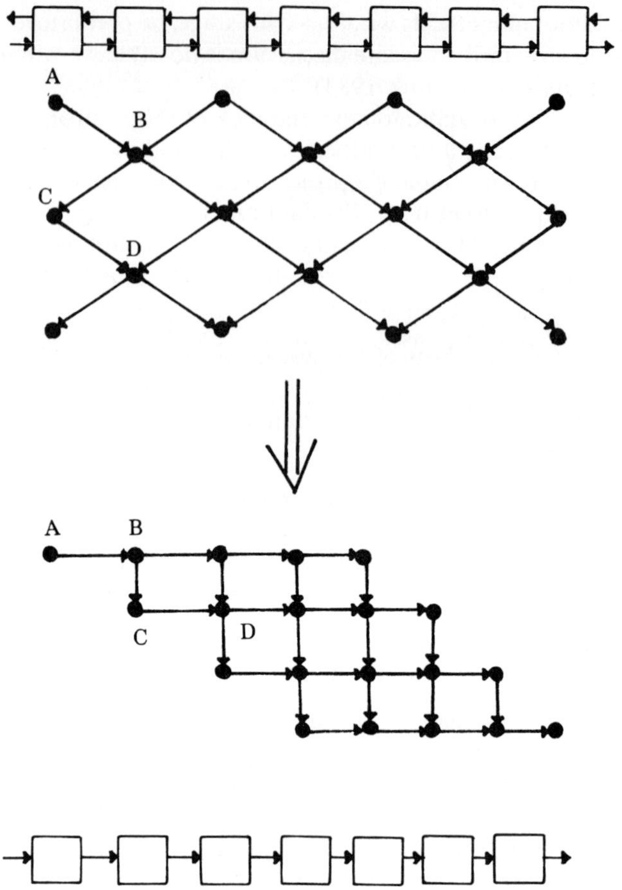

Fig. 2.11 Array unrolling

systolic design greatly simplifies the design process. As a result it is often useful to generate the simplest array using the space–time mapping method and then use array unrollings to reason about modifying data flow characteristics. This last statement is especially true when the space–time representation is difficult to visualize, for example when greater than three dimensions are involved. Indeed we will see some examples in the next chapter where it is profitable to unroll only one or two loops of a program and to generate a subgraph of the complete space–time graph. The full graph is then recovered by unrolling (or replicating) the subgraph for the remaining loops.

Array unrolling can be regarded as the 'inverse' operation to projection. However, it is important to note that an exact copy of the space–time data dependency graph will not be produced. The reason for this is that an array includes extra information about the routing of the input–output data sequences to and from the array boundaries. In the first case sequences have to be moved to their correct starting positions inside the array and in the second case paths have to be determined for output data leaving the array. In an actual implementation of the array we will have to add extra steps to the computation for the data to reach the correct cells. For complex designs it is not at all obvious how this routing can be achieved or whether any extra control is required to prevent cells altering data before the computation starts. Similarly, once we have evaluated all the computations associated with nodes of the data dependency graph we will have to extract the result from the array. In some cases the data will emerge naturally from a projected array but in many cases additional unloading steps will be required to force sequences to leave from cells on the boundary of the design. It follows that the array must be controlled properly to prevent cells from destroying the final result before it has had a chance to emerge from the array.

The correct input and output paths from the boundaries of the array can be determined quite easily using the *envelope* algorithm. Enveloping is a three-stage process.

Stage 1. Determine an envelope in space–time that encloses the data dependency graph. This is achieved by finding the perimeter of the projected array and unrolling it in space–time.

Stage 2. Unroll the dependency graph forwards in time by extending the data flow to the boundary of the envelope. This determines the output routing.

State 3. Unroll the dependency graph backwards in time extending the data flow to the envelope boundary. This determines the input–output routing.

Figure 2.12 demonstrates the envelope algorithm for the problem of matrix–vector computation and the array in Fig. 2.8(c). In this example, the data sequences must be synchronized correctly otherwise they will be out of phase with each other and generate incorrect computations. The first step requires a projection direction which for Fig. 2.8(c) is $(-1, -1)^t$. The perimeter of the array amounts to just the endpoints of the array so that unrolling produces the dashed lines in Fig. 2.12(a). Next we need to determine how the x and y values which are non-stationary will leave the array. This is achieved by tracing the data pipelining and extending forwards past the end of the computation to generate the open circles in Fig. 2.12(b). The process terminates when all the output sequences reach the boundary defined by the envelope. We then repeat the process but extend the graph backwards in time until all the inputs to the dependency graph have been mapped onto the boundary of the envelope. This creates additional open circles as shown in Fig. 2.12(c). Projecting out the extended data dependency graph produces an array in which all the data input and output are confined to the

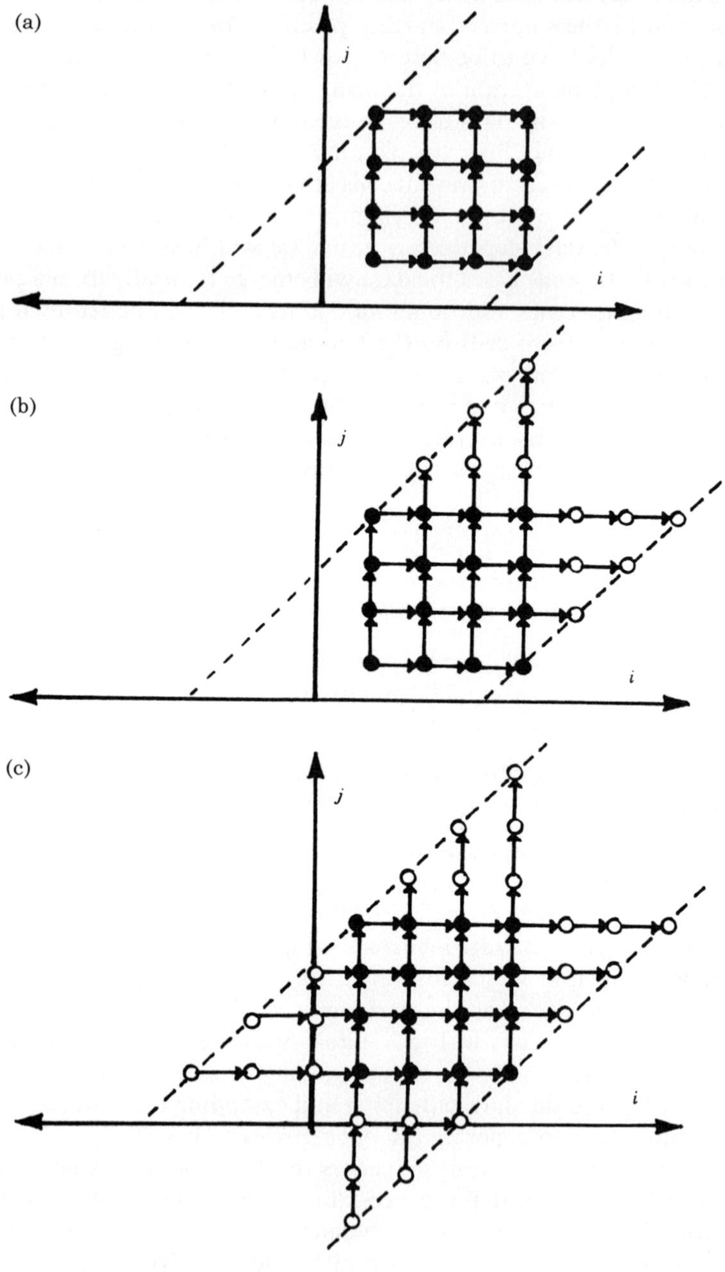

Fig. 2.12 Routing input–output using envelopes: (a) array; (b) roll forward; (c) roll back

boundaries of the array. Indirectly the process also gives us information about how long to delay the input of data sequences so that they will synchronize correctly. For example, in this case the path of the first x value to enter the graph to the envelope is three steps, the same as the path for the first y value so that no delay is required. If there had been more steps in one direction than the other some initial synchronizing steps would have been necessary. Finally it should be pointed out that the envelope method will only work for non-stationary data sequences. If data are stationary it moves parallel to the direction of projection in space–time, and consequently roll-forward and roll-back are infinite procedures that never terminate. Nevertheless the technique is quite useful in determining array data sequences once an initial projection of a graph has been obtained.

2.5 Retiming and cuts

From our examples so far it is clear that a significant degree of design time is spent ensuring that the right data arrive at the right place at the right time. Indeed, the ability to spot good transformations that achieve this goal is the essential art in systolic design. The design process would be more flexible if it were possible to be fairly loose in the specification of timing and placement of data. For example, it is often easier to produce a semi-systolic design involving broadcasting than a purely systolic design with strictly nearest-neighbour connections (see the matrix product example above). In this section we will show that such flexibility can be gained by retiming an underlying graph representing a projected array or dependence graph.

Retiming is based on the physical reality that data takes time to propagate down connections. If a design has only nearest-neighbour connections then all connections can be assumed to have the same propagation delay and this delay can be built into the cost of the cell operation and ignored. In more general connection structures such assumptions are not valid and this makes them difficult to manipulate. For systolic design the idea of limited propagation delay is essential, otherwise it becomes difficult to maintain a synchronous method of timing. For example, long propagation delays such as broadcasts produce clock skew and mistiming of data resulting in erroneous computations. To model a propagation delay we interpret the data as being passed through a number of unit delay registers. The number of these registers on a link can be expressed as a weighting function associated with a digraph. Retiming a graph can now be defined as the process of changing the delay (or weighting) function of the graph in a way that does not alter the computation of its associated array. Some facts about graphs with delay modelling are immediately apparent. For example, if a cycle of zero delay exists it is inevitable that collision of data must occur somewhere in the cycle; it follows that any sensible cycle must involve some delays. It should also be clear that introducing delays can often produce pipelining and improve the throughput of design. This follows because cells can be freed for more computations while data is moving along a link. Finally, if a graph is acyclic it is possible to remove or add delays associated with links by retiming—this is the result of the famous retiming lemmas due to Leiserson and Saxe (1983).

***k*-slowing lemma** If all the delays of a timing graph are multiplied by $k > 1$ then the cells can be redesigned so that the array works correctly but at $1/k$ the speed (i.e. k-slowed).

Proof (i) The array will form the same function if the delay of data sequences arriving at each cell are multiplied by a constant—simply change the cell timing so it requires k cycles instead of 1. (ii) Two data sequences a and b travelling between cells u and v along different paths P_1 and P_2 have delays $l = d^*(P_1)$ and $m = d^*(P_2)$ respectively (where d^* is a function representing the total delay of a path) and arrive at times differing by $|l - m|$. Multiplying this by k ensures that they arrive at times differing by $k|l - m|$ so k-slowing the design preserves operation.

Timing shift lemma Suppose $k > 0$ and that cell v has outgoing links which all have delay greater than k. Then we can add k delays to all the incoming links and subtract from all outgoing links. Provided the cells are modified correctly the array will still work correctly. [Remark: The reverse procedure of moving delays from incoming links to outgoing links is also valid.]

Proof Delays before and after a cell provide a certain amount of slack time. k represents the largest shift in time that a cell can make and still produce its result before or at the time required by other cells depending on its output.

Next we consider the retiming method. The essential feature is the definition of a lag function which determines how much a cell must lag behind other cells in the network. More formally, the lag of cell v is given by

$$\text{lag}(v) = \max(|P| - d^*(P))$$

where $|P|$ is the number of edges in a path from S to v, and $d^*(P)$ is the total delay associated with these edges. Recall that S is a node representing a global input source.

Retiming lemma (Leiserson and Saxe 1983) Let $D = (V, E, \varphi_-, \varphi_+)$ be a digraph with no cycle of zero delay. Then let lag: $V_U\{S, T\} \to Z$ and define $d\colon E \to Z$ as a weighting function of D and let $w\colon E \to Z$ be a new weighting function such that

$$w(e) = kd(e) + \text{lag}(\varphi_+(e)) - \text{lag}(\varphi_-(e))$$

where $k > 0$ is an integer. If, for all $e \in E$, $w(e) \geq 0$ then D with a weight function of w is a retiming of D with weight function d.

Proof Let D be the original graph with no zero-delay cycles. Define lag(v) of every cell to be the longest path of zero-delay links ending at v. (i) lag(v) is finite and equal to the amount cell v must lag behind cells with zero lag. (ii) There is at least one node with zero lag otherwise we could trace back along the links and find a cycle of zero delay, because D is finite and cells must be repeated eventually. (iii) A link from u to v with delay zero in D will be given by lag(v) − lag(u) when the largest path to u must be shorter than the largest path of v making the delay positive. (iv) In the event that v is the source of a link with non-zero delay z to node t with a lag much less than v, we would have to subtract lag(v) − lag(t) from the link with delay z. This follows because $\text{lag}(t) - \text{lag}(v) < 0$ and consequently $z + \text{lag}(t) - \text{lag}(v)$ could be negative. In this case we choose some k such that $zk > \text{lag}(v) - \text{lag}(t)$ for all nodes, making the delay for the link from v to t positive.

By extending the definition of w and d to deal with paths of links the equivalent result $w^*(P) = d^*(P) + \text{lag}(\varphi^*_+(P)) - \text{lag}(\varphi^*_-(P))$ for a given path P in D is easily derived. It follows that a necessary and sufficient condition for a retiming of D in which every link has non-zero delay is that, for every cycle C in D, $d^*(C) \geq |C|$. Unfortunately this condition may not always be satisfied and one must multiply the delay of each link in D by some integer value $k > 0$ which forces the condition to be true.

We conclude that graphs can be retimed in a two-stage process. First select k using the k-slowing lemma and then apply the retiming lemma. Delay each cell of lag(z) by z cycles and then for all links from u ending at v with zero delay replace the delay with lag(v) − lag(u), and for links with non-zero delay replace with $d(e)k + \text{lag}(v) - \text{lag}(u)$ where e is the link from u to v. Examples of retiming are shown in Figs 2.13 and 2.14. Figure 2.13(a) is an example of a graph with zero-delay paths but no cycles; each edge on the graph is labelled with its associated delay and each node has a lag value associated with it shown inside a dashed circle. Now, applying the retiming lemma produces the new delay assignment shown in Fig. 2.13(b)—notice that there are no zero-delay edges. The delay for edge (v_4, v_2) is computed by subtracting the lag values for v_2 and v_4. Other delays are calculated similarly. Readers should take a moment to convince themselves that the arrival of data is exactly the same in Fig. 2.13(a) as Fig. 2.13(b) so the latter is a valid retiming of the former. Next we can see that some edges have more delays than others. To try and balance the delays on each edge we will apply the timing shift lemma. Figure 2.13(c) shows the result. The delay of 3 on (v_1, v_2) has been reduced to 2 by moving v_1 forward in time. Likewise, v_3 has also been shifted (remember that T is for notational convenience and is not part of a physical implementation). All the cells on the top path from S to T now have delays of 2. Next consider the bottom path. We remove the delay of 3 on (v_4, v_5) by moving one delay forward; this must affect all incoming edges so the delay on (v_2, v_5) is reduced to zero. Alternatively we could have moved

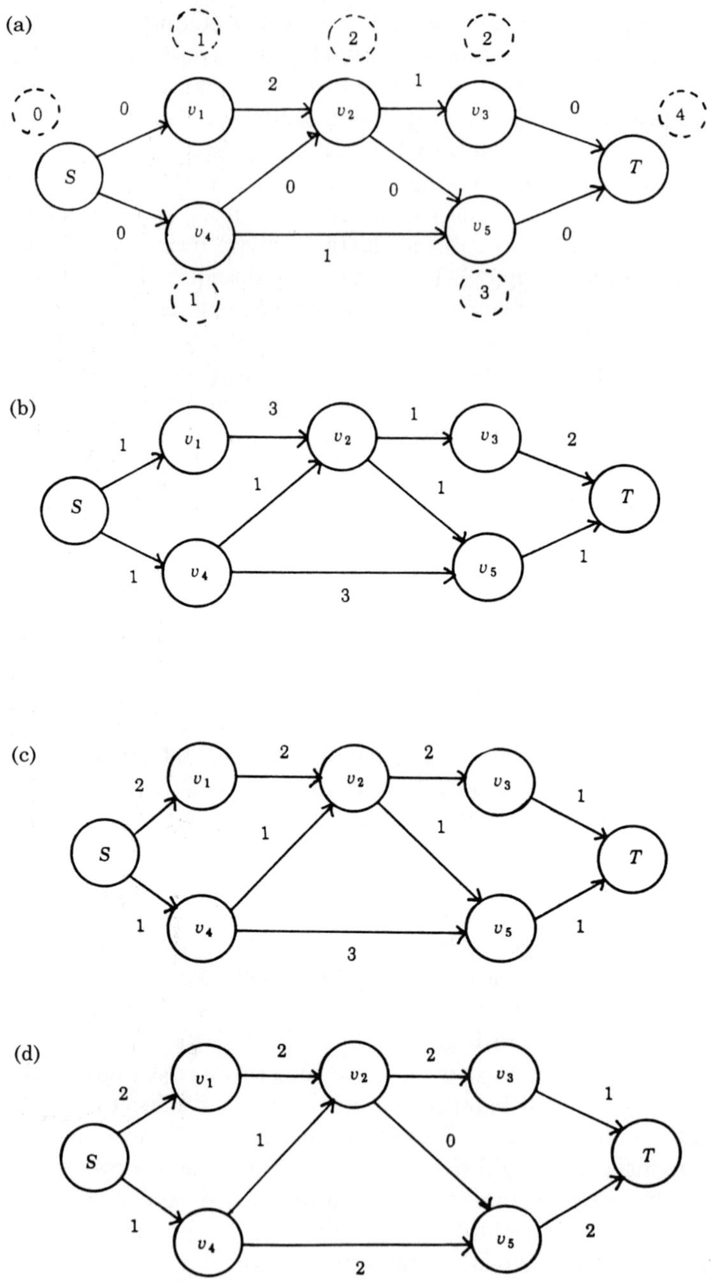

Fig. 2.13 Retiming without cycles: (a) lag computation; (b) retiming; (c), (d) timing shift

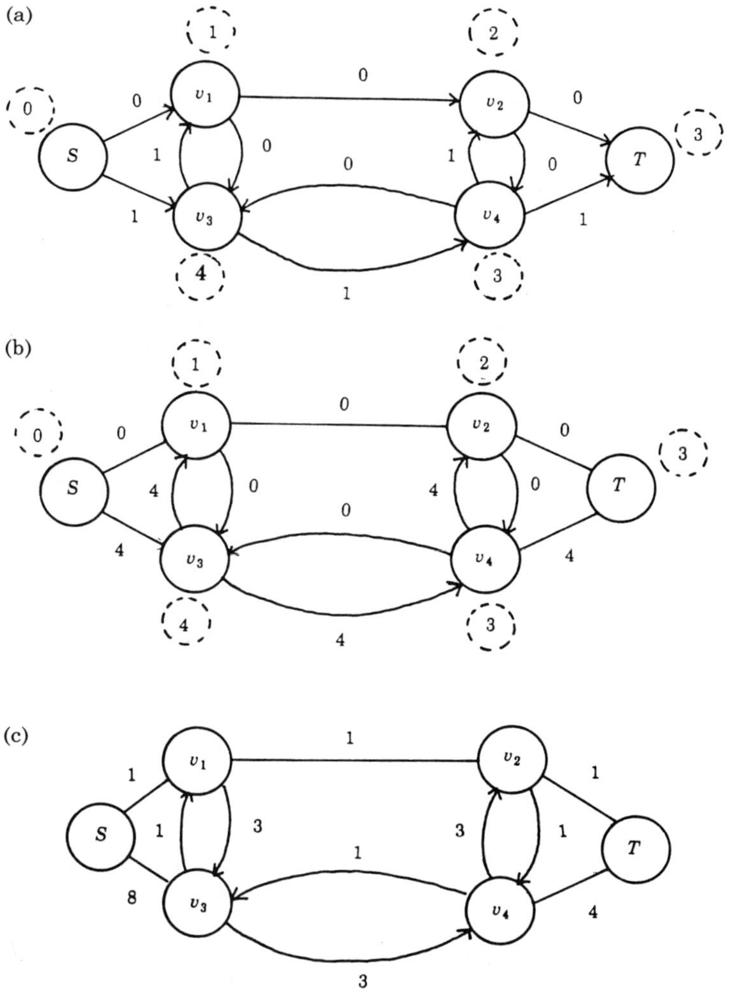

Fig. 2.14 Retiming with cycles (of non-zero delay): (a) assignment of lags; (b) *k*-slowing and new lags; (c) retimed version

v_4 forward to make (v_4, v_5) have delay 2, but (v_4, v_2) would have become zero. Next consider Fig. 2.14(a); this is an example of a graph with cycles, but there are no cycles of zero delay. Again the lags are shown in dashed circles beside a node and delays are edge labels. If we apply the retiming lemma immediately we find that some edges will have negative delay. For example, edge (v_3, v_1) has delay $1 - 4 = -3$, which is due to the path of zero delay. Before we can retime this graph we must apply the *k*-slowing lemma by choosing some appropriate value of *k*. It is easy to see that increasing the delays on the edges will eventually produce a non-zero result because the definition of lag involves only the path length, when a path of zero delay is involved, which is static for a given graph. Trial and error (in fact ensuring that the above subtraction of lags gives any value greater than zero) determines $k = 4$ and all delays in Fig. 2.14(a) are multiplied to produce Fig. 2.14(b). Applying the retiming method in the normal fashion produces the retimed graph in Fig. 2.14(c) which has no edges of zero delay. Readers should again take a few moments to convince themselves that the arrival of data at each cell is identical to that of Fig. 2.14(c) but possibly shifted in time.

Figure 2.15 illustrates a more practical example of retiming. Here we have a graph which involves some broadcasting to cells. Each of the long connections in Fig. 2.15(a) have zero delay so that the data travelling along the associated connection require zero time to arrive at the indicated cells. Meanwhile, other data are travelling on point-to-point connections from one cell to another. To retime the graph we first compute the associated lag functions for each node as shown in Fig. 2.15(b). Applying the retiming lemmas then produces the retimed graph in Fig. 2.15(c) where each of the zero-delay broadcast connections have been replaced by non-zero delays. Finally it is simple to show that Fig. 2.15(c) is equivalent to Fig. 2.15(d) by a suitable sharing of delays. It follows that we can use retiming as a method for determining a suitable pipelining in cases such as the matrix–vector and the matrix product examples of previous sections. Hence the retimings give us a mechanism for localizing data flow. More powerful and simpler methods are considered below and in Chapter 8.

We can see that the application of the retiming lemma requires the assignment of a lag value to every cell—a complex, time-consuming, and error-prone task. Fortunately related work by Kung and Lin (1983) and Kung and Lam (1984) has resulted in a simpler process which can be summarized by the so-called cut theorem. Before this important result can be stated we require some additional definitions. First the undirected graph $\bar{D}$ of D is constructed by adding a copy of each link in E but with opposite direction (i.e. for each $e \in E$ make an $\bar{e}$ link with the property $\varphi_+(e) = \varphi_-(\bar{e})$ and $\varphi_-(e) = \varphi_+(\bar{e})$. We say that D is connected if for every pair of cells u and v in D a path from u to v can be found in $\bar{D}$. Finally, if D is connected, we define a *cutset* of D to be a subset of links which disconnects D when they are removed. C is minimal if a subset of C cannot be found that still disconnects D.

Cut theorem (Kung and Lam 1984) Let $D = (V, E, \varphi_+, \varphi_-)$ be a connected digraph with no zero-delay loops, and let C be a minimal cutset for D. In the disconnected graph resulting from the removal of links in C from E let $\bar{S}$ be the connected component containing S. If d is a weight function on E

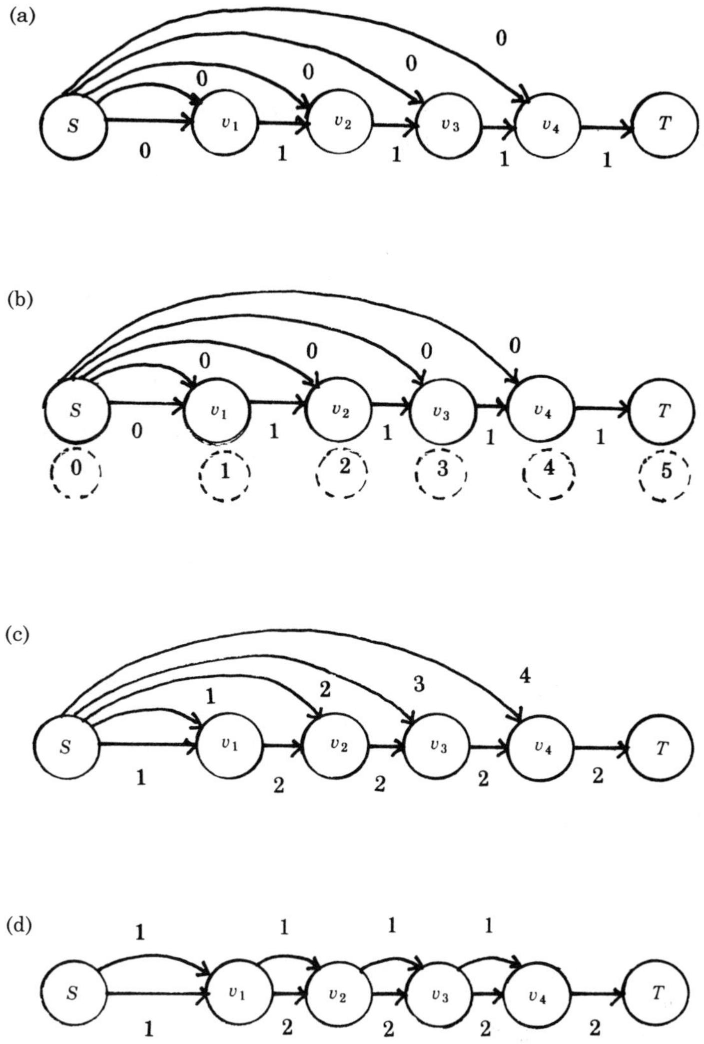

Fig. 2.15 Pipelining variables: (a) broadcast graph; (b) assignment of lags; (c) retimed graph; (d) localized array

then w: $E \rightarrow Z$ is defined as

$$w(e) = \begin{cases} d(e) + k & \text{if } e \in C \text{ and } \varphi_{-}(e) \in \bar{S} \\ d(e) - k & \text{if } e \in C \text{ and } \varphi_{-}(e) \notin \bar{S} \\ d(e) & \text{if } e \notin C. \end{cases}$$

If, for every e in E, $w(e) \geq 0$, then D with weighting function w is a retiming of D with weighting function d.

Proof First define lag: $V_U\{S, T\} \to Z$ as

$$\text{lag}(v) = \begin{cases} 0 & \text{if } v \in \bar{S} \\ k & \text{otherwise} \end{cases}$$

for each node in D. Now if edge e is in C either

$$\varphi_-(e) \in \bar{S} \quad \text{and} \quad \varphi_+(e) \notin \bar{S}$$

or

$$\varphi_+(e) \in \bar{S} \quad \text{and} \quad \varphi_-(e) \notin \bar{S}$$

and if we let $u = \varphi_-(e)$ and $v = \varphi_+(e)$ then $\text{lag}(v) - \text{lag}(u) = k$. For e not in C, $\text{lag}(u) = \text{lag}(v)$ so that $\text{lag}(u) - \text{lag}(v) = 0$ and the result follows from the retiming lemma because $w(e) = d(e) + \text{lag}(\varphi_+(e)) - \text{lag}(\varphi_-(e))$.

The upshot of this result is that if we find a minimal cutset for a given graph we can add k delays to every link in the cutset with a given direction and subtract k from the remaining links in the cutset. The resulting array is a retiming provided all the delays are still positive. Intuitively the cut is a line which partitions the graph D by severing all the links from the source S to sink T; we can add as many delays as we wish to the cutset provided that the computation is preserved. More recently Dew and McEvoy (1988) have presented a more general notion of a cut which allows delays on all arcs of the cutset. Kung (1984) also considers some extensions. As an example of cuts and cutsets we will attempt to retime the convolution arrays in Fig. 1.1. The example also allows us to distinguish between the graphs used for retiming, data dependencies, and arrays. In Fig. 1.1 we showed the array as a graph in which input and output edges have one edge not attached to a node (we use S and T to force the array to be a true graph in this section). The data dependency graph is produced directly from the array snapshots as described in the previous section so that cells still represent atomic operations. In retiming the array graphs are interpreted differently. We associate delays with edges and also expand the cell so that the actual computations are more explicit as shown in Fig. 2.16(i). The circle containing a plus represents an addition, and the circle with an asterisk multiplication. There is no delay associated with the passage of data through circles but timing is retained by adding delays to edges. Each array cell or computational site of a dependency graph is a pair of add and multiply circles which require unit time. Note that there is zero delay between the adder and multiplier of each cell—this implies natural propagation of data during the unit step. To retime the design using cuts we note that the vertical dashed line in Fig. 2.16(ii) forms a cutset. Choosing $k = 1$ we can subtract one delay off the upper link and add it to the lower link to produce the delays shown. The process can be repeated for the next set of edges along the array which are also a cutset so that we produce Fig. 2.16(iii) and then again to produce Fig. 2.16(iv). Now the adders form a path of zero delay and because addition is

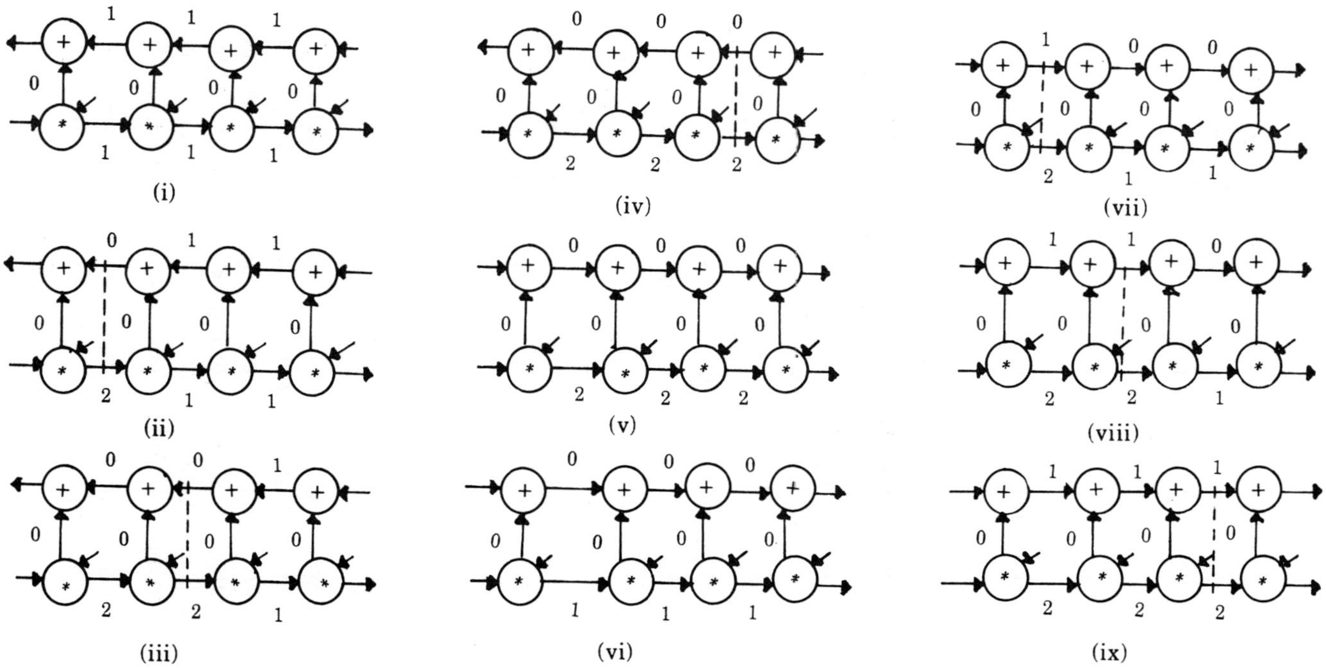

Fig. 2.16 Application of the cut theorem

associative we can simply reverse the direction of the communication path to produce a unidirectional array as shown in Fig. 2.16(v). This design is 2-slow so applying the k-slowing lemma in reverse allows all the delays to be divided by 2 to speed up the design as shown in Fig. 2.16(vi). Next we apply the cut theorem again to introduce a single delay onto each of the top links as shown in Fig. 2.16(vii). The process can be repeated along the array to produce Fig. 2.16(viii) and Fig. 2.16(ix), the final array.

2.6 Design methodology

Now that we have encountered some methods for defining and manipulating systolic algorithms we can begin to move away from an *ad hoc* approach to systolic design. The *ad hoc* philosophy is this: we sit down with a pen, piece of paper, and a recurrence equation and sketch various array organizations until we stumble across an organization that works. In the light of the preceding sections it is surprising that the *ad hoc* method is still quite prevalent among parallel algorithm designers. This may, in part, be due to the lack of widely available software tools for visualizing and transforming data dependency graphs (although usable software is now emerging; see Chapter 8). The developmental process we suggest follows closely the established and disciplined approach of Horowitz and Sahni (1978) for program development. In the systolic paradigm the design cycle requires the following five stages.

1. *Specification.* Take the recurrence form or *seed* algorithm for a problem and map it into space–time to create a space–time data dependency graph. Attention should be given to representing the computation correctly rather than exposing any particular features of the problem and often involves pipelining variables.

2. *Design.* Perform some transformations on the representation in space–time to bring out particular features suitable to your design objectives (e.g. making certain data sequences stationary or non-stationary). Project the design into pure space dimensions and determine the data flow sequences for the resulting array. Notice that the physical space can be greater than two dimensions although a plane is highly suited to VLSI techniques. More than one projection is allowed to reduce the required space to two dimensions but this may have adverse effects on the allocation of computation to cells (such as mapping a number of different operations to the same cell).

3. *Analysis.* Evaluate the design with respect to the area ($\mathscr{A}$) and time ($\mathscr{T}$) of the design and establish the efficiency (e). Consider the $\mathscr{A}\mathscr{T}^2$ criterion, or one more suited to your problem domain, and compare the array with any other existing solutions (not necessarily systolic). The unit area of one design may be different from that of another especially if renormalization

and/or multiple projection are employed because the basic operations of cells could be different. These problems should be taken into account when analysing the design.

4. *Refinement*. Does the design meet your requirements? Perhaps further manipulations of space–time would produce a better form. Alternatively can retiming and cuts be used to improve the pipeline properties of the array (e.g. two-level pipelining)? Are there any different *seed* algorithms which might produce a modified partial ordering of instructions or a different space–time representation?

5. *Verification*. Does the design actually do what it was intended to do? Test the design with trial implementations/simulations, or produce a formal proof that the array meets the specifications. The former may be achieved by writing a suitable version in an appropriate parallel language, or mapping the design into a suitable programmable architecture. The latter is generally non-trivial and requires iteration of 1–4 as inaccuracies are detected.

It is important to notice the role of retiming and representation in space–time. The latter is used to produce an initial array while the former improves upon existing designs. Quite often a design is easily specified with the aid of broadcasting and rather than perform space–time manipulation directly it is better to project out the semi-systolic array and then apply retiming to produce a truly systolic version. Conversely if a design already exists and all we want to do is refine it, retiming can be an important first step. If further improvements are required array unrolling can be adopted to map the array back into space–time for further geometric manipulations.

The techniques considered in this chapter are very simple but can take us a long way in systolic design. Indeed they can be quite effective for a wide range of problems including a number of imporatnt applications—we will consider some in detail in the next few chapters. It should be clear that mapping out space–time representations is both tedious and time consuming, and unless software tools are available, it is virtually impossible for large and complex computations. These difficulties can be alleviated by applying the principle of abstraction. Abstraction leads to a hierarchical method of design, which starts with a recurrence and unrolls loops selectively to produce array components which are familiar. The art in systolic design is choosing the correct loops to unroll and the right cell components to reduce the area and time requirements of a design. The naive and brute-force approach is to unroll all the loops of a recurrence and generate a complete space–time representation which can be manipulated. Unfortunately the more complex the design the more difficult it becomes to separate the phases of computation. While a full space–time description is satisfying in its completeness, an array produced by divide and conquer principles using levels of abstraction is often faster for the more experienced designer. One can always recover the full space–time representation by unrolling the component arrays. If the components are standard arrays they have already been analysed in space–time and can form subgraphs of the final space–time representation.

Finally, although modelling algorithms geometrically in space–time is simple and gives an intuitive insight into the objectives of design, more sophisticated methods exist. We favour the simplistic approach described above because, as pointed out by Cappello and Steiglitz (1984), such models allow one to visualize the data flow and to make informed decisions on how to improve the space or time properties of algorithms. Such insights are invaluable to the inexperienced designer. The lemmas on retiming and the cut theorem are more involved and have formed the basis for automated design techniques in synchronous systems and so deserve adequate discussion in their own right if only from a historical point of view. More complex techniques simply generalize retiming methods and develop more involved transformations (e.g. non-linear transformations). In particular we have been rather naive in our choice of time directions. More sophisticated methods provide techniques for determining optimal timing schedules for nodes in the dependency graph (see Chapter 8), area–time minimal arrays, and the automatic production of control sequences. However, the underlying design methodology of modelling recurrences in space–time remains the same, the essential feature being the representation of time in recurrences.

2.7 Notation

Finally, to conclude this chapter a few brief words are in order about the representation of systolic arrays in the rest of the text. A suitable choice of notation must be made because it plays an important role throughout the text. Many representations for systolic algorithms are possible. For example, McKevoy (1986) considers directed graphs as a syntax and state-transition semantics for timing. Kung (1984) has adopted a signal flow graph model while Kung and Lin (1983) favour an algebraic representation based on z-graphs. Other representations such as dependency graphs, denotational semantics (synchronous circuits), and the transformation of data index sets among others have been suggested. Alternatively, interconnection topologies can always be represented as virtual topologies in an appropriate parallel language. For example, a message-passing language such as Occam allows a natural mapping of cells to processes and data sequences to messages. The problem is, what representation should we adopt? On the one hand, a rigorous analysis of each algorithm presented is both precise and satisfying but tends to alienate the less formally minded reader. On the other hand, specifications in terms of code are also concrete and unambiguous but the final form of presentation depends upon specific features of the given language rather than the algorithm itself. For example, even simple Occam programs can be quite large once the generation of input and output data sequences, interfacing, and cells have been defined.

In this text we have opted for the middle ground and will not burden the reader with reams of mathematical definitions and equations, nor shall we present pages and pages of code. Instead we will continue to use graphs as representations of arrays. These graphs will be suitably augmented with appropriate algorithmic definitions for cells, and implied structures for data sequences which can be derived from the cell input–output and the array input. Our motivation for this representation is two-fold. First, experience shows that novice designers feel quite comfortable with the idea of pictorial representations of systolic algorithms. Indeed, the majority of research literature on systolic algorithms adopts the same convention as this text for relating new designs. Consequently the interested reader should have no problems in coping with more advanced literature on the topic. Second, graphs are intuitive objects which allow immediate comprehension of problems in a more direct way than offered by textual information in the form of program code or mathematics. The former is supported by the natural affinity of humans for pattern recognition while the latter requires a more formal training. It is, however, important to note that there is no loss of information or accuracy in our representation, simply that some features may be more explicit than others.

It remains only to clarify the specification of algorithms and arrays. Systolic algorithms will be treated as graphs as described in Section 2.1; these graphs represent a connection topology and are augmented with data sequences, which show how data is entered into the array (see Figs 2.4, 2.6, 2.7, and 2.10. The actual nodes of the graphs are the cells. In our examples so far we have used only a single cell type (the inner product step, IPS) but in general several different cell types will appear in a design. To clarify the operation of the cells we will include a cell description which consists of an internal connection structure or a sequential algorithm when cell computations are more complex. Figure 2.17 shows cells' definitions for the arrays developed in this chapter using the first method (the small square cells are latches which hold data in a cell and can be interpreted as delays or registers). The second method is illustrated by the convolution arrays in Fig. 1.1. Which method is used for a design depends on the particular features that need to be emphasized. In addition it is useful to show the duality between hardware and algorithm. It is these complementary features that hold the key to successful systolic design.

Exercises

1. A point (x, y) in a 2-D coordinate system is represented by the 3-D vector $(x, y, 1)^t$. Show that the 3×3 matrices

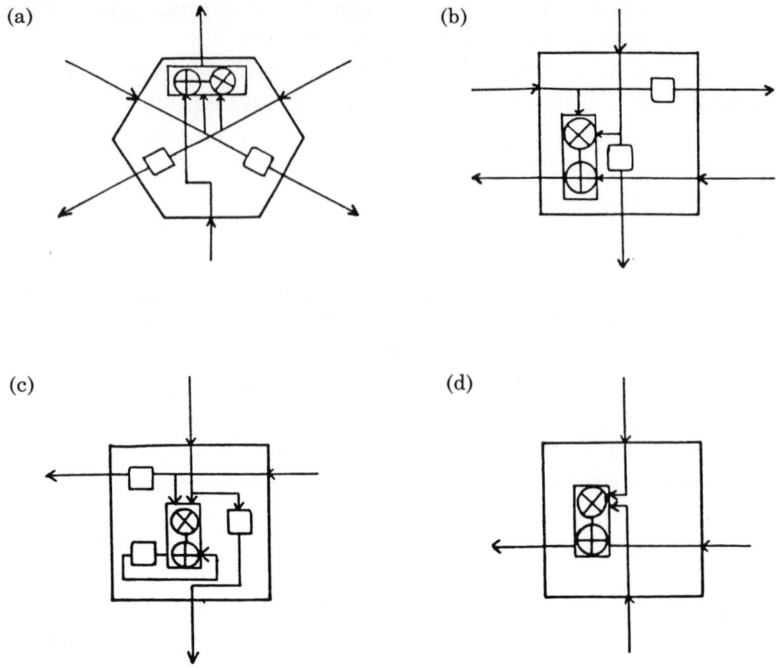

Fig. 2.17 Basic inner product cells: (a) hex; (b) three way; (c) accumulating; (d) one-way instant

$$T = \begin{bmatrix} 1 & 0 & -Tx \\ 0 & 1 & -Ty \\ 0 & 0 & 1 \end{bmatrix}, \quad S = \begin{bmatrix} Sx & 0 & 0 \\ 0 & Sy & 0 \\ 0 & 0 & 1 \end{bmatrix}, \quad R = \begin{bmatrix} \cos\theta & \sin\theta & 0 \\ -\sin\theta & \cos\theta & 0 \\ 0 & 0 & 0 \end{bmatrix}$$

can be used to translate, scale, and rotate a 2-D space. What is the effect of $S \times R \times T$ (where $\times$'s denote matrix product)?

2. Demonstrate that the following changes in space are equivalent:

   (a) moving space by (Tx, Ty) is equivalent to translating the axes by $(-Tx, -Ty)$;

   (b) stretching space by a factor Sx in the x direction and Sy in the y direction is equivalent to scaling the x axis by Sx and the y axis by Sy.

   (c) rotating space by an angle θ is equivalent to rotating the axes by $-\theta$.

3. Suppose that a point (x, y, z) in a three-axis coordinate system is

represented by the vector $(x, y, z, 1)^t$. Show that the 4×4 matrices

$$T = \begin{bmatrix} 1 & 0 & 0 & -Tx \\ 0 & 1 & 0 & -Ty \\ 0 & 0 & 1 & -Tz \\ 0 & 0 & 0 & 1 \end{bmatrix}, \quad S = \begin{bmatrix} Sx & 0 & 0 & 0 \\ 0 & Sy & 0 & 0 \\ 0 & 0 & Sz & 0 \\ 0 & 0 & 0 & 1 \end{bmatrix}$$

will translate and scale the point, and that

$$\begin{bmatrix} c & s & 0 & 0 \\ -s & c & 0 & 0 \\ 0 & 0 & 1 & 0 \\ 0 & 0 & 0 & 1 \end{bmatrix}, \quad \begin{bmatrix} c & 0 & -s & 0 \\ 0 & 1 & 0 & 0 \\ s & 0 & c & 0 \\ 0 & 0 & 0 & 1 \end{bmatrix}, \quad \begin{bmatrix} 1 & 0 & 0 & 0 \\ 0 & c & s & 0 \\ 0 & -s & c & 0 \\ 0 & 0 & 0 & 1 \end{bmatrix}$$

rotate by an angle θ about the z, y, and x axes respectively, where $c = \cos\theta$ and $s = \sin\theta$.

4. A permutation matrix P is a matrix that has precisely one entry whose value is one in each column and each row, and all of whose other entries are zero. Show that for certain angles θ the matrices above reduce to permutation matrices. Comment on the use of this property in manipulating systolic designs.
5. Show that a data dependency graph with n nodes can be represented (for manipulation purposes) as an $m \times n$ matrix Γ of $m \times 1$ column vectors for a *p-dimensional* space–time coordinate system when $m = p + 1$. When $p \leq 3$ what is the effect of $S \times \Gamma$, $T \times \Gamma$, $R \times \Gamma$? Use this result to formalize the manipulation of space–time.
6. Cappello and Steiglitz (1984) represent recurrences with p indices in a $p + 1$ coordinate system with p space dimensions and one time dimension. Consider how you would represent the designs for the matrix–vector and matrix product in this system. Discuss the role of the time axis in the system and derive permutation matrices for interchanging space and time axes.
7. Derive an inner product array in which the matrix A is non-stationary and the vectors x and y are non-stationary. How many processors do you require and how much time? What is the efficiency?
8. Show that the convolution problem is a special case of the matrix–vector problem. Use the result to derive different arrays from those in Fig. 1.1 and comment on their area/time/efficiency trade-off.
9. Produce space–time diagrams for the rectangular matrix product $C = AB$ where A is $n \times m$ and B is $m \times n$. Derive the actual arrays and compare them to the designs for square matrices.
10. Derive a hexagonally connected matrix product array which requires no synchronizing spaces between matrix inputs, require $w_1 w_2$ cells for

banded matrices with bandwidths w_1 and w_2 and time $T = n + \min(w_1, w_2)$. Comment on the efficiency of the design. [Hint: Reverse the order of accumulation for the partial products of the results.]

11. Produce orthogonally connected matrix product arrays in which (a) the matrix A is stationary and the matrix B and the resulting matrix C are non-stationary, (b) B is stationary and A and C are non-stationary.
12. Modify the designs for matrix product and matrix–vector computation so that they are optimized for triangular matrix problems.
13. Show that a timing graph with a cycle of zero delay cannot be retimed without use of the k-slowing lemma.
14. Define cuts for (a) the convolution arrays, (b) the hexagonal array, (c) the orthogonally connected array. Show that in each case an arbitrary number of delays can be added to links to provide additional pipelining properties of the designs.

3
MATRIX ALGORITHMS

The previous two chapters have established the basic steps required for the synthesis of systolic algorithms. The level of sophistication in synthesis techniques continues to improve and it is now possible to automate some functions in the design process (such as representing and manipulating restricted recurrences in space–time). Perhaps one day it will be possible to perform the entire design process automatically. Unfortunately, at present systolic design is still as much of an art as it is a science. This statement is particularly true when more complex designs are considered, where the recurrences are not simple to analyse (e.g. non-uniform), or where a problem consists of a number of complicated subalgorithms pipelined together. It is beyond the scope of this text to survey all the systolic algorithms that have appeared in the literature. However, we can consider a selection of frequently used arrays which constitute a *working set* for the construction of more complex systolic algorithms.

In the next three chapters we will build a reference set of useful arrays. This chapter deals with arrays for basic linear algebra problems which, apart from being of significant historical importance to the development of systolic design, account for a substantial portion of computations performed by computers. Chapter 4 deals with the problem of systolically generating tables of data. Such applications arise in a wide range of numerical and non-numerical problems such as interpolation and extrapolation. Finally, in Chapter 5 non-numerical and miscellaneous examples such as sorting, pattern matching, and the representation of data structures (like stacks and queues) are considered. The format of each chapter is the same: we describe the basic algorithms and then introduce systolic versions. In addition to providing a specific set of basic arrays the examples discussed also introduce a number of design principles which are summarized at the end of the chapter.

The basic themes in this chapter are the principles of *array building blocks*, *control sequences*, and *generification* of cell and array functions. The concept of array building blocks is concerned with the idea of using existing (off-the-shelf) arrays to build up larger and more complex composite arrays. The concept of control sequences introduces the possibility of treating cell inputs as either control or data. In particular, we adopt the technique of tagging control to the data in order to change the cell operations on-the-fly, switch data between stationary and non-stationary states, and act as a cell reset mechanism. The possibility of control tags leads directly to the concept of generification where cells with multiple operation types and arrays capable of performing a number of algorithms are permitted.

3.1 Linear systems

Linear systems of equations can be used to represent many practical problems that occur naturally in areas such as science and engineering, social science, and economics. A general set of linear equations has the form

$$a_{i1}x_1 + a_{i2}x_2 + \cdots + a_{im}x_m = b_i, \quad i = 1(1)n \tag{3.1}$$

where the x_i are unknown and the a_{ij} and b_i are known and real respectively. The linear system of equations (3.1) can also be represented by

$$Ax = b \tag{3.2}$$

where A is an $n \times m$ coefficient matrix and x and b are $m \times 1$ and $n \times 1$ vectors respectively, the latter being termed the right-hand side (RHS). The system is homogeneous with $b_i = 0$, $i = 1(1)m$, and any solution with some $x_i \neq 0$ is termed a non-trivial solution. A non-homogeneous system has a particular solution if a vector satisfies (3.2) when substituted for x. The set of all vectors satisfying the equation is the general solution. We will restrict ourselves to linear systems with mainly square matrices which arise in many physical problems—and if solvable they will have unique solutions. Many matrices have elements whose positioning forms special structures (e.g. bandedness, sparsity) which together with the numerical value of their entries produce certain properties such as diagonal dominance and positive definiteness. These quirks are essential for deriving relationships between different matrices and classifying sets of systems which are in some sense easier to solve than others. For example, in Chapter 2 we saw how the property of bandedness together with the data dependencies of the matrix–vector computation could be exploited by systolic algorithms to reduce the number of cells and improve efficiency. In this chapter we consider systolic methods for constructing the solution of linear systems like (3.2). For convenience it is assumed that A is non-singular (i.e. A^{-1}, the inverse of A, exists). The choice of the solution method depends on a number of factors including the structure and size of the matrix, the number of arithmetic operations required to construct the solution, the amount of storage available/required, and the control of rounding error by the machine. In systolic terms we are concerned with minimizing the area and time and maximizing the efficiency of an array for solving a particular problem.

Triangular matrices and substitution

Systems like (3.2) which have lower (or upper) triangular matrix structures are easy to solve because all the elements on or above (or below) the main diagonal are zero so that the components of x can be written explicitly. For example, if A is lower triangular the solution to (3.2) is represented by the recurrence

$$
\begin{aligned}
y_i^{(1)} &= 0 \\
y_i^{(j+1)} &= y_i^{(j)} + a_{ij}x_j \\
x_i &= (b_i - y_i^{(i)})/a_{ii}
\end{aligned}
\tag{3.3}
$$

for $i = 1(1)n$, $j = 1(1)i$, and where $y_i^{(j)}$ is an additional set of variables used to accumulate the partial results. In matrix notation we usually write

$$Lx = b \qquad \text{or} \qquad Ux = b$$

where L and U are lower and upper triangular matrices respectively. When solving a lower triangular system the equation (3.3) is referred to as a forward substitution process. For an upper triangular system a simple reassignment of the indices produces a backward substitution. Now, triangular matrices of order n have $(n/2)(n + 1)$ non-zero elements each of which appears once in (3.3), so $O(n^2)$ sequential arithmetic operations are required for the solution of (3.2).

Direct solution methods

These are techniques for solving (3.2) which guarantee a solution after a fixed number of arithmetic steps dependent on the problem size (i.e. the order of the matrix). In general (3.2) is an implicit system so that the solution vector x cannot be derived without modifying the original system of equations. This modification must be performed in a way that preserves the solution. A brute-force approach is to make the equation explicit by assuming that A^{-1} is known or easy to compute, so we can write

$$x = A^{-1}b. \tag{3.4}$$

x is then constructed explicitly by matrix–vector multiplication (we have already seen systolic arrays which perform this operation). Generally, however, A^{-1} is not known and is not easy to compute, so direct methods modify A to produce a semi-explicit form

$$\bar{A}x = \bar{b} \tag{3.5}$$

where x can be bound from a substitution process, and $\bar{b}$ is a modified version of b. Clearly $\bar{A}$ has to have a structure which allows easy solution. We have seen that triangular structures are easy to solve, and consequently direct methods are based on the simple proposition that the time taken to transform the original matrix, to a triangular form using operations which preserve the solution, will minimize the computational work. Direct methods are further subdivided into two forms:

(1) triangularization methods, which convert A to L or U form (e.g. Gaussian elimination, QR methods, etc.);

(2) factorization (or decomposition) methods, which replace A by a product of triangular matrices.

In matrix form (1) is equivalent to

$$MAx = Ux = b \tag{3.6}$$

where M is a matrix determining the modifications to A which reduce it (in this case) to upper triangular form. In (2) the matrix form is

$$Ax = LUx = b \tag{3.7}$$

so that x is produced by solving the coupled equations

$$Ly = b, \qquad Ux = y \tag{3.8}$$

using a forward substitution followed by a backward substitution.

For problems in class (1) the simplest technique for reducing the matrix to triangular form, and thereby producing M explicitly, is the Gaussian elimination algorithm. This method relies on the use of three operations applied to the rows of A which preserve the solution of (3.2):

(1) row_i can be multiplied by any non-zero constant α and the result used in place of row_i (i.e. scalar multiplication of a row vector);

(2) two rows i and j can be added together and used in place of one of the rows (e.g. $row_i = row_i + row_j$, that is vector addition);

(3) two rows can be interchanged.

These rules, when applied to the augmented $n \times (n+1)$ matrix $\bar{A}$ (which is A with the additional column corresponding to the RHS of (3.2)), yield a sequence of matrices $\bar{A}^{(1)}, \ldots, \bar{A}^{(k)}$ for $k = 1(1)n$ using the recurrence

$$k = 1, \qquad \bar{A}^{(1)} = A$$

$$k > 1, \qquad a_{ij}^{(k)} = \begin{cases} a_{ij}^{(k-1)} & i = 1(1)k-1, j = 1(1)n+1 \\ 0 & i = k(1)n, j = 1(1)k \\ a_{ij}^{(k-1)} - m_{i,k-1}^{(k-1)} a_{k-1,j}^{(k-1)} & i = k(1)n, j = k(1)n+1 \end{cases} \tag{3.9}$$

where $m_{i,k}^{(k-1)} = [a_{i,k-1}^{(k-1)}/a_{k-1,k-1}^{(k-1)}]$ and when $k = n$ the matrix $\bar{A}^{(n)}$ is upper triangular. The element $a_{k-1,k-1}$ at each step is called the pivot. A range of pivoting strategies based on avoiding the condition $a_{k-1,k-1} = 0$, which cause breakdown of the method because m_{ik} cannot be formed, and reducing the rounding error are known (e.g. see Burden *et al.* 1981).

1. *Maximal column (or partial) pivoting.* This is the simplest method which selects an element, in the same column but below the current pivot, with the largest modulus and interchanges the pivot and element rows.

2. *Scaled column pivoting.* The same as method 1 but it scales the rows first by dividing the row elements by the maximum row element and then chooses the pivot.

3. *Maximal (total) pivoting.* The most general form which scales rows and uses a combination of row and column interchanges to produce the best pivot.

Now, although pivoting is useful for controlling error and avoiding breakdown it involves additional work and as a result the simplest schemes are normally adopted. In systolic arrays the additional work associated with pivoting creates added data dependencies which constrain the possible array structures. It follows that systolic arrays incorporating pivoting tend to exhibit poor area–time trade-offs. For the record an elimination scheme without pivoting requires

$$\sum_{i=1}^{n-1} (n-i)(n-i+2) = \tfrac{1}{6}(2n^3 + 3n^2 - 5n) \tag{3.10a}$$

$$\sum_{i=1}^{n-1} (n-i)(n-i+1) = (n/3)(n^2 - n) \tag{3.10b}$$

mults/div and add/subs respectively so that recurrence (3.9) is evaluated in $O(n^3)$ sequential arithmetic operations.

Many variations on the Gaussian elimination technique exist. For example, the Gauss–Jordan method includes a second elimination recurrence which reduces the triangular form resulting from (3.9) to a diagonal matrix which is easily inverted. We shall not consider the Gauss–Jordan technique explicitly but concentrate, instead, on another variation, namely the Givens (orthogonal) rotation method. In the Givens technique, we follow a procedure identical to Gaussian elimination except that the modification

$$a_{ij}^{(k)} = a_{ij}^{(k-1)} - m_{i,k-1}^{(k-1)} a_{k-1,j}^{(k-1)}$$

in (3.9) is replaced by the 2×2 rotation matrix operation

$$\begin{bmatrix} c & -s \\ s & c \end{bmatrix} \begin{bmatrix} a_{k-1,j}^{(k-1)} \\ a_{ij}^{(k-1)} \end{bmatrix} = \begin{bmatrix} a_{k-1,j}^{(k)} \\ 0 \end{bmatrix} \tag{3.11}$$

which yields the non-linear equations

$$s a_{k-1,j}^{(k-1)} + c a_{ij}^{(k-1)} = 0$$

$$s^2 + c^2 = 1$$

with solution

$$c = a_{k-1,j}^{(k-1)}/D, \qquad s = a_{ij}^{(k-1)}/D$$
$$D = \sqrt{[a_{ij}^{(k-1)}]^2 + [a_{k-1,j}^{(k-1)}]^2}. \tag{3.12}$$

These equations have inherent stability properties so that no pivoting is required. Consequently more flexible partial orderings of the required data dependencies can be exploited. However, the basic computation in (3.11) uses a square root which in most situations is computationally expensive compared with operations such as the inner product. The added flexibility in possible array configurations is offset against the increase in the complexity of the basic step. Other forms of the Givens rotation, such as Gram–Schmidt, fast Givens, and square-root-free forms which minimize these problems, are possible (see Chen and Yao 1987). We shall not describe the computations here but simply note that, when they are adopted, only the formation of the 2×2 matrix and hence the basic cycle time and complexity of a cell is affected, not the general data dependencies of the triangularization technique.

Next consider matrix factorization as described by (3.7). This is an alternative to triangularization which avoids modification of the RHS vector. The advantage is that only one factorization is required for multiple RHSs. Generally these methods avoid pivoting although some pivoting strategies are known. The basic principle is to replace the coefficient matrix by two coupled matrices (factors) which are easy to solve but when multiplied together produce A. For example, when the factors are triangular (3.7) is solved by the coupled equations (3.8). A number of methods are known for producing L and U factors which differ only according to whether the L_{ii} and U_{ii} elements are set to one or zero respectively, or if both are equal. Again, the change in the method does little to disrupt the general partial ordering of instructions. A simple recurrence form of the calculation is given as

$$a_{ij}^{(1)} = a_{ij}$$
$$a_{ij}^{(k+1)} = a_{ij}^{(k)} + l_{ik}(-u_{kj}) \tag{3.13a}$$

where

$$l_{ik} = \begin{cases} 0 & i < k \\ 1 & i = k \\ a_{ik}^{(i)}/u_{kk} & i > k \end{cases} \tag{3.13b}$$

$$u_{kj} = \begin{cases} 0 & k > j \\ a_{kj}^{(k)} & k \le j. \end{cases} \tag{3.13c}$$

A simple analysis of these equations shows that a factorization requires $O(n^3)$ sequential operations for a matrix of order n.

Iterative solution methods

A significant problem with direct methods is that the triangularization process tends to fill in the sparse (zero parts) of the matrix. Iterative methods preserve the sparse structure of a matrix and avoid the fill-in that occurs with direct methods. This highly desirable property is achieved by computing a potentially infinite sequence of approximations to the solution vector which (hopefully) converges quickly to a solution of (3.2). Iterative methods provide arbitrary accuracy (subject to machine precision) depending on the number of iterations performed and whether the iteration matrix is convergent or not. A general iterative scheme is formed by making a splitting of A in (3.2) into two matrices E and F such that

$$A = E - F \tag{3.14}$$

so that on substitution in (3.2)

$$Ex = Fx + b.$$

If $x^{(0)}$ is an arbitrarily selected starting vector and $x^{(k)}$ denotes the kth approximation to x, then we can write

$$Ex^{(k)} = Fx^{(k-1)} + b \tag{3.15}$$

and consequently if E^{-1} exists $x^{(k)}$ is easily found. The amount of work to construct $x^{(k)}$ depends on the structure of E and F. If E is a diagonal matrix we have the so-called simultaneous displacement methods (e.g. Jacobi, Richardson, etc.), and when E is lower triangular, successive displacement methods (e.g. Gauss–Seidel and SOR). In the simultaneous case the order in which the components of $x^{(k)}$ are updated is flexible, while in successive methods a sequential order is imposed.

We shall consider systolic schemes for both types of method using the well-known Jacobi and Gauss–Seidel methods. The Jacobi method results from the splitting $A = D - B$, where D is a diagonal matrix, so that (3.15) becomes

$$Dx^{(k)} = Bx^{(k-1)} + b \tag{3.16}$$

or

$$x^{(k)} = D^{-1}Bx^{(k-1)} + D^{-1}b$$

and with

$$x^{(k)} - x^{(k-1)} = D^{-1}(b - Ax^{(k-1)})$$

it is clear that successive approximations are proportional to the difference between the solution (x) and the $x^{(k-1)}$ estimate. On the other hand, the Gauss–Seidel method adopts the splitting $A = D - L - U$, where L and U

are strictly lower and upper triangular, producing

$$(D - L)x^{(k)} = Ux^{(k-1)} + b. \tag{3.17}$$

The successive over-relaxation (SOR) method with a relaxation parameter ω for accelerating convergence yields

$$(x^{(k)} - x^{(k-1)}) = \omega D^{-1}[Lx^{(k)} + Ux^{(k-1)} + b - Dx^{(k-1)}] \tag{3.18}$$

or

$$(I - \omega D^{-1}L)x^{(k)} = \omega D^{-1}(U - D + \omega^{-1}D)x^{(k-1)} + \omega D^{-1}b.$$

It is well known that, provided the original matrix A is strictly diagonally dominant, (3.16), (3.17), and (3.18) converge to a solution of (3.2). Furthermore, each iteration requires only matrix–vector and substitution processes so that each iteration requires $O(n^2)$ sequential steps. Thus for r iterations we require $O(rn^2)$ steps; when $r \ll n$ a significant improvement over direct methods is apparent. Further improvements to the actual computing times can be made when the special structure of the matrix A, for particular problem instances, is exploited.

Matrix inversion

This is the process of computing the inverse A^{-1} of a known $n \times n$ matrix which has the property $A^{-1}A = AA^{-1} = I$. It can be shown that when the determinant of a matrix A is non-zero the inverse exists and the matrix is then said to be non-singular. We have used the inverse property several times already in the above discussion and noted that for an arbitrary non-singular matrix the inverse is not usually easy to compute. One of the most obvious ways to compute an inverse is to consider the problem

$$AX = I \tag{3.19}$$

where X is an unknown $n \times n$ matrix and I is the identity matrix of order n. Denoting $x^{(i)}$ as the ith column of X implies that (3.19) can be solved by the solution of n linear systems of the form

$$Ax^{(i)} = e^{(i)} \tag{3.20}$$

for $i = 1(1)n$ where $e^{(i)}$ is the ith column of I. Equation (3.20) can clearly be evaluated by applying one of the direct methods described above. [Note: The most popular is the Gauss–Jordan algorithm because the final solution step involves only a diagonal matrix.] It follows that one triangularization and n substitutions are required, making the sequential computing time for the inverse $O(n^3)$.

When the matrix to be inverted has a special structure the work involved in finding the inverse can be considerably reduced. For example, when A is a diagonal matrix the inverse is given by computing the reciprocal of the diagonal elements, requiring $O(n)$ arithmetic operations. Alternatively, if A is an orthogonal matrix it satisfies the property $A^{-1} = A^{\mathrm{T}}$ where A^{T} is the transpose of A. As matrix transposition is simply defined by the mapping

$$a_{ij} \to a_{ji} \tag{3.21}$$

for $i, j = 1(1)n$, only $O(n^2)$ sequential operations are required. Under normal circumstances direct inversion of a matrix is not recommended because significant rounding errors are produced and generally sparsity in a problem is destroyed by the filling-in of zero matrix elements. Exceptions to this latter condition are triangular matrices whose inverses are themselves triangular. Many other methods for inverting matrices are known, for example bordering, escalator, and rank updating methods. We shall not deal with them explicitly but the latter method for updating a known inverse is considered in the exercises.

3.2 Substitution arrays

The first array we consider is for the important task of computing forward or backward substitutions using eqn (3.3). The design itself illustrates how to deal with the difficult problem of feedback in recurrence equations. According to our design methodology the first step is to model the computation using a recurrence and then map the problem into space–time to produce a data dependency graph. Equation (3.3) describes an appropriate recurrence.

3.2.1 A linear array

The recurrence has two indices so a mapping into 2-D space is expected once the equations have been fully indexed. The revised equation has the form

$$y_{i,j} = y_{i,j-1} + a_{ij}x_{0j}, \quad i = 1(1)n, j = 1(1)i \tag{3.22a}$$

$$x_{ii} = b_{i0} - y_{ii}/a_{ii} \tag{3.22b}$$

where the b_{i0} and x_{0j} are non-uniform and have to be pipelined (see Chapter 2). The revised equation is of the form

$$y_{i,j} = y_{i,j-1} + a_{ij}x_{i-1,j} \tag{3.23a}$$

$$x_{ii} = b_{i,i-1} - y_{ii}/a_{ii} \tag{3.23b}$$

$$x_{ij} = \begin{cases} x_{i-1,j} & i > 1 \\ x_j & i = 1. \end{cases} \tag{3.23c}$$

Next we take all the variables appearing on the right side of (3.23) and define them as input, and all the variables on the left side of the equations become outputs. The matrix, RHS, and $y_i^{(0)}$ values are easily identified as inputs and the x_j as outputs. Note that x_j also appears on the right side of a recurrence implying that it is an input to the array. Now the initial value for each x_j is determined by an output variable—the recurrence equations in (3.23) are coupled by feedback. How do we resolve this problem in space–time? It is clear from the definition that the form of the computation can be broken into two parts each of which involves no feedback, the accumulation of the y_i values being a lower triangular matrix–vector computation (a special case of the matrix–vector problem studied in Chapter 2) while the evaluation of (3.23b) consists of n independent computations. Figure 3.1(a) and 3.1(b) illustrate data dependency graphs for each problem ($n = 5$). In the former we compute an instance of (3.23a) at each node and in the latter (3.23b). It follows from the diagrams that the composite graph in Fig. 3.1(c) can be constructed by combining the two previous graphs together. The two arrays work together to evaluate (3.23) with each component array producing results for the other just when they are required.

The next step in the design process is to project out a representation of the array. Because the space is 2-D any projection will produce a 1-D array. We consider the projection associated with the direction indicated in Fig. 3.1(c) because it will result in two simple cell types: one for (3.23a) and another for (3.23b). Any other direction would demand that a cell was capable of evaluating both equations, requiring more hardware and control. Figure 3.1(d) illustrates the final array ($n = 4$). For a triangular matrix of bandwidth q we require q cells because null subdiagonals produce cells which are never used. The input length of the data is $2n$ because there are n values for y_i, b_i, and x_i each separated by a synchronizing zero. We require $\mathscr{A} = q$ cells. The total computing time is $\mathscr{T} = 2n + q$ because the last value y_n requires $q - 1$ steps to reach the circular cell, and an extra step is then required to compute x_n. A step is the maximum cost of performing the circular or the square cell computations.

The design considered illustrates two important design principles. First, the resolution of mutual feedback in recurrences is achieved by sectioning the recurrence equations into components each of which involves no feedback. Each of the components is then represented in space–time using the normal procedure. Second, the component arrays are used as building blocks to construct a composite array and feedback difficulties are resolved by pipelining data between the components. Finally, the array for the whole computation is projected, taking care to choose a direction that minimizes cell complexity and area. There are a number of issues here. By a careful choice of the recurrence sections we can reduce the problem to a set of component recurrences that have already been analysed in space–time (e.g. one component is a special case of the matrix–vector array). Consequently

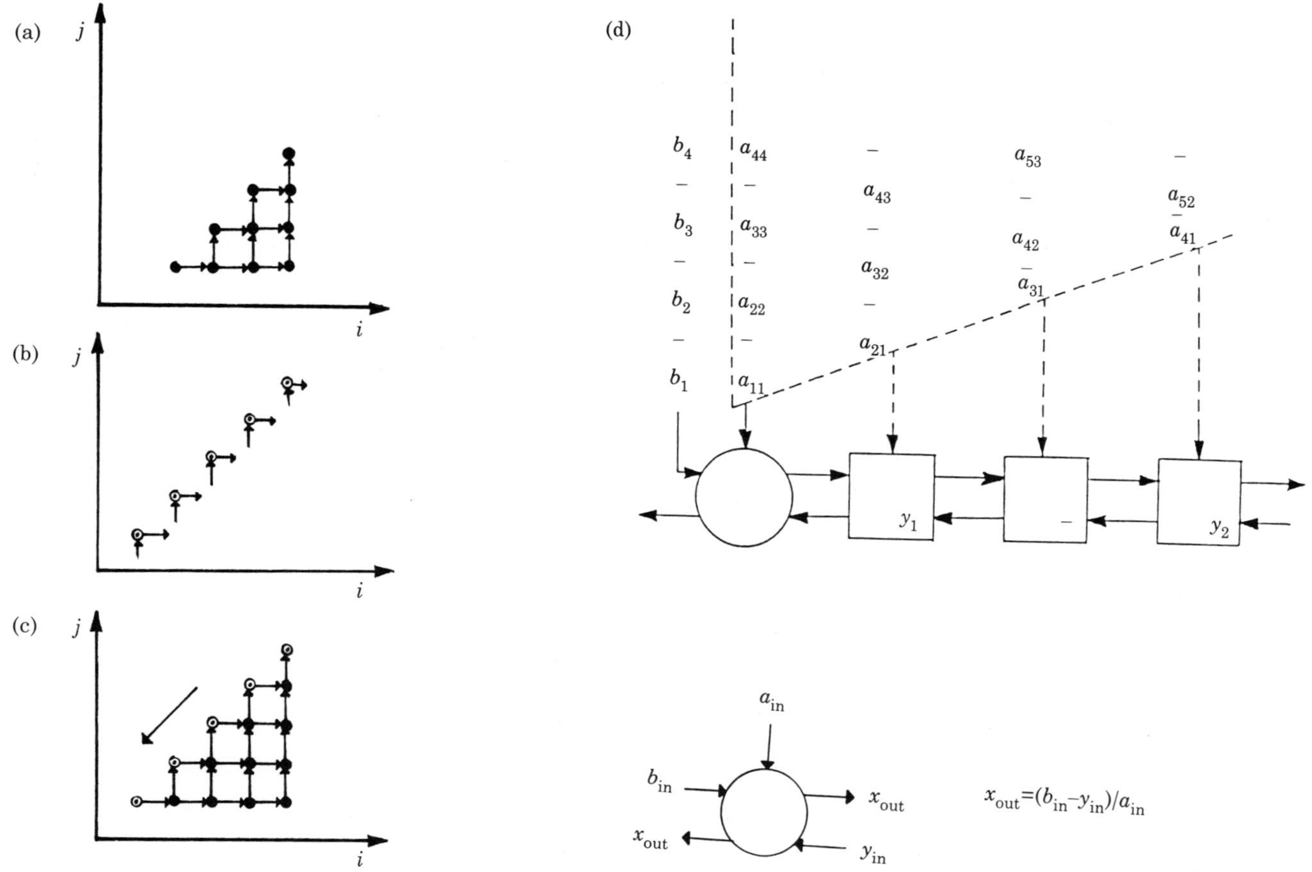

Fig. 3.1 Linear substitution array: (a) triangular matrix vector; (b) divisions; (c) composite graph; (d) bidirectional array (C. Mead and L. Conway, *Introduction to VLSI systems*, © 1980, Addison-Wesley Publishing Co. Inc., Reading, Massachusetts, reprinted with permission)

the need to model the problem in space–time explicitly is diminished, and we can concentrate on the simpler problem of resolving the input–output format between component arrays. The data dependency graphs associated with the component recurrences are treated as subgraphs and add additional dependencies which resolve the feedback. In the former case blocks can be modified by retiming to produce appropriate input–output formats, in the latter transformation and projection of a more complex data dependency graph will produce complete arrays directly. Clearly, as the complexity of a problem increases so does the difficulty of identifying component recurrences. One useful tip is to try and section recurrences so that the nodes of a subgraph perform only a single operation. Each subgraph then corresponds to a single equation in the recurrence formulation—intuitively this simplifies the design of arrays for each array component. In this chapter we will develop the idea of arrays as building blocks because it limits the complexity of space–time representations and also subscribes to the important principle of divide and conquer in algorithm design.

Finally, it should be noted that, although space–time representation helps in designing component arrays, selecting and interfacing the appropriate arrays to reduce the time and area of a design is one of the basic skills in systolic design. Recently, more powerful transformation techniques than those in Chapter 2 have been used to tackle this problem by manipulating the form of the recurrence to produce a canonical form before determining data dependencies. We shall consider this issue again in Chapter 8.

3.2.2 Multiple right-hand sides

Quite often when we triangularize a linear system the work involved is justified by computing the solution to more than one right-hand side. For example, in (3.19) we require the solution to n right-hand sides to produce the inverse of a matrix. A recurrence for solving r RHSs can be derived simply by adding a loop of the form $k = 1(1)r$ to (3.23) so that it is repeated r times using a different RHS but the same matrix on each iteration. This yields the recurrence

$$y_{i,j,k} = y_{i,j-1,k} + a_{i,j,k-1}x_{i-1,j,k} \tag{3.24a}$$

$$x_{i,i,k} = b_{i,i-1,k} - y_{i,i,k}/a_{i,i,k} \tag{3.24b}$$

$$b_{i,j,k} = b_{i,j-1,k}, \qquad a_{i,j,k} = a_{i,j,k-1} \tag{3.24c}$$

where $x_{i,i,k} = x_{ik}$ and $b_{i,0,k} = b_{ik}$. This equation simply pipelines the matrix elements in the k direction. Applying the building block principle a composite array can be constructed by using Fig. 3.1(c) as a basic component and performing a loop unrolling on the outer loop $k = 1(1)r$. This is equivalent to laying out r copies of Fig. 3.1(c) in the k direction as shown in Fig. 3.2(a)

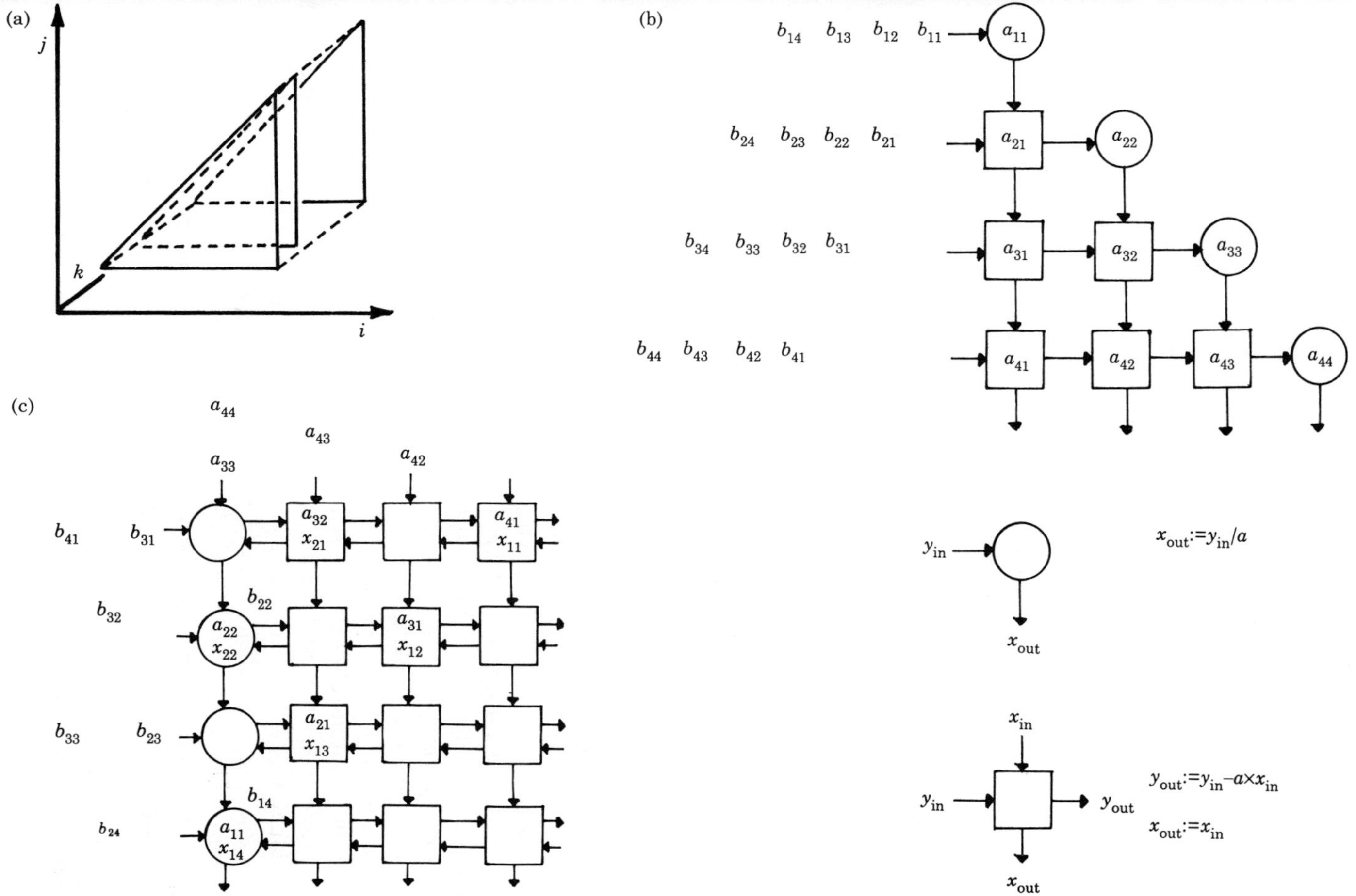

Fig. 3.2 Triangular substitution array: (a) unrolling into three dimensions; (b) triangular array; (c) bidirectional array

and connecting nodes of each subgraph according to $a_{i,j,k} = a_{i,j,k-1}$. Projections of the composite graph will produce 2-D arrays. We could project out the i axis to produce an $n \times r$ array but this would again map (3.24a) and (3.24b) onto a single cell and make the derivation of the data sequences for A non-trivial.

Alternatively a projection in the k direction produces a triangular array as shown in Fig. 3.2(b) in which each cell computes only a single operation. The array is orthogonally connected, triangular, and has only one unidirectional connection between two adjacent cells in a row or column. The matrix elements a_{ij} are stationary and loaded one element per cell. The array is operated by feeding in the b_i value into row i of the array on the ith time step (b_{ij} denote different RHSs). If we let $y_i^{(0)} = b_i$ the value y_i is accumulated as the horizontal inputs move left to right. On encountering a circular cell the accumulation $b_i - a_{i1}x_1 - \cdots - a_{i,i-1}x_{i-1}$ is complete in row i and x_i is produced by a division. The resulting x_i is propagated down the ith column so that it encounters partially accumulated y_j values with $j > i$. The x_i eventually emerge from the bottom of column i in the last tier of the array. A simple analysis shows that $\mathscr{A} = n/2(n+1)$ cells and $2n$ steps are required to produce a single right-hand side including input–output time. For r right-hand sides we require $\mathscr{T} = 2n + r$ steps, so $3n$ steps are needed when $r = n$. As each cell of the array receives at most r values the efficiency is $e = r/(2n + r)$ or $e = 0.33$ when $n = r$.

A third design suitable for banded matrices is produced by a projection in the $(-1, -1, 0)^t$ direction. In this case each subgraph of the composite design projects an array like that in Fig. 3.1(d). The matrix A is pipelined through the arrays by adding connections between arrays corresponding to the projections of connections between component subgraphs. The resulting array is shown in Fig. 3.2(c) where the kth linear array computes the backward substitution to problem k. The r right-hand sides are evaluated by staggering or *skewing* the input of the y_i and b_i for each problem (k) so that they synchronize with the matrix filtering through the array. From the previous section a single tier of the array requires q cells, when the matrix has bandwidth q, so $\mathscr{A} = rq$ cells are required in total. The last value of the first row is output after $2n + q$ steps, so allowing r steps for the skew of other tiers makes the total computation time $\mathscr{T} = 2n + q + r$ steps. As the individual tiers of the array have efficiency $e = 0.5$ it is not surprising that the whole array has an efficiency of 50 per cent. When $r = n$ the solution to the n problems associated with (3.19) requires just $3n + q$ steps and n^2 cells for an arbitrary non-singular matrix. The latter array appears slower than the triangular version but in the former array the matrix is stationary which requires at least $O(n)$ loading steps. Unfortunately the banded design requires a number of input–output connections proportional to $q + r$ compared with $O(n)$ for the triangular array. Which array is better depends upon the criteria (e.g. $\mathscr{A}\mathscr{T}$ etc.) and circumstances in which the design will be used.

These new arrays are composite designs produced by pipelining arrays with compatible input–output formats together. The composite data dependency graph was produced entirely from knowledge of previously developed arrays by a simple unrolling of the recurrence outer loop. The space–time representation of the design can be reconstructed by performing an array unrolling from any of the arrays. Alternatively, we can construct an array unrolling of (3.24) by simply replicating Fig. 3.1(d) r times and resolving the array interfaces by adding additional connections for the movement of the matrix A.

3.3 Triangularization

In this section we will consider the more difficult problem of reducing A in (3.2) to triangular form using the recurrences (3.6)–(3.13). The first design performs Gaussian elimination or Givens rotations depending upon the cell definition, incorporates a simplified method of pivoting based on swapping adjacent matrix rows, and is due originally to Gentleman and Kung (1981). We then consider a composite array due to Megson (1990*c*) that allows partial pivoting. The next design performs triangularization using Givens rotations but annihilates elements using the bottom-up scheme developed by Sameh and Kuck (1978). This latter design is again due to Gentleman and Kung and is suitable for banded matrices. An improved version of the array due to Heller and Ipsen (1982) is considered in the exercises. The fourth design performs LU factorization on a hexagonally connected array as discussed by Kung and Leiserson in their famous introductory paper.

3.3.1 Gaussian elimination

The Gentleman and Kung approach to matrix triangularization exploits the recurrence (3.9) for Gaussian elimination. Since the equation involves feedback, a number of different operations, and three indices, we shall derive the array by constructing a composite 2-D data dependency graph and unrolling this graph into three dimensions. Subsequent projections will then produce the required arrays. To start rewrite eqn (3.9) as

$$a_{i,j,k} = a_{i,j,k-1} - m_{i,k-1,k-1}a_{k-1,j,k-1}, \quad i = k(1)n, j = k(1)n + r \qquad (3.25a)$$

$$m_{i,k-1,k-1} = a_{i,k-1,k-1}/a_{k-1,k-1,k-1} \qquad (3.25b)$$

where $r \geq 0$ is the number of columns added to A to produce an augmented matrix. The variable k corresponds to the elimination of all the values in the $(k-1)$th column below the pivot which is required at step k. Intuitively k represents time. A 2-D recurrence is produced trivially by making k constant and assuming that data moving in the k direction are stationary. Hence

$$a_{ij} = a_{ij} - m_{i,k-1}a_{k-1,j}, \quad i = k(1)n, j = k(1)n + r \tag{3.26a}$$

$$m_{i,k-1} = a_{i,k-1}/a_{k-1,k-1}. \tag{3.26b}$$

Both the $m_{i,k-1}$ and $a_{k-1,j}$ in (3.26a) produce non-local connections which can be removed by suitable pipelining arguments. Thus $m_{i,k-1}$ is replaced by the equivalent term $m_{i,j}$ where $m_{i,j} = m_{i,j-1}$. Now when $k = 2$ the data dependency graph in Fig. 3.3(a) is produced ($n = 4$, $r = 1$). The non-local connections associated with $a_{k-1,j}$ can be removed in a similar manner to the m values. Projections of the graph will produce 1-D arrays for a single elimination step. For example, when $k = 2$ projecting out the i axis will produce an array with $n + r$ cells. One cell computes (3.26b) and the rest evaluate (3.26a). The input to the array is simply the augmented matrix appropriately skewed and entered row by row (there is one cell for each column). The first row of the matrix is loaded into the cells and then subsequent rows generate a multiplier (m) value and pump it across the array to update the row.

The complete array is now constructed as follows. Observe that at step k a graph identical to that in Fig. 3.3(a) but of size $(n - k + 1) \times (n - k + r - 1)$ is required. A 3-D data dependency graph is produced by replicating subgraphs of appropriate size in the k direction and connecting them using the fact that $a_{i,j,k} = a_{i,j,k-1}$. Neglecting columns once they have been eliminated produces the solid in Fig. 3.3(b) which shows the shape of the space taken by the dependency graph. Shadows (or images) of the solid indicate the overall shape of arrays that can be produced by projection. For example, projecting out the i axis produces the design in Fig. 3.3(d)—the perimeter of the array is identical to the shadow cast by the solid on to the j–k plane. The method of operation is simple:

1. The first element of the augmented matrix to reach an empty cell is loaded (stored) in the cell and is not passed on to the next row of the array.
2. Subsequent matrix values entering the cell are updated using the modifier input from the horizontal connection and the value already stored in the cell. The updated value and the modifier are passed vertically and horizontally to the next cell.

The boundary (circular) cells correspond to the locations of pivotal values in the $A^{(k)}$ matrices with row k of the array performing the eliminations associated with the kth pivot. The boundary cell uses the loaded value as the pivot, computes multipliers from subsequent values entering the cell, and sends them horizontally across the array. The square cells on row k perform the update to a matrix row passing the updated row on to the $(k + 1)$th row of the array. As the computation proceeds the tiers of the array fill up with the stationary and triangularized augmented matrix. [Remark: Trace out some array snapshots to make sure you understand the data flow.]

The top row of the array contains $n + r$ cells so that the first element of the rth right-hand side is input on the $(n + r)$th step. There are n rows in the augmented matrix so the last element of the matrix enters the last column of the array on the $(2n + r)$th step. The array itself contains n rows (one for each matrix row) so the last element of the triangularized matrix is loaded into the appropriate cells after $\mathcal{T} = 3n + r$ steps, which is the total computation time. We have used $\mathcal{A} = (n/2)(n + 1) + nr$ cells. It follows that we can triangularize an $n \times n$ dense matrix in $\mathcal{T} = 3n$ steps ($r = 0$) and produce a form suitable for a substitution process in $\mathcal{T} = 3n + 1$ steps ($r = 1$). The array has been used extensively for least-squares tasks where the objective is to minimize $\|Ax - b\|_2$. Our description of Fig. 3.3(d) is still incomplete. As described the array computes Gaussian elimination without pivoting and consequently suffers from (a) breakdown of the algorithm due to zero pivots, and (b) rounding error. The cell definitions included with the array perform a limited form of pivoting known as *pairwise pivoting*. In this method the boundary cell checks all incoming values against the stored pivot value and decides if a row interchange is necessary. If an interchange is required the c output is set to one, otherwise to zero, and pumped along with the modifier. Square cells use the c value associated with the modifier to determine whether or not to swap the stored value with the incoming value thus maintaining the correct ordering of rows. The multipliers and c values eventually emerge from the array and can be used to recover the original ordering of the matrix rows. The c value is a control tagged to the data (the multiplier) which informs the cells when to perform different functions (swap or no swap). Another control tag can be used to trigger the loading of empty cells. In this case the tag is input to the boundary cell in the first array row with a_{11} causing it to be loaded into the cell. The tag is then pumped along the row to load the square cells and output to the next boundary cell, using the diagonal connection, in time to synchronize with a_{22}. It is normal practice to omit loading details from array descriptions so this tag is not included in the cell definition provided by Fig. 3.3(d).

Figure 3.3(c) is produced in a similar manner to Fig. 3.3(b) but employs the fact that in general only a submatrix of $(n - k + 1) \times (n + r + k - 1)$ values needs updating at step k. This observation allows the first $k - 1$ rows and columns to be omitted from the data dependency graph at stage k. The new solid yields the same array as above when the i axis is projected out, but when the j axis is removed the resulting graph is triangular. In this alternative form only $(n/2)(n + 1)$ cells are required, which is independent of r, so the design is attractive for solving systems of equations with many RHSs. The array is due to Ahmed *et al.* (1982) and operates in a similar manner to the previous array except that data are input columnwise, the

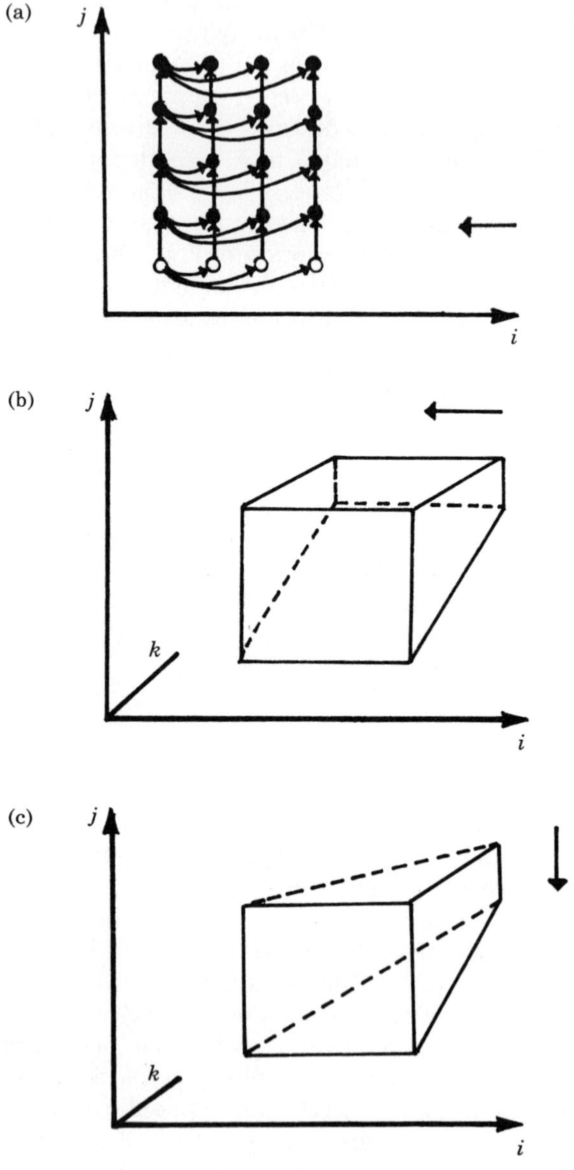

Fig. 3.3 Gaussian elimination array: (a) single elimination subgraph; (b) unrolled space–time solid

(d)

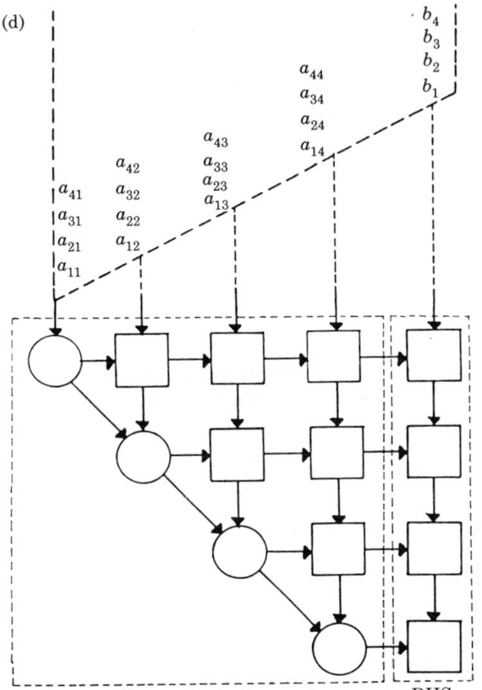

Shape	Procedure: Gaussian elimination	Procedure: Orthogonalization

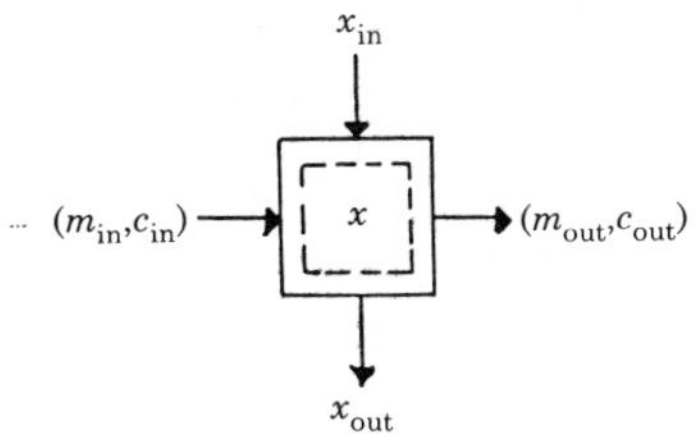	IF c_{in} THEN
	$\{x_{out}=x+m_{in}x_{in}$
	$x=x_{in}$
	$\}$
	ELSE
	$x_{out}=x_{in}+m_{in}x$
		$x_{out}=c_{in}x_{in}-s_{in}x$
		$x=s_{in}x_{in}+c_{in}x$

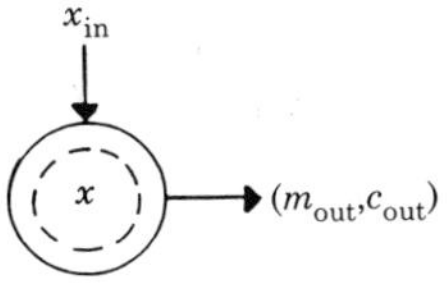	IF $\lvert x_{in}\rvert \geq \lvert x\rvert$ THEN
	$\{$IF x_{in} <>0 THEN $m_{out}=-x/x_{in}$
	ELSE 0
	$x=x_{in}, c_{out}=1$
	$\}$
	ELSE
	$\{m_{out}=-x_{in}/x, c_{out}=0\}$
		IF $x_{in}=0$ THEN
		$\{c_{out}=1,\ s_{out}=0\}$
		ELSE
		$\{\Delta=(x^2+x_{in}^2)^{1/2}$
		$c_{out}=x/\Delta$
		$s_{out}=x_{in}/\Delta$
		$x=\Delta$
		$\}$

Fig. 3.3 (*cont.*) Gaussian elimination array: (c) unrolling for square matrix; (d) array (Courtesy W. M. Gentleman and H. T. Kung, *SPIE IV*, Vol. 298, 1981)

multipliers are stationary, and the triangularized matrix is non-stationary. The exact details are left as an exercise.

Note that the derivation of the elimination arrays involves no notion of pivoting or control. Indeed these properties are not represented in the recurrences. The recurrences can be augmented to cater for the former but the latter has no meaning. Indeed the space–time representation we have adopted deals directly with data flow; control flow is not represented explicitly. Control tags must be added to a design to cope with the practicalities of array implementation. It is not normally apparent until we choose a particular projection that control might be needed (e.g. to switch between different operations projected on to the same array cell).

3.3.2 Arrays with pivoting

For the next design let us return to the problem of pivoting, one reason for doing so being the following. The pairwise pivoting method has been analysed by Sorenson (1985) and shown to be stable but the error bound is significantly worse than partial or full pivoting. Arrays with improved pivoting properties have been suggested by Barada and El-Amawy (1989) and Hochet *et al.* (1989) and are based on extensions to the triangular array just considered. They require $O(n^2)$ time and $O(n^2)$ cells to implement partial pivoting, a rather disappointing characteristic since the sequential algorithm requires $O(n^3)$ steps. With $O(n^2)$ cells we should expect $O(n)$ time. Figure 3.4 shows an array for performing Gaussian elimination with partial pivoting which requires $O(n^2)$ cells arranged in an orthogonally connected mesh but only $O(n)$ are true arithmetic processors. There are four types of basic cell. The circular cell in the bottom left corner is responsible for evaluating the multiplier (m) values associated with a particular pivot, while the remaining $n - 1$ square processors in the last row update the relevant rows of A in a pipelined fashion. The first $n - 1$ processors of the first column are comparison cells which compare two matrix elements and output the largest and save the smallest; the horizontal output is set if a swap occurs. Finally, the remaining $(n - 1)^2$ cells in the first $n - 1$ rows and the last $n - 1$ columns are simple switches that swap elements according to the state of the horizontal input. It is simple to observe that the bottom row of the array is the first tier of Fig. 3.3(d) which implements nearest-neighbour pivoting. The first column is also a zero-time sorter but more about that in Chapter 5.

The actual operation of the array is quite complex and is best illustrated with a small example. Suppose we have the following 4×4 matrix

$$A = \begin{bmatrix} 2 & 3 & 1 & 1 \\ 4 & -2 & -3 & 2 \\ 1 & 3 & -3 & 0 \\ 3 & -4 & 0 & 2 \end{bmatrix}$$

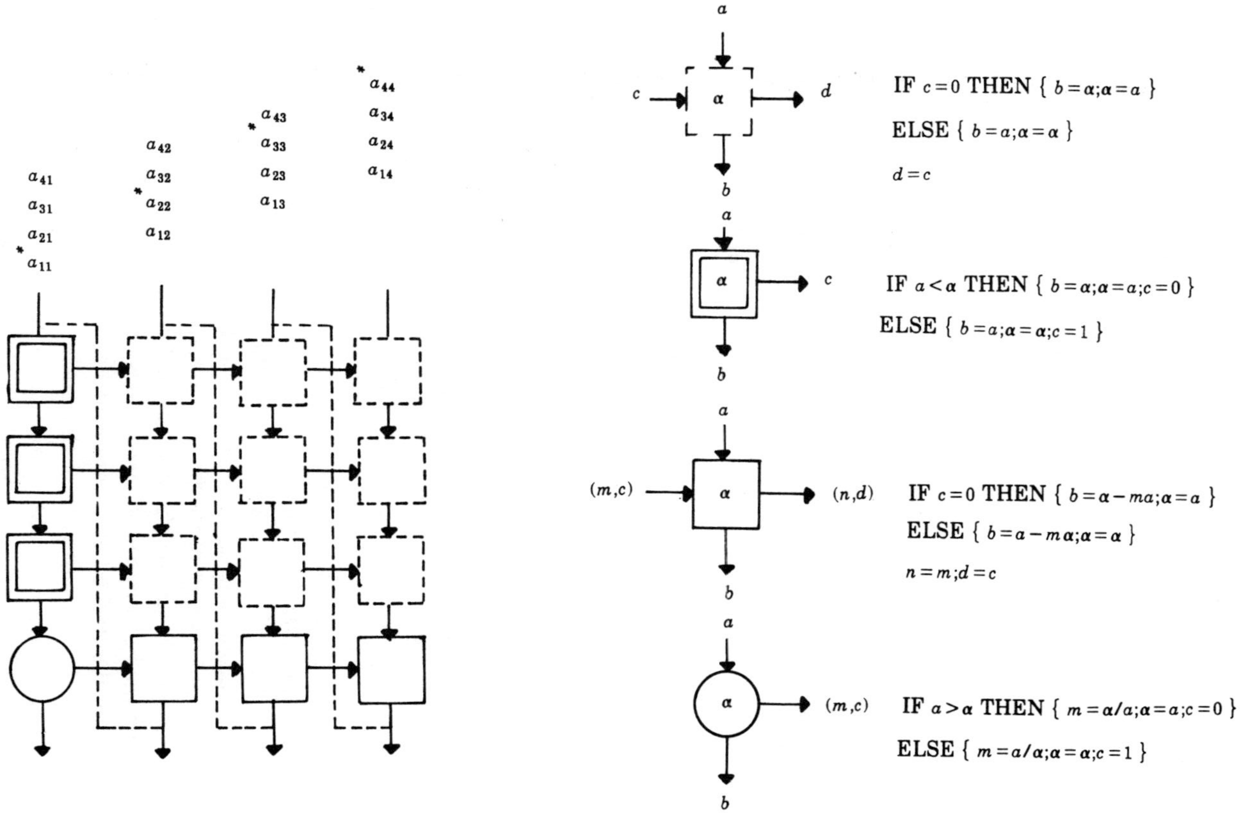

Fig. 3.4 Elimination array with partial pivoting

then the triangularized form is given by

$$\bar{A} = \begin{bmatrix} 4 & -2 & -3 & 2 \\ 0.5 & 4 & 2.5 & 0 \\ 0.25 & 0.875 & -4.437 & -0.5 \\ 0.75 & -0.625 & -0.859 & 37.04 \end{bmatrix}$$

where the entries below the main diagonal are the multipliers. A series of snapshots demonstrating the array operation for this example are shown in Fig. 3.5.

The general idea behind the computation is to input the matrix row-wise (as shown) and to sort rows according to values in the first matrix column using the first column of the array. The relevant row swaps are produced using control tags pumped left to right across the mesh which by virtue of the natural data skew realign the matrix rows as they filter through the array. By the time the data reach the last row of the array, the first column of cells has determined the first two maximum elements (in the first column), and the circular cell chooses the actual pivot by a single nearest-neighbour pivoting step. The natural delay of the row data allows the first column of the matrix to be eliminated and the rest of the matrix to be updated. The first row of A is stored in the last row of the array and the updated $(n-1) \times (n-1)$ submatrix is output from the array. Now, observe that the array cells can be reused by shifting the emerging matrix one column to the left and inserting it back into the array. The first column now determines the best pivot in the second column, the last row of cells eliminates the second column, ejects the first row, and loads the second. An updated $(n-2) \times (n-2)$ submatrix emerges from the array. In general the ith pass of data through the array eliminates the ith column of the matrix and produces an updated $(n-i) \times (n-i)$ submatrix for further elimination.

The delay associated with each comparison and switching cell is two steps so that the total time for an element to move down a column is $2n$ steps. It follows that the updated a_{ii} value is output in $(2n+1)i$ steps. Now, when a_{ik} is output, the element $a_{n,k-1}$ (for $k = i = 1, \ldots, n$) must have reached the $(n/2)$th cell from the top of the $(k-1)$th column of the array (because each cell contains two elements). We conclude that if the $(n-i) \times (n-i)$ submatrix output from the bottom row of the array is input directly back into the array (as shown by the dashed connection in Fig. 3.4) it will never catch up and interfere with the data already in the array. The ∞ symbol in Fig. 3.5 is a value used for synchronization that guarantees that real matrix elements always stay together as they move down the column (i.e. a value compared with ∞ always loses). At the end of the submatrix data we insert synchronizing zeros so that matrix elements do not get disrupted from behind. On the feedback of the output submatrix from the bottom of the array cells must

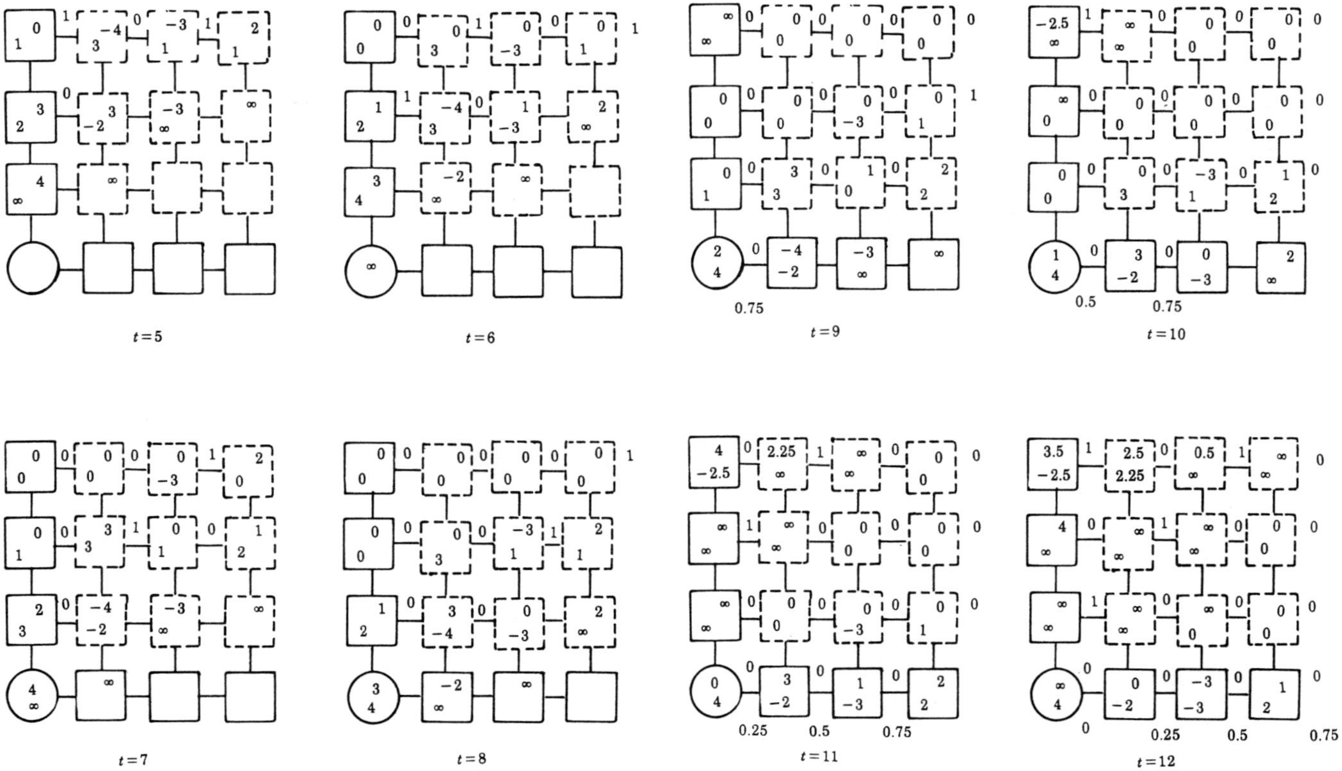

Fig. 3.5 Snapshots for pivoting array

be reset to avoid trailing zeros already in the array from a previous pass. All these tasks plus the control of the loading and unloading of rows from the bottom tier of the array can be produced by control tags attached to the a_{ii} (shown by asterisks in Fig. 3.4). The tag in the first column resets the comparator cells and then is pipelined along the last row to load/unload the cell contents. It should be clear that the total computing time is $\mathscr{T} = (2n + 1)n$ steps which includes input/output time of the original and eliminated matrix.

The feedback connections avoid the contentious problem of repeatedly storing and retrieving updated submatrices from some external source, but demand a time of $2n$ steps for locating the next pivot. As triangularization proceeds the number of rows which can affect the pivot value diminishes. Figure 3.6 shows an alternative array which requires $2(n - k)$ steps to select

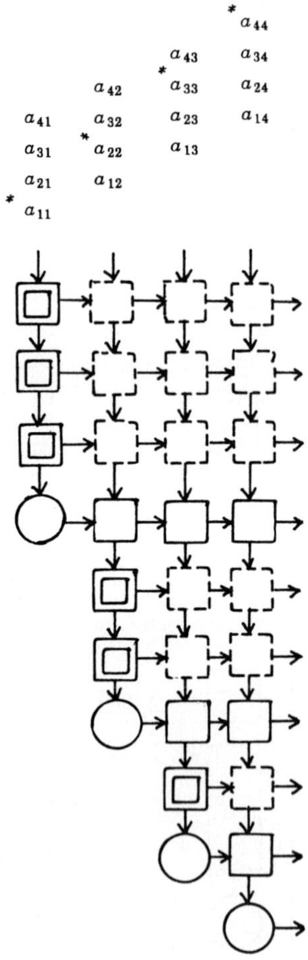

Fig. 3.6 Unrolled pivoting array

the pivot at stage i. The idea is to use an $(n - k + 1) \times (n - k + 1)$ version of the array in Fig. 3.4 (without feedback connections) to locate a pivot for row k and eliminate column k. Arrays for $k = 1, \ldots, n$ are pipelined together and constitute a loop unrolling of recurrence (3.9). The effect is to reduce overall efficiency but improve throughput. Indeed many triangularization problems can be pipelined behind one another. The time delay of the nth column in the unrolled design is given by

$$2 \sum_{i=1}^{n} (n - i + 1) = n(n + 1)$$

and the last element of A enters the array after $2n - 1$ steps so the total computation time is $\mathcal{T} = (2n - 1) + n(n + 1) = n^2 + 3n - 1$ steps. The number of cells is given by

$$\mathcal{A} = \sum_{i=1}^{n} (n - i + 1)^2 = (n/6)(n + 1)(2n + 1) = O(n^3).$$

Fortunately the vast majority of these cells are simple switch cells, and we require only n^2 arithmetic processors. An additional property of the design is that the array is completely planar so that it satisfies the heuristics in Chapter 1. The previous design required long connections and violated the rule of 2-D planar designs. It is, however, interesting to note that the first design in Fig. 3.4 forms a helix with nearest-neighbour connections in three dimensions.

3.3.3 Givens rotation and banded matrices

An equivalent array to that in Fig. 3.3 which performs a triangularization using orthogonal Givens rotations is produced by simply substituting the appropriate cell definitions (encoding (3.11)–(3.12)). Of course orthogonal rotations are inherently stable and there is no need to be concerned about pivoting. The latter property can be exploited to good effect by adopting the annihilation ordering due to Sameh and Kuck (1978). To illustrate this method consider the 8 × 8 example

$$\begin{array}{cccccccc}
x & x & x & x & x & x & x & x \\
7 & x & x & x & x & x & x & x \\
6 & 8 & x & x & x & x & x & x \\
5 & 7 & 9 & x & x & x & x & x \\
4 & 6 & 8 & 10 & x & x & x & x \\
3 & 5 & 7 & 9 & 11 & x & x & x \\
2 & 4 & 6 & 8 & 10 & 12 & x & x \\
1 & 3 & 5 & 7 & 9 & 11 & 13 & x
\end{array}$$

where the x values represent non-zero values and the numbers indicate the time step when the element at that position in the matrix is annihilated. Note that elements are removed by subdiagonals from the bottom of the matrix towards the diagonal rather than by columns and away from the diagonal as used in the previous scheme. We conclude that the method is well suited to banded matrices, because subdiagonals falling outside the band are already zero and can be omitted from the input. Figure 3.7 illustrates an array for triangularizing a matrix using the new ordering. From our previous discussion it should be clear that each tier of the array is a component array that annihilates one subdiagonal of the matrix. Thus Fig. 3.7 is an unrolling with respect to the number of subdiagonals. Delays between tiers are added so that values being shifted left in a tier synchronize with the data entering the tier. The number of delays is determined by comparing the input and output formats of the component array. If the matrix A is of bandwidth $w = p + q - 1$, where q is the number of subdiagonals, we require q tiers of the array and each tier is of length w. Data are input in a diagonal format (like that for the matrix product array). The circular cell computes the 2×2 matrix corresponding to the Givens rotation and annihilates the appropriate subdiagonal element. Square cells update matrix elements by applying the rotation matrix. As data move through the array the matrix sub(super)diagonals are shifted left along the array so that they synchronize with rotation matrices moving left to right. Eventually a subdiagonal element reaches a boundary cell where it is annihilated. Observe that each tier of the array must be of length w to allow for fill-in that occurs in the upper triangular part of the matrix as the annihilation process proceeds. The total area is $\mathscr{A} = wq$ ignoring the delay registers between cells and the time is $\mathscr{T} = 3n + 3q$ steps, because the input data are of length $3n$ and the array has a latency of at most $3q$. A faster version which requires only one synchronizing element between inputs and no delays between tiers (see Heller and Ipsen 1982) can be produced by retiming (see exercises).

3.3.4 Factorization arrays

Finally, we turn to the problem of matrix factorization and consider the famous hexagonal array solution of Kung and Leiserson shown in Fig. 3.8(c). In this problem the recurrence (3.13) involves feedback of the l_{ik} and u_{kj} values which are used to update the $(n - k) \times (n - k)$ matrix which still has to be factorized after the kth step. The problem produces a three-loop program and demands a 3-D mapping. Consequently the important parts of the fully indexed system can be written as

$$a_{i,j,k+1} = a_{i,j,k} + l_{i,k,k+1}(-u_{k,j,k+1}) \quad (3.27a)$$

$$l_{i,k,k+1} = a_{i,k,k}/u_{k,k,k+1}, \quad i = k + 1(1)n, j = k + 1(1)n \quad (3.27b)$$

$$u_{k,j,k+1} = a_{k,j,k}. \quad (3.27c)$$

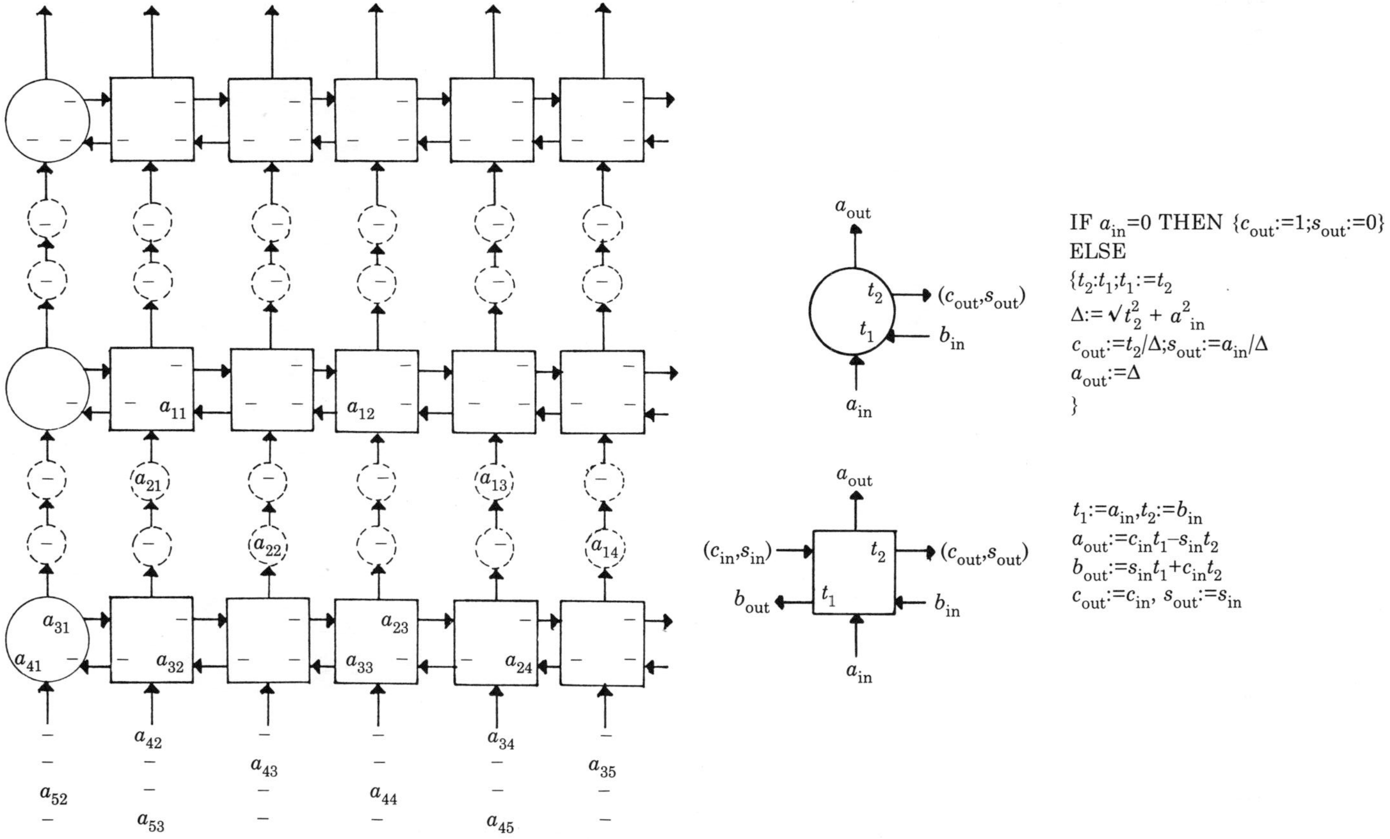

Fig. 3.7 Givens array for banded matrices

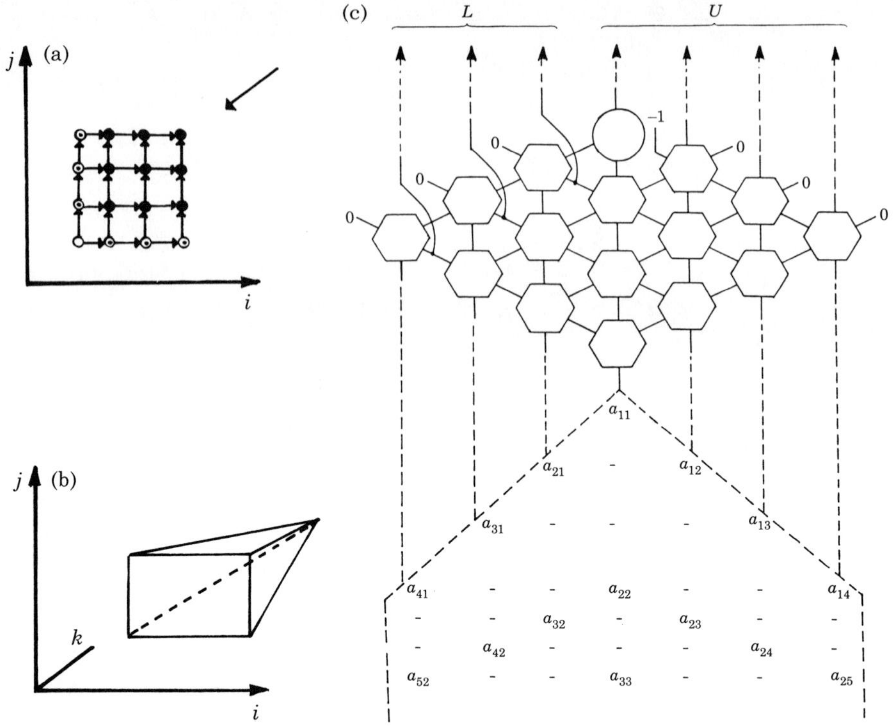

Fig. 3.8 *LU* decomposition array: (a) single decomposition step; (b) unrolled space–time solid; (c) array (C. Mead and L. Conway, *Introduction to VLSI systems*, © 1980, Addison-Wesley Publishing Co. Inc., Reading, Massachusetts, reprinted with permission)

Equation (3.27) tells us quite a lot about the design, for example the matrix elements are pipelined in the k direction and consequently a 2-D plane subgraph can be produced by making A stationary. The variables $l_{i,k,k+1}$ and $u_{k,j,k+1}$ involve long connections which can be localized by a suitable retiming (see Chapter 2). A similar argument allows the pipelining of $1/u_{k,k,k+1}$. In addition, the unary minus can be removed from (3.27a) by rewriting (3.27c) as $-u_{k,j,k+1} = (-1) \times a_{k,j,k}$ and pipelining the minus value. It follows that (3.27) can be rewritten as

$$a_{i,j,k+1} = a_{i,j,k} + l_{i,j,k+1} u_{i,j,k+1} \tag{3.28a}$$

$$\begin{aligned} l_{i,j,k+1} &= \begin{cases} l_{i,j-1,k+1} & j > k \\ a_{i,k,k} * c_{i,k,k+1} & j = k \end{cases} \\ c_{i,k,k+1} &= \begin{cases} c_{i-1,k,k+1} & i > k \\ 1/u_{k,k} & i = k \end{cases} \end{aligned} \tag{3.28b}$$

and

$$u_{i,j,k+1} = \begin{cases} u_{i-1,j,k+1} & i > k \\ a_{k,j,k} * d_{i,j,k+1} & i = k \end{cases}$$
$$d_{i,j,k+1} = \begin{cases} d_{i,j-1,k+1} & j > k \\ -1 & j = k. \end{cases} \tag{3.28c}$$

These equations result in the composite array shown in Fig. 3.8(a) for some value k. The bottom row represents the pipelining of c values and the creation of l_{ik} values in (3.28b). Similarly the first column of nodes corresponds to the movement of d values and (3.28c) and the creation of u_{kj} terms. The rest of the graph corresponds to (3.28a) with the l and u values pipelined from node to node. To construct the whole graph we unroll the loop associated with k and replicate Fig. 3.8(a) adjusting the size of the subgraph appropriately for each value of k and connecting a_{ijk} to $a_{i,j,k-1}$. The solid generated by this unrolling is shown in Fig. 3.8(b), which for $n \times n$ matrices has a front face of dimension $n \times n$. Various arrays can be produced from the solid by choosing appropriate projections. The hexagonal array is produced by a projection in the $(-1, -1, -1)^t$ direction which ensures that each cell in the array only performs a single type of operation. Drawing out a number of snapshots will clarify the array operation. In particular the computation times of the l_{ik} and u_{kj} values can be established as

0	1	2	3	4	5	6	7
1	3	4	5	6	7	8	9
2	4	6	7	8	9	10	11
3	5	7	9	10	11	12	13
4	6	8	10	12	13	14	15
5	7	9	11	13	15	16	17
6	8	10	12	14	16	18	19
7	9	11	13	15	17	19	21

for $n = 8$, which is the time schedule generated from the snapshots of the matrix product array. In particular it is clear that $t = i + j - 2$ is a schedule for the computation. The upper boundary of the array corresponds to the first row and columns of the graph in Fig. 3.8(a) while the rest is a simple hexagonal matrix product array which computes the modification to the submatrix with first element $u_{k+1,k+1}$. More precisely, the circular cell receives u_{kk} from the south input and sends it north, and computes the reciprocal u_{kk}^{-1}, outputting it south-west. The cell represents the current pivot. All the remaining cells are hexagonal inner product cells except that the upper boundary cells to the left are rotated 120° clockwise and perform the l_{ik} computations denoted by the vertical lines in the sketch, while cells on the right upper boundary are rotated 120° anticlockwise and correspond to the horizontal rows computing $-u_{kj}$ terms. Thus the wavefronts of the input data correspond to the chevrons formed by the horizontal and vertical lines together, the delay between successive wavefronts being the time to move from one pivot to the next (the feedback loop length). The data input format and the number of synchronizing elements between matrix elements are easily determined from the differences between diagonal values in the above sketch.

Clearly for a matrix with bandwidth $w = p + q - 1$ we require $\mathscr{A} = pq$ cells. The computation time is determined as follows.

1. The total length of the input data sequence is $3n$ allowing for synchronizing delays (include an extra two steps after the last element).
2. The computation depicted in the sketch above begins when a_{11} has filtered through the array to the circular cell—this requires $\min(p, q)$ steps.

It follows that the last element of the factorization is produced in $\mathscr{T} = 3n + \min(p, q)$ steps. The array has an efficiency of $e = 0.33$ because each cell works for one in three steps. Note that when A is dense ($p = q = n$) we require n^2 cells and $4n$ cycles. In the case of a symmetric matrix only the l_{ik} have to be computed explicitly (because $a_{ij} = a_{ji}$), which reduces the cell count further (see exercises).

Finally, observe that projections in the $(-1, 0, 0)^t$, $(0, -1, 0)^t$, and $(0, 0, -1)^t$ directions are also possible. The first two imply triangular arrays of $(n/2)(n + 1)$ cells where the input and output formats are row and column orientated and the L or U matrices are stationary. The third possibility produces an $n \times n$ orthogonally connected mesh with the initial matrix preloaded which computes with efficiency $e = 0.33$, $\mathscr{T} = 4n$ steps, and $\mathscr{A} = n^2$. Detailed specification of these designs is left to the reader.

3.4 Iterative arrays

Systolic arrays for the solution of (3.15) were first reported in Berzins *et al.* (1983) and Dew (1984). Recently the technique has been extended by Megson and Evans (1989) to include preconditioned iterative systems. The basic principle is to devise a component systolic array for performing a single iteration of the method and then cascade iterations by pipelining a number of the components together. The general structure of an array for (3.15) is shown in Fig. 3.9(d), which is a composite array derived by unrolling the loop associated with k, that is $k = 1(1)r$. The solution vector (x) is successively approximated by cascading it through r linear arrays before finally outputting the rth approximation. The coefficient matrix A is

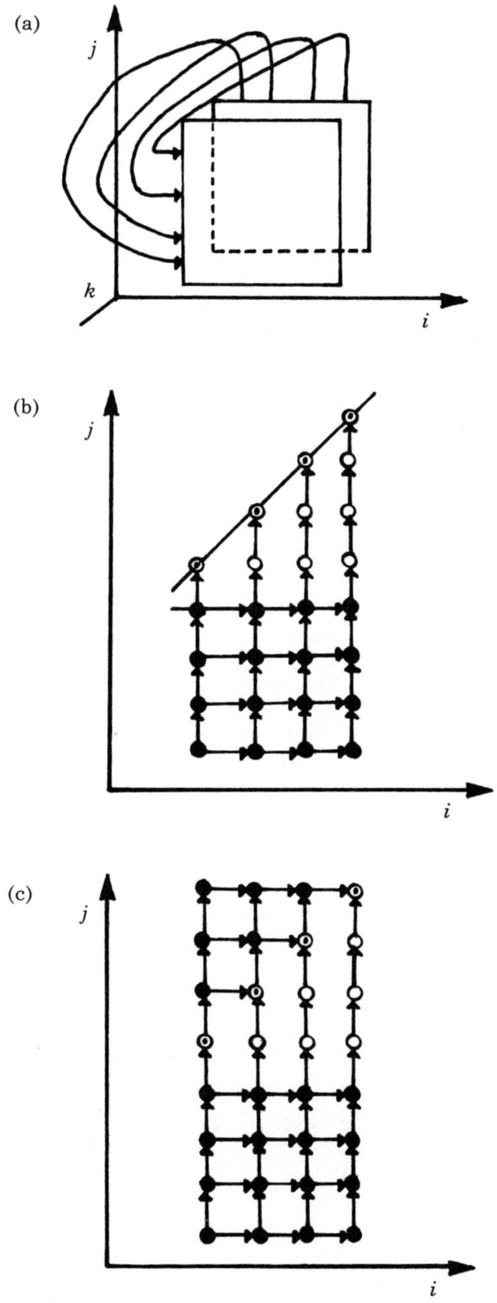

Fig. 3.9 General iteration array: (a) unrolled iterative method; (b) composite Jacobi graph; (c) composite Gauss–Seidel

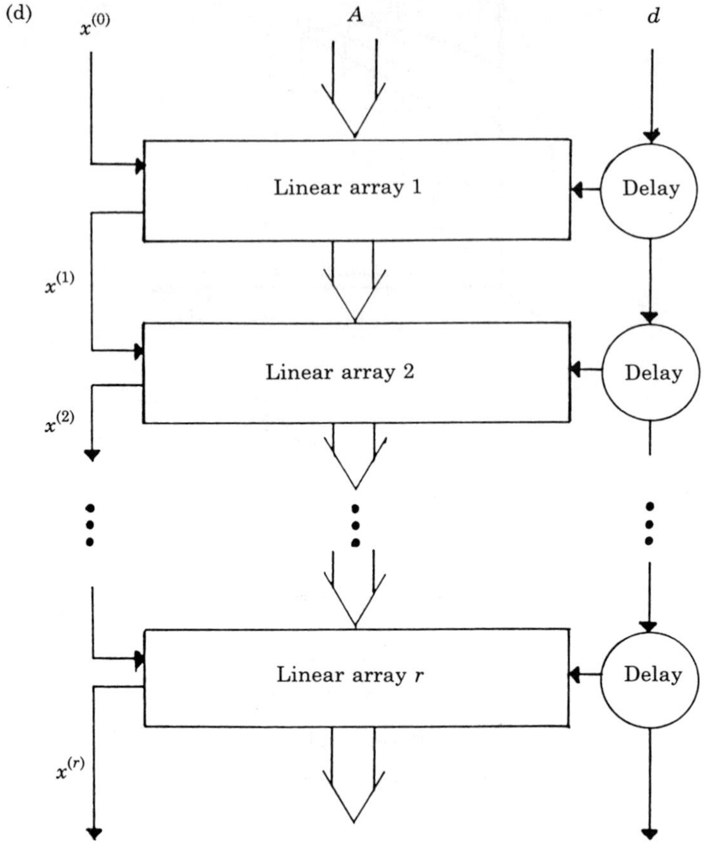

Fig. 3.9 (*cont.*) General iteration array: (d) cascaded iteration array (Source M. Berzins *et al.*, *Parallel Computing 83*, North-Holland, Elsevier Science Publishers)

pipelined through the r arrays and synchronized with $x^{(i)}$ and the right-hand-side vector d on each level. When A has a simple splitting for E and F it is usually possible to construct the linear array from the designs already considered. Below we use this idea to produce arrays for the Jacobi and Gauss–Seidel methods.

3.4.1 General iteration

Suppose that the iteration matrix M, and vector c, make up a general iterative scheme of the form

$$x^{(k)} = Mx^{(k-1)} + c. \tag{3.29}$$

If M is banded (which is often the case in partial differential equation problems), each iteration is simply a matrix–vector problem so that a recurrence form of the method can be written as

$$x_{i,j,k} = x_{i,j-1,k} + m_{i,j,0}x_{j,n,k-1}, \quad i, j = 1(1)n,\ k = 1(1)r \qquad (3.30a)$$

$$x_{i,0,k} = c_{i,0,k} = c_i \qquad (3.30b)$$

for $n \times n$ matrices. Both $m_{i,j,0}$ and $x_{j,n,k-1}$ involve non-local connections. The former can be removed by the pipelining and the latter modified to produce

$$x_{i,j,k} = x_{i,j-1,k} + m_{i,j,k}z_{i,j,k} \qquad (3.31a)$$

$$m_{i,j,k} = \begin{cases} m_{i,j,k-1} & k > 1 \\ m_{ij} & k = 1 \end{cases} \qquad (3.31b)$$

$$z_{i,j,k} = \begin{cases} z_{i-1,j,k} & i > 1 \\ x_{j,n,k-1} & i = 1 \end{cases} \qquad (3.31c)$$

$$x_{i,0,k} = c_{i,0,k} = c_i \qquad (3.31d)$$

which pipelines the matrix in the k direction. Similarly the c vector can also be pipelined but this is omitted. Equation (3.31) is essentially a matrix–vector problem so that a data dependency graph for constant k is the same as that derived in Chapter 2. A composite graph is produced by replicating the matrix–vector graph in the k direction and connecting nodes in each subgraph according to (3.31b). Finally, the input x^k to the kth subgraph is the output of the $(k-1)$th subgraph as indicated by the non-local dependency $x_{j,n,k-1}$ (and the variable z). Figure 3.9(a) illustrates the situation for a 4×4 case with $r = 2$ iterations. Projecting in the $(-1, -1, 0)^t$ direction produces the cascaded array in Fig. 3.9(d) directly where the linear arrays are bidirectional matrix–vector arrays. For a band matrix with bandwidth $w = p + q - 1$ the first component of $x_1^{(i)}$ would emerge $2p$ steps after the $x_1^{(i-1)}$ entered the array on the ith tier, and p steps after it met m_{11}, the first matrix element input to the array. It follows that the matrix input has to be delayed by $2(p-1)$ steps between corresponding cells in linear arrays i and $i-1$ for successive iterations to synchronize correctly. To achieve the required delays the matrix output of each cell of the linear array must be augmented with a queue of $2(p-1)$ delay registers. The synchronization of the right-hand-side vector c (in this case) is also necessary. The required delay is dependent on p and q so the length of the delay in the boundary cells of Fig. 3.8(d) is easily determined. Now, the following facts are easily established from array snapshots or reasoning about the array latency and data sequence structure.

1. Initialization for the first linear array is $\max(p-1, q-1)$ steps and the first component is output after an additional p steps.
2. Each array has an output latency of $2p-1$ steps. Thus, the first result after r iterations is ready to emerge from the pipeline after $(r-1)(2p-1)$ steps.
3. There are $2n$ cycles required to output all components of the solution vector.

After summing the times in 1–3 and some simple manipulations it is evident that the total number of steps for r iterations of the cascaded array is given by

$$\mathscr{T} = 2n + r(2p-1) + \max(p-1, q-1) - p + 1. \tag{3.32}$$

Of course other projections are possible. The surprising feature of the design suggested is that the non-local connections between composite arrays produce only local connections in the projected array. A simple explanation can be found by applying the envelope method to produce the correct delays for the input and output sequences of a single linear array.

3.4.2 Jacobi iteration

When M and c are unavailable alternative composite linear arrays can be constructed by choosing E and F in (3.14) to be diagonal or triangular matrices. For example, a linear array for the Jacobi iteration scheme (3.16) is illustrated in Fig. 3.10, which consists of a matrix–vector array to compute $z = Bx^{(k-1)} + b$ and a boundary cell which evaluates $x^{(k)} = D^{-1}z$. The central cell in the matrix–vector array associated with the zero main diagonal of B can be replaced by a delay cell that performs no computations. The boundary cell consists of a divider and accepts the elements of D. Timing of the iterative array using the Jacobi linear array is easily derived from (3.32) by substituting $\bar{p} = p + 1$ for p to allow for the extra delay through the boundary cell.

The array is derived from first principles as follows. First take the data dependency graph for the matrix–vector computation ($n = 4$ in the diagram) and apply the envelope method to extend the graph to show the routing of results from the array. The graph produces z. Next produce a subgraph for computing $D^{-1}z$ using the discussion for backward substitution. The composite design is shown in Fig. 3.9(b) and a projection in the $(-1, -1)^t$ direction produces the array in Fig. 3.10.

3.4.3 Gauss–Seidel iteration

For the Gauss–Seidel method (3.17) a single iteration is a composite array constructed from an upper triangular matrix–vector array for $z = Ux^{(k-1)} + b$,

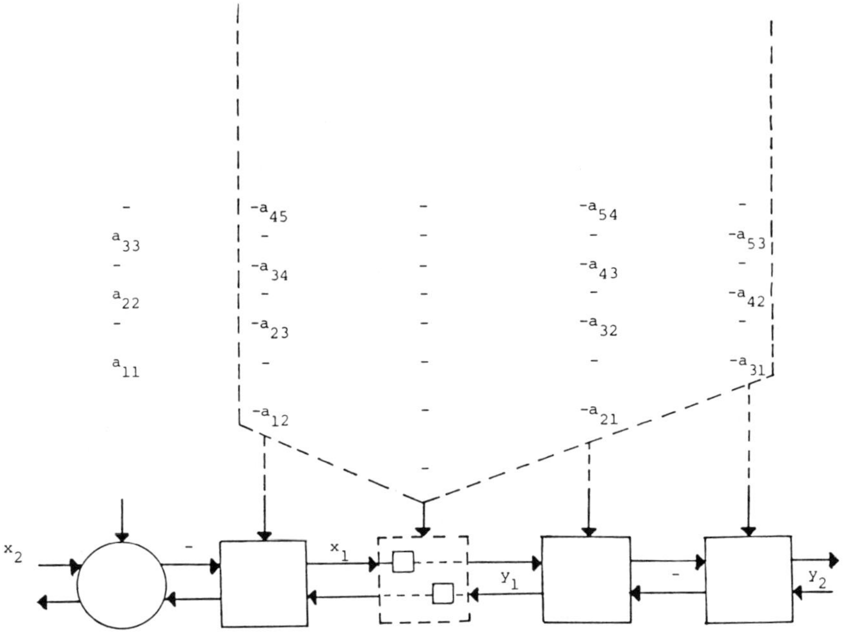

Fig. 3.10 Array for Jacobi iteration

and a back-substitution array for $(D - L)x^{(k)} = z$. Figure 3.9(c) shows how a data dependency graph can be constructed from two subgraphs for these two computations. Again a projection in the $(-1, -1)^t$ direction will produce the required linear array which is simply Figs 2.8(c) and 3.1(d) pipelined together. When this composite array is incorporated into Fig. 3.9(d) the timing of the array can be derived as follows.

1. The upper triangular matrix–vector array has $p - 1$ cells and thus a component input to the linear array for iteration takes $2(p - 1)$ steps to produce the equivalent z component from $Ux^{(k-1)} + b$.

2. The back-substituter can be arranged so that the vector z enters as the right-hand side to the boundary cell and requires only a single delay to produce the $x^{(k)}$ component.

3. The total delay is $2p - 1$ cycles between input and output of components so the first result arrives at the output of the rth linear array after $r(2p - 1)$ steps.

4. There are $2n$ steps to output all the components of $x^{(r)}$.

After a simple summation we conclude that r iterations of the Gauss–Seidel iterative method for an $n \times n$ band matrix A with bandwidth $w = p + q - 1$ requires $\mathscr{A} = rw$ cells (augmented with delays) and $\mathscr{T} = 2n + r(2p - 1)$ steps.

Improvements to these basic schemes are possible. For example, in the Gauss–Seidel array the solution of the L and U forms can be interleaved on a single array with $\max(p, q)$ cells by folding the L data to fit the synchronizing spaces left by the U matrix. Folding is not specific to iterative schemes—it is an attribute of many systolic algorithms that contain synchronizing delay elements. We will consider some of these techniques in Chapter 6. For the moment we will content ourselves by pointing out that as long as $w \ll n$, r iterations of an iterative scheme with the general form (3.15) can be computed in $O(2n)$ steps.

Finally, observe that the cascaded design builds in some features that are common to all iterative schemes. For example, a single pass of the data through the array outputs a solution approximation every r iterations. Intuitively when an iterative scheme starts it will be far away from the true solution, and consequently we probably do not want to test for convergence immediately—the array prevents us from doing so. This also illustrates a second assumption: when we get close to the answer, r iterations will not be needed. As we cannot change the size of the array we have to assume that once an iteration has converged it stays at the solution, otherwise later iterations would destroy the answer before it emerged from the array. Fortunately the convergence criterion (or consistency condition as it is more formally known) is satisfied for most iterative schemes in popular use. We conclude that when convergence has occurred redundant iterations will not affect the final result.

3.5 Inversion and transposition

Next we consider two arrays for transposing an $n \times n$ matrix, a task that arises in many situations. For example, if the matrix concerned is orthogonal a transposition is also equivalent to finding the inverse. The case for general square matrix inversion will be considered later. Alternatively, transposition arrays can be used for *data turning* or *reformatting*. For instance, suppose we have two arrays, one that accepts a row-ordered input and the other that produces column-ordered output. We can pipeline the data from one array to the other provided we change the data format between the two. For completeness two designs are considered, one suited to banded matrices and the other for dense matrices.

3.5.1 Transposing banded matrices

Before we can develop any arrays for the transposition eqn (3.21) has to be represented as a suitable recurrence. One form is the following:

$$t_k = \begin{cases} t_{k-1} & k > 1 \\ a_{i,j} & k = 1 \end{cases} \tag{3.33a}$$

$$r_k = \begin{cases} r_{k-1} & k > 1 \\ a_{j,i} & k = 1 \end{cases} \quad i = 1(1)n,\ j = i(1)n,\ k = 1(1)|j-i| \tag{3.33b}$$

$$a_{j,i} = t_{|i-j|}, a_{i,j} = r_{|j-i|} \tag{3.33c}$$

which swaps $a_{i,j}$ and $a_{j,i}$ in a non-destructive way by routing them through $|j - i|$ temporary variables. The term $|j - i|$ measures the shortest distance between the two elements $a_{i,j}$ and $a_{j,i}$ in the matrix. In sequential computing (3.33) would be very inefficient because a swap can be achieved with just a single variable, but in parallel computing we can pipeline the exchanges by reusing the variables. Indeed a fully indexed version of (3.33) produces

$$t_{i,j,k} = \begin{cases} t_{i+1,j-1,k-1} & k > 1 \\ a_{i,j} & k = 1 \end{cases} \tag{3.34a}$$

$$r_{j,i,k} = \begin{cases} r_{j-1,i+1,k-1} & k > 1 \\ a_{j,i} & k = 1 \end{cases} \quad i = 1(1)n,\ j = i(1)n,\ k = 1(1)|j-i| \tag{3.34b}$$

$$a_{j,i} = t_{i,j,|j-i|}, \qquad a_{i,j} = r_{j,i,|i-j|} \tag{3.34c}$$

which can be plotted in 3-D space to produce a locally connected data dependency graph. Subsequent projections will produce arrays. For example, projecting in the $(-1, -1, -1)^t$ direction (because we want an array suitable for banded matrices) produces the graph shown in Fig. 3.11(a). The matrix is input to the bottom boundary in diagonal format. A problem with this design is that the paths for swapping elements on different sub(super)diagonals are of different length. Consequently, it is not obvious how data should be routed out of the array to produce a convenient output format. In addition the diagonal elements of the matrix are not treated explicitly. Other projections produce similar difficulties and we need to adjust our recurrence model of the computation.

An alternative method for transposing elements is to notice that (3.21) can be rewritten as

$$a_{ij} \rightarrow a_{ii} \rightarrow a_{ji}$$

so that swapping requires two paths with orthogonal directions. First we move $j - i$ steps in the j direction and then $i - j$ steps in the i direction. More formally

$$t_{i,j,k} = \begin{cases} t_{i,j+1,k-1} & k = 1(1)d \\ t_{i-1,j,k-1} & k = (d+1)(1)2d \\ a_{ij} & \mathrm{k} = 0 \end{cases} \tag{3.35a}$$

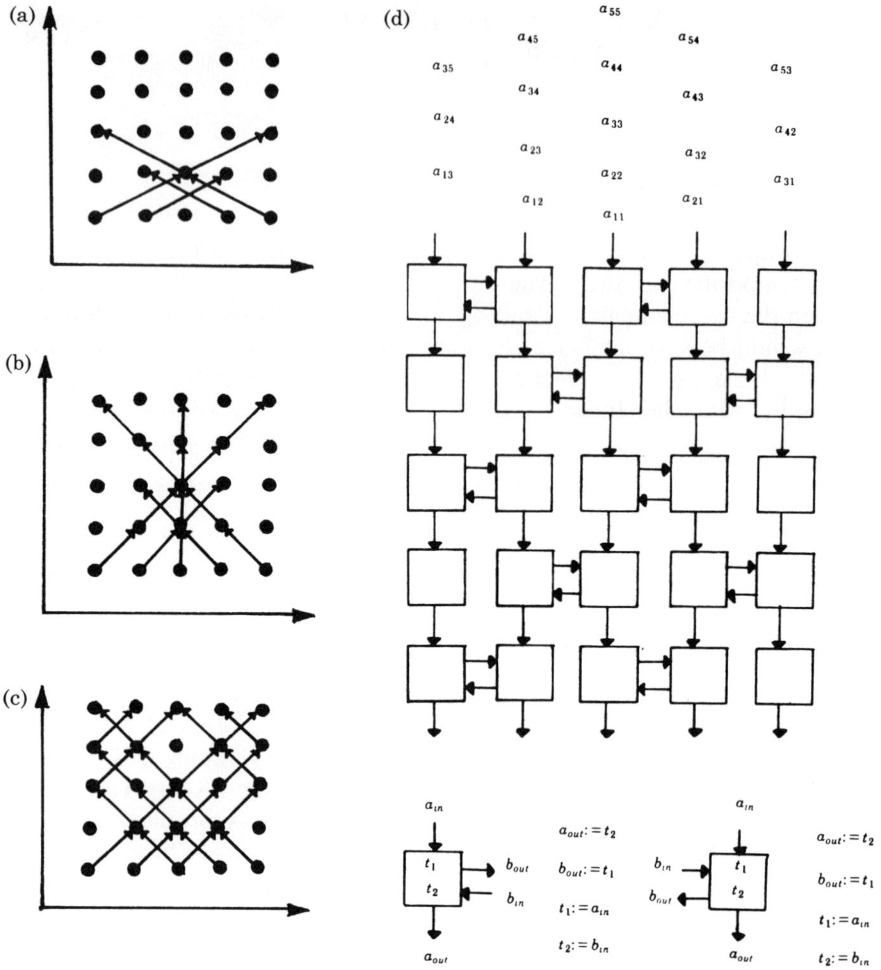

Fig. 3.11 Transposition array (banded systems): (a) simple routing; (b) mutually exclusive routing; (c) routing with equal path lengths; (d) array based on sorting

$$r_{j,i,k} = \begin{cases} r_{j,i-1,k-1} & k = 1(1)d \\ r_{j+1,i,k-1} & k = (d+1)(1)2d \\ a_{ji} & k = 0 \end{cases} \qquad (3.35b)$$

where $d = |j - i|$ and $i = 1(1)n$, $j = i(1)n$. The r and t values still swap elements $a_{i,j}$ and $a_{j,i}$ but now t and r use mutually exclusive paths that do not share the same nodes. Plotting a projection of the associated data dependency graph produces the graph in Fig. 3.11(b) which is similar to Fig. 3.11(a) except that the interconnections are nearest neighbour rather than next-nearest neighbour. Unfortunately paths for different swaps are still of different lengths. The longest path is described by the corner elements of the matrix (i.e. $(1, n)$ and $(n, 1)$) which require paths of length $2(n-1)$ steps. Furthermore, the difference in path length between the longest path and the path for element a_{ij} can be represented as

$$d_{ij} = d_{ji} = 2(n-1) - 2|i-j| = 2(n - |i-j| - 1)$$

which is always even. It follows that a delay path with $n - |i-j| - 1$ steps in one direction and $n - |i-j| - 1$ in the reverse direction does not affect the computation so that putting $d = |i-j| + (n - |i-j| - 1)$ in (3.35) does not change the computation but simply shifts it in space–time. In particular, we can treat the line $(1, 1, 1)^t$ as time so that a projection in the $(-1, -1, -1)^t$ direction produces the 2-D graph in Fig. 3.11(c). The resulting array accepts a matrix input by diagonals and outputs the transpose also in diagonal format. Because all the data paths are of the same length the input and output formats are completely compatible and it is easy to determine the area and time requirements of the design. For an $n \times n$ matrix with bandwidth w each tier of the graph requires w cells, and the maximum path length is w. The input data length is $2n$ allowing for synchronizing elements so that the total time is $\mathcal{T} = 2n + w$ steps and total area is $\mathcal{A} = w^2$. Each of the cells works once every two cycles so $e = 0.5$.

Finally, we show that transposition is also equivalent to sorting. Recall that a matrix A has p subdiagonals and q superdiagonals when the bandwidth is $w = p + q - 1$. Now, each of the diagonals can be numbered uniquely by using the mapping $d_k = i - j$ so that the ith subdiagonal is numbered $i - 1$ and the jth superdiagonal is numbered $1 - j$. Now sorting the diagonals into non-decreasing order using d_k as the key and swapping diagonals when they are out of order will transpose the matrix. Chapter 5 considers systolic sorting networks, but we point out here that transposition of a banded matrix is equivalent to sorting n lists of length w. A network to transpose a banded matrix can then be constructed by pipelining suitable sorting arrays together—such an array is shown in Fig. 3.11(d) and requires w^2 cells. Notice the similarity between this array and the graph in Fig. 3.11(c).

3.5.2 Transposing dense matrices

The previous discussion and the graphs in Fig. 3.11 can be used to derive arrays more suited to the problem of dense matrix transposition. We will not pursue these arrays directly but instead introduce another formulation for the transposition problem. The emphasis here is on the modelling of data which change from non-stationary to stationary states (and vice versa) during a single computation. We will divide the computation into two phases, which amounts to turning the data from movement in one direction into movement in another. The two phases are then used as subgraphs to build a composite array.

In phase I we pipeline data in direction k and then turn them to move in direction i. More formally

$$t_{i,j,k} = \begin{cases} t_{i,j,k-1} & k \le i \\ t_{i-1,j,k} & k > i \\ a_{ij} & k = 0. \end{cases} \tag{3.36}$$

Plotting this recurrence in 3-D space produces the solid shown in Fig. 3.12(a). Intuitively row i moves i steps in the k direction and then turns towards the i direction. For $n \times n$ matrices and $k = n$ steps a prism shape is produced. Any arrays for the computation can be projected in the normal way. In particular projecting out the i axis produces an $n \times n$ mesh of orthogonally connected cells. The boundary BC in the diagram shows that input is by rows. Similarly, directions parallel to the i axis become stationary. The data dependency tells us how to load a mesh with a matrix so that the matrix is stationary at the end of loading. For phase II we first pipeline the matrix in the k direction and then turn the data into the j direction. That is

$$r_{i,j,k} = \begin{cases} r_{i,j,k-1} & k \le i \\ r_{i,j-1,k} & k > i \\ a_{ij} & k = 0. \end{cases} \tag{3.37}$$

Plotting this recurrence in 3-D space produces the solid shown in Fig. 3.12(b). This time a projection in the k direction produces an $n \times n$ orthogonally connected array in which the initial matrix is stationary. It follows that data moving in the j direction are non-stationary. Consequently, Fig. 3.12(b) tells us how to unload a mesh in a way that outputs the first column first and the last column last.

The way forward should now be clear. In phase I element $a_{ij} \to a_{kj}$ and in phase II $a_{ij} \to a_{jk}$. Now, treating k as i and pipelining the two computations together produces $a_{ij} \to a_{ij} \to a_{ji}$ which is a transposition. We can use the subgraphs in Fig. 3.12(a) and (b) to derive a composite array for transposition by putting the blocks together as shown in Fig. 3.12(c) where the faces joined are indicated by ABCD. Projecting in the direction shown produces the $n \times n$ orthogonally connected array in Fig. 3.12(d). The array transposes its input by simply preloading the input matrix into the array and then recovering the desired output pattern by unloading in column order. The design works as follows.

1. The input matrix percolates down through the array and the first element to enter an empty cell is loaded into the cell.

2. The stationary matrix is then made non-stationary by pipelining row elements left to right across the array; a value becomes non-stationary when its cell is the leftmost non-empty cell in the row.

These rules are encoded in Fig. 3.12 where the asterisks denote control tags which change the data direction. The first phase of computation is controlled by tags moving vertically while in the second phase tags move horizontally. In the first phase the loading of the matrix proceeds by setting the tag associated with the first row of the matrix. Each tag moves twice as slowly as the matrix so that they are delayed one extra cycle in each cell; this realigns the tag with successive matrix rows as the data move vertically through the array. It follows that row i of the matrix input is loaded into row i of the array. For the second phase we use a similar idea with tags shifted horizontally from left to right along a tier. If the tag for row i is entered at time $t + i$ the tag for row $i + 1$ enters at time $t + i + 1$. The horizontal tag moves at half the speed of the matrix values to ensure that it enters a new cell only when the cell is the leftmost non-empty cell. Consequently horizontal tags can be used to mobilize the stored matrix in correctly transposed order. The array requires $\mathscr{T} = 4n$ steps: n to load the first column of the input matrix, n to mobilize the first row of the stationary matrix, and $2n$ to unload the transposed matrix. This timing can be verified by finding the shortest path from the first vertex of the solid to the last in Fig. 3.12(c) (which is $3n$) and then adding n steps to allow for the skew of the input data.

The role of the control tags is self-evident: they mark the edges of subgraphs in a larger data dependency graph indicating where the projected cells need to change to a different function (in this case from stationary to non-stationary states and vice versa). Also, observe that the space–time representation itself models only the data flow; the fact that nodes of the graph incorporate different functions at different times is not explicit. One way to overcome this problem is to imagine the component subgraphs to be different colours (we have used full and open circles in the previous examples). Control tags are then added to correspond to changes in node colour that are projected on to a single array cell. At this stage it may appear that pipelining computations in the manner just described is obvious and intuitive. Indeed, as a designer gains experience it is not necessary to reduce computations to the level of coloured space–time graphs. However, some problems are intrinsically difficult and hard to visualize especially when a number of component arrays, recurrence unrollings, and phases are all used simultaneously. The next example illustrates the point.

3.5.3 Matrix inversion

For more general non-singular matrices the problem of inversion is non-trivial. Indeed, apart from the partial pivoting array in Section 3.3.2 the

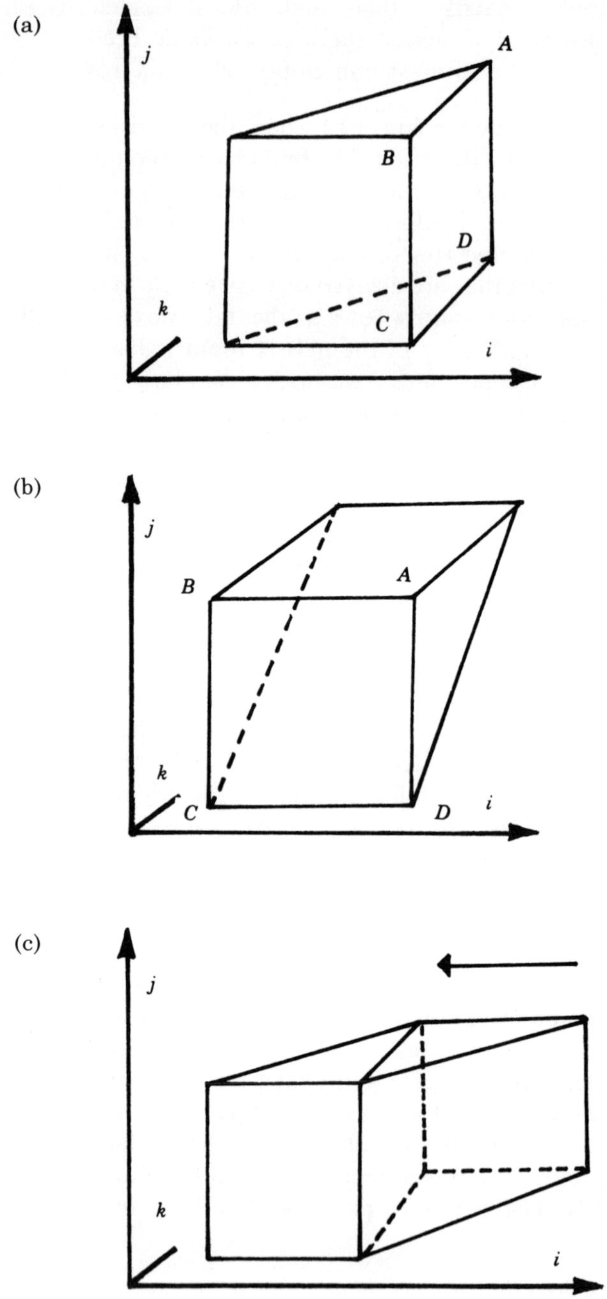

Fig. 3.12 Transposition of dense matrices: (a) solid for loading a square array; (b) solid for unloading a square array; (c) composite solid for transposition; (d) projected array

(d)

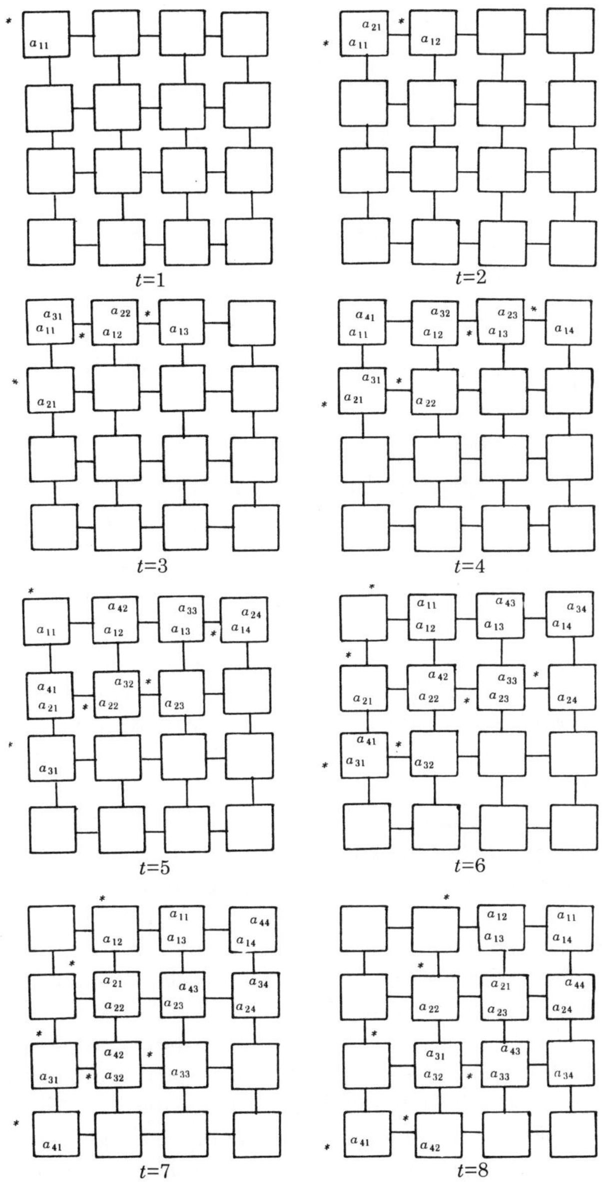

(d)

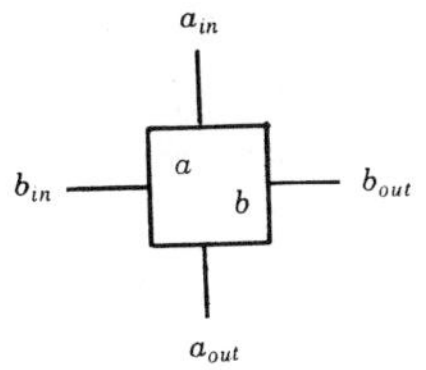

IF a_{in} tag = * THEN $\{a = a_{in}\}$
ELSE $\{a_{out} := a_{in}\}$
IF b_{in} tag = * THEN $\{b_{out} := b\}$
a_{out}.tag := tag.a
tag.a := a_{in}
b_{out}.tag := tag.b
tag.b := b_{in}

Fig. 3.12 (*cont.*)

array described next is the most complex we have seen so far. The method adopted is that described by Robert and Trystram (1985) for inverting the matrix $(I - A)$. In particular we note that the matrix can be factorized to give

$$(I - A) = (I - L)(D^{-1} - U) \tag{3.38}$$

so that

$$(I - A)^{-1} = (D^{-1} - U)^{-1}(I - L)^{-1} = W^{-1}Z^{-1} \tag{3.39}$$

for $W = (D^{-1} - U)$ and $Z = (I - L)$. The inverse of the matrix can now be found using the following three-phase algorithm.

1. Compute $Z^{-1}[(I - A)|I] = [W|Z^{-1}]$ using an appropriate triangularization algorithm.
2. Solve $WW^{-1} = I$ to get W^{-1}.
3. Evaluate $W^{-1}Z^{-1}$ to produce the final inverse.

An array for computing the matrix inverse is then produced by noting the following facts. Phase 1 is the same as matrix triangularization so a Gaussian-elimination-type array can be used. Phase 2 requires triangular matrix inversion, which according to (3.20) can be solved by n back-substitutions. Phase 3 requires the matrix product of triangular matrices, which was considered in Exercise 2.12. The required array is developed by taking existing arrays already discussed or apparent from previous sections and using them as building blocks to construct a composite array. We then resolve any difficulties between input and output formats so that data can be pipelined directly from one array to the next. Pipelining allows different phases to be overlapped on different arrays.

For the first phase we need to use the subgraph developed in Section 3.3, Fig. 3.3(c). In this case $(I - A)$ and I are both $n \times n$ matrices so that the front face is of dimension $n \times 2n$ and n steps are required for triangularization. A projection in the j direction produces a triangular array of $(n/2)(n + 1)$ with the matrices input columnwise and I following $I - A$, that is the array of Ahmed *et al.* (1982) where the multipliers are stationary and the upper triangular matrix W is output from the side of the array projected from the face CDE in Fig. 3.13(a). Likewise the matrix I following $I - A$ is transformed into Z^{-1} and is pipelined behind W due to the projection of face ABDC on to the i–k plane. For the second phase we need to find an array for back-substitution of n right-hand sides which is compatible with the array for the first phase. Section 3.2.2 considers such arrays and shows that a triangular solid describing the computation can be produced; we represent it here by Fig. 3.13(b). The solid must be orientated so that the output of face CDE in Fig. 3.13(a) can be input directly. Thus we require that the right-hand side I is preloaded and stationary when W arrives (given our knowledge of the problem this is not difficult to achieve by choosing an appropriate projection). In the third phase we require a matrix product of two triangular matrices. It is easy to show, using the discussion of matrix product in Chapter 2, that triangular orthogonally connected arrays for this problem exist (treat the dense case as a matrix with bandwidth $n-1$ instead of $2n-1$). Consequently we can use the solid in Fig. 3.13(b) as a shape for the required subgraph.

Now we need to build a composite array from these building blocks such that all the interfaces are compatible. Figure 3.13(c) shows the composite solid. We know that face CDE of Fig. 3.13(a) outputs W, and that the data must be pipelined into the subgraph for the second phase; hence the lower triangular block in Fig. 3.13(c) describes back-substitution for n right-hand sides. Similarly the output of face ABDC in Fig. 3.13(a) produces Z^{-1} so that the top triangular block in Fig. 3.13(c) describes the triangular matrix product. Next we must ensure that the inverse W^{-1} produced in the bottom triangular block is available in the top triangular block. A simple way to achieve this is to make W^{-1} stationary and interpret the j axis as time so that a projection in the $(0, -1, 0)^t$ direction produces a lozenge-shaped array. This array is shown in Fig. 3.13(d) where the dashed line is the boundary AB in Fig. 3.13(c).

We require $2 \times (n/2)(n+1)$ or $\mathscr{A} = n(n+1)$ cells, and a time of $\mathscr{T} = 5n - 2$ steps. The former follows from the dimensions of the subgraphs and the latter can be shown by finding the shortest path along the boundaries of the solid (i.e. $4n$) and then adding n steps for the skew of the input data. The array actually computes $(I - A)^{-1}$ so substituting $I - A$ for the first matrix input computes A^{-1}.

Finally, and to end this section, we note that an array with exactly the same connection structure as Fig. 3.13(d) can be used to perform matrix inversion by the Gauss–Jordan elimination technique using a row-ordered input. In this case the computation has the form

$$AX = I \rightarrow LAX = L \rightarrow (D + U)X = L \tag{3.40}$$

where L is a multiplier matrix that triangularizes A. Further,

$$M(D + U)X = ML \rightarrow \bar{D}X = ML \rightarrow X = \bar{D}^{-1}W \tag{3.41}$$

where M is upper triangular and diagonalizes $(D + U)$, $W = ML$, and $A = L^{-1}M^{-1}$. The three phases are now as follows.

1. Triangularize A in the left part of the array. $D + U$ is stationary and L is moving right (because the data are input in row order).

2. Diagonalize $(D + U)$ in the left part and load L into the right part. M is non-stationary and follows L.

3. $\bar{D}$ follows M and the right part of the array evaluates W followed by $\bar{D}^{-1}W$ to complete A^{-1} which is non-stationary and emerges from the bottom boundary.

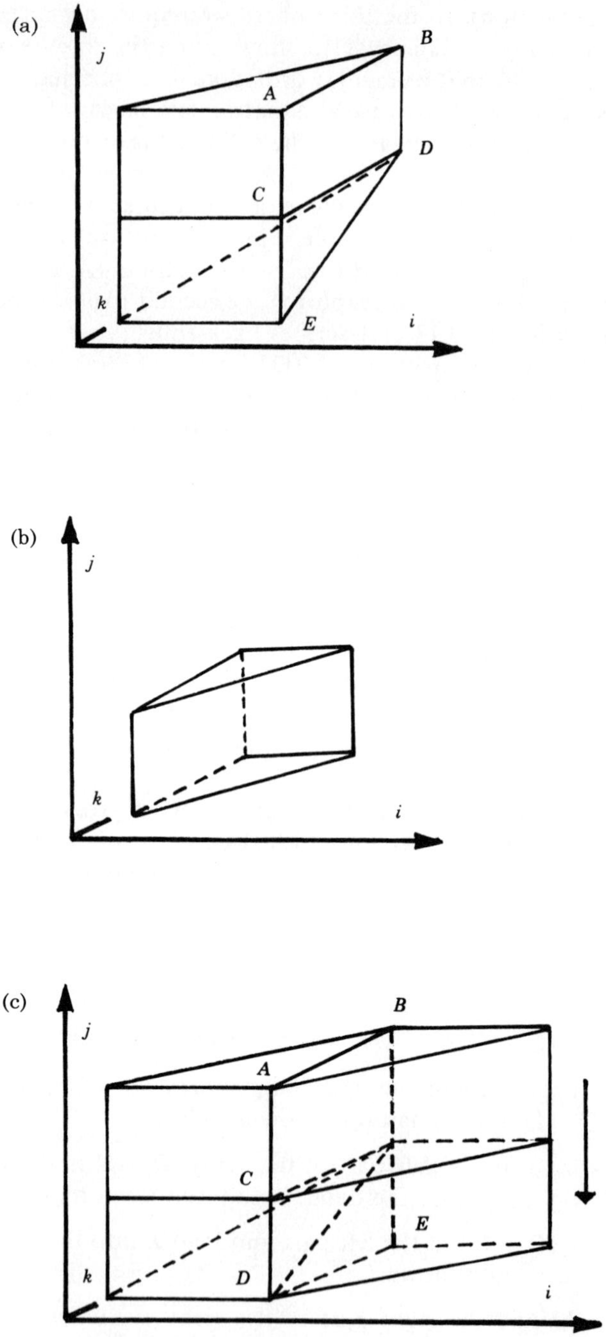

Fig. 3.13 Matrix inversion array: (a) solid for elimination; (b) solid for back-substitution and product; (c) composite solid; (d) projected array

(d)

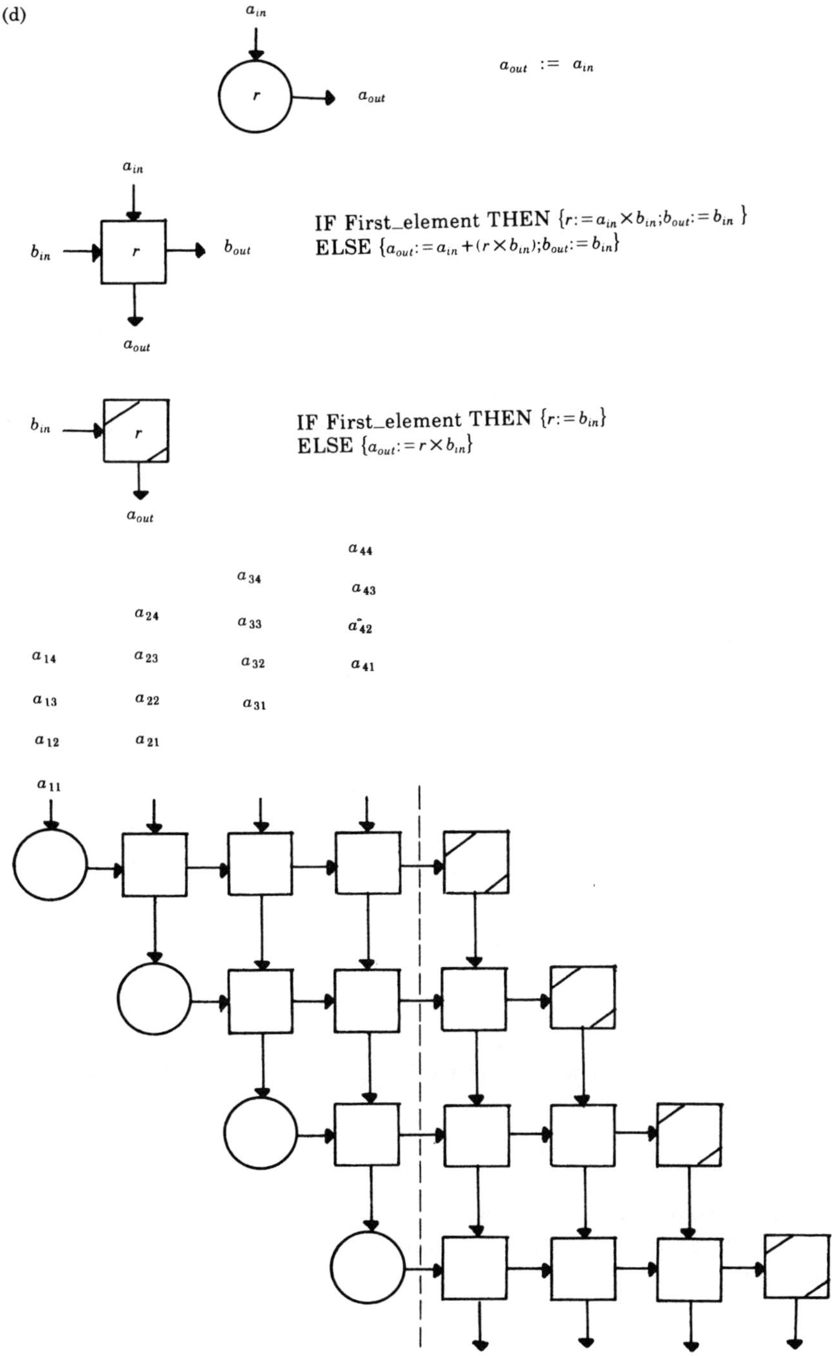

Fig. 3.13 (*cont.*)

The time and cell requirements are the same as the previous design. The construction of the composite data dependency graph and the cell descriptions are left as an exercise.

3.6 The Faddeev algorithm

In the previous sections we have considered a number of different systolic algorithms for frequently used linear algebra problems. It is clear that one or two designs such as the triangular and orthogonally connected arrays recur. The connection topologies between these arrays are very similar—all that we change are the data inputs, the direction of communication, and the cell functions. In the transposition problem we produced a design in which a control tag was used to change the cell function during the computation. In the matrix inversion array we showed that tags and pipelining could be used to overlap computations with matching topologies on to the same cells. Can we apply the same principle to different algorithms and construct one array which uses control flows (as well as data flows) to change the cell functions and data directions for different problems? A general solution to this problem will be delayed until Chapter 7 where we examine practical implementation issues. In this section we will show that a simple systolic array for computing the majority of linear algebra problems considered in this chapter does indeed exist. Furthermore this array requires only a simple control tag mechanism and the array function is determined by the choice and form of the input data.

The design considered is the so-called Faddeev array, named after a famous mathematician who discovered a powerful elimination technique for computing matrix functions (Faddeeva and Faddeev 1963). The general principle of the technique can be stated simply as follows. Let

$$\begin{bmatrix} E & F \\ -G & H \end{bmatrix} \tag{3.42}$$

be a compound matrix where E, F, G, and H are $n \times n$, $n \times p$, $q \times n$, and $q \times p$ matrices respectively (i.e. an $(n+q) \times (n+p)$ matrix). Suppose that we apply a matrix transformation T to the upper blocks of (3.42) to produce

$$\begin{bmatrix} TE & TF \\ -G & H \end{bmatrix} \tag{3.43}$$

where TE is triangular. Next apply a transformation W which nullifies the bottom left block of (3.43) by performing row operations between TE and $-G$ so that

$$\begin{bmatrix} TE & TF \\ 0 & H + WTF \end{bmatrix} = \begin{bmatrix} TE & TF \\ 0 & H + GE^{-1}F \end{bmatrix}. \tag{3.44}$$

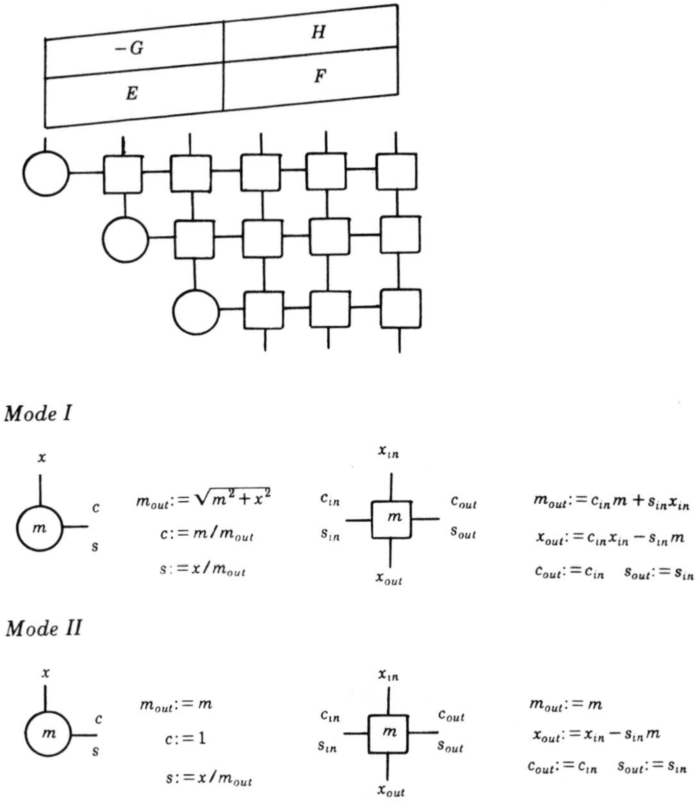

Fig. 3.14 Faddeev array

Hence $G = WTE$, implying that $W = GE^{-1}T^{-1}$.

A trapezoidal array for computing the Faddeev algorithm is shown in Fig. 3.14 which is similar to Fig. 3.3 except that the cells have two modes of operation corresponding to the elimination and annihilation phases in the algorithm. The rows of E and F are input into the array in row order with the basic cells operating in mode 1 to triangularize E and load the updated elements of E and F into the array cells. Once the last element of either E or F has entered a cell in a particular column the cell changes to mode 2. In mode 2 the boundary cells generate multipliers (using Gaussian elimination) to annihilate the matrix $-G$ which is pipelined behind E and updates H. We change from Givens rotation to Gaussian elimination to avoid modifying TE and TF as demanded by the nullification step. Clearly the array requires $\mathscr{A} = (n/2)(n + 1) + pn$ cells and $\mathscr{T} = (n + p) + (n + q) + (n)$ steps to compute (3.44).

Finally, it remains only to show that the Faddeev array is generic. Table 3.1

Table 3.1 Matrix parameters for Faddeev array

E	F	G	H	Computation
A	b	I	0	$A^{-1}b$
A	I	I	0	A^{-1}
A	B	C	0	$CA^{-1}B$
A	B	I	0	$A^{-1}B$
A	I	C	0	CA^{-1}
I	C	B	0	BC
I	x	A	0	Ax
I	A	x^t	0	x^tA
I	x	y^t	0	y^tx
I	x^t	y	0	yx^t

lists different choices for the E, F, G, and H matrices along with the final term $H + GE^{-1}F$. Inspection of the table shows that all the matrix problems (apart from transposition) can be computed by this one array. For example, the matrix inverse requires $p = q = n$ so that $\mathscr{A} = (3n/2)(n + 1)$ cells and $\mathscr{T} = 5n$ steps are needed for the computation. Note that the time for a matrix inversion is approximately the same on the Faddeev array as it is for the array in Section 3.5.3. Of course some of the more specific designs are faster and require less cells, which is the price one pays for flexibility.

3.7 Design principles

This chapter has considered a number of systolic solutions to common linear algebra problems and introduced a number of design principles. On first reading the algorithm and array descriptions may appear rather shallow. Indeed the inexperienced designer may be forgiven for expecting a tight and detailed interplay between space–time mappings, data dependencies, and the projection of array forms. This expectation, although understandable, clearly misses the point. All the necessary details required of an algorithm description are present. The relations between the input, intermediate variables, and output which describe the 'state' of an algorithm are specified precisely albeit implicitly by the cell descriptions and connection topologies. Explicit representations of problems can always be recovered by tracing snapshots for a small example or unrolling the arrays in space–time. In this chapter techniques for minimizing the amount of explicit space–time mappings have been introduced. Below we briefly review them, and indicate why they are useful.

Arrays as building blocks

The first concept introduced was the idea of array components or building blocks. This approach combines the three important principles in algorithm design: *modularity*, *divide and conquer*, and *abstraction*. Good designers are able to distinguish between what a component array does and how it does it. In systolic algorithm design component arrays are black boxes where the input–output format is given in terms of specific patterns. These black boxes are defined once and then used to assemble arrays for different algorithms. It is imperative that designers familiarize themselves with standard arrays, and build up a sufficiently large working set of components, so that prototyping and design time is reduced. A working set should consist of several arrays for the same task with different area, time, efficiency, and input–output formats. For example, we developed row-, column-, and diagonal-ordered input–output formats. In linear algebra applications the first two are predominantly used for dense and the last for banded matrices.

The real skill in systolic design is to choose the correct level of abstraction for the array components. Choosing the correct level minimizes problems with interfacing different blocks and in particular reduces the need to become involved with very complex space–time representations. Only very basic components have to be analysed in terms of space–time mappings of recurrences and array projections. In Chapter 2 we expressed data dependencies at the variable level (each node of the dependency graph was identified with a variable of the recurrence), but there is no need to limit the space–time mapping technique in this way. For instance, we can consider nodes as representing blocks of computation such as procedures and functions, expressions, or even bit level computations. As an example we interpreted Fig. 3.9 as a loop unrolling of (3.15) where the block of computation is itself a matrix–vector computation. Component arrays for matrix–vector computations are known so the overall design is simple. The level of abstraction is determined by the number of loops unrolled in the recurrence equation; when all the loops have been unrolled the space–time representation is explicit. At high levels of abstraction the nodes of the data dependency graph represent component arrays and the space–time representation has difficulties in resolving the input–output format required for the array. This is because the implementation of the block determines the input–output structure but only the data dependencies between blocks are explicitly represented.

Phases and control tags

The building block approach works well for simple algorithms like the matrix–vector, matrix product, and substitution arrays where the data are completely non-stationary. This is because the arrays require very little control and provided the input–output formats are compatible blocks can be pipelined together to solve more complex problems. Where data formats are similar but not compatible additional reformatting blocks can be used (e.g. row to column conversion), or a component array retimed to produce the correct format. However, completely non-stationary designs are limited. Often the building block method introduces large array latencies, poor efficiency, and high cell count because many blocks are used. The data flowing through the composite array tend to occupy only one or two blocks at any instance.

In contrast problems such as triangularization, inversion, and transposition change the state of the data flow during different periods or phases of the computation so that cells can be reused and efficiency improved. For example, it is often necessary to change data from non-stationary to stationary states or vice versa. Changing state requires control and implies that cells are capable of a number of different functions. More compact designs are sometimes possible if the underlying connection topology and input–output format of some component blocks are the same. This is because different blocks of the composite array can be mapped on to a single generic block and data for different phases pipelined through the block (e.g. the matrix inversion array has two triangular blocks). Control tags are added to the data in order to distinguish between different computational phases and flip the cell into different functions appropriate for the context of the computation. It should be noted that a certain duality between data sequences and instruction sequences exists. For example, a pure instruction sequence can be constructed by using a data sequence of synchronizing elements (dummy data) with appropriate tags. Such a sequence was adopted in Fig. 3.12 for recovering the transposed matrix.

Designing composite systolic arrays using generic components is generally more difficult than simple design. Considerable skill is required to exploit all the possible pipelining and cell reuse. Indeed, the control tags required for the pipelining of multiphase algorithms are not explicit in the original recurrences and are not easy to generate using an explicit space–time representation because data dependency graphs tell us nothing about the functions evaluated at the nodes of the graph. We have used colouring of nodes to make the computations more explicit but this is not described by the basic design methodology. Using the building block approach allows composite arrays to be unrolled in space–time so that the boundaries between phases of computation are more explicit. Unfortunately one already needs to know a great deal about the final form of the systolic algorithm.

Generification

Use of multiphase algorithms and control tags leads naturally to the concept of generic arrays. For example, why not produce one square, one hexagonal, and one triangular array and map all the problems considered so far onto these arrays using control tags to switch the cell function? This idea is a powerful one and leads ultimately to the ideal of general-purpose cells and reconfigurable array topologies which produce programmable systolic arrays. The general topic of programmable arrays is considered in Chapter 7; we remark here that such flexibility is accompanied with increases in step time and cell area. The step time is longer because cells must decide which function is applicable on each step of the algorithm. The area of a cell is also affected because more functions need to be implemented, requiring more hardware. Restricted generalization is often more attractive. For example, in the Faddeev array (Fig. 3.14) we produce a design with a fixed topology and limited cell functionality (only two modes). The array is generic in the sense that it computes many linear algebra tasks but achieves this desirable property only by a careful choice of data, not by additional and more intelligent cell hardware. We will develop the idea of generic arrays further in subsequent chapters.

Exercises

1. Using a space–time transformation modify the design in Fig. 3.1 so that the x_i are stationary. Comment on the array efficiency.
2. Devise a Gaussian elimination array which uses an orthogonally connected $n \times n$ grid of cells with the matrix A preloaded before computation starts.
3. Consider how you would implement Gaussian elimination with partial pivoting using a modified triangular array like that in Fig. 3.3.
4. Apply the retiming and cut theorems to Fig. 3.7 so that no delays are required between tiers, and only one synchronizing delay is necessary between elements of the input.
5. Consider the LU decomposition array in Fig. 3.8 and modify it so that it (a) computes the determinant of A, (b) produces the Cholesky factorization $A = LL^{\mathrm{T}}$, and (c) produces the $A = LDU$ factorization where L and U are strictly lower and upper triangular with D a diagonal matrix.
6. Repeat Exercise 2 for LU decomposition, and show how to compute $A = UL$ instead of the LU factorization. Can the existing arrays be extended for this task?
7. Pipelining the output of one array directly into another is often desirable but not always possible because the input–output formats of arrays are not compatible. To alleviate this difficulty devise arrays for the following tasks: (a) changing row-, column-, and diagonal-ordered inputs into each of the other forms (e.g. row to column and diagonal); (b) modifying existing arrays to accept different input formats (e.g. make the

matrix–vector array accept hexagonal-type inputs). [Hint: Use the retiming and cut theorems.]

8. Devise an alternative Faddeev array which accepts the matrix in a column-ordered input format. [Hint: Consider the solid in Fig. 3.3(c).]
9. Design arrays for inverting a non-singular matrix B by the rank annihilation formula

$$B^{-1} = (A + uv^t)^{-1} = A^{-1} - \frac{(A^{-1}u)(v^t A^{-1})}{1 + v^t A^{-1} u}$$

where A^{-1} is known and u, v are vectors determining the change in a row and column of A.
(a) By use of matrix–vector and transposition arrays
(b) Faddeev arrays
(c) Discuss how r updates satisfying the recurrence

$$A^{(0)} = A$$

$$A^{(i)} = A^{(i-1)} + u_i v_i^t$$

$$B = A^{(r)}$$

could be implemented.

10. Broyden's algorithm for solving n non-linear equations $F(x) = 0$ can be expressed as the iteration

$$A_i^{-1} = A_{i-1}^{-1} + \frac{(s_i - A_{i-1}^{-1} y_i) s_i^{\mathrm{T}} A_{i-1}^{-1}}{s_i^{\mathrm{T}} A_{i-1}^{-1} y_i}$$

$$x^{(i+1)} = x^{(i)} - A_i^{-1} F(x^{(i)})$$

where $y_i = F(x^{(i)}) - F(x^{(i-1)})$, $s_i = x^{(i)} - x^{(i-1)}$, and A_0 is an approximation to the Jacobian matrix $J(x^{(0)})$. Use the Faddeev array to formulate a systolic solution to this problem. [Hint: Use the solution to Exercise 9.]

11. By pipelining a number of systolic arrays develop systolic solutions to the following problems:
(a) generating the sequence $A, A^2, A^3, \ldots$
(b) $I + A + A^2 + A^3 + \cdots$ (the Neumann expansion)
(c) the sequence $A, A^2, A^4, A^6, \ldots$.
12. Indicate how your solutions to Exercise 11 could be used: (a) to compute the largest eigenvalue λ of a square matrix A satisfying $Ax = \lambda x$ using the power method; (b) to produce the matrix power series EXP(A), LOG(A), SIN(A), COS(A), etc.
13. A preconditioned iterative scheme can be used to accelerate the convergence of iterative methods for solving systems of the form $Ax = d$.

Derive arrays for the following preconditioned methods:
(a) $(I - B^2)x = (I + B)d$
(b) $x = L^2x + (I + L)(Ux + d)$
where $A = (I - B)$ and $A = I - L - U$ respectively. What effect would improved convergence have on the area requirements of an iterative scheme?

4
TABLE GENERATION

Many problems in numerical analysis result in the generation of data in a tabular form, for example finite differences used for estimating derivatives, Padé tables, binomial coefficients, continued fractions of rational functions, extrapolation and interpolation tables, to name only a few. The use of tables in numerical computation dates back to the time of Isaac Newton when calculation was mainly performed by hand. Tables were introduced to minimize the number of errors in manual arithmetic by use of highly organized and regimented approaches to computation. Fortunately, because of their inherent simplicity and recurrent forms these techniques are particularly amenable to a systolic interpretation. Indeed, the solution of systems of equations considered in the previous chapter evolved for similar reasons, and consequently it is sometimes convenient to regard matrix methods as a subset of the more general table-generating algorithms. In this chapter we will demonstrate the derivation of systolic table algorithms by considering some important applications in function approximation and polynomial manipulation. The examples, although simple, establish the basic principles and can be readily extended to more complicated problems.

The basic design themes for this chapter are *two-level pipelining*, *systolic rings*, and *problem duality*. The first is concerned with the improvement of array throughput and deals directly with modifications to the internal arrangements and functionality of basic cells. The second deals with reuse and reduction of the number of cells in an array and leads on to the concepts of *fixed-size* arrays and *multipass* algorithms. We will consider the use of these techniques for potentially infinite data sequences and tables that arise in many iterative algorithms. The third and final theme emphasizes the fact that problems may have a number of representations which can be used to trade off area, time, and efficiency. In particular the idea of an algorithmic versus geometric interpretation of a problem is introduced. More involved techniques for improving the efficiency of designs will be introduced in Chapter 6.

Finally, recall that in Chapter 1 we indicated that the appeal of systolic algorithms was the close interplay between algorithmic and architectural forms of a problem. Indeed this is one form of duality, because the array topology is an architectural interpretation of the algorithm data dependencies. At the basic cell level the functionality of a cell can be interpreted as a procedure or as a hardware description. In the previous chapter we used a procedural description for cell definitions, but in this chapter a cell will be described by a hardware configuration. One reason for adopting this form of description is to demonstrate the changes that occur in the underlying cell implementation as a result of different design decisions. In particular the difference between stationary and non-stationary data flow is made explicit. Another justification is, of course, to promote the concept of duality.

4.1 Tables and space–time

Any undergraduate textbook on the numerical approximation of functions will introduce the concept of generating tables of data (e.g. Burden *et al.* 1981; Householder 1970). In this section we will consider the type of tables that frequently occur and establish the relationship between tables and space–time. Take a few moments to think about what types of table might occur. Figure 4.1 illustrates a representative selection divided into three types: finite, semi-finite, and infinite. Other more complicated tables can often be reduced to these forms by reorganizing the elements.

All tables consist of the same basic components: a table structure which shows its geometric form, a rule or set of rules for relating elements, and a set of boundary or initial values. The table rules show how to generate new table elements from existing ones and are usually simple mathematical formulae which relate elements according to their geographical position in the table. For example, the rule

$$a_{ij} = a_{i-1,j-1} + a_{i-1,j} + a_{i,j-1} \tag{4.1}$$

will generate an infinite table like Fig. 4.1(b) provided the boundary elements $a_{0,j}$ and $a_{i,0}$ as $i, j \to \infty$ are specified. The same rule produces a finite $(m \times n)$ table like Fig. 4.1(b) when $a_{0,j}$ and $a_{i,0}$ are defined only for $i = 0(1)n$ and $j = 0(1)m$. Alternatively the rule

$$a_{ij} = a_{i-1,j-1} + a_{i,j-1} \tag{4.2}$$

produces an infinite trapezoidal table like that in Fig. 4.1(d) when the boundary elements a_{i0} for $i = 1, \ldots$ and a triangular table like Fig. 4.1(a) when $i = 1(1)n$. It should be clear that an $m \times n$ table requires $O(mn)$ applications of the rectangle rule while a triangular table with $(n/2)(n + 1)$ elements needs $O(n^2)$ applications of a rule similar to (4.2). These estimates give a bound on the sequential computing time for constructing the tables. Infinite and semi-infinite tables by definition have unbounded computation time and are normally associated with iterative solution techniques that converge to within a specified accuracy of the desired solution.

Equations (4.1) and (4.2) have the desirable property that the values required by the rule are all nearest neighbour. Fortunately this property remains true for many useful applications and can be exploited for the purposes of systolic design. Visually, table-generating rules can be represented by *computational molecules* (because they look like simple molecules). For

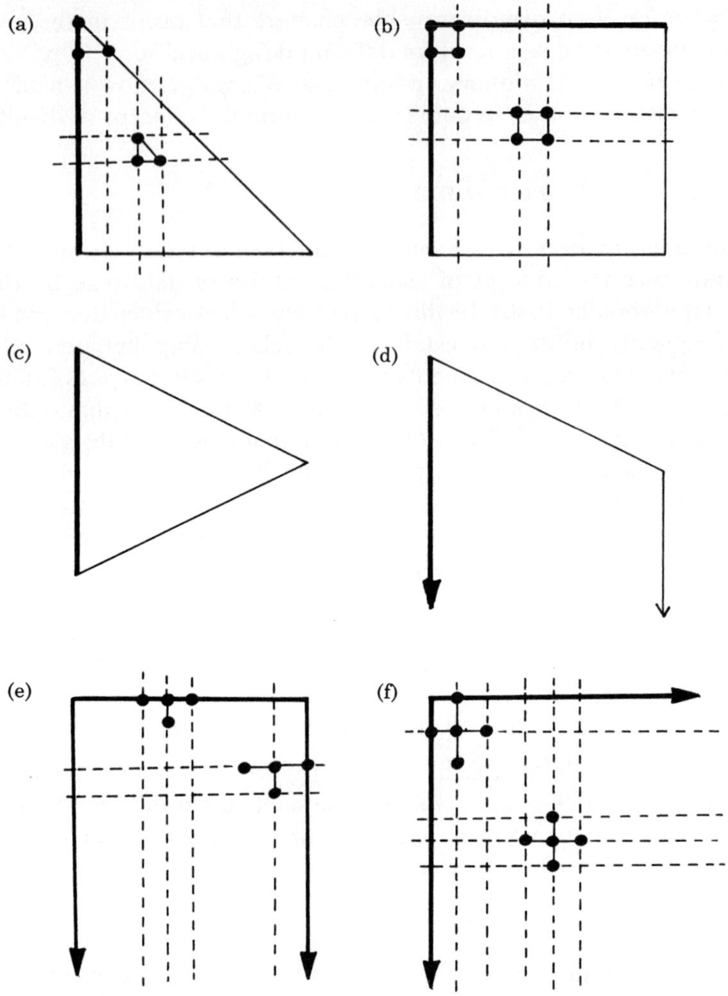

Fig. 4.1 Types of table: (a) triangular; (b) rectangular; (c) skew triangular; (d) open trapezoidal; (e) open rectangular; (f) doubly infinite

example, (4.1) is sometimes called a rectangle rule because its molecule looks like a rectangle. The nodes of the molecule represent data and the connections between them indicate data dependencies. We draw out a table by applying the molecule such that all but one of the nodes is covered by existing table values. The order in which the molecule is applied defines a partial ordering of the computations required for table construction. It follows that the table together with the rule represents a data dependency graph. As we have seen previously many construction rules can have the same molecule but involve different arithmetic operations so the molecules will produce generic array structures. In Fig. 4.1 the tables are all 2-D and can be interpreted as space–time representations of the table computation with one space and one time dimension. Projecting out the time dimension implies that linear systolic arrays will generate 2-D tables. Below we examine some specific examples and show how to produce the required arrays.

4.2 Systolic differencing

To begin let us consider arrays for common differencing techniques and rational function approximation. These types of tables can be used to extract coefficient data for the calculation of polynomials $P(x)$ and rational functions $R(x)$ of a given function $y(x)$. Many formulae are available and we shall confine our attention to simple forms which emphasize the design technique rather than the complexities of different table-generating rules. More sophisticated algorithms can be tackled in the same manner except that further consideration must be given to the internal arrangement of cell functions.

4.2.1 Equally spaced arguments

Now, given a discrete function (i.e. a set of arguments x_k and a corresponding value y_k for $k = 0(1)n$) such that the arguments are equally spaced by a distance $h = x_{k+1} - x_k$ we can define the difference operator as

First difference: $\Delta y_k = y_{k+1} - y_k$

Second difference: $\Delta^2 y_k = \Delta(\Delta y_k) = \Delta y_{k+1} - \Delta y_k = y_{k+2} - 2y_{k+1} + y_k$

and generally as

$$\Delta^j y_k = \Delta^{j-1} y_{k+1} - \Delta^{j-1} y_k \tag{4.3}$$

which generates a table with the form shown in Fig. 4.2(a) for $j = 1(1)n$. If we let $y_{kj} = \Delta^j y_k$, eqn (4.3) can be written as

$$y_{kj} = y_{k+1,j-1} - y_{k,j-1} \tag{4.4}$$

so that the table is a skewed form of the triangular table in Fig. 4.1(a) and the rule is similar to (4.2). The data dependency graph for the table generation is obtained by connecting y_{kj} values according to (4.4). Now suppose that the index k represents space and the index j is time; then a projection on to the $j = 0$ axis produces a unidirectional array. The values y_k are preloaded into the kth cell and the array computes by shifting $y_{k,j-1}$ to cell $k - 1$ on step j, evaluating (4.4), and overwriting the stored cell value with the result. After n steps $y_{0n} = \Delta^n$ resides in the $k = 0$ cell. The total computation time is $\mathscr{T} = 2n$ allowing n steps to load the y_{n0} values and n steps to compute the table. A step is the cost of performing (4.4) and we

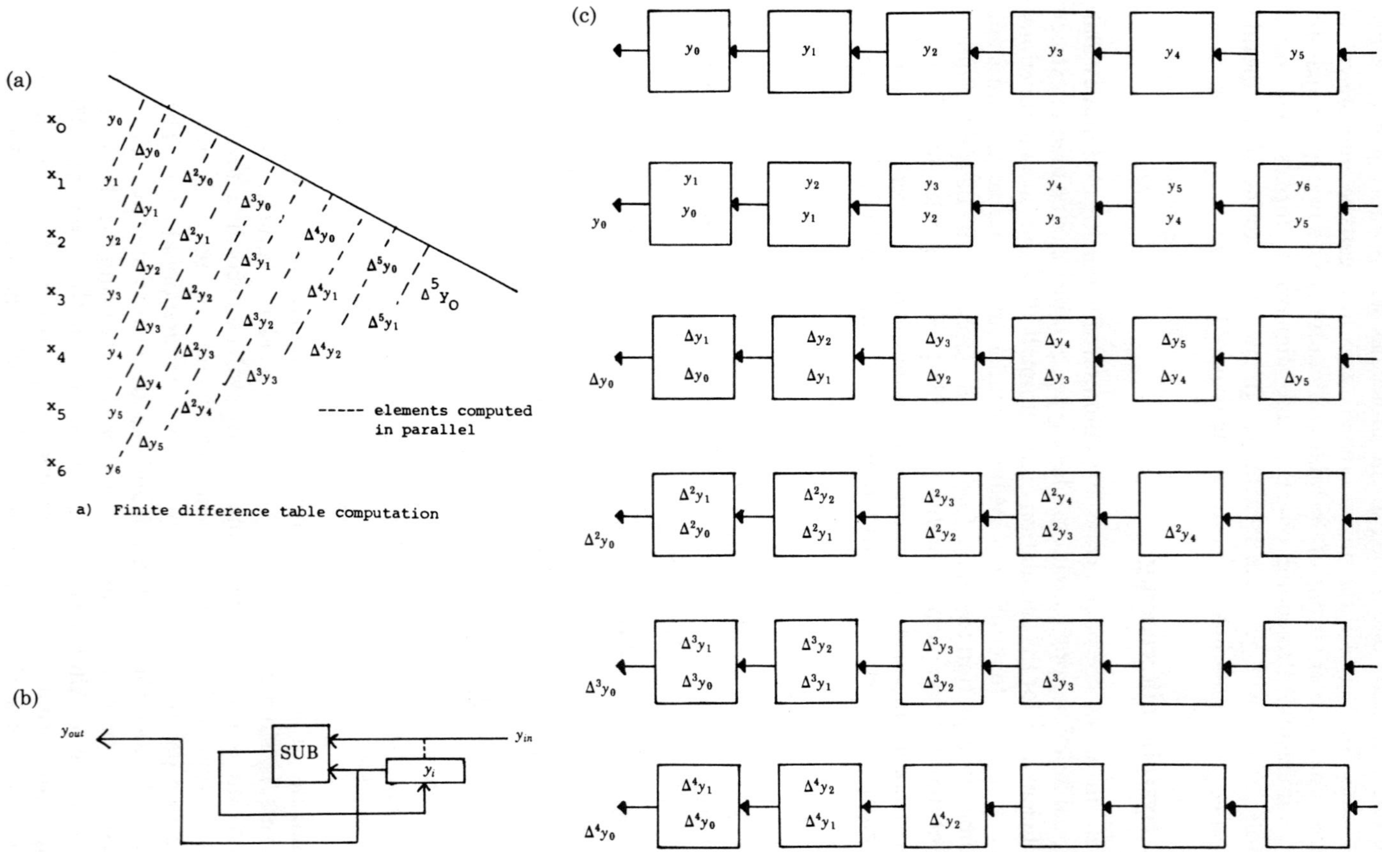

Fig. 4.2 Finite difference table (equally spaced arguments): (a) computation, — — — elements computed in parallel; (b) basic cell; (c) array snapshots

require $\mathscr{A} = n - 1$ cells. The efficiency of the design is 25–50 per cent because cell k computes $n - k$ values.

The first design is not very satisfactory because we waste n steps loading the data. Can we pipeline the loading and computation? For such a design the initial y_{k0} must become non-stationary, which is achieved by interchanging the assignment of space and time so that the k axis represents time and the j axis space. Projecting out time on to the $k = 0$ axis should produce another array but notice that $y_{0,j}$ for $j = 1(1)n$ cannot be computed simultaneously. To avoid this problem transform the data dependency graph so that the node at coordinate (k, j) moves to position $(k + 2j, j)$. This is equivalent to aligning values on the dashed lines shown in Fig. 4.2(a), where all the values on the same diagonal can be computed simultaneously. The $y_{0,j}$ values are pipelined so a projection on to the space axis (j in the current context) produces the array snapshots in Fig. 4.3(a). A basic (Δ) cell consists of a single delay register and subtractor for evaluating (4.3) as shown in Fig. 4.3(b). The cell is two-level pipelined, meaning that in addition to the pipelining exhibited in the snapshots at the array level the computations at the cell level are also pipelined. Let the cost of subtraction and delay be τ_1 and τ_0 respectively. The basic cell computation time is also τ_1 and the cell latency is $2\tau_1$ when we shall assume that $\tau_0 < \tau_1$ (which is usually the case). Indeed, Fig. 4.3(a) demonstrates that a single cell produces one result every cycle after an initial delay of two cycles. After n cycles the last boundary value has been input but data have only propagated as far as the $((n/2) + 1)$th cell. Allowing for a latency of $2\tau_1$ for the remaining $n/2$ cells means that the value $\Delta^n y_0$ is available after at most $(n + 2(n/2))\tau_1$ cycles. Normalizing with respect to τ_1 produces $\mathscr{T} = 2n$ steps for at most $\mathscr{A} = n - 1$ cells. A new problem can be pipelined into the array and begin computation after only $n + 2$ steps.

An alternative but similar differencing scheme is the backward difference method which can be defined as

$$\nabla y_k = y_k - y_{k-1} \tag{4.5}$$

and leads to a table with a similar form to Fig. 4.2(a). The construction of the table for successive differences is also similar except that the table elements are computed from bottom to top rather than top to bottom. It is trivial to observe that (4.3) and (4.5) and hence the data dependencies are isomorphic. It follows that similar arrays to those above exist for backward difference generation—in fact by a simple reversal of the argument input orders and rerouting of the subtractor operands the forward difference array can be used. A generic or unified array for forward and backward differencing is now derived easily using a non-stationary instruction sequence in the form of control tags which operate a switch to force the correct ordering of operands in the subtractor (see Fig. 4.3(c)). For example, if $c_i = 1$ then $z_i = y_{i0}$, otherwise when $c_i = 0$, $z_i = y_{n-i}$.

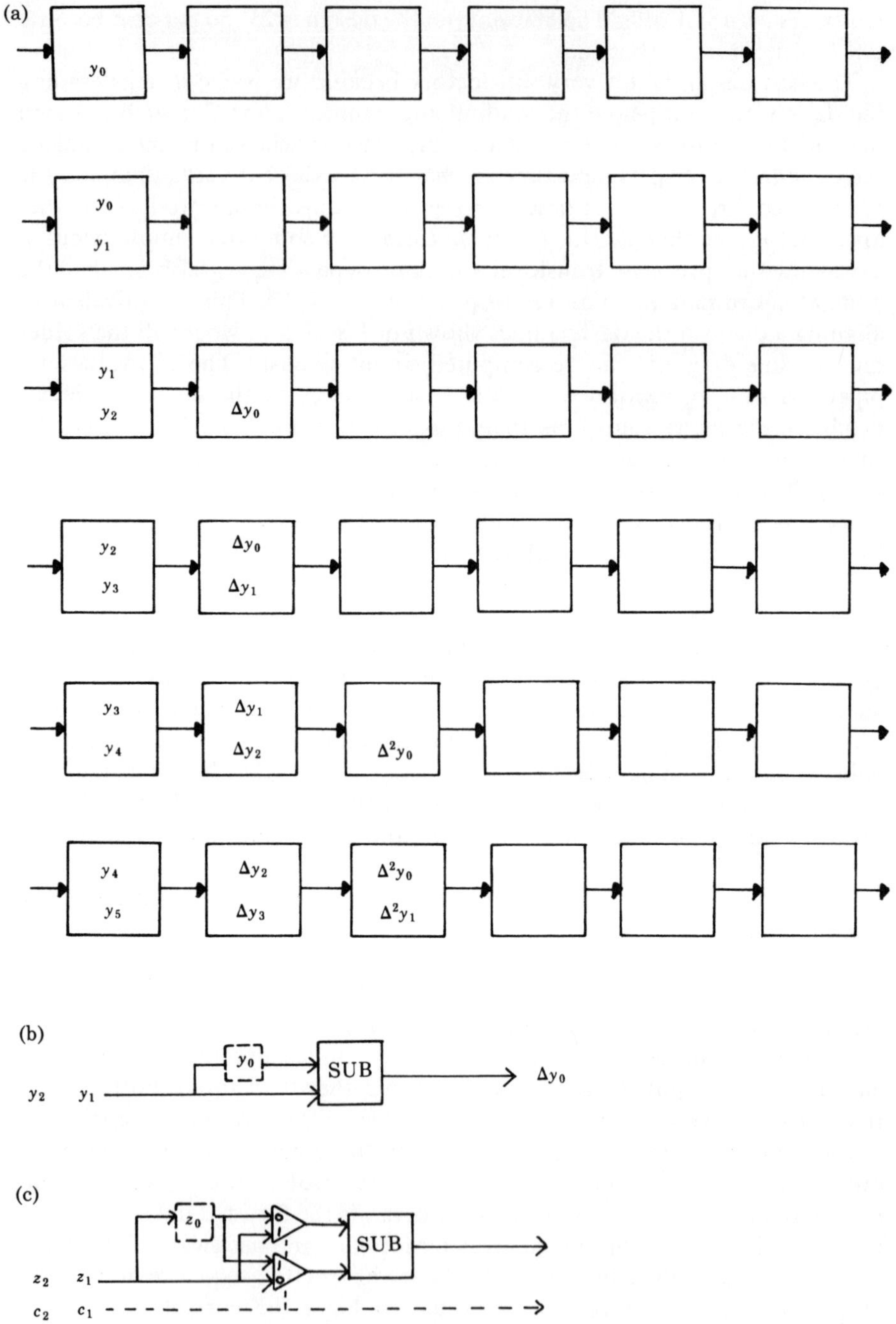

Fig. 4.3 Finite difference table (two-level pipelined): (a) array snapshots; (b) two-level cell; (c) generic cell

4.2.2 Unequally spaced arguments

Equally spaced arguments are simply a special case of more general table generators that allow unequally spaced arguments and have wider applications. It follows that a systolic array for unequally spaced arguments should incorporate the equally spaced array as a special case (and in this sense be generic). For purposes of illustration we shall consider divided differences which can be formulated as

First divided differences: $$y(x_0, x_1) = \frac{y_1 - y_0}{x_1 - x_0}$$

Second divided differences: $$y(x_0, x_1, x_2) = \frac{y(x_1, x_0) - y(x_0, x_1)}{x_2 - x_0}$$

Higher differences:

$$y(x_k, \ldots, x_p) = \frac{y(x_{k+1}, \ldots, x_p) - y(x_k, \ldots, x_{p-1})}{x_p - x_k} \tag{4.6}$$

where the step size is evaluated explicitly so that the x_i as well as the y_i values are required in the cell function. The table generated by (4.6) is given in Fig. 4.4(a). To produce a space–time representation simply make the assignment $y_{k,p-k} = y(x_k, \ldots, x_p)$ and put $j = p - k$ so that (4.6) becomes

$$y_{k,j} = \frac{y_{k+1,j-1} - y_{k,j-1}}{(x_{j+k} - x_k)}. \tag{4.7}$$

Now interpret the k axis as space and the j axis as time. A projection on to the space axis produces the snapshots shown in Fig. 4.4(c). The array consists of $n - 1$ cells and cell k is preloaded with the pair x_k, y_k. At step j the values x_{j+k}, $y_{k+1,j-1}$ are shifted from cell $k + 1$ to cell k, (4.7) evaluated, and the $y_{k,j-1}$ value overwritten. The basic cell for the computation is shown in Fig. 4.4(b) and consists of two subtractors, a divider, two preloadable registers, and a delay register to latch the x_{in} value. The cell computation is broken down into two parts.

1. Preload cell i with x_i and y_i, the starting values, $i = 0(1)n$.
2. Compute the next column element as follows:
   (a) evaluate $a = x_{\text{in}} - x_i$, $b = y_{\text{in}} - y_i$ in parallel;
   (b) set $y_i = b/a$, the new divided difference.

After preloading successive cycles of the array construct the table by evaluating a column every cycle. If we compare this design to the first design for forward differences the global array data flow is similar but the cell functions are completely different. The current array is more flexible than

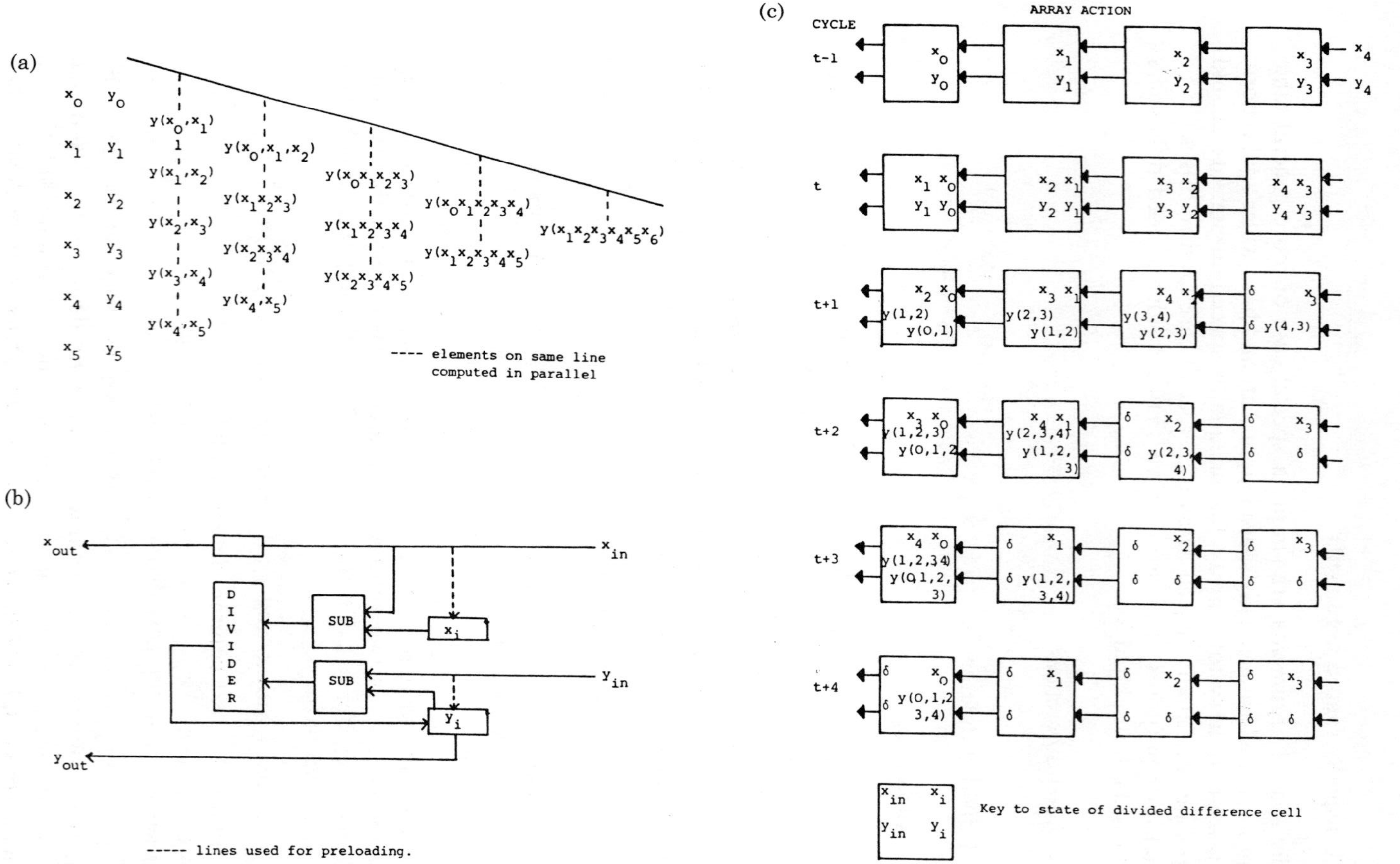

Fig. 4.4 Divided difference table (unequally spaced arguments): (a) parallel divided difference table computation, — — — elements on some line computed in parallel; (b) divided difference cell, — — — lines used for preloading; (c) array snapshots

the previous equally spaced version because equally spaced cases can be solved easily. Indeed, as promised the problem reduces to the finite difference case when both the x_i subtractor and the divider are removed to leave just a single subtractor. As the x input and output is now redundant it can be removed to reproduce the design considered briefly in Section 4.2.1.

The timing of the divided difference array has the general form

$$\mathscr{T} = (\text{preload time}) + (\text{array latency}) = n + (c \times n). \tag{4.8}$$

The cell latency is $c = \tau_1 + \tau_2$ where τ_2 is the cost of a division. This implies that loading is faster than actual computation (which is usually the case). For comparative purposes suppose that we let a loading step take c cycles (longer than is actually needed), then $\mathscr{T} = 2cn$. The finite difference array required $2\tau_1 n$ for a basic cell operation so the first array is c/τ_1 cycles faster than the more complex divided difference array. This difference is obviously due to the complexity and organization of the cell hardware and exhibits a measurable effect of flexibility. That is, less hardware reduces basic cell cycle time, while more general cells increase cycle time. Where generic arrays are concerned these facts can be of utmost importance.

Section 4.2.1 presented two alternative designs for differencing, one that demanded and one that avoided preloading of the boundary values. In the first design the columns of the table were non-stationary and the rows stationary; for the second, the situation was reversed with columns stationary and rows non-stationary. To produce the latter for unequally spaced arguments proceed as follows. Transform the data dependency graph in the same way as for the forward difference table, associating k with time and j with space. Projecting out the time dimension produces the array snapshots given in Fig. 4.5(a). Observe that for two arguments x_k and x_j the successive values of j cause the value $d = |k - j|$ to increase. When k and j are identified with space and time increases in d imply temporal and spatial separation of data and impose restrictions on the admissible array structures. The problem can be avoided by duplicating the x_i data sequence and adjusting the offset between the two x sequences in each cell by appropriate delays. The cell layout shown in Fig. 4.5(b) is easily derived from the data flow, and is two-level pipelined. Data entering the cell are delayed a cycle so that they synchronize with the next input and compute (4.7) correctly. Let the total delay through the arithmetic units be $c = \tau_1 + \tau_2$ and suppose this is also the length of the delay. The latency of an individual cell is $2c$ cycles so the array timing can be given in a general form

$$\mathscr{T} = (\text{input length}) + (\text{array latency}). \tag{4.9}$$

The input length is clearly nc and the array latency is $2c(n-1)$, giving a time of $c(3n-2)$ altogether. This is the maximum time for the last input element to filter through and leave the array. The actual table construction requires less time than this because once the last input arrives data have

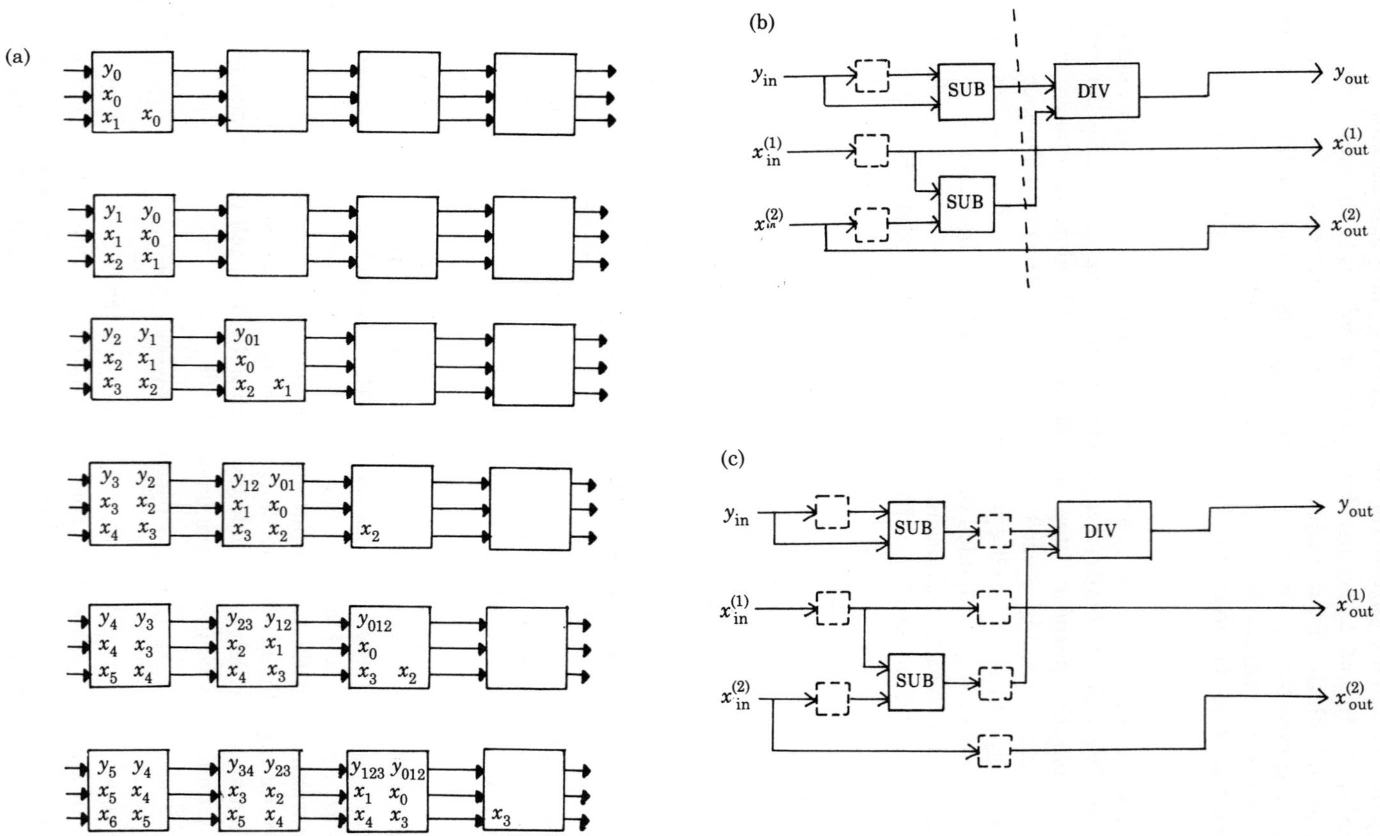

Fig. 4.5 Divided difference table (two-level pipelined): (a) array snapshots; (b) cell definition; (c) two-level cell

reached the $((n/2)+1)$th cell and require only a further $2c(n/2)$ steps to produce the last element of the table. Thus $nc + nc = 2nc$ cycles or $\mathscr{T} = 2n$ steps where the length of a step is c. For the case of the forward difference table the divider and x subtractor can be removed from Fig. 4.4(b) to reproduce the cell in Fig. 4.2(b). In the modified design the cell latency is $2\tau_1$ confirming our earlier result on the speed difference between cells for the equally and unequally spaced arrays.

Two-level pipelining can be used to improve the throughput of a design. For example, consider the cell in Fig. 4.5(c), which is a retimed version of the cell in Fig. 4.5(b) obtained by applying the cut theorem (see dashed line) to add a delay between the subtractor and divider. The cell operates in three pipelined stages: delaying the initial input, computing the subtractions, and finally the division. Each stage is independent of the others so that different steps can be overlapped in the same cell. The cell cycle can now be defined as $\bar{c} = \tau_2$ where we assume that division requires more time than subtraction or delay. The cell latency is $3\bar{c}$ and by (4.8) the maximum time for the table construction is $n\bar{c} + 3\bar{c}(n-1) = \bar{c}(4n-3)$. Although this appears to make things worse, $\bar{c} < c$ in the previous design and the array speed-up is given by

$$\frac{(3n-2)c}{(4n-3)\bar{c}} \to \frac{3c}{4\bar{c}}. \tag{4.10}$$

Consequently if $\bar{c} < (3/4)c$ the new array is faster. In any case the initial values will have been input after only $n\bar{c}$ cycles rather than nc cycles and $\bar{c} < c$ is guaranteed. It follows that we can input more data into the second array than the first in the same time period, that is throughput has been improved. Note that the same argument cannot be applied to the cell in Fig. 4.4(b) because the feedback connection overwriting the stationary y_i demands that the cell cycle time is at least as long as the cost of evaluating the whole cell function. We can use two-level pipelining only if the data are non-stationary and the cell functions can be broken into a number of arithmetic segments not connected by feedback. The more complex the cell the more scope there is for improving the array performance. Also observe that the cell hardware is utilized in a much more efficient way with a two-level cell and that the array can be operated at much higher clock speeds.

4.2.3 Rational functions

Divided differences are often used as substitutes for derivatives of functions in formulae such as Taylor and Newton series. Although these formulae are of undoubted importance for function approximation, divided differences can only approximate polynomial functions. Rational functions represent a much wider class of functions because they are quotients of polynomials. For example, a function like $\tan x$ cannot be accurately approximated around its asymptotes by a polynomial whereas with a rational function it can. Generally, a rational function has the form $R(x) = P(x)/Q(x)$ with $P(x)$ and $Q(x)$ polynomials. When $Q(x) = 1$ we generate the class of polynomial approximations so the arrays considered so far are a special case of rational function generators. It follows directly that systolic arrays for generating rational functions not only have a wider range of applications but also incorporate the array designs considered so far in this chapter. The link with previous designs can be made explicit by using reciprocal differences. Rational functions can be represented by continued fractions which in turn are made up of reciprocal difference components. For example,

$$y(x) = y_1 + \cfrac{(x - x_1)}{\rho_1 + \cfrac{(x - x_2)}{\rho_2 - y_1 + \cfrac{(x - x_3)}{\rho_3 - \rho_1 + \cfrac{(x - x_4)}{(\rho_4 - \rho_3)}}}} \tag{4.11}$$

where the ρ_i are the reciprocal differences with the form

$$\rho_i(x_{i-1}, x_i, \ldots, x_n) = \frac{x_n - x_{i-1}}{\rho_{i-1}(x_i, \ldots, x_n) - \rho_{i-1}(x_{i-1}, x_i, \ldots, x_{n-1})} + \rho_{i-2}(x_i, \ldots, x_{n-1})$$

and can be constructed using the table in Fig. 4.6(a). The method is best illustrated by a simple example. Suppose we are given the data set (0, 1), (1, 0.5), (2, 0.2), (3, 0.1), (4, 0.0588), (5, 0.0384), and wish to find some function to fit the data. According to the above formulae we can construct the following table

1				
0.5	−2.0			
0.2	−3.3333	−1.0		
0.1	−10	−0.1	0.0	
0.0588	−24.2857	−0.25	40.0	0
0.0384	49.1111	−0.0217	140.0	0

which is just a skewed form of the table in Fig. 4.6. The main diagonal of the table gives the coefficients for (4.11) so that direct substitution produces

$$y(x) = 1 + \cfrac{(x - 0)}{-2 + \cfrac{(x - 1)}{-1 - 1 + \cfrac{(x - 2)}{0 + 2 + \cfrac{(x - 3)}{(0 + 1)}}}}$$

which is simply $y(x) = 1/(1 + x^2)$.

An array with stationary rows and non-stationary columns which will generate this table is illustrated in Fig. 4.6(c). Each cell consists of an adder, divider, two subtractors, three preloadable registers, and a delay for x_{in}, connected as shown in Fig. 4.6(b). The cell computes as follows for a single step:

$$\begin{aligned}
t:&\quad r_0 = x_{\text{in}} - x_i, \quad r_1 = \rho_{\text{in}} - y_i \\
t+\tfrac{1}{2}:&\quad y_i = (r_0/r_1) + \rho_{\text{tmp}} \\
t+1:&\quad \rho_{\text{out}} = y_i, \quad \rho_{\text{tmp}} = \rho_{\text{in}}
\end{aligned}$$

so that the cycle time is $c = \tau_2 + 2\tau_1$ assuming the cost of subtraction is the same as addition. The whole array requires $\mathscr{T} = 3cn$ cycles and $\mathscr{A} = n - 1$ cells to construct a table with n initial values. Observe that the array cannot be two-level pipelined because of the feedback connection from the add/divide block which overwrites the y_i. To exploit two-level pipelining we need to make the data non-stationary. From previous work on divided differences an array where the table columns remain stationary in cells, and the rows are non-stationary, is easily derived. The actual array derivation is left as an exercise but it should be clear that the non-stationary cells can be sectioned into four pipeline segments (an initial delay, subtraction, division, and addition). It follows that the cell latency is $\hat{c} = 4\tau_2$ where division is assumed to be more time consuming than addition, subtraction, or delay. Employing (4.9) the computing time is $\hat{c}n + 4\hat{c}(n-1) = \hat{c}(5n-4)$ and will be faster than the row stationary scheme provided $\hat{c} < (2/5)c$. In any case the initial data are input at least four times faster than the row stationary scheme because $\hat{c} < c$. It should be clear that by selectively removing parts of the cell definitions corresponding divided difference cells can be reproduced. Adding a control tag to the data which masks out certain parts of the hardware allows the reciprocal difference cell to implement any of the cell functions discussed so far.

Finally, to conclude this section consider the ε algorithm due to Wynn (1962). This method deserves special attention because it is a powerful technique for accelerating the convergence of a slowly convergent sequence of values which is potentially infinite in length. For the moment we will assume that we know in advance how many boundary values are required to guarantee convergence. This situation is far from satisfactory for a number of reasons which shall become clear shortly, so we will simply present the array as another example consistent with previous designs. The basic step in the ε table generation has the form

$$\varepsilon_{(s+1)}^{(m)} = \varepsilon_{s-1}^{(m)} + \frac{1}{\varepsilon_s^{(m+1)} - \varepsilon_s^{(m)}} \tag{4.12}$$

yielding the table in Fig. 4.7(a). The algorithm has the interesting property of being very similar to the reciprocal differences considered above. As a

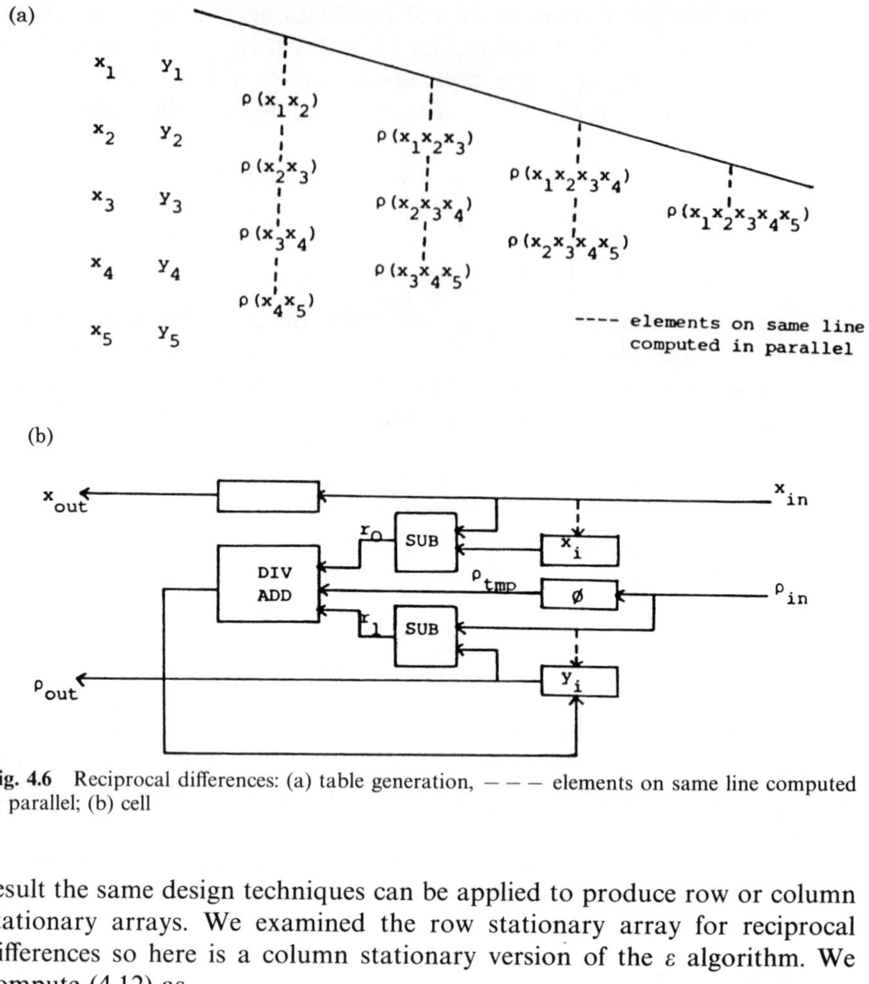

Fig. 4.6 Reciprocal differences: (a) table generation, — — — elements on same line computed in parallel; (b) cell

result the same design techniques can be applied to produce row or column stationary arrays. We examined the row stationary array for reciprocal differences so here is a column stationary version of the ε algorithm. We compute (4.12) as

$$t\colon \quad \text{In } \varepsilon_{-1}^{(0)}, \quad \text{In } \varepsilon_{0}^{(0)}$$

$$t + \tfrac{1}{4}\colon \quad \varepsilon_{-1}^{(1)}, \quad \varepsilon_{0}^{(1)}, \quad r_0 = \varepsilon_0^{(1)} - \varepsilon_0^{(0)}$$

$$t + \tfrac{1}{2}\colon \quad \varepsilon_{1}^{(2)}, \quad \varepsilon_{0}^{(2)}, \quad r_1 = \frac{1}{r_0}, \quad r_0 = \varepsilon_0^{(2)} - \varepsilon_0^{(1)}$$

$$t + \tfrac{3}{4}\colon \quad \varepsilon_{-1}^{(3)}, \quad \varepsilon_{0}^{(3)}, \quad r_2 = \varepsilon_{-1}^{(1)} + r_1, \quad r_1 = \frac{1}{r_0}, \quad r_0 = \varepsilon_0^{(3)} - \varepsilon_0^{(2)}$$

to produce the cell in Fig. 4.7(b) which involves no feedback and can be two-level pipelined. Applying the cut theorem allows each cell to be divided into four segments corresponding to each of the stages in the basic step. The

(c)

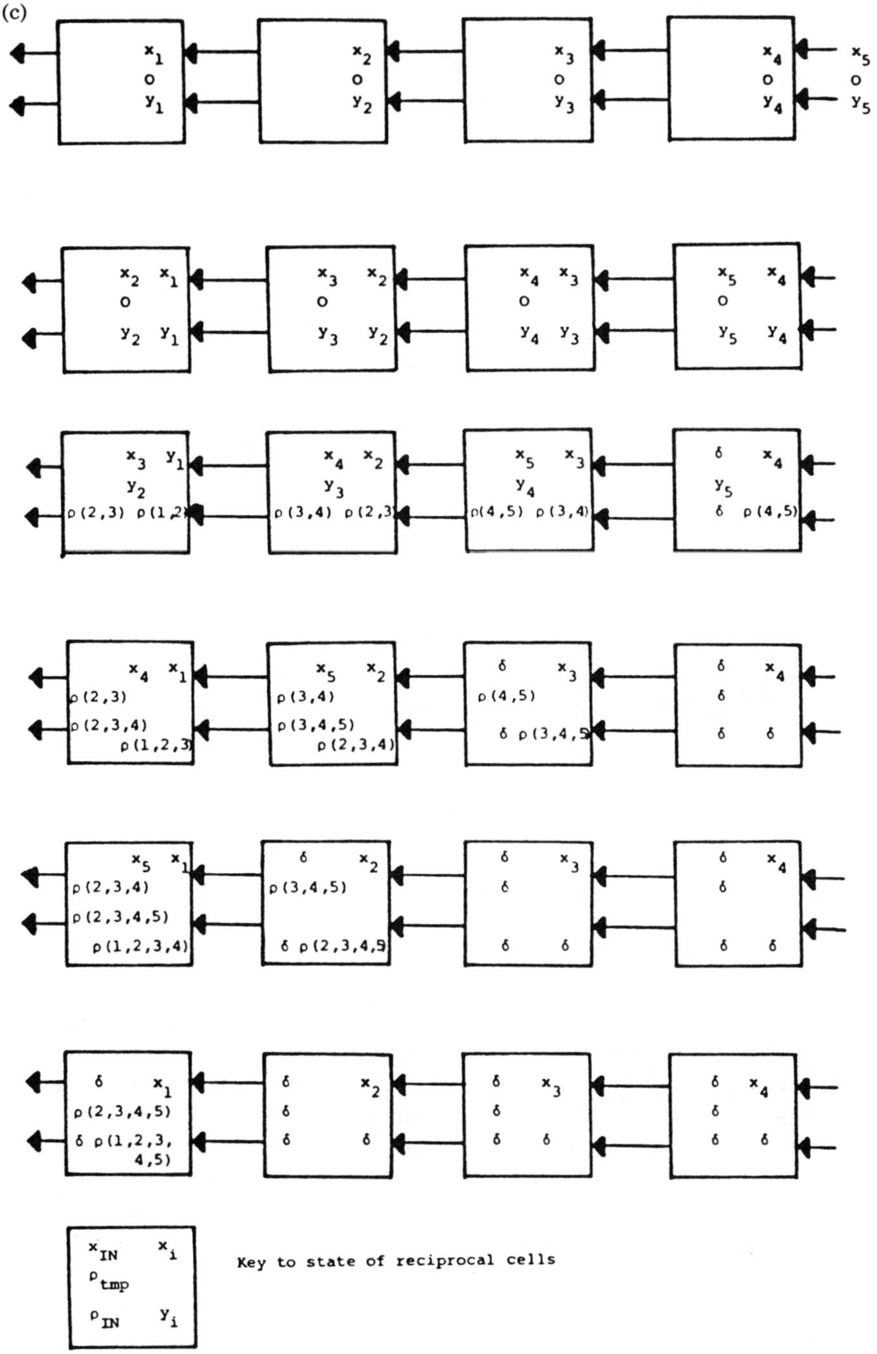

Fig. 4.6 (*cont.*) Reciprocal differences: (c) array snapshots

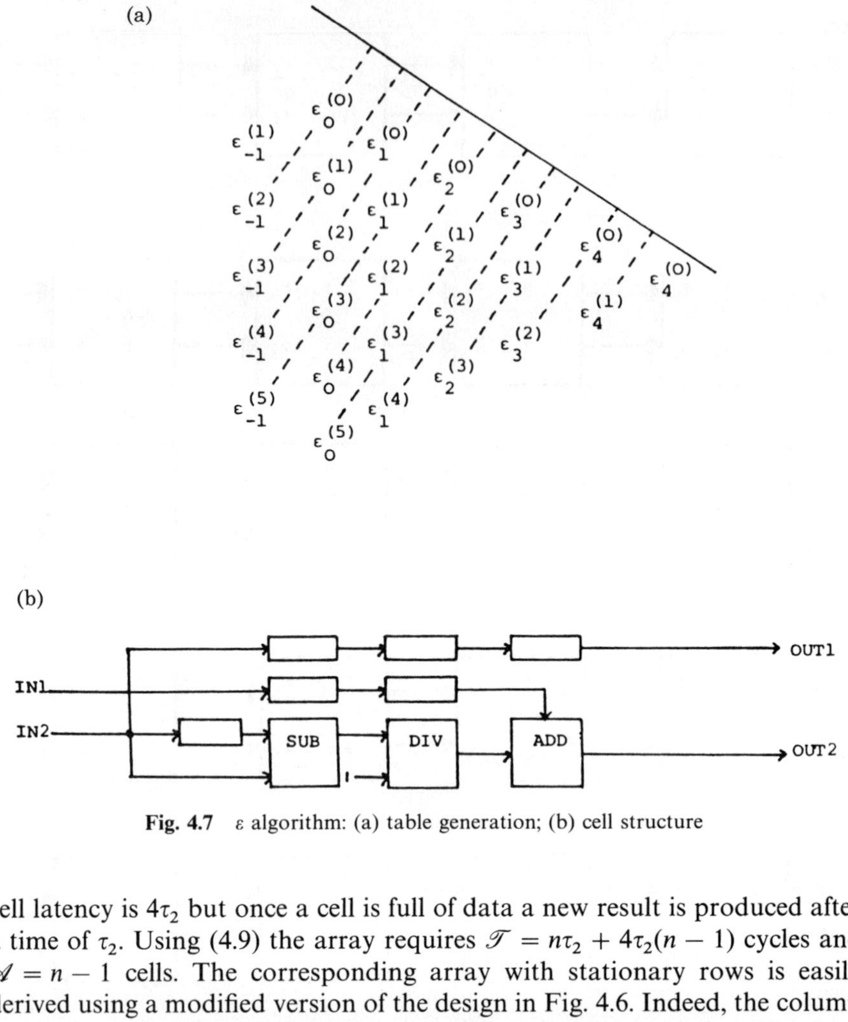

Fig. 4.7 ε algorithm: (a) table generation; (b) cell structure

cell latency is $4\tau_2$ but once a cell is full of data a new result is produced after a time of τ_2. Using (4.9) the array requires $\mathscr{T} = n\tau_2 + 4\tau_2(n-1)$ cycles and $\mathscr{A} = n - 1$ cells. The corresponding array with stationary rows is easily derived using a modified version of the design in Fig. 4.6. Indeed, the column stationary version of Fig. 4.6 can be produced by considering modifications to Fig. 4.7. Both these problems are left as exercises.

In the examples considered so far we have implicitly assumed that the number of boundary values is known in advance so that tables are finite. These assumptions have practical merit because an array with an unbounded number of cells cannot be implemented. We have also assumed that the tables computed are the same size—change the size of the table and we are forced to change the size of the array. For arrays that are to be implemented in hardware this is not a practical assumption. A simple and obvious solution to this problem is to impose a bound on the maximum table size and implement the array for this size. For example, in the ε algorithm we placed a bound on the number of values required to construct a table whose final value had converged. If a larger table is required for convergence it cannot be computed by the array. For tables smaller than the array the last row is destroyed as data move through the excess cells and create further difficulties. A solution to this tricky problem requires some further examples which are given in the next two sections. From a design viewpoint it should be noted that the space–time representation and projection techniques used so far tell us nothing about the fine details of implementation. The arrays generated are for the specific instance of the problem considered—this includes the problem size. This property is natural and should not be overly criticized because the representation is based on data dependencies which encode no information about implementation. Indeed these are features that we impose on an algorithm to meet our design constraints.

4.3 Extrapolation and interpolation

Improving the throughput of a systolic array is not the only advantage of two-level pipelining. From the previous examples it is clear that a cell with pipelined cell functions increases the latency of the array and only a portion of the array is in full computation at any particular time. We can exploit such features to improve the efficiency of a systolic design using a ring topology. To illustrate the technique we will explore the more complex problems of extrapolation and interpolation of a given function $f(x)$.

4.3.1 Romberg extrapolation

For example, suppose we wish to compute the integral

$$I = \int_a^b f(x)\,\mathrm{d}x \tag{4.13}$$

of some integrable function $f(x)$. It is well known that (4.13) can be approximated using the trapezoidal rule

$$\int_a^b f(x)\,\mathrm{d}x = \frac{h}{2}\left(f(a) + f(b) + 2\sum_{j=1}^{m-1} f(x_j)\right) - \frac{(b-a)h^2}{12} f''(\mu)$$

where $h = (b-a)/m$ and $x_j = a + jh$ for $j = 0(1)m$. The trapezoidal rule is easy to apply but often does not give the kind of accuracy required, so the value I is computed for a range of the h (e.g. $h/2, h/4, \ldots, h/2^n$) producing the successively more accurate estimates R_{i1}, $i = 1(1)n$, of I. The convergence of this sequence to the value of I can be accelerated by the Romberg extrapolation procedure

$$R_{ij} = \frac{4^{j-1}R_{i,j-1} - R_{i-1,j-1}}{4^{j-1} - 1}, \quad i = 2(1)n, j = 2(1)i \tag{4.14}$$

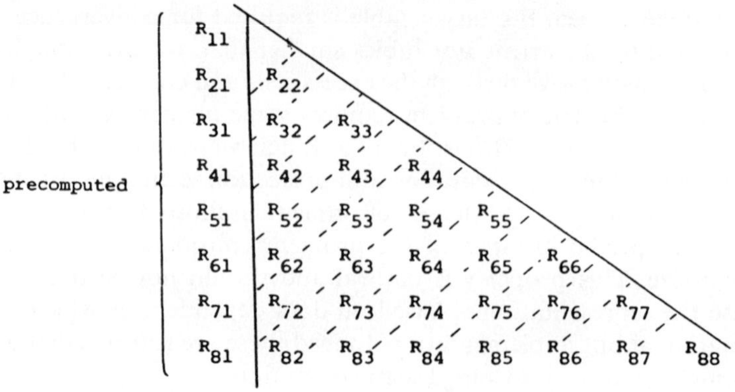

Fig. 4.8 Romberg extrapolation table: – – – elements on same line computed in parallel

which generates the table illustrated in Fig. 4.8. The entries R_{ii}, $i = 1(1)n$, represent improvements to the value I and generally the sequence $[R_{m,1}]_{m=1}^{\infty}$ converges more slowly than $[R_{ii}]_{i=1}^{\infty}$. We stop the table construction when $|R_{ii} - R_{i-1,i-1}| < \text{Tol}$, where Tol is some required accuracy. To illustrate the method suppose we want to compute the following

$$I = \int_0^{10} \frac{1}{(1 + x^2)} \, dx.$$

First we evaluate a number of estimates using different numbers of points shown in the first two columns of the table below. The first column is the number of points used in the trapezoidal rule. The rest of the table is then produced by applying (4.14) repeatedly

2	5.0595				
3	2.7170	1.9395			
5	1.7470	1.4236	1.3892		
9	1.4916	1.4064	1.4053	1.4055	
17	1.4711	1.4643	1.4682	1.4692	1.4694

where the table entries have been truncated to four digits but the final result is accurate to six figures.

Row and column stationary designs for generating the Romberg table are easily derived using the same principle as that in Section 4.2.1, but we shall concentrate on the two-level pipelined version. In addition we note two important facts:

1. The array has to be of fixed size and the size must be sufficient to yield the required accuracy.

2. For some problems convergence will occur before the full table size is constructed.

In the former case we choose n to be the size of the table and describe the array in terms of this parameter, while in the latter a partially constructed table already in the array must not be affected if premature termination occurs. The case of tables larger than the array will be postponed until Section 4.4. Also observe that evaluation of the function values $f(x)$ required for the R_{i1} is assumed to have taken place outside the array and before input starts, otherwise the cells in the array must be given a cycle time proportional to the cost of evaluating the (arbitrary) function $f(x)$, and the actual evaluation would require arbitrary amounts of hardware. An unfortunate side effect of these assumptions is that if premature convergence of the table does occur we will have wasted some time evaluating the more costly R_{i1} elements at the bottom of the table.

Figure 4.9(a) illustrates a linear array for computing the extrapolation table. The design is column stationary and consists of $n - 1$ Richardson extrapolation procedure (REP) cells with two inputs and two outputs with the form shown in Fig. 4.9(b). Snapshots of the array operation are shown in Fig. 4.9(c). The fan-in network is used for filtering out the results R_{ii}, $i = 2(1)n$, forming the diagonal table elements which are then used to determine convergence. Cell i computes column $i + 2$ of the table, and if c is the latency of the cell, the fan-in line is active on cycles c, $2c$, $3c$, etc. It follows that each of the cells can share the line without interfering with one another's outputs. The basic cell consists of an inner product step (multiply and add), a multiplier, and a divider, from which the latency $c = 3\tau_3$ is derived when τ_3 is the cost of the inner product cell. Each cell also calculates the 4^j value for the next cell; hence the use of two input and output lines. Finally, a control tag is attached to the R_{ij} inputs and is used to activate the fan-in connection. As the tag moves systolically from cell to cell it uses the natural delay of the cell components to remain synchronized with the R_{ii} values. The snapshots illustrate the timing of the array and $\mathscr{T} = c \times$ (no. of cells) $= 3(n - 1)$.

If a problem converges before all the rows of the table are computed we simply replace the input with zeros and ignore the R_{ii} values until the remaining table elements are flushed out of the array. It follows that any table of size $m < n$ can be computed on the array of size $n - 1$ cells in $3(m - 1)$ cycles (where a cycle is an inner product step). The fan-in connection makes the design semi-systolic and introduces long wires which according to the heuristics in Chapter 1 are to be avoided. Fortunately two-level pipelining can be further exploited. The latency of a cell is $3\tau_3$ so that the fan-in line is active every three cycles. It follows that the fan-in connection can be retimed by adding delays between each cell so that diagonal outputs are pipelined behind one another. The design is then purely systolic and solves any table problem up to and including size n provided that only the diagonal values are required.

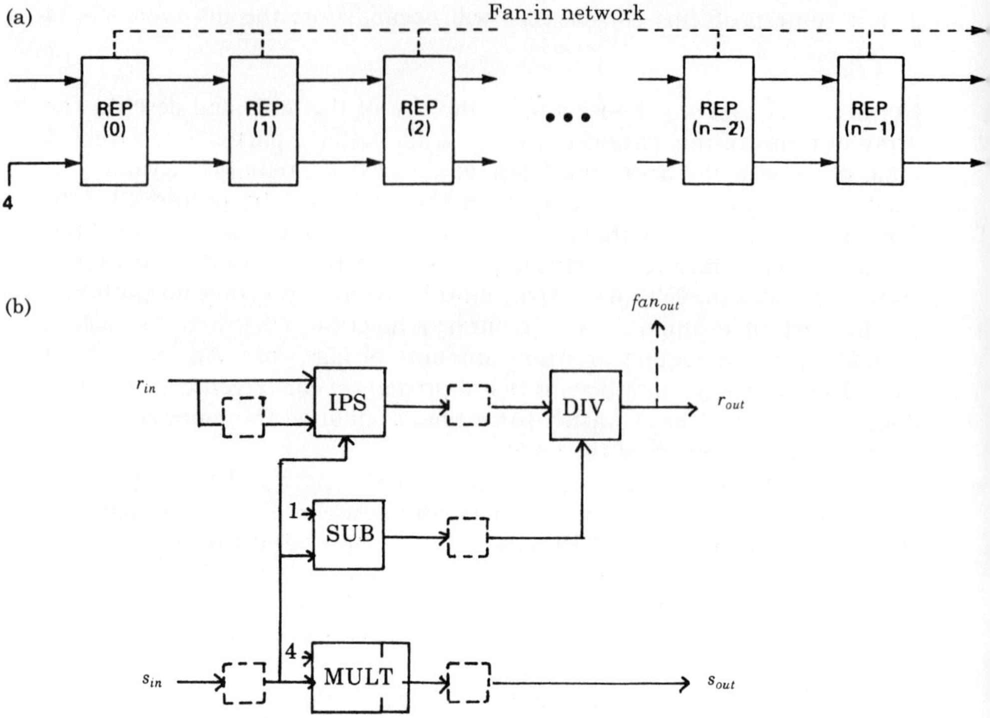

Fig. 4.9 Romberg array: (a) array; (b) basic cell

Next, observe that in Fig. 4.9(c) the last input R_{61} enters the array as the second cell is about to output the R_{ij} value. In general the first result of the $(1/3n)$th cell is output when the last R_{n1} value is input into the first cell. It follows that only one-third of the cells work at any one time so by truncating the array to $(1/3)n$ cells, and wrapping the output of the last cell back to the array input, a more compact array is produced. The only problem is that values wrapped back to the front of the array (i.e. on a second tour of the circuit) will encounter the wrong 4^j value stored in REP cells. Now, whenever the tag bit controlling the fan-in line enters a cell, the cell is empty (or unused) so the control tag can be used to overwrite the old 4^j values. The overwrite is performed by preloading a register in each cell with the input value from the previous cell. The tag bit can also be used to control connections between the host and the wraparound connections (the former must be switched out after the first cycle). This new array, a systolic ring, is shown in Fig. 4.10(a) and requires $n/3$ cells. Snapshots of the array operation appear in Fig. 4.10(b). We conclude that only n inner product cells (with subtractor and multiplier etc. equivalent to half an IPS cell) are required to

(c)

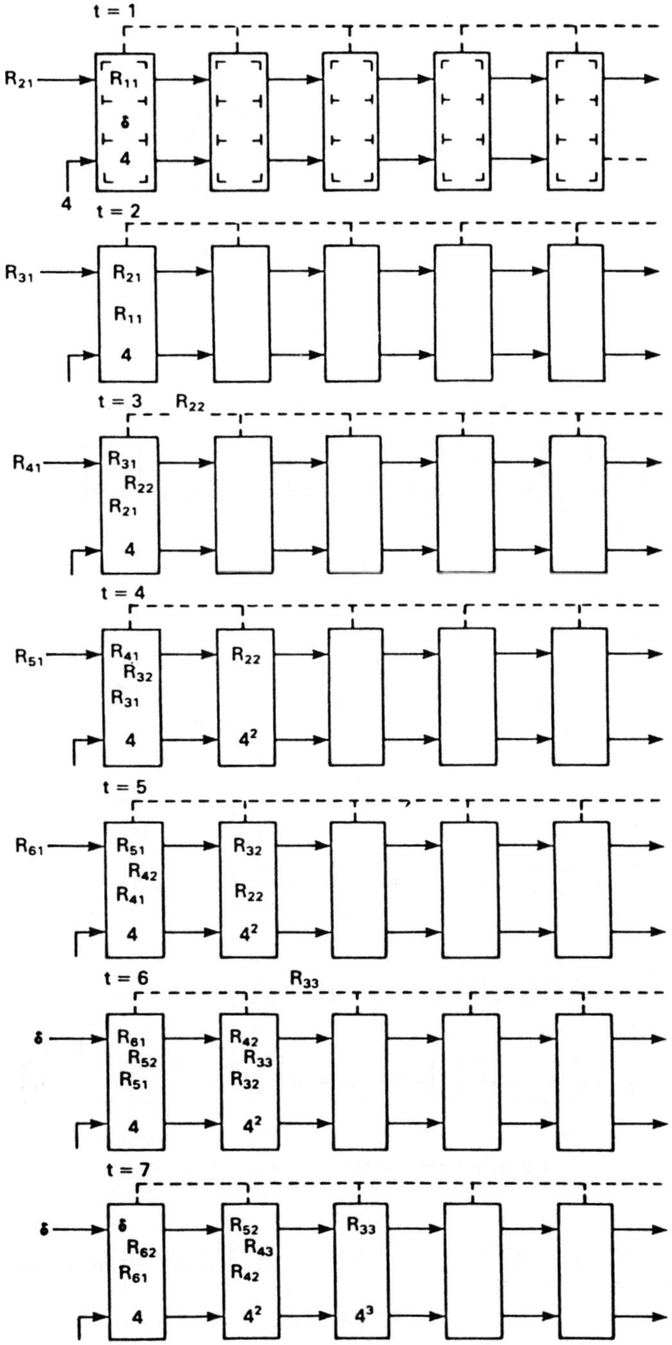

Fig. 4.9 (*cont.*) Romberg array: (c) snapshots

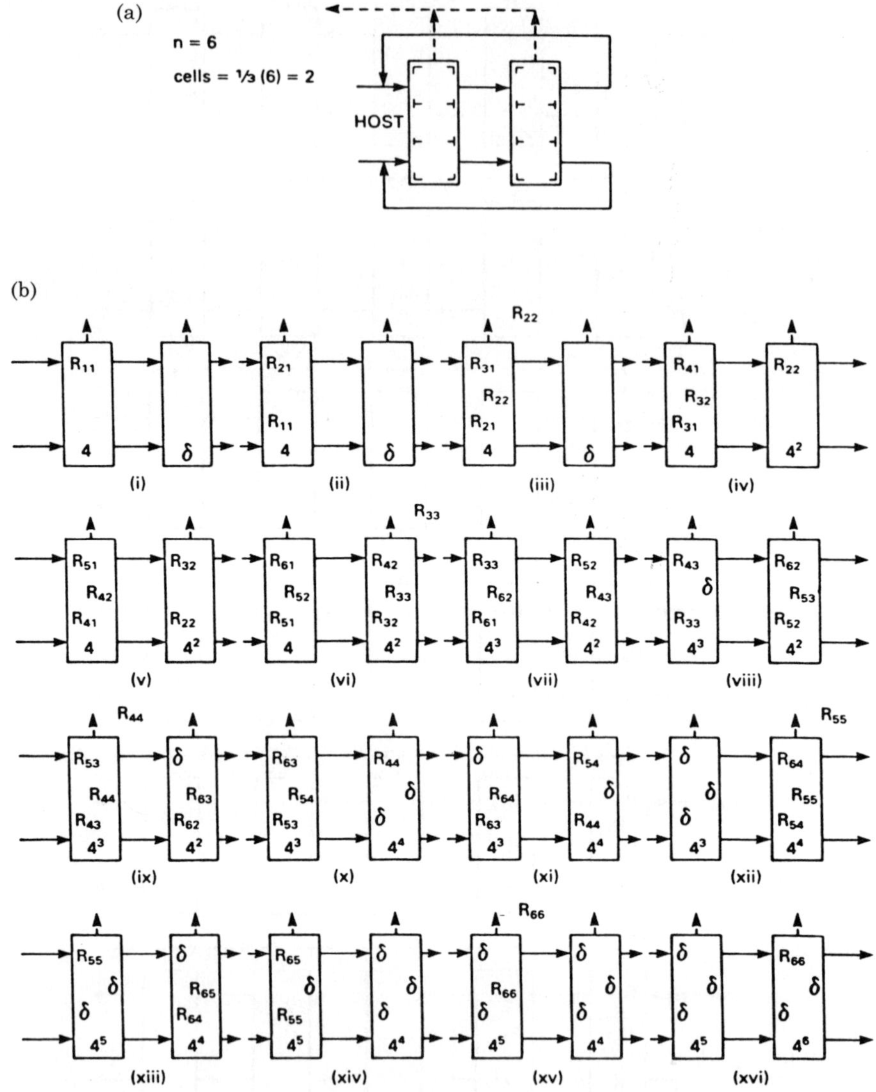

Fig. 4.10 Systolic ring: (a) ring; (b) computation

compute the same table as the linear array. The potentially long wires due to the feedback of the array output back to the input can be avoided by arranging the cells in a circle. In particular an area-efficient layout such as that shown in Fig. 4.10(c) can be employed when only the table entries on the diagonal are to be output.

(c)

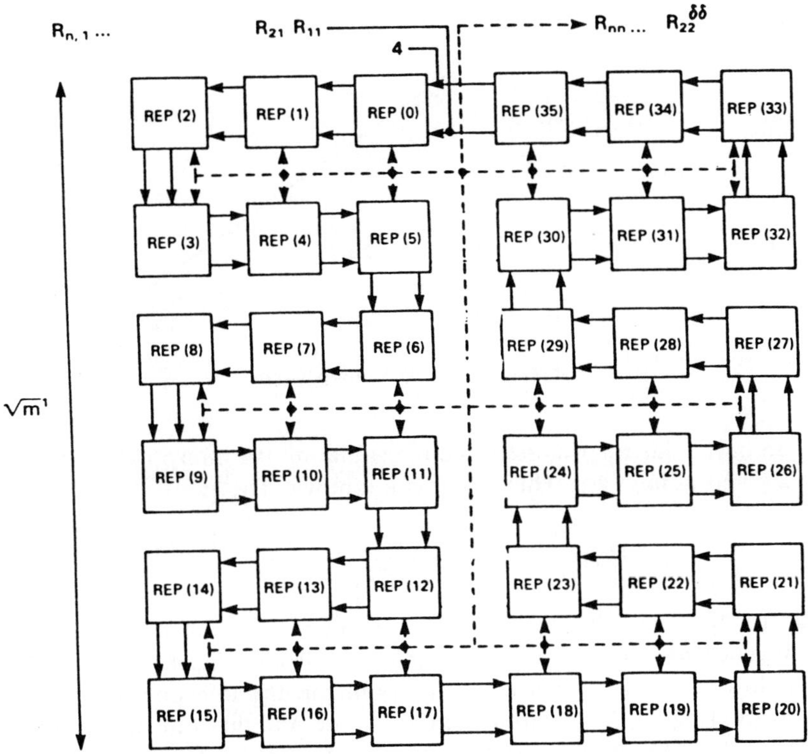

Systolic Ring for Romberg Integration n = 3m m' = 36 cells

Fig. 4.10 (*cont.*) Systolic ring: (c) area-efficient layout

4.3.2 Iterated interpolation

Clearly the amount of hardware we save by employing systolic rings depends on the complexity of the basic cell. Indeed, the latency of the basic cell determines the number of cells that can be removed from an array. Greater savings are possible for more complex basic cells because their cell functions can be partitioned into larger numbers of pipelined segments. Of course the cell saving is offset by the increased area required to implement the complex cells in the first place. To illustrate the point let us consider another example.

The problem of polynomial interpolation may be stated briefly as follows. Given a function $f(x)$ and a series of numbers $x_0, \ldots, x_n$ at which $f(x)$ is known can we find a polynomial (i.e. a function with the form $P(x) = a_0 + a_1x + a_2x^2 + \cdots + a_nx^n$) which approximates $f(x)$? Many methods are known for constructing such functions but we are interested in an interpolating polynomial, that is one that agrees with $f(x)$ at the points

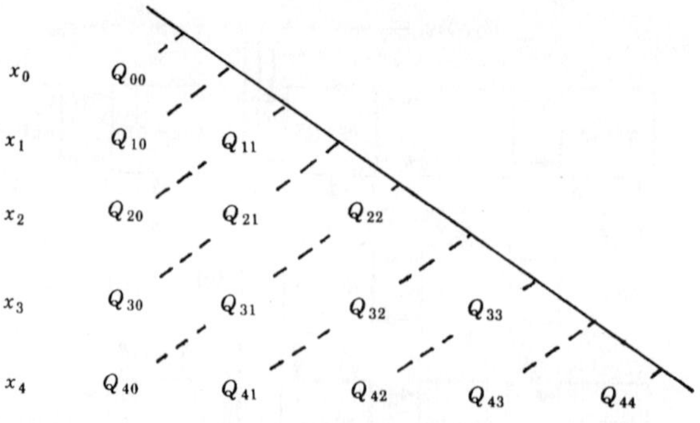

Fig. 4.11 Neville's interpolation table

x_i. In particular we are interested in evaluating the interpolating polynomial at a given point x for which $f(x)$ is unknown. The rule

$$Q_{ij} = \frac{(x - x_i)Q_{i-1,j-1} - (x - x_{i-j})Q_{i,j-1}}{x_{i-j} - x_i} \tag{4.15}$$

due to Neville, will construct such a polynomial when $Q_{i0} = f(x_i)$. The recurrence generates a triangular table as shown in Fig. 4.11 and $P(x) = Q_{nn}$. It follows that (4.15) generates any point on the interpolating polynomial by evaluating the $f(x_i)$, supplying the x value, and then constructing a table.

Snapshots of an array, stationary with respect to columns, are shown in Fig. 4.12(a) and the corresponding cell suitable for two-level pipelining is given in Fig. 4.12(b). Notice that the cell is considerably more complex than previous designs and requires a non-planar layout. Without two-level pipelining a cycle time of $2\tau_1 + 2\tau_2 + \tau_0$ is required where the cost of multiply is assumed to be the same as division. Applying the cut theorem to isolate sections of the cell and pipeline data, the cell latency becomes $5\tau_2$ because the cycle time τ_2 is the maximum delay through any of the arithmetic sections. Once the cell is full a result is produced every cycle. After n inputs the Q_{i0} values are exhausted and data have reached only the $(n/2)$th cell. The array can be truncated to just $n/5$ cells to form a systolic ring similar to that in Fig. 4.10 saving $4n/5$ cells in total—a considerable hardware reduction. Notice that once the array is full of data the cells are 100 per cent efficient.

From the discussion so far one might get the impression that the point in two-level pipelining is to increase cell latency so that a systolic ring can be produced. Although it is true that rings are useful for minimizing hardware there are some occasions when they should be avoided. For example, suppose that we wish to generate several points on the interpolating polynomial for $f(x)$. Using a linear array the high throughput obtained by the two-level effect allows successive constructions of the table to be pipelined. If a systolic ring is adopted generation of the next table would have to wait until the current table was on the last cycle of the ring. The more complicated a cell function the more hardware is saved, leading to more cycles around the ring.

4.4 Polynomial root finding

Another interesting and important task involving polynomials is the problem of finding all the values of x for which $P(x) = 0$ (i.e. the roots of the polynomial). For example, if $p(\lambda) = \det(A - \lambda I) = 0$, the roots of $p(\lambda)$ are the eigenvalues associated with the matrix A of a linear system. Next we will derive some arrays for computing the roots of a polynomial of degree n where we assume the roots are distinct. From the viewpoint of systolic design these problems illustrate the difficulties associated with potentially infinite tables. Indeed, we will examine schemes that consist of open-ended trapezoidal and rectangular tables and show how a fixed number of cells can be used to compute an infinite number of table elements.

4.4.1 QD algorithm

A method for the root-finding problem by table generation is the quotient difference (QD) algorithm. A table of root approximations is produced whose columns converge to the actual roots. To start the array development let the polynomial in question be

$$P(x) = a_0 x^n + a_1 x^{n-1} + \cdots + a_n x \tag{4.16}$$

which we assume has all roots distinct, and denote the dominant root by r_1. This root can be found by computing the solution sequence of the associated difference equation

$$a_0 x_k + a_1 x_{k-1} + \cdots + a_n x_{k-1} = 0 \tag{4.17}$$

and by setting

$$r_1 = \lim_{k \to \infty} (x_{k+1}/x_k). \tag{4.18}$$

Now, because $P(x) = 0$ is the characteristic equation of the difference form it has solutions of the form

$$x_k = c_1 r_1^k + c_2 r_2^k + \cdots + c_n r_n^k \tag{4.19}$$

where r_i, $i = 2(1)n$, are the remaining roots of $P(x)$. If $c_1 \neq 0$ then a simple manipulation yields

$$\frac{x_{k+1}}{x_k} = r_1 \frac{1 + (c_2/c_1)(r_2/r_1)^{k+1} + \cdots + (c_n/c_1)(r_n/r_1)^{k+1}}{1 + (c_2/c_1)(r_2/r_1) + \cdots + (c_n/c_1)(r_n/r_1)^k} \tag{4.20}$$

(a)

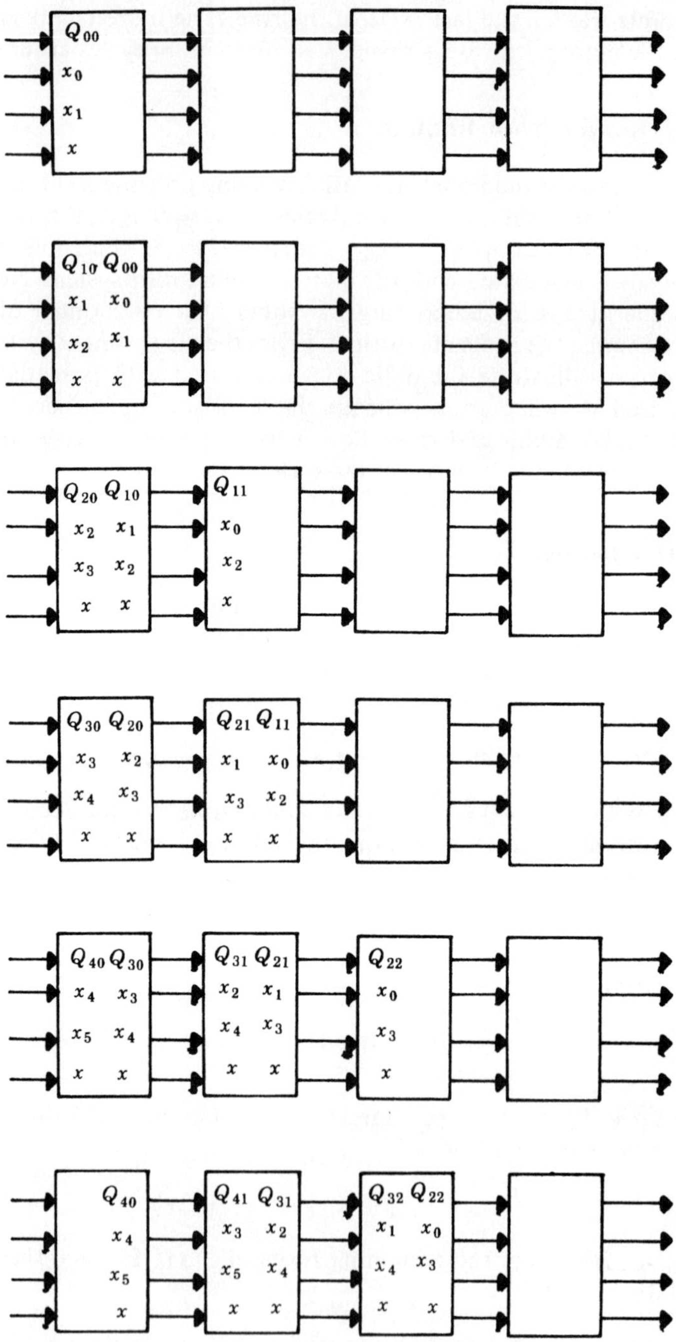

Fig. 4.12 Neville's array and description of cells: (a) array snapshots

(b)

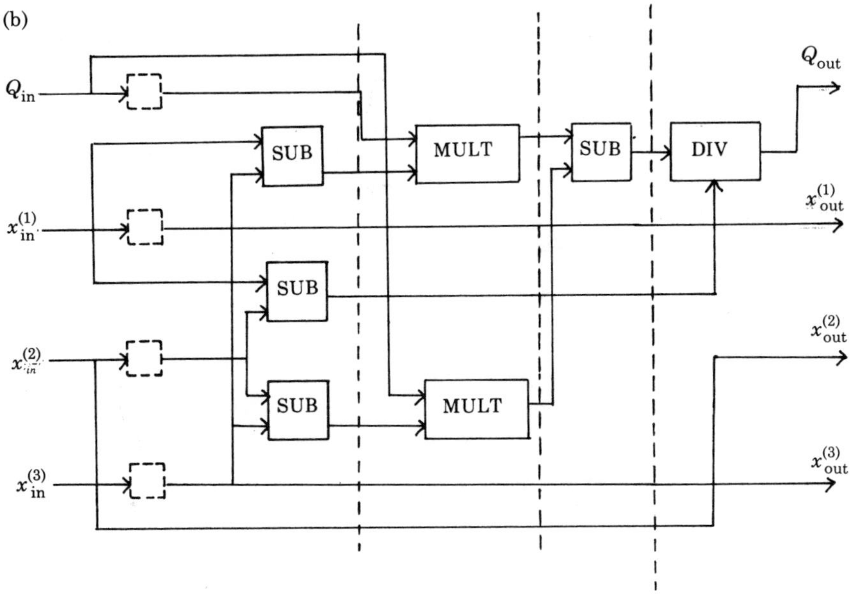

(c)

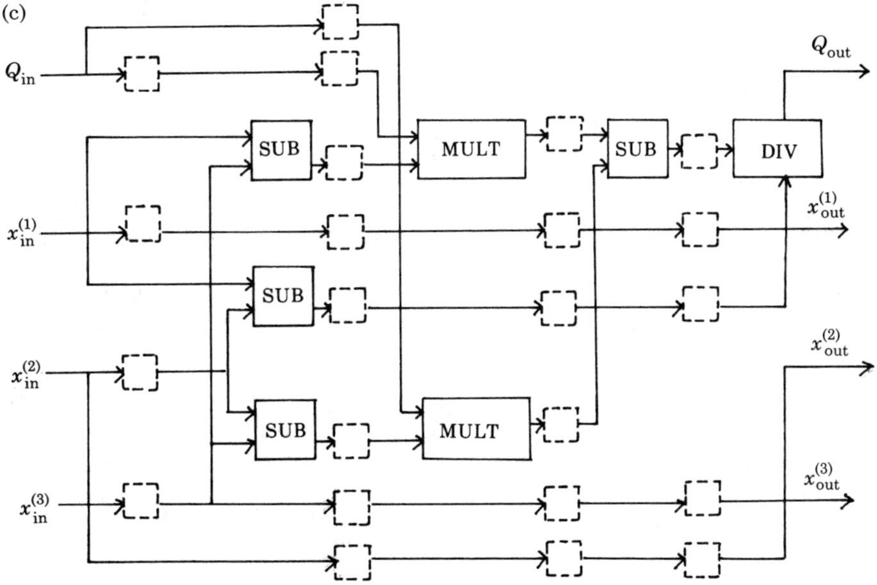

Fig. 4.12 (***cont.***) Neville's array and description of cells: (b) basic cell; (c) two-level cell

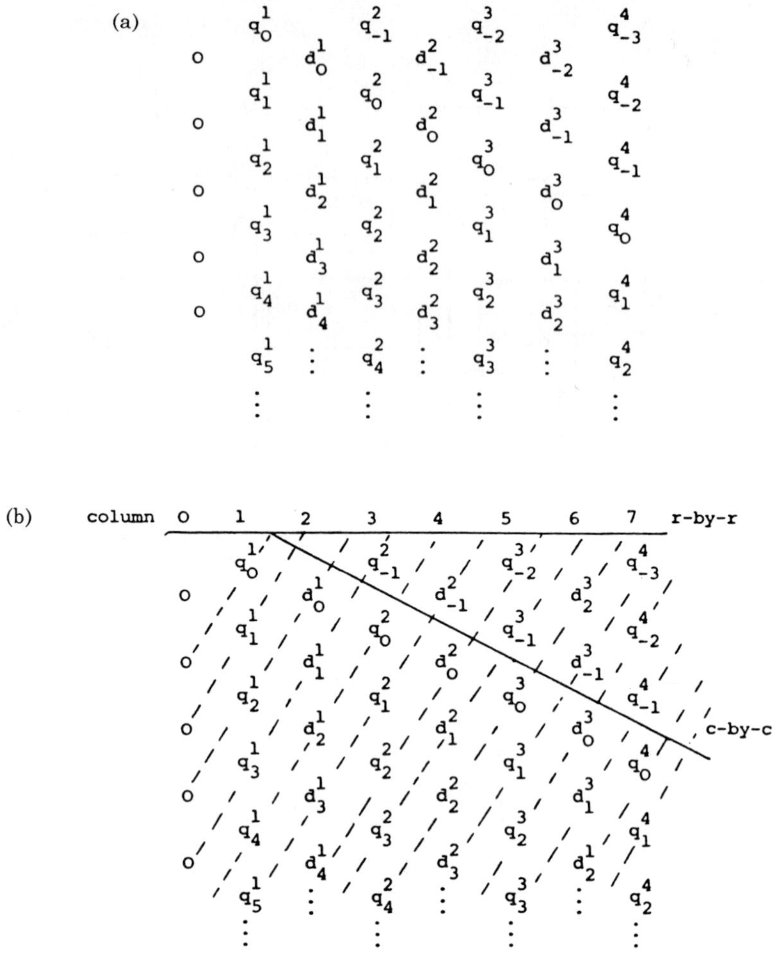

Fig. 4.13 Quotient difference tables: (a) generalized; (b) parallel evaluation of QD table entries (– – – elements on same line computed in parallel, ——— upper boundaries of tables for differeing QD methods)

and, as r_1 is the dominant root,

$$\lim(r_i/r_1) = 0, \quad i = 2(1)n \tag{4.21}$$

from which (4.18) follows immediately. By extending (4.21) and putting $q_k^1 = (x_{k+1}/x_k)$, $d_k^0 = 0$ the generalized QD table in Fig. 4.13(a) can be constructed using the following rhombus rules:

1. rhombus centred in a q column: $q_k^j + d_k^j = d_{k+1}^{j-1} + q_{k+1}^j$ (4.22a)
2. rhombus centred on a d column: $d_k^j q_k^{j+1} = q_{k+1}^j d_{k+1}^j.$ (4.22b)

These rules produce the forms

$$\text{(a)}\ d_k^j = q_{k+1}^j - q_k^j + d_{k+1}^{j-1} \quad \text{or} \quad \text{(b)}\ q_{k+1}^j = q_k^j + d_k^j - d_{k+1}^{j-1} \tag{4.23}$$

and

$$\text{(a)}\ q_k^{j+1} = (q_{k+1}^j * d_{k+1}^j)/d_k^j \quad \text{or} \quad \text{(b)}\ d_{k+1}^j = (d_k^j * q_k^{j+1})/q_{k+1}^j \tag{4.24}$$

which indicate that

$$\lim_{k \to \infty} q_k^j = r_j, \quad j = 1(1)n. \tag{4.25}$$

In addition when no two roots have the same absolute value and no division by zero occurs

$$\frac{d_{k+1}^j}{d_k^j} = \frac{q_k^{j+1}}{q_{k+1}^j} \to \frac{r_{j+1}}{r_j} > 1 \tag{4.26}$$

and the d_k^j-converge (geometrically) to zero. If the d_k^j values do not converge $P(x)$ has some roots with equal absolute values and more sophisticated techniques, such as the Newton–Raphson method, are required. The q_k^j approximate r_j and the d_k^j define a measure of the error between successive root approximations. If d_k^j is not convergent but d_k^{j+1} and d_k^{j-1} do converge, the presence of a complex conjugate root is indicated. The root can be found by solution of the quadratic

$$p_j = x^2 - A_j x + B_j \tag{4.27}$$

where

$$A_j = \lim_{k \to \infty} (q_{k+1}^j + q_k^j) \quad \text{and} \quad B_j = \lim_{k \to \infty} (q_k^j q_k^{j+1}).$$

The generalized QD table can be generated in two ways according to the choice of k:

1. *the 'column-by-column' (c-by-c) method*, which results when $k \geq 0$ for all j making the table an opened trapezium;
2. *the 'row-by-row' (r-by-r) method*, which results when $k < 0$ for some j making the table an open-ended rectangle of elements.

The c-by-c method is extremely sensitive to rounding error while the r-by-r method controls the error by forcing the correct behaviour on to the upper boundary of the c-by-c table. This additional stability is achieved by filling the top two rows of the table with fictitious entries as follows:

$$\begin{array}{lccccccccccc} \text{row 1:} & 1 & a_1/a_0 & 0 & 0 & 0 & \cdots & 0 & \cdots & 0 & \cdots & 0 \\ \text{row 2:} & 0 & a_2/a_1 & a_3/a_2 & a_4/a_3 & a_5/a_4 & \cdots & \cdots & \cdots & \cdots & \cdots & a_n/a_{n-1} \end{array} \tag{4.28}$$

and Fig. 4.13(b) indicates a suitable ordering of the elements for the systolic construction of the QD table. The pattern is similar to that used in the previous sections and suggests a linear systolic array of $2n$ cells for a QD table with n roots (or $2n$ columns). The first step is to define two types of cell corresponding to the rhombus rules centred in the q and d columns. Next allocate Q cells to odd-numbered columns and D cells to even-numbered columns of the table. Now observe that a D cell requires only multiply and divide operations while the Q cell uses only addition and subtraction. Next merge pairs of adjacent odd and even cells to create a single QD cell with a hardware equivalent of two inner product cells (i.e. $y = y + a * x$ and $y = y - a/x$) to produce a linear array with n QD cells. The array utilizes the fact that the QD table can be partitioned by odd and even columns to create two distinct but related tables of size n, one for root approximations and the other for root convergence. The QD array interleaves the construction of both tables on the same linear array.

A QD cell computation is determined by (4.23) and (4.24), but also note that part (a) must be computed before part (b) and demands a two-level pipelined approach to the cell design. Choosing (4.23a) and (4.24a) produces a cell for the column-by-column (c-by-c) method and selecting (4.23b) and (4.24b) gives the row-by-row (r-by-r) method. The basic cells for these operations are shown in Fig. 4.14(a) and (b). Tracing the data flow in the respective cells reveals interesting relations regarding array data flow and the type of table generation. The c-by-c QD cell creates a non-stationary array in the sense that every input q_k^j, d_{k+1}^j to cell j produces an output q_k^{j+1}, d_k^j tying columns $2j - 1$ and $2j$, $j = 1(1)n$, of the QD table to cell j. Consequently, the successive root approximations q_k^j, $k = 1(1)\cdots$, to r_j remain stationary so the array must contain n cells to evaluate all the roots. Now, in order to judge root convergence we must obtain the values d_k^j. Assuming that a host machine supplies values to and from the array, the collection of the d_k^j implies fan-in-type networks with an output associated with each cell (similar to that for Romberg extrapolation). Once convergence is achieved we encounter the additional problem of stopping the array and unloading the results. In contrast the r-by-r QD cell produces a non-stationary array, with inputs q_k^j, d_{k+1}^{j-1} of cell j producing the output q_{k+1}^j, d_{k+1}^j. It follows that successive approximations to the roots r_j, $j = 1(1)n$, are pumped systolically from left to right along the array. Furthermore, this non-stationary array requires $z > 0$ cells where z is the number of approximations to each root (see Fig. 4.14(d)). Results emerge from the right-hand end of the array without any special effort. Thus the fact that the r-by-r method is more stable than the c-by-c scheme, together with the non-stationary QD cell arrangement, makes the r-by-r table construction preferable. Figure 4.15 clarifies the operation of the r-by-r cell for a worked example.

Further improvements to the r-by-r array are possible. First, the latency is $c = 4$ cycles where a cycle is the cost of division (the most complex arithmetic operation). If $z = n$, after n cycles the $n/c = (n/4)$th QD cell has performed one complete computation, and the last input a_n/a_{n-2} of the top two table rows has been input to the first cell. It follows that a systolic ring (Fig. 4.14(e)) with $n/4$ QD cells will generate an infinite table of root approximations with $n/4$ rows of the table computed on each complete circuit of the ring. Allowing a trade-off of two inner product cells for each QD cell implies that all the real roots of $P(x)$ can be found with $2n$ inner product cells. If more root approximations are required on a single cycle around the ring we just need to increase the value of z and hence the array size. Of course the array becomes less efficient as more cells are added. The timing of the r-by-r array is complicated by the fact that convergence is dependent on the polynomial $P(x)$. Suppose we let l be the total number of QD table rows required for convergence of all roots. A linear array of z cells requires l/z passes of the root approximations through the array. The approximation to r_1 on the first pass is output after $cz = 4z$ cycles, and has to wait $n - 4z$ cycles for the remaining roots of the pass to be input, before the second pass can start. Thus, the total computation time is

$$\mathscr{T} = (l/z)n4z.$$

Note that z can be independent of n provided that the outputs required for the next pass of data through the array are buffered when $z < n/4$. For a systolic ring where $z = n/4$ the time is approximately

$$\mathscr{T} = \frac{4l}{n} n + n < 2n + 4l.$$

Finally, consider the generation of the top two starting rows in the r-by-r table. The required computations can be pipelined with the array operation by adding a boundary cell consisting of a negator and divider to produce the required quotients—this is left as an exercise.

4.4.2 Aitken's method

A method closely related to the QD method is Aitken's algorithm. This method can be used to find the roots of a function with the form

$$f(z) = 1 + a_1 z + a_2 z^2 + \cdots. \tag{4.29}$$

To formulate the problem we let

$$g(z) = 1 + b_1 z + b_2 z^2 + \cdots \tag{4.30}$$

and suppose that $f(z)$ and $g(z)$ are analytic and have no root in common. Next, suppose that

$$h(z) = g(z)/f(z) = 1 + c_1 z + c_2 z^2 + \cdots \tag{4.31}$$

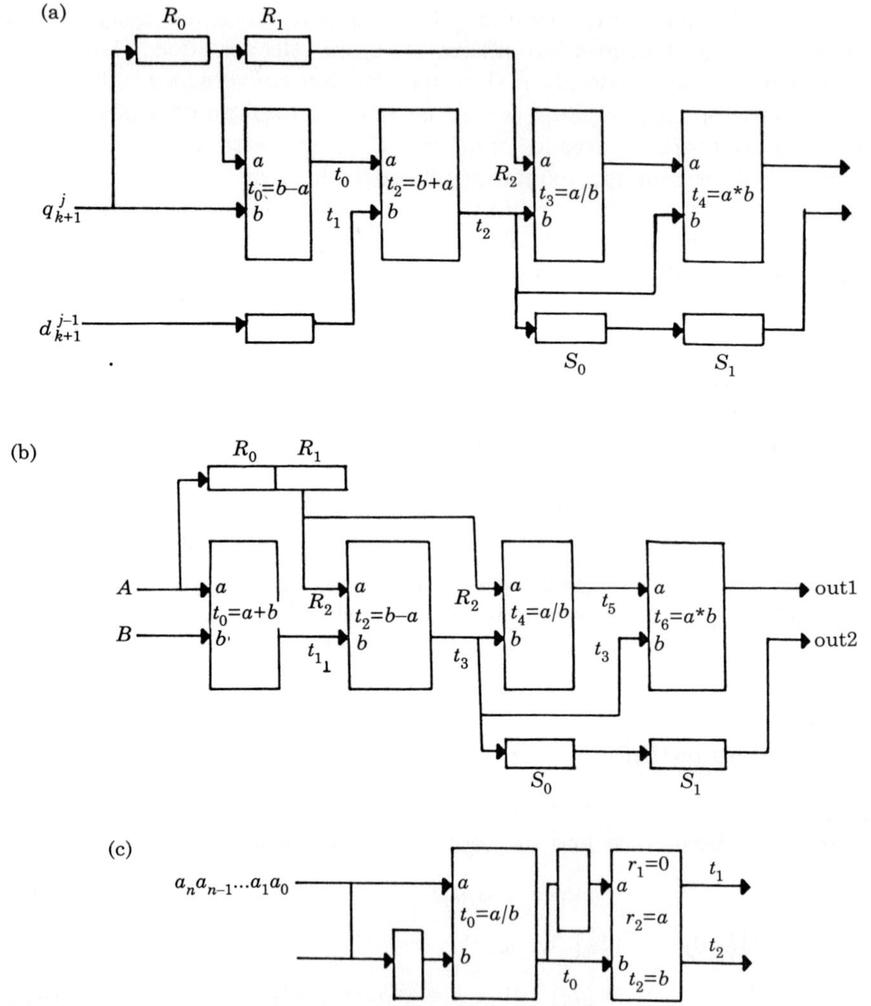

Fig. 4.14 QD cells and array: (a) stationary c-by-c cell; (b) non-stationary r-by-r cell; (c) boundary cell generating to produce starting values

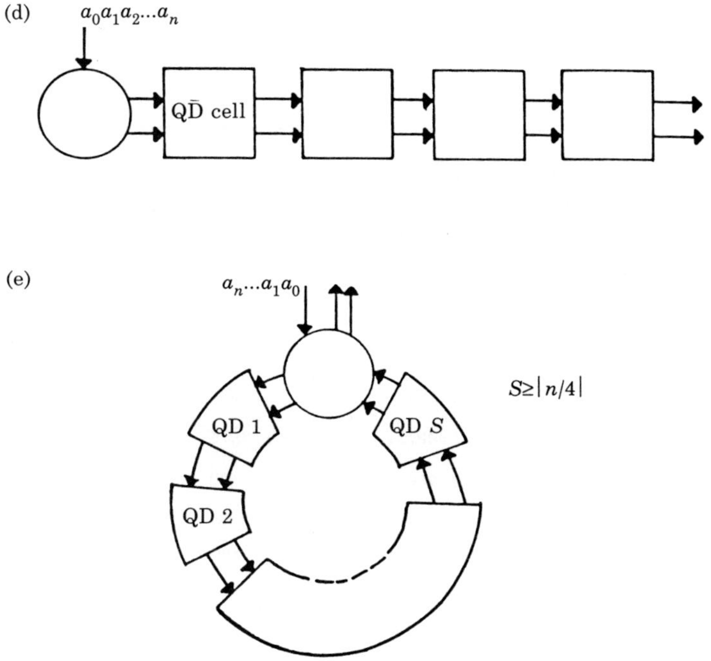

Fig. 4.14 (*cont.*) QD cells and array: (d) linear array; (e) systolic ring (with modified boundary cell)

then

$$\lim c_v/c_{v+1} = r \tag{4.32}$$

where r is the root of $f(z)$ with smallest modulus. Aitken's method is a generalization of this method and involves two steps. First we compute the c_i (by noting that $f(z)h(z) = g(z)$ is a matrix–vector product, see exercises), and second we construct a table of Hankel determinants using the rule

$$H_{v,p-1}H_{v,p+1} = H_{v+1,p}H_{v-1,p} - H^2_{v,p} \tag{4.33}$$

where $H_{i,j}$ is a Hankel determinant (the exact definition need not concern us here). The first two columns of the table are known because $H_{v0} = 1$ and $H_{v1} = c_v$; in addition the H_{0v} can be computed so that the table has the form shown in Fig. 4.16(a). Now for any column, if the ratio $H_{vp}/H_{v+1,p}$ has a limit, then

$$H_{vp}/H_{v+1,p} \to r_1 r_2 \cdots r_p$$

where $r_1, r_2, \ldots, r_p$ are zeros of $f(z)$. Furthermore, if $f(z)$ has any other zeros they are all greater in modulus than the ones already computed. Clearly if limits exist in any two adjacent columns the exact value of a root can be found by a simple division.

(a)

k	d	q	d	q	d	q	d	q	d
		10		0		0		0	
1	0		-3.5000		-1.4286		-.4800		0
		6.5000		2.0714		.9486		.4800	
2	0		-1.1154		-.6542		-.2329		0
		5.3846		2.5326		1.3599		.7229	
3	0		-.5246		-.3513		-.1291		0
		4.8600		2.7059		1.5821		.8520	
4	0		-.2921		-.2054		-.0695		0
		4.5679		2.7926		1.7180		.9215	
5	0		-.1786		-.1264		-.0373		0
		4.3893		2.8448		1.8071		.9588	
6	0		-.1158		-.0803		-.0198		0
		4.2735		2.8803		1.8676		.9786	
7	0		-.0780		-.0521		-.0104		0
		4.1955		2.9062		1.9093		.9890	
8	0		-.0540		-.0342		-.0054		0
		4.1415		2.9260		1.9381		.9944	

(b)

	t_0	t_1	t_2	t_3	t_4	t_5	t_6
R[0]	0.0	-3.5	-1.4286	-0.48	0.0	0.0	0.0
R[1]	0.0	0.0	-3.5	-1.4286	-0.48	0.0	0.0
R[2]	0.0	0.0	0.0	-3.5	-1.4286	-0.48	0.0
t[0]	0.0	6.5	-1.4286	-0.48	0.0	0.0	0.0
t[1]	0.0	0.0	6.5	-1.4286	-0.48	0.0	0.0
t[2]	0.0	0.0	6.5	2.0714	0.9486	0.48	0.0
t[3]	0.0	0.0	0.0	6.5	2.0714	0.9486	0.48
t[4]	0.0	0.0	0.0	-0.53846	-0.6897	-0.5060	0.0
t[5]	0.0	0.0	0.0	0.0	-0.53846	-0.6897	-0.5060
t[6]	0.0	0.0	0.0	0.0	-1.1154	-0.6542	-0.2429
s[0]	0.0	0.0	0.0	6.5	2.0714	0.9486	0.48
s[1]	0.0	0.0	0.0	0.0	6.5	2.0714	0.9486
A	-3.5	-1.4286	-0.48	0.0	0.0	0.0	0.0
B	10	0.0	0.0	0.0	0.0	0.0	0.0
out 1	0	0	0	0.0	0.0	-1.1154	-0.6542
out 2	0	0	0	0.0	0.0	6.5	2.0714

etc.

Fig. 4.15 Numerical example of cell operation: (a) r-by-r QD table for $p(x) = x^4 - 10x^3 + 35x^2 - 50x + 24 = 0$ (exact solutions $x = 1, 2, 3, 4$); (b) snapshots of r-by-r cell operation for problem in (a)

(a)

1	1	-1	-1	1	1	-1
1	c_1	H_{12}	H_{13}	H_{14}	H_{15}	H_{16}
1	c_2	H_{22}	H_{23}	H_{24}	H_{25}	H_{26}
1	c_3	H_{32}	H_{33}	H_{34}	H_{35}	H_{36}
1	c_4	H_{42}	H_{43}	H_{44}	H_{45}	H_{46}

(b)

1	1	-1	-1	1	1	-1
1	$-a_1$	$-a_2$	a_3	a_4	$-a_5$	$-a_6$
1	H_{21}	H_{22}	H_{23}	H_{24}	H_{25}	H_{26}
1	H_{31}	H_{32}	H_{33}	H_{34}	H_{35}	H_{36}
1	H_{41}	H_{42}	H_{43}	H_{44}	H_{45}	H_{46}

Fig. 4.16 Aitken tables for root finding: (a) first method; (b) second method

The table may be constructed a column at a time by applying (4.33) and it is obvious from our previous designs that either columns or rows can be made non-stationary. If we make the rows stationary one cell for each c_v value is required, which according to (4.31) is not generally known. Likewise making columns stationary requires a number of cells equivalent to the degree of the polynomial which is also unknown. The table is doubly infinite and rectangular so how do we map the computation into a systolic array that could be implemented? The answer is simple: limit one of the dimensions to a finite size and treat the associated axis as space in the space–time representation. For example, Fig. 4.17(a) shows the snapshots for an Aitken array with stationary columns. Table rows are non-stationary and can be pipelined into the array at one end while the last column emerges row by row from the other. An appropriate cell description suitable for two-level pipelining is shown in Fig. 4.17(b). Observe that the whole table can be constructed by multiple passes of data through the array. The idea is to insert c_i values until the output column converges to a limit and then stop the array. Note that because the columns are stationary all knowledge of intermediate columns is lost unless special stop and unload features (such as control tags and fan-in connections) are added to the array. The pth column may now be used to construct columns $(p + 1)$ to $2p$, and generally

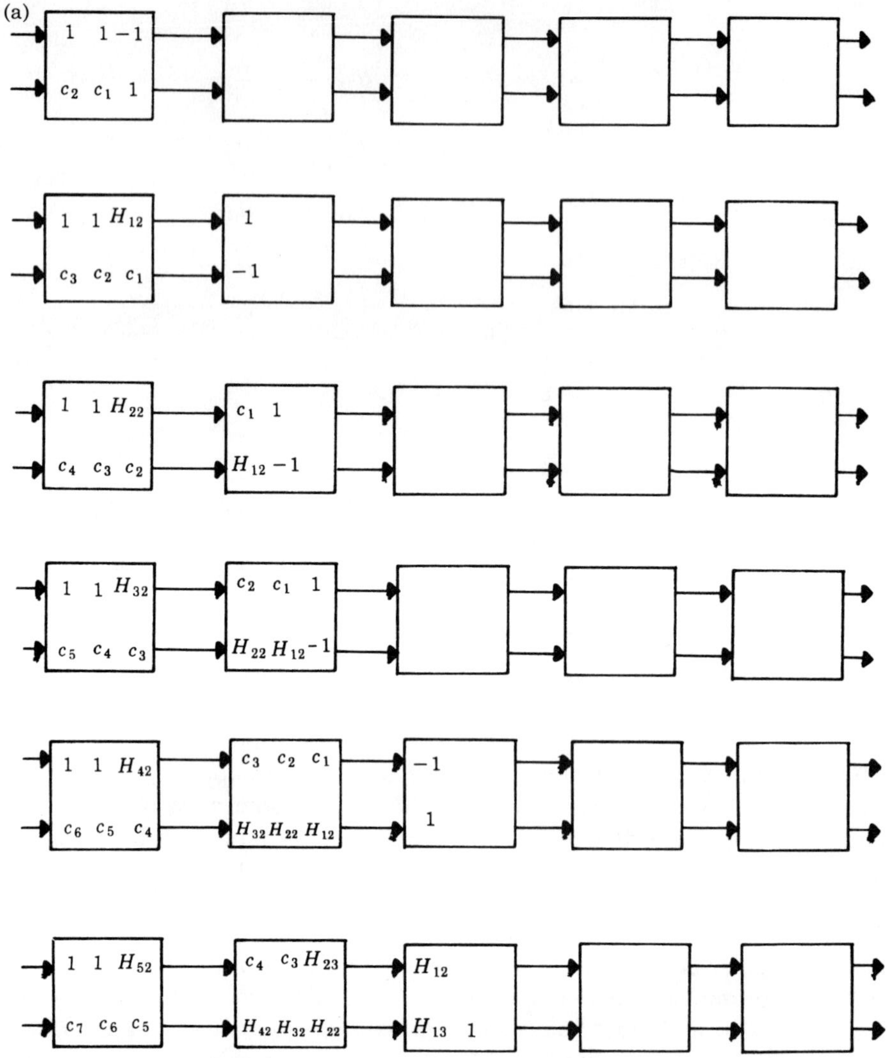

Fig. 4.17 Aitken array and cells: (a) array snapshots

the ith pass of data through the array will generate columns $(i - 1)p + 1$ to ip.

Remark. If later columns require more iterations the array can run for more steps because the output column of the previous pass has converged so that all its values are known.

It follows that the whole table is constructed by computing blocks of columns. As the array length is proportional to the number of columns in

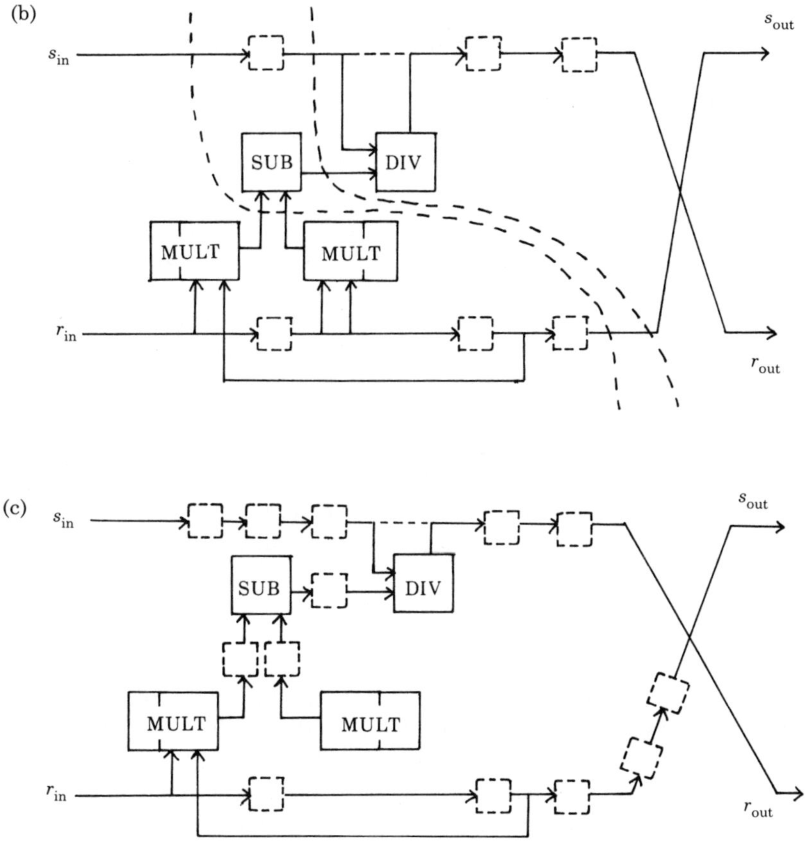

Fig. 4.17 (*cont.*) Aitken array and cells: (b) basic cell; (c) two-level cell

a block the design is of fixed size (independent of the problem size). An array of any size can be implemented by choosing the block size appropriately. The time for a single pass is given by $\mathcal{T} = l + cz$ where l is the number of inputs required for convergence, z is the number of cells in the array, and c is the cell latency. A systolic ring implementation can also be used to reduce cells further but this would prohibit the overlapping of successive passes and is not worthwhile because z can be chosen arbitrarily in any case.

Finally, we briefly consider another scheme due to Aitken which demands that $g(z) = 1$. The resulting table is shown in Fig. 4.16(b) where it should be noted that the first two rows and the first column are known. The table is again constructed using rule (4.33) but the ratios of consecutive row elements determine the product of the roots for $f(z)$. Clearly an equivalent array to that in Fig. 4.17, where the root data flow is non-stationary, can be derived easily. The advantage of this second method is that only the coefficients a_i are required, removing the need to compute c_i as an additional step.

4.5 Geometric versus algorithmic interpretations

So far in this chapter we have used the table structure and the construction rule to determine data dependency graphs for table generation. In the examples discussed such a *geometric* interpretation is both natural and convenient. It is, however, important to remember that table structures can always be written in an *algorithmic* form, such as for-loop programs, so that the table is really a loop unrolling. For some applications this latter formulation can be used to produce a different or dual interpretation of the problem which leads to an alternative perspective on the design process. To illustrate this point we will consider a simple example from the numerical solution of partial differential equations.

Problems involving time as a single independent variable often lead to parabolic or hyperbolic equations. The former arise in conduction- or diffusion-type problems and the latter are normally associated vibration problems or where discontinuities in pressure, density, speed, etc. can occur (e.g. shock waves). In general a parabolic equation has the form

$$\frac{\partial U}{\partial T} = \frac{\partial^2 U}{\partial X^2} \tag{4.34}$$

where x and t are independent variables. A finite difference solution to (4.34) is found by choosing $\delta x = h$ and $\delta t = k$ and defining grid lines by the equations $x_i = ih$ for $i = -\infty, \ldots, +\infty$ and $t_j = jk$ for $y = 0, \ldots$. Lines intersect at points (ih, jk) and the value of (4.34) at this point is denoted by U_{ij}. The partial derivatives can be approximated by finite differences so that

$$\frac{\partial U}{\partial t} \approx \frac{U_{i,j+1} - U_{i,j}}{k}$$

and

$$\frac{\partial^2 U}{\partial t^2} \approx \frac{U_{i,j+1} - 2U_{i,j} + U_{i-1,j}}{k^2}$$

and

$$\frac{\partial^2 U}{\partial x^2} \approx \frac{U_{i+1,j} - 2U_{i,j} + U_{i-1,j}}{h^2}$$

to produce

$$\frac{u_{i,j+1} - u_{i,j}}{k} = \frac{u_{i+1,j} - 2u_{i,j} + u_{i-1,j}}{h^2} \tag{4.35}$$

or

$$u_{i,j+1} = ru_{i-1,j} + (1 - 2r)u_{i,j} + ru_{i+1,j} \tag{4.36}$$

where $r = k/(h^2)$. Figure 4.1(e) shows the geometric interpretation of this problem along with the molecule for (4.36). Clearly if three boundaries are known all the grid points can be determined explicitly.

The problem is a special case of the table-generating problem, and consequently the grid can be interpreted as a data dependency graph and an array with stationary columns produced by projection on to the $t = 0$ axis. Applying the technique developed throughout this chapter leads to several arrays for computing the differential equation solution. Alternatively we can number the grid points from left to right along a particular grid line and formulate the problem in terms of matrix algebra to derive

$$U_{j+1} = Au_j + b_j \tag{4.37}$$

where $U_{j+1} = (u_{1,j+1}, u_{2,j+1}, \ldots, u_{N-1,j+1})$, $b_j = (ru_{0,j}, 0, \ldots, 0, ru_{n,j})$ and

$$A = \begin{vmatrix} (1-2r) & r & & & & \\ r & (1-2r) & r & & 0 & \\ & r & (1-2r) & & & \\ & & r & & & \\ & & & \ddots & & \\ & & & & r & \\ & 0 & & & (1-2r) & r \\ & & & & r & (1-2r) \end{vmatrix}$$

so that (4.37) can be solved by an iteration array (described in Chapter 3, Fig. 3.9) with a matrix–vector array forming a single iteration. As the matrix A is tridiagonal each linear array requires only three inner product cells.

The finite difference method extends to a wide range of physical problems (using hyperbolic and elliptical as well as parabolic equations). Consequently table-generating or iterative arrays can be produced for many important applications. In general any table in which new elements can be generated from a linear combination of known values can be reformulated as linear algebra problems. This formulation is achieved by numbering the table elements in a way that allows a single row or column to be generated from previously computed rows and columns. If the numbering is done carefully a banded matrix–vector problem will usually result and the bandwidth will be proportional to the number of known elements in the generating rule. The key point for systolic design is that the problems have a dual interpretation either as a geometric table-generating or as an algorithmic matrix form. Which approach you choose for a particular application depends upon the exact circumstances in which the array will be used.

4.6 Design principles

In this chapter numerous designs for generating finite, semi-finite, and infinite tables have been considered. The discussion has centred about a small number of simple but illustrative examples each of which has highlighted a specific design technique. It should be clear that all the techniques will generalize in a straightforward manner to more complex problems and can be used simultaneously on a single design. The general principles of these techniques are summarized in the following paragraphs, but before continuing it is worthwhile to review the general design strategy. Chapter 2 emphasized the use of hierarchical levels of design and the application of abstraction to minimize manipulation of space–time. We have continued this theme by opening up the black boxes represented by basic cells and considering the internal cell organization. A number of important and yet subtle changes have occurred as a result. First, cell descriptions have slipped from an algorithmic (procedural) to an architectural (hardware) form. Of course we could have forced a procedural description on to the cell but this overlooks one of the most important features of systolic processing. The second point is that we can now begin to appreciate the problems involved with physical implementations of cell functions. Indeed it is relatively straightforward to construct some of the cells described above by using standard off-the-shelf components such as adders and subtractors.

Two-level pipelining

This was introduced as a mechanism for improving array throughput. Any basic cell which consists of a number of arithmetic steps can be two-level pipelined provided that no feedback occurs between the pipe segments. Note that this does not mean that array cells cannot contain any feedback at all. But if feedback does occur it must occur wholly inside a pipeline segment. A basic cell is pipelined by applying the cut theorem (Chapter 2) to introduce latch registers between segments so that partial results moving through a cell are not destroyed when new input data arrive. Normally the basic step of an algorithm is the time taken for data to propagate from the input, through the arithmetic units, and to settle on the output. In a two-level pipelined cell a basic step is divided into a number of smaller cycles, a cycle being the maximum time required for data to propagate through any of the arithmetic segments. A basic step time is always a multiple of the cycle time and denotes the cell latency. For example, if τ is the cycle time and there are four segments in the pipelined cell, the basic step time is 4τ and the latency is four cycles. The name two-level pipelining is appropriate because pipelining occurs at the global array level from cell to cell, and also within a cell. Two-level cells affect the throughput and efficiency of a design because the array can be operated at the cycle speed allowing more data to be entered in the same time period when compared with an ordinary cell which is operated at the basic step speed. This is ideal when long sequences of input are expected because the individual pieces of cell hardware are utilized much more effectively and improve efficiency. Indeed once a two-level cell is full of data a new result is produced every cycle compared with every basic step in an ordinary cell.

Systolic rings

These can be used when the number of cells in an array is similar to the data input length, and cells can be two-level pipelined. The short cycle time and the latency of a two-level cell conspire so that only a small proportion of the array works at any one time. For example, if c is the cell latency of an array with n cells and only n inputs the data run out when the first input has penetrated as far as the (n/c)th cell. A ring is constructed by truncating the original array to n/c cells and feeding the output back to the input thus avoiding unnecessary inefficiency. Once the original data have been entered the array becomes 100 per cent efficient. In general, c cycles around the ring will be required to perform the same computations as the original linear array. The concept of cell reuse extends naturally to the idea of multiple-pass computation where a fixed-size array is used repeatedly to construct the solution to a single problem. For instance, any systolic ring can be simulated on a linear array by feeding the output data back through the host machine (which is providing the initial data). It follows by extension that any array capable of generating output which is compatible with its own input can form a ring. When the latency of the array is less than the total data input length the host machine must buffer the output data until the array input connections become free and feedback can be made. When the array latency is longer than the data input length no buffering is required and feedback can occur immediately. We conclude that the designs presented above are special cases of systolic rings where the input length and array latency are perfectly matched.

Problem duality

This is the relationship between geometric and algorithmic forms of a problem. Tables are natural geometric forms because the table structure has an inherent geometrical representation. In this chapter we have exploited the geometrical form by interpreting it as the space–time representation from which systolic designs can be projected. When the table-generating rules are particularly simple (i.e. linear combinations of known table elements) the generation problem can be formulated as an iterative matrix problem and solved by applying standard linear algebra arrays already developed. Duality establishes links between table algorithms and matrix algorithms by exploiting a mathematical correspondence, but there are other informal similarities related to the design technique. In Chapter 2 we produced arrays with row-ordered, column-ordered, and diagonal-ordered input by choosing different projections of data dependencies from space–time into pure space dimensions. Similarly, in this chapter we have produced arrays in which the tables were generated with stationary columns or stationary rows. Row stationary, table-generating arrays often lead to basic cells which involve feedback by virtue of elements being stored in the cell from step to step. Column stationary designs tend to involve no intermediate cell storage, no feedback, and can be used for two-level pipelining. By extension it should be clear that more table-generating arrays with non-stationary rows and columns also exist. Such designs have not been developed explicitly here because they often involve bidirectional data flow which prevents effective use of two-level effects and systolic rings. For completeness an example is given in the next chapter.

It should be clear that three-array forms of an algorithm are produced because we consider only two axes in space–time. The only possible projections of an array are on to one axis or the other, or a mixture of the two. This implies more degrees of freedom for the design process when higher dimensionality space–time representations are considered. A simple and natural example is to consider the problem of updating rather than generating a table. For example, we have tacitly assumed throughout this chapter that the design objective is to generate a table from a set of boundary values. In some problems (e.g. three-dimensional partial differential equations, linear programming) the initial values are already in the form of a table. For these cases a natural geometric interpretation is a wave rolling across the table. Elements behind the wavefront have already been updated, those in front of it have yet to be modified, and those on the wave crest are currently being updated. In space–time we interpret the table dimensions as space and the wavefront as time so that the table itself is a projection from 3-D space–time into 2-D pure space dimensions. The array topology is recovered directly from the table molecule. A new family of systolic algorithms for updating rather than generating tables can be produced using two-level pipelining and rings. Such designs are appropriate where multiple updates (wavefronts) to a table are required but grossly inefficient otherwise. Of course systolic rings translate to cylinders and torus shapes in the new arrays but the basic design principles are the same.

Exercises

1. Given the unequally spaced points (x_i, y_i) for $i = 0(1)n$ construct an

array for evaluating Aitken's interpolation table using the rule

$$Q_{i,j} = \frac{(x - x_i)Q_{j-1,j-1} - (x - x_{j-1})Q_{i,j-1}}{x_{j-1} - x_i}$$

where $Q_{i0} = y_i$.

2. Given the power series $P(z) = c_0 + c_1 z + c_2 z^2 + \cdots$ the Padé table is a doubly infinite table whose entry in position (m, n) is a polynomial of degree at most m divided by a polynomial of at most degree n and whose expansion agrees with as many terms of $P(z)$ as possible. The following formulae can be used for Padé table construction:
   (a) $p_{vp}(z) = p_{v+1,p}(z) + e_{vp} z p_{v,p-1}(z)$
   (b) $p_{vp}(z) = p_{v,p+1}(z) + q_{v,p+1} z p_{v-1,p}(z)$
   (c) $e_{vp} q_{vp} = e_{v-1,p} q_{v,p+1}$
   (d) $q_{vp} + e_{vp} = q_{v+1,p} + e_{v,p-1}$
   where $e_{v,0} = 0$ and $q_{v,1} = c_{v+1}/c_v$ for $v \geq 0$, and $q_{0,p} = 0$ for $p > 1$, and p_{vp} is one of the polynomials mentioned above. Derive arrays for computing the Padé table.
3. Discuss methods for generating tables with the following generation rules
   (a) $U_i = U_i(U_{i+1})^{-1}$, $U_{i+2j} = U_{i+2j} - U_i U_{i+2j+1}$,
   $i = 1(1)N, j = 1(1)\cdots i + 2j \leq N.$
   (b) $U_i = U_i(U_{i+1})^{-1}$, $U_{2n+2-i} = U_{2n-2-i}(U_{2n+1-i}^{-1})$, $i = 1(1)n$,
   $U_{i+2j} = U_{i+2j} - U_i U_{i+2j+1} - U_{2n+2-i} U_{i+2j-1}$,
   $j = 1(1)n - i, i = 1(1)n - 1.$
4. Construct a generic array for computing the following table functions: (a) divided differences, (b) finite differences, (c) reciprocal differences, (d) continued fractions, (e) the ε algorithm (Wynn 1962). [Hint: Use control tags and switching to design a unified basic cell.]
5. What are the main differences between table-generating arrays with (a) stationary columns, (b) stationary rows? Under what circumstances would you prefer column stationary to row stationary data flow? Do you think that it is possible to generate table-generating arrays with non-stationary rows and columns?
6. How does two-level pipelining improve throughput and how can it be used to reduce hardware in a systolic design?
7. When would it be inadvisable to use a systolic ring? Give an example which illustrates your argument.
8. Gragg's extrapolation formula may be stated as follows

$$y_{ij} = \frac{h_{i-2}^2 y_{i,j-1} - h_{i-1}^2 y_{i-1,j-1}}{h_{i-2}^2 - h_{i-1}^2}$$

where $y_{i,1} = w(t, h_{i-1})$ and w approximates $y(t)$ at step size h. Derive systolic arrays for generating the required table.

9. The Burlisch and Stoer (1966) extrapolation formula uses rational function approximations to $y(t)$ to allow larger step sizes. The extrapolation table can be generated using the formula

$$T_k^{(i)} = T_{k-1}^{(i+1)} + \frac{T_{k-1}^{(i+1)} - T_{k-1}^{(i)}}{\left(\dfrac{h_i}{h_{i+k}}\right)^2\left(1 - \dfrac{T_{k-1}^{(i+1)} - T_{k-1}^{(i)}}{T_{k-1}^{(i+1)} - T_{k-2}^{(i+1)}}\right) - 1}.$$

   Produce a two-level pipelined systolic array.
10. Show that the product $R(x) = P(x)Q(x)$ of two polynomials can be written as a band matrix–vector computation and use this to construct an array for generating the coefficients of eqns (4.31). Consider ways in which you might pipeline this array together with the root-generating array.
11. The following finite difference formulae can be used to solve parabolic partial differential equations

   (a) $(u_{i,j} - u_{i,j-1})/k$
   $= (u_{i+1,j} - 2u_{i,j} + u_{i-1,j} + u_{i+1,j-1} - 2u_{i,j-1} + u_{i-1,j-1})/2h^2$

   (b) $-2ru_{i-1,j+1} + (3 + 4r)u_{i,j+1} - 2ru_{i+1,j+1} = 4u_{i,j} - u_{i,j-1}$

   for $i = 1(1)N - 1, j = 1, \ldots,$ and known boundary values. Derive linear algebra formulations of these problems and devise suitable systolic arrays. Attempt to produce table-generating arrays for the same problems and comment on any difficulties you encounter.
12. The simplest finite difference approximation to the elliptical partial differential equation

$$\frac{\partial^2 \varphi}{\partial x^2} + \frac{\partial^2 \varphi}{\partial y^2} + 2 = 0$$

   is given by

$$\frac{1}{h^2}(\varphi_{i+1,j} - 2\varphi_{i,j} + \varphi_{i-1,j} + \varphi_{i,j+1} - 2\varphi_{i,j} + \varphi_{i,j-1}) + 2 = 0$$

   where $x = ih$, $y = jh$ on a cross-section of size $N \times M$ where $N = nh$, $M = mh$, and n and m are the number of grid lines separated by distance h. You can assume that the elements on the boundary are known. Interpret this problem in both the geometric and algorithmic senses and derive suitable arrays.

5

NON-NUMERICAL ALGORITHMS

Non-numerical algorithms are as important to computer science as numerical problems. Indeed, from the viewpoint of providing a basic infrastructure (or operating system) efficient and fast non-numerical algorithms are of great concern. For example, the fast retrieval and ordering of information from large (relational) databases is an increasingly important aspect in many modern businesses. Databases continue to increase in size and short retrieval times can only be maintained by the exploitation of parallel processing techniques. Another area of interest is the so-called human–computer interface (HCI). HCI considers ways in which humans interact with computing equipment through a range of different input–output media. For example, one might consider problems of continuous speech recognition or pattern matching which have obvious applications in customer services for face and/or voice recognition. The emphasis in such applications, is on the fast manipulation of large volumes of symbolic data in order to maintain interactive performance. Below we consider some basic algorithms for supporting these types of application.

As in the previous chapters, we introduce some design principles to guide the discussion. The themes considered here are (i) *the exploitation of semi-rings*, (ii) *recursive data structures*, and (iii) *the use of conditional operations in algorithms.* In Chapter 3 we briefly mentioned the fact that many numerical algorithms have the same loop and data dependency structures but require different operations to be performed on data. This relationship can be represented formally by the mathematical concept of a semi-ring. The similarity between computations in numerical and non-numerical instances of semi-rings can be exploited so that use of existing or modified arrays reduces design time considerably. In the second case the principle of loop unrolling is extended to the representation of data structures that can be expressed in a recurrent form. The extension of systolic concepts to data structures is not as straightforward as it may first appear; this is because data structures themselves are passive, meaning that they support an algorithm, and in themselves do not constitute computations in the normal sense. Probst and Li (1988) distinguish two groups of systolic network termed *data flow* and *control flow* architectures respectively. In the former the sequence of computation is completely determined and independent of the input data, in the latter the sequence of computation is not known in advance but depends upon the input data. Chapters 3 and 4 have dealt largely with data flow arrays, and this chapter deals with basic control flow arrays. In particular it should be appreciated that the exact computations required by a control flow array change from one problem instance to another and demand some type of decision making at each node of the data dependency graph. This brings us to the third topic of concern: the role of conditional statements when they appear in algorithm definitions and the effects they have on the general design methodology.

Finally, to illustrate the design principles we will consider systolic solutions to simple and intuitive problems for basic data structures (e.g. stacks, queues, etc.), and algorithms such as sorting, searching, and pattern matching which can be used as basic components for supporting essentially non-numerical computations. It should be clear that such techniques form the basis for the construction of embedded algorithmically specialized arrays which can be used as building blocks to provide significant performance improvements for non-numerical applications.

5.1 Pattern matching

The first task we consider is the so-called pattern matching problem. Pattern matching arises in many applications mainly concerned with searching large volumes of data. A simple example from text processing is the problem of searching a document for a word that is to be replaced by an alternative. Pattern matching is also of significant interest in image processing where the identification of objects such as lines and corners of an image in real time is important. Indeed it is the speed of response offered by systolic pattern matchers that motivates their inclusion in this book. Other, more exotic, applications include speech recognition and matching DNA sequences. From a historical viewpoint the pattern matching problem was one of the first systolic designs to be considered suitable for VLSI implementation (Foster and Kung 1980).

Essentially, pattern matching can be regarded as an operation on two strings of characters (or symbols) S and P where $S > P$ in length. The smaller string P is called the pattern and the long string S is a sequence which must be searched to find all the subsequences of consecutive symbols that match the pattern. For example, let $P = abc$ and $S = abbaababcbabbb$; the pattern P matches at only a single place mid-way along the string. Clearly as the length of P grows the number of possible matches is reduced so that finally, when the two strings are of similar length, pattern matching reduces to the problem of string comparison (a basic step in sorting and searching). Systolic designs for the two cases $m \gg n$ and $m \approx n$ are considered below. In particular we shall exploit the principles of previous work on linear algebra and table-generating arrays to produce a range of designs.

5.1.1 Matching strings of different length

A more formal definition of a pattern matcher is derived by representing the strings as indexed sequences of symbols, that is

$$S = S_1S_2S_3\cdots S_m, \qquad P = P_1P_2P_3\cdots P_n. \tag{5.1}$$

The first few tests to match the pattern P to substrings of S would have the form

$$\begin{array}{ccccc} S_1 & S_2 & S_3 & S_4 & S_5 \\ P_1 & P_2 & P_3 & & \\ & P_1 & P_2 & P_3 & \\ & & P_1 & P_2 & P_3 \end{array}$$

and in recurrence notation the whole procedure can be defined by the equation

$$M_i = P_1S_i + P_2S_{i+1} + \cdots + P_nS_{n+i-1}, \quad i = 1(1)m - n + 1 \tag{5.2}$$

where we temporarily interpret '+' as logical 'AND' and juxtaposition as the comparison of the two symbols. In practice (5.2) requires a two-loop sequential program which gives the alternative form

$$\begin{aligned} M_i^{(0)} &= 0 \\ M_i^{(j)} &= M_i^{(j-1)} + P_jS_{i+j-1}, \quad i = 1(1)m - n + 1, j = 1(1)n. \end{aligned} \tag{5.3}$$

Intuitively a sequential algorithm for pattern matching must check P with every subsequence of consecutive symbols in S (three in the above case). It follows that if n and m are the lengths of P and S respectively the sequential time for pattern matching must be bounded by $O((m - n + 1)n) = O(mn)$ operations. Observe that in this context an operation is a comparison of two symbols and the update of a Boolean variable indicating whether or not a match has occurred. Many variations on this straightforward pattern matching approach can be made. For example, rescanning the string S as little as possible when a match is not found. For simplicity we shall concentrate only on the simple form given above.

To design a systolic algorithm from first principles the design methodology demands a representation of (5.3) in space–time followed by various transformations and projections to produce an array. Now (5.3) has two dimensions and it is trivial to observe that the recurrence, when written in this form, is very similar to the definition for the convolution problem (Chapter 1, eqn (1.3)). In fact all that has changed is the interpretation of the basic operations '+' and juxtaposition (or '.'). Consequently in matrix notation we have

$$\begin{bmatrix} P_1 & P_2 & - & P_n & & \\ & P_1 & & & \ddots & \\ & & \ddots & & & P_n \\ & & & \ddots & & | \\ & & & & & P_1 \end{bmatrix} \begin{bmatrix} S_1 \\ S_2 \\ \vdots \\ S_m \end{bmatrix} = \begin{bmatrix} M_1 \\ M_2 \\ \vdots \\ M_m \end{bmatrix} \tag{5.4}$$

where the matrix is of order m and the $m \times 1$ right-hand-side vector components yield logical '0' or '1' values depending on the match of each pattern row with S. It follows directly that any of the convolution arrays described in Chapter 1 or the matrix–vector designs in Chapter 2 can be used for pattern matching provided that we modify the cell definitions accordingly (i.e. replace the adder by a logical 'AND' and the multiplier by a comparator). The matrix–vector computation, pattern matching algorithm, and convolution problem all have a common data flow and differ only by the nature of operations (i.e. they are different instances of a semi-ring). We can exploit this template relationship by observing that pattern matching will require just n cells (the bandwidth of the matrix) and that the computation time should be $2\max(m, n) + \min(m, n)$ using the matrix–vector array in Fig. 2.8 so that $\mathscr{T} = 2m + n$ steps are required.

An alternative approach is to formulate the recurrence as an outer product computation with the form

$$\begin{bmatrix} P_1 \\ P_2 \\ \vdots \\ P_n \end{bmatrix} [S_1 \quad S_2 \quad \cdots \quad S_m] = \begin{bmatrix} P_1S_1 & P_1S_2 & \cdots & P_1S_m \\ P_2S_1 & P_2S_2 & \cdots & P_2S_m \\ \vdots & \vdots & & \vdots \\ P_nS_1 & P_nS_2 & \cdots & P_nS_m \end{bmatrix} \tag{5.5}$$

where the matrix is $n \times m$ and the element (i, j) is '1' or '0' depending on the result of the comparison between P_i and S_j. It follows that the logical 'AND' of elements on the ith superdiagonal produces the M_i value. In space–time the computation P_iS_j is located at the (i, j) position and it is simple to observe that element (i, j) of the matrix is computed at time $t = i + j - 1$ (again this follows from the banded matrix–vector example shown in Fig. 2.8). Now, in order to accumulate the result of matching the pattern with different subsequences of S we would like the M_i and hence the superdiagonal elements of (5.5) to remain stationary. To achieve this task rotate the dependency graph (45°) with respect to the i–j axes so that the line with direction $(1, 1)^t$ is mapped on to the j axis. The set of points (i, j) for particular values of t define a family of (equitemporal) lines which are

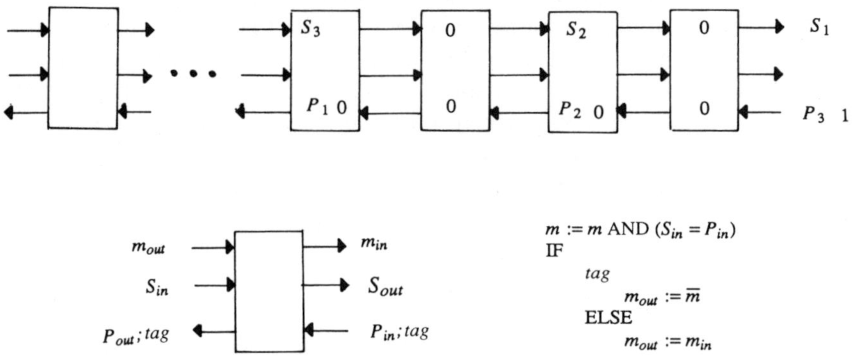

Fig. 5.1 Pattern matching array (Source M. J. Foster and H. T. Kung, © 1980, *IEEE Computer*)

parallel to the horizontal axis. A projection in the direction $(0, -1)^t$ on to the axis produces a bidirectional array, with the M_i values accumulated in the array cells. There are two data sequences, one for P and another for S with directions $(-1, 0)^t$ and $(1, 0)^t$ respectively. In each sequence the string symbols are separated by a neutral or synchronizing dummy element. A sketch of the array is shown in Fig. 5.1. The efficiency is $e = 0.5$. Notice that in the cell definition the superdiagonal computations are accumulated in the variable m and a control tag has been added to unload the final result of the matches. The tag is set to mark the end of the string P so that when accumulation of the match is complete it is made non-stationary and travels with the S_j to mark the end of the matched subsequence. This additional data flow required for unloading is a technical detail and is not part of the original computation. As a result it is not represented explicitly in the space–time representation.

Finally observe that the subdiagonals of the outer product matrix are mapped into the positive space–time quadrant. As these values provide no useful computations they can be omitted from the projected design thus removing $n - 1$ cells. Similarly, notice that there is no point in comparing P_1 with any symbols after S_{m-n+1} because the pattern cannot possibly match the remaining symbols. It follows that only $(m + n - 1) - (n - 1) - (n - 1)$ or $\mathscr{A} = m - n + 1$ cells are required. The timing of the array is derived from the data sequence length and the array latency. The longest input sequence has $2m$ elements (allowing for dummy elements) and so the last value enters the array after $2m$ steps. The array latency is $m - n + 1$ so that the last match will have left the array after $\mathscr{T} = (m - n + 1) + 2m$ steps which includes input–output time. However, computation begins only after the first symbol of S has reached the rightmost cell, so the actual computation time is $2m + n - 1$ steps.

The first design required only n cells and $\mathcal{T} = 2m + n$ time but the matrix–vector formulation of the problem implies that the pattern must be preloaded (the time for this is not included in $\mathcal{T}$). In the second design we require $m + n - 1$ cells and $\mathcal{T} = 3m - n + 1$ but this includes input–output time. Both designs yield 50 per cent efficiency. Clearly, when the pattern is significantly smaller than the target string the first method has both area and time advantages; unfortunately it also requires extra control for loading the initial pattern which increases the cell complexity.

5.1.2 Matching strings of similar length

The above method works well when the pattern is much smaller than the target string. When both strings are of approximately the same length the number of pipelined matches that can be accommodated is significantly reduced and it is necessary to seek other ways of representing string similarity. An interesting systolic design for matching long strings (due to Lipton and Lopresti (1986)) is based on the idea of computing the edit distance between two strings. For example, if

$$S = S_1 S_2 S_3 \cdots S_m \qquad \text{and} \qquad T = T_1 T_2 \cdots T_n \tag{5.6}$$

where $m \approx n$, the edit distance is the number of insertions and deletions of symbols that would be required to change one string into the other. The idea is to generate an $m \times n$ table according to the following rule

$$d_{ij} = \min\left(d_{i,j-1} + 1,\, d_{i-1,j} + 1,\, d_{i-1,j-1} \begin{cases} +0 & \text{if } S_i = T_j \\ +2 & \text{otherwise.} \end{cases} \right) \tag{5.7}$$

For example, the strings SYSTOLIC and SYMBOLIC produce the table shown in Fig. 5.2. If we arbitrarily assign the cost of insertion/deletion and symbol replacement (i.e. insertion followed by deletion) to be one and two respectively, adding one to the edit distance implies an insertion or deletion and adding two implies replacement. The last table entry, d_{mn}, is the minimum edit distance. In the example given the table tells us that at least

		S	Y	M	B	O	L	I	C
	0	1	2	3	4	5	6	7	8
S	1	0	1	2	3	4	5	6	7
Y	2	1	0	1	2	3	4	5	6
S	3	2	1	2	3	4	5	6	7
T	4	3	2	3	4	5	6	7	8
O	5	4	3	4	5	4	5	6	7
L	6	5	4	5	6	5	4	5	6
I	7	6	5	6	7	6	5	4	5
C	8	7	6	7	8	7	6	5	4

Fig. 5.2 Edit distance table

two replacements are required to change the string SYSTOLIC into SYMBOLIC—this is obviously correct. Clearly, as mn table elements must be computed $O(mn)$ sequential steps are required to generate the table.

We have already seen numerous examples of systolic table-generating algorithms in Chapter 4—perhaps some of those techniques can be used to good effect here. The table in Fig. 5.2 and the rule (5.7) can be used to interpret the 2-D table as a data dependency graph in 2-D space–time. Clearly a suitable projection will produce a linear array. To make this fact explicit let us redefine (5.7) as follows

$$d_{ij}^{(k)} = \min\left(d_{i,j-1}^{(k)} + 1, d_{i-1,j}^{(k)} + 1, d_{i-1,j-1}^{(k)} \begin{cases} +0 & \text{if } S_i^{(k)} = T_j^{(k)} \\ +2 & \text{otherwise} \end{cases} \right) \tag{5.8}$$

where $k > 0$, and define a series of k string pairs for which the edit distance is to be determined. Three indices imply 3-D space–time and it should be obvious that a 3-D cube is constructed simply by piling tables for $k = 1, \ldots$ on top of one another. That is, the direction of the k axis is perpendicular to the page. Now, by using the rectangle rule (5.7) elements $d_{i,j}$ of the table can be computed at time $t = i + j - 1$ while elements $d_{i,j}^{(k)}$ of (5.8) can be evaluated at time $t = i + j + k - 1$. This implies that the k axis can be used to represent time because the edit distance computation for string k starts at time k. If k represents time a projection on to the i–j plane will be an array. Indeed such a topology is shown in Fig. 5.3 for a single pair of strings at step $t = (1 + 6 - 1) = 6$. Cell (i, j) in the design computes the rule (5.7) and requires three additions and three comparators (one for comparing string symbols, and two others to find the minimum d value). The whole table is generated using a wavefront pattern. Cells in front of the wave are blank because they have performed no useful computations so far. Cells behind the wave contain the corresponding edit distance table entry. Cells on the wavefront itself contain the symbols to be matched and are currently computing their table entries. Because the only table element required is held in the bottom right cell it follows that a cell can be reset as soon as the wave has passed through it, so a new problem instance can start evaluation immediately. As a result a number of edit distance computations can be pipelined behind one another to improve array throughput significantly. The array itself requires $\mathscr{A} = O(mn)$ cells and becomes 100 per cent efficient only when more than $m + n$ string matches are pipelined.

Remark. The idea of a wavefront was used earlier in Chapter 2. The reader is encouraged to compare the current design with the matrix product arrays in Fig. 2.10 and the transposition array in Fig. 3.12.

When only a single pair of strings is to be compared the 2-D array is clearly inefficient. In fact in this case $k = 1$ so we can revert back to the original recurrence in (5.7). As eqn (5.7) only uses two indices the topology

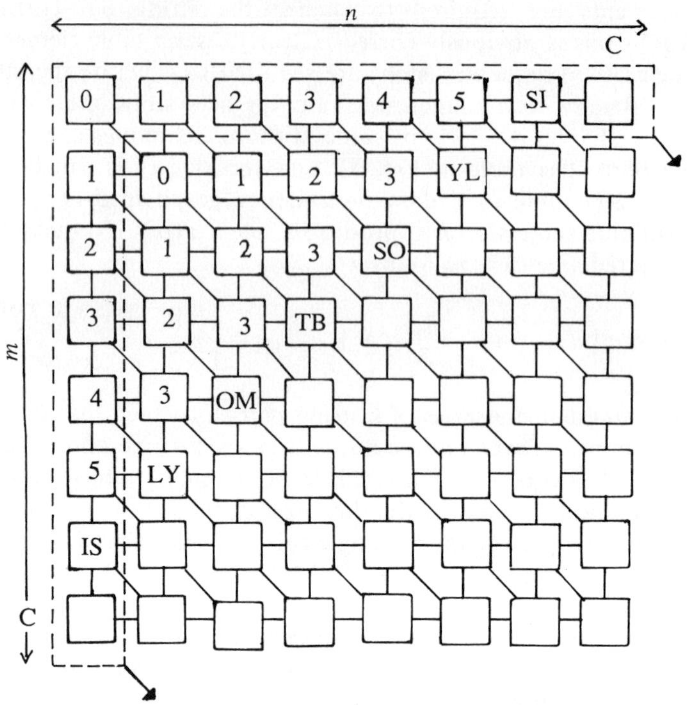

Fig. 5.3 Two-dimensional edit distance array

in Fig. 5.3 can be interpreted as a data dependency graph. It is clear from the previous discussion that the antidiagonals represent equitemporal lines so that projecting in the $(-1, 1)^t$ direction maps the 2-D graph on to a bidirectional linear systolic array. Some snapshots of this array which is attributed to Lipton and Lopresti are shown in Fig. 5.4. The bandwidth of the table is $m + n - 1$ so there are this many cells in the design. Tracing through a number of wavefront movements in the 2-D array reveals the data sequence structure and direction. Observe that because the subdiagonals and superdiagonals of the table are parallel to the direction of projection they become stationary in the linear array—this implies that d values are overwritten as computation progresses. Each cell in the new array stores the current diagonal element, and the relevant row and column values are pumped along the array with their corresponding string symbols. The total time for table construction is $m + n - 1$ steps because this is the time required for the single wavefront to propagate over the 2-D array shown in Fig. 5.3. In addition we must also add $\max(m, n)$ steps to synchronize the two input strings inside the array before computation starts.

The above discussion illustrates the connection between 2-D and 1-D

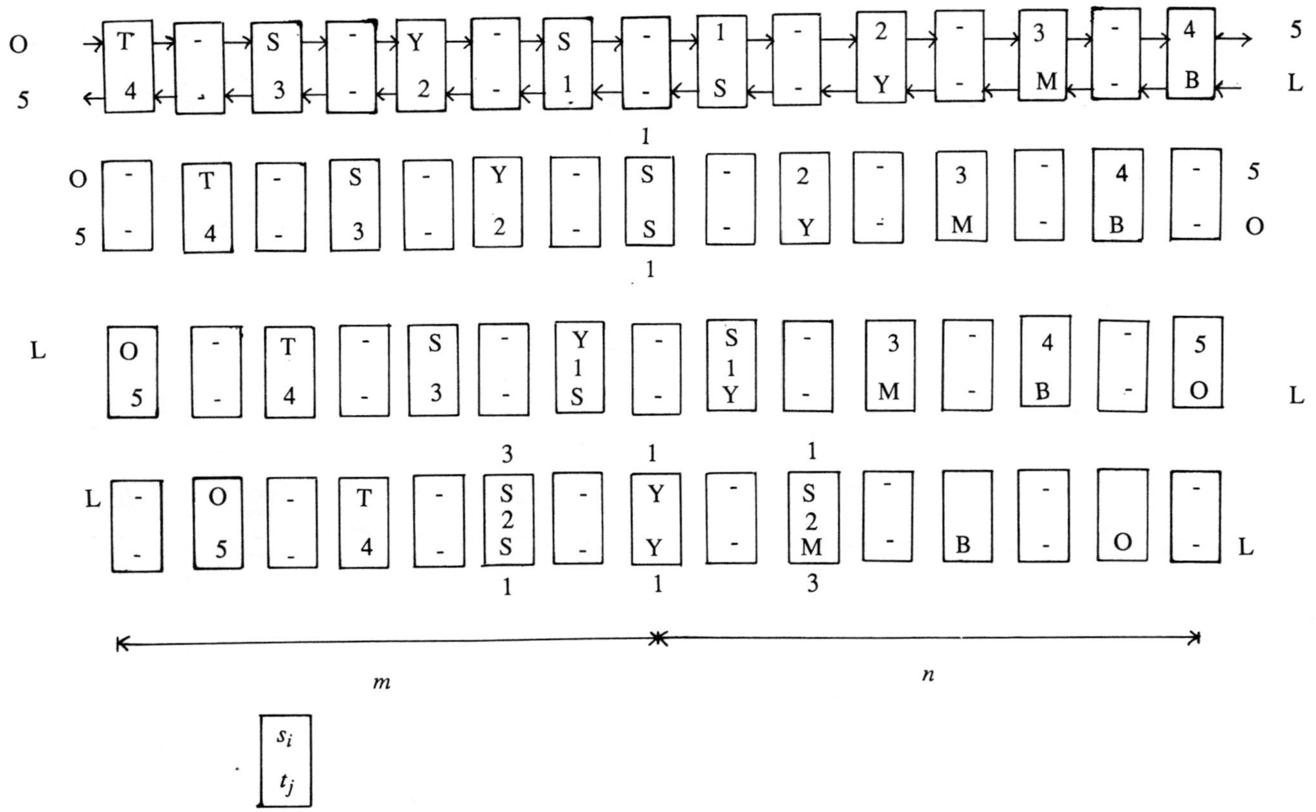

Fig. 5.4 One-dimensional bidirectional edit distance array

arrays. A 2-D array is useful when high throughput is required for 2-D table generation; the 1-D version is better when just a single problem is to be solved. The 2-D version can also be exploited when the task is to update an existing table (preloaded into the array) rather than generate a new one. In general the mapping technique is of great value in deriving systolic designs for algorithms which employ rectangular tables and single wavefronts (see Yang and Lee 1986). In particular we point out that a similar design can be used for the related problem of speech recognition (see Frison and Quinton 1985). The idea of a generic wavefront array processor architecture for supporting computations with a wavefront form has been investigated extensively by Kung (1985) (see Chapter 7). Further improvements to the edit distance array are also possible and some are considered in Chapter 6.

5.2 Systolic sorting

Sorting is another important area of interest for computer science. The basic sequential techniques are excellently covered in Knuth (1973), where it is asserted that up to 25 per cent of non-numerical computer time is spent on sorting in one form or another. The basis of sorting can be stated simply as follows. Suppose we have n items

$$I_1, I_2, \ldots, I_n \tag{5.9}$$

which have to be sorted, where I_i could itself be a record of information. Each item has some key k_i that can be used to control the sorting mechanism. To sort we define some kind of ordering relation such as '$<$' which satisfies rules for three of the keys a, b, and c, for example

(1) $a < b$, $a = b$, and $a > b$

(2) $a < b$ and $b < c$ implies $a < c$.

If after sorting the keys satisfy

$$k_1 < k_2 < \cdots < k_n \tag{5.10}$$

the list is fully sorted and we have what is termed a total ordering. If $\leq$ is permitted some elements can be the same and a partial order exists. For example, if the keys represent the time steps of instructions for a particular algorithm we could recover the program operation by sorting the instructions into ascending order. If some instructions have the same key value they could be executed in parallel. Thus total orderings define deterministic (or sequential) computation, partial orderings non-deterministic (or parallel) computation. The sorting algorithm therefore needs only to produce a permutation of the indices $i = 1(1)n$ which places keys k_i in non-decreasing order. In the following discussion we will develop simple systolic sorting algorithms for two basic sequential algorithms. To facilitate easy discussion the special values $+\infty$ and $-\infty$ are introduced and used as neutral elements. Intuitively these values represent the largest and smallest possible numbers which can be represented in the hardware and do not occur in the actual lists to be sorted.

5.2.1 Selection sort

The simplest technique for sorting is called selection sort and the basic method can be written as a two-loop sequential program:

```
For j := 1 to n-1 do
  {min := k[j];
   For i := j+1 to n do
     If k[i] < min THEN
       {SWAP(k[i], k[j]);
        min := k[i]
       }
  }
```

where $k[j] = k_j$ and SWAP exchanges the two keys. The comparisons involved in this algorithm can be expressed as a tableau, that is

$$\begin{array}{cccccc} (1,2) & (1,3) & (1,4) & \text{———} & (1,n) & \\ & (2,3) & (2,4) & & (2,n) & \\ & & (3,4) & \searrow & | & \\ & & & & (n-1,n) & \end{array} \qquad (5.11)$$

where row j corresponds to the jth iteration of the code above. The pair (i, j) implies that keys k_i and k_j are compared and correspond to the IF–THEN statement in the program. Observe that these comparisons are always made, but that elements in the list can change their affiliation (i.e. get exchanged) as the result of a comparison. For example, row 1 of the table implies that we start with the first element and compare it with all other elements in the list; when a smaller value is found we exchange the two values and continue. Thus after the computations in row 1 have been completed the element in the first position of the list is the minimum. We now repeat the process by performing the comparisons in row 2 using the second list element. In general, row j of the table finds the jth smallest element and uses a sublist of size $n - j + 1$. Clearly, selection sort requires $O(n^2)$ comparison–exchange operations in the worst case. In fact the tableau (5.11) is a loop unrolling of these necessary comparison exchanges. A space–time representation of the problem can be constructed by determining data dependencies among these comparisons. The statement forming the body of the program involves values with only a single index. Fully indexing the system produces

$$k_{ij} = \min(k_{i-1,j}, k_{i,0})$$

where $k_{i-1,j}$ represents the variable min. The value $k_{i,0}$ makes the system non-uniform, but application of the pipelining principle produces

$$k_{0,j} = k_j, \qquad k_{j+1,j-1} = -\infty \tag{5.12a}$$

$$k_{i,j} = \min(k_{i-1,j}, k_{i,j-1}), \quad j = 1(1)n-1,\ i = j+1(1)n \tag{5.12b}$$

which is uniform. Indeed, observe that once comparisons (1, 2) and (1, 3) have been made the comparison (2, 3) can proceed. Thus (1, 4) and (2, 3) can be computed simultaneously as can (1, 5), (2, 4), and (1, 6), (2, 5), (3, 4), etc. This ordering of the comparisons obeys the wavefront principle used in the previous section so that $k_{i,j}$ is evaluated at time $t = i + j - 2$.

Plotting the tableau (5.11) in 2-D space and connecting nodes using (5.12) produces the graph in Fig. 5.5. As the table dimensions are $O(n)$ the result of a projection will produce arrays with $O(n)$ cells and we should expect $O(n)$ time because there are only $O(n^2)$ sequential comparisons. In fact $\mathcal{T} = n + n - 2 = 2(n-1)$ steps should be sufficient. To derive the first array suppose we project out the i dimension. A linear array is produced with the list elements preloaded and stationary. Some snapshots for the array are shown in Fig. 5.6(a). The minimum for row i can be input as $+\infty$ at the left of the array and filters through the cells from left to right to be output

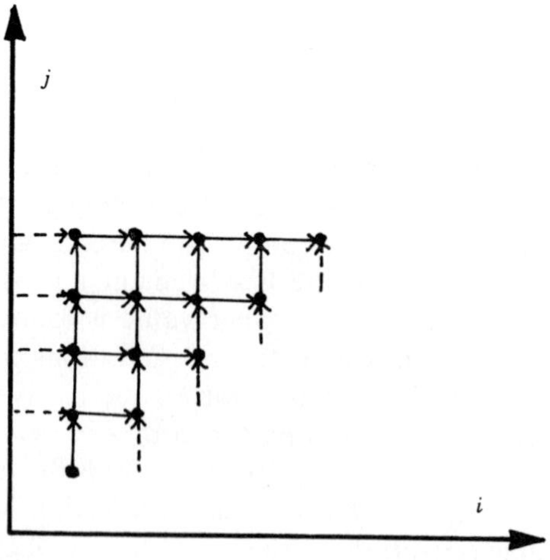

Fig. 5.5 Data dependency graph for selection sort

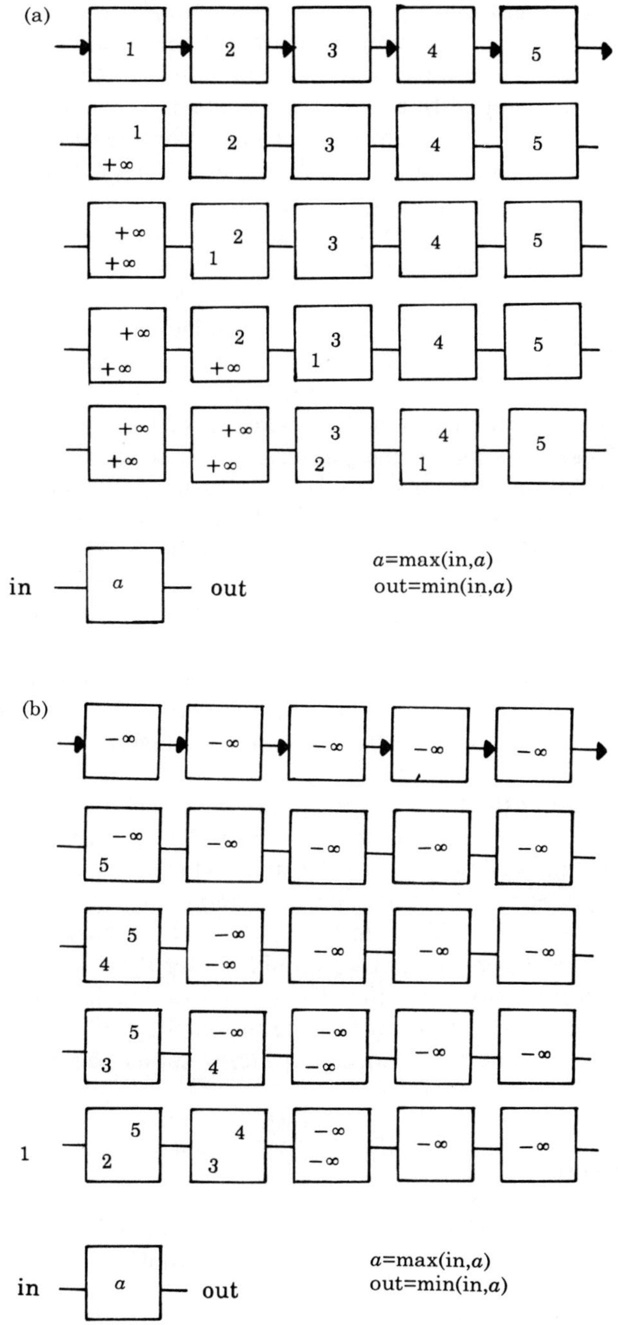

Fig. 5.6 Arrays for selection sort: (a) projection from $(-1, 0)^t$ direction; (b) projection from $(0, -1)^t$ projection

eventually at the right end by which time it contains the minimum of the list. The comparisons and exchanges ensure that the minimum is propagated right so that the first cell value is overwritten with the $+\infty$ element inserted into the array. As computation progresses the first i cells contain $+\infty$ when computation of the $(i+1)$th row starts. Clearly computations on successive rows can be overlapped and pipelined so that n consecutive $(+\infty)$ values are input. The array contains n cells (i.e. length of the first row) so that $\mathscr{A} = n$ cells and $\mathscr{T} = 2n$ steps are required, where a step is the time to perform a comparison and determine the minimum. In the design each cell receives n values so the efficiency is $e = n/2n = 0.5$. The final time is different from that given above because we use n cells; in fact only $n - 1$ are necessary when one of the list elements is used as the first input instead of $+\infty$.

An alternative array which avoids preloading of the initial list is derived by projecting out the j axis. Again a linear array of n cells is produced (i.e. length of last column) and all the computations associated with row i of the table are mapped on to processor i. Initially assume that all the processors contain $-\infty$ values (this is achieved by flushing the array beforehand). A sketch of the array together with some snapshots is shown in Fig. 5.6(b). To operate the array we pump the values k_i into the leftmost cell. Generally when k_i enters a cell it is delayed a single cycle and compared with k_{i+1}. The maximum value is retained inside the cell and the minimum is sent on to the next cell. It follows that row i of (5.11) remains stationary inside cell i as indicated by the projection. The snapshot shows that cell i contains the ith largest key, and thus once the last key has entered, flushing the array with $+\infty$ values forces the list to propagate from left to right. On reaching the end of the array the list is output in non-decreasing order. As the input data have length n, the array has length n, each cell has a delay of two cycles, and the total time is $\mathscr{T} = 2n + n = 3n$ steps, where a step is again the cost of a comparison. Each cell receives n values and computes true comparisons (i.e. on real list elements) for n steps so that $e = 0.33$. Now on comparison of the two designs it appears that we should opt for the first because $\mathscr{T} = 2n$ and $e = 0.5$. Notice, however, that the second design includes the input–output time. Allowing n steps for loading makes the two designs equivalent in cell and time count so the deciding factor should be efficiency which favours the first.

5.2.2 Bubble sort

Another intuitive way of sorting a list is the so-called bubble-sort algorithm. The basic method can be described by the following two-loop program

```
For j := n to 1 do
   For i := 2 to j do
      {IF k[i-1] > k[i] THEN
```

```
        SWAP(k[i-1], k[i])
    }
```

Again, representing the comparison exchanges as a tableau produces the form

$$
\begin{array}{llllll}
(1, 2) & (2, 3) & (3, 4) & \text{———} & (n-2, n-1) & (n-1, n) \\
(1, 2) & (2, 3) & (3, 4) & & (n-2, n-1) & \\
| & & & & & \\
(1, 2) & & & & &
\end{array}
\qquad (5.13)
$$

As in the previous example each row represents a single iteration of the algorithm and the pairs (i, j) indicate which elements of the list to compare. Clearly row 1 of the table will force the maximum element to the end of the list. Row 2 repeats the process but, on a list of size $(n-1)$ and in general, row p locates the pth largest element using a list of length $n-p+1$. We could derive systolic arrays from this table using the same technique as that in the selection sort example. Unfortunately the pairs here are duplicated in successive rows and this hides the true data dependencies of the problem. To illustrate this feature try plotting the pairs from (5.13) in a 2-D space. Notice that (1, 2) must be evaluated before (2, 3) and (3, 4) before (4, 5), and so on, so that the data dependencies are easily produced. The whole algorithm reduces to a single line of points with direction $(1, 1)^t$ and computations on different rows of (5.13) are strictly pipelined behind one another. It is trivial to note that a projection in the $(0, -1)^t$ direction would produce a linear array with elements preloaded into the cells. To make the details more explicit consider the following recurrence form of the bubble-sort algorithm. A single iteration of the algorithm can be formulated as

$$k_i = \max(k_i, k_{i-1}), \quad i = 2(1)j \qquad (5.14a)$$

$$k_{i-1} = \min(k_i, k_{i-1}) \qquad (5.14b)$$

and the whole sort is given by evaluating these expressions for $j = n(-1)1$. It should be clear that (5.14a) and (5.14b) together constitute a comparison exchange. Only one index is present in the recurrence so we need to add another to get a 2-D representation. This yields

$$k_{i,0} = k_i \qquad (5.15a)$$

$$k_{ii} = \max(k_{i,i-1}, k_{i+1,i-1}), \quad i = 1(1)j, j = n(-1)1 \qquad (5.15b)$$

$$k_{i+1,i} = \min(k_{i,i-1}, k_{i+1,i-1}) \qquad (5.15c)$$

$$k_{ip} = k_{i,p-1}, \quad 0 < p < i, p > i+1. \qquad (5.15d)$$

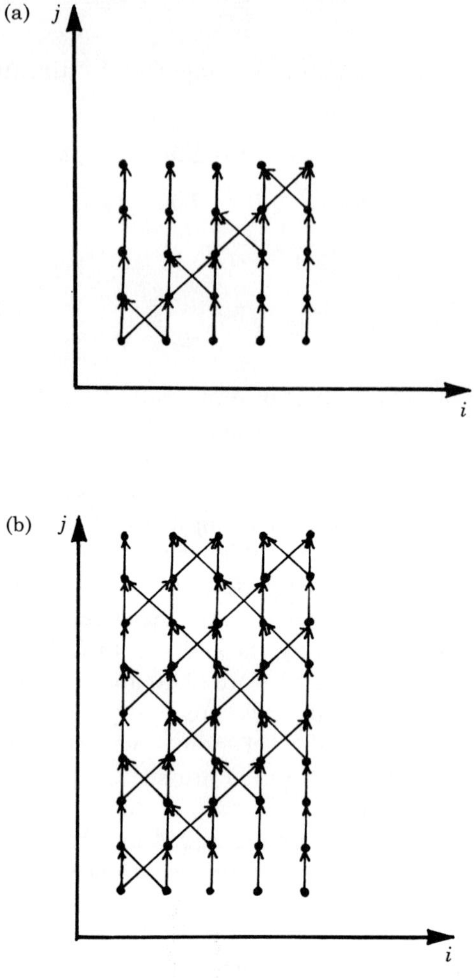

Fig. 5.7 Data dependency graph for bubble sort: (a) single iteration; (b) pipelined iteration

Plotting (5.15) in 2-D space produces the data dependency graph for a single iteration of the method as shown in Fig. 5.7(a). Indeed, by interpreting the second index as time we have a space–time representation. A projection in the $(0, -1)^t$ direction to remove the j axis produces a bidirectional array with n cells which are preloaded with the keys such that k_i is in cell i. Sketching some snapshots clarifies the cell operation. On odd time steps (assuming the first computation after preloading is step 1) odd-numbered cells read the value from the right adjacent cell and perform a comparison, store the minimum, and return the maximum value. Similarly an even-numbered cell sends its element left and waits for a value to be returned by the left adjacent cell. On even-numbered time steps the situation is reversed, with even-numbered cells computing comparisons and odd-numbered cells being passive. Although this behaviour appears complicated it is quite easy to control and is implied by the cross-over connections in the data dependency graph resulting from (5.15). From the viewpoint of control each array cell requires two modes of operation dependent upon the time cycle; this is easily produced by introducing a stationary control toggle inside each cell. After preloading the list the odd-numbered cells have the control toggle set and the even-numbered cells have it cleared. A single bit can be used and logical negation at the end of every cycle will keep the cells properly coordinated.

Now (5.15) only describes how to compute a single iteration of the bubble-sort method. It is, however, trivial to notice that the smaller and smaller sublist computations can be pipelined behind one another on the array so that the operations described above will sort the whole list. Extending the dependence graph in this way produces Fig. 5.7(b). A more symmetric recurrence

$$k_{i0} = k_i \tag{5.16a}$$

$$\left.\begin{aligned} k_{(2i-1),j} &= \max(k_{(2i-1),j-1}, k_{(2i),j-1}), \quad j \text{ is odd} \\ k_{(2i),j} &= \min(k_{(2i-1),j-1}, k_{(2i),j-1}) \end{aligned}\right. \tag{5.16b}$$

$$\left.\begin{aligned} k_{(2i),j} &= \max(k_{(2i),j-1}, k_{(2i+1),j-1}), \quad j \text{ is even} \\ k_{(2i+1),j} &= \min(k_{(2i),j-1}, k_{(2i+1),j-1}) \end{aligned}\right. \tag{5.16c}$$

includes the odd–even computation as a subgraph and has the advantage that the odd–even activation is made explicit. The usage of cells is also improved. The final dependence graph is shown in Fig. 5.8(a), and projecting out the j axis produces the array in Fig. 5.8(b). It should be clear that the additional computations added to give the data dependency graph regularity are overlapped with the required computations and consequently do not add additional cells or additional time overheads. Figure 5.8(b) shows some snapshots for the projected array; $\mathscr{A} = n$ cells are required. The cells at the end of the array are supplied with appropriate $+\infty$ or $-\infty$ values to prevent the cell elements leaving the array accidentally. As each cell is active every alternate cycle the efficiency must be $e = 0.5$. The timing of the array is more complicated to derive. Using Fig. 5.8(a) it is clear that the maximum (or minimum) of a list can be found in at most n steps. Thus the array in Fig. 5.8(b) has the effect of computing two bubble sorts simultaneously: one computes maximums, the other minimums, and both are interleaved on the same array. The practical value of this interleaving is that the minimum and maximum are placed in the correct cells after n steps. Now the remaining

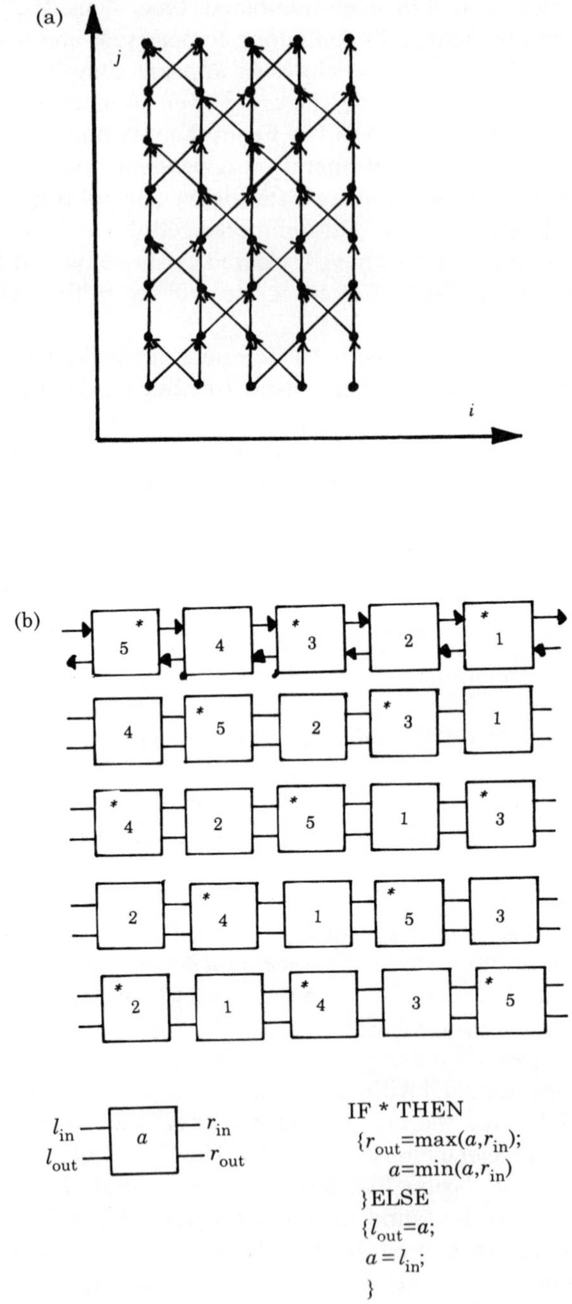

Fig. 5.8 Odd–even sorter: (a) regular graphs; (b) array and snapshots

sublist of $n-2$ elements resident in cells 2 to $n-1$ requires $n-2$ steps to place its largest and smallest elements. In general the jth sublist has size $n-2j$ and requires $n-2j$ steps. It follows that the computation of the successive lists can be started up on consecutive cycles so that the fully sorted list is generated in at most $\mathcal{T}=n$ steps. Comparing this time to the arrays for selection sort appears to produce a better computation time for the same hardware and approximately the same efficiency. Unfortunately the array has to be preloaded with the start list and unloaded at the end, which adds at most $2n$ further steps, so this array also requires $3n$ steps in total.

So far we have considered the problem of sorting just a single list. What happens when we have $m>0$ lists to sort? A trivial and naive solution to the problem is to use m copies of a 1-D array. The solution is naive because we will require $O(m)$ connections to the external controlling device for input–output. Clearly we need to be able to pipeline successive instances of the sorting problem through the same array. From this viewpoint the arrays for systolic selection sort appear to have some advantages because the final list is output as a natural consequence of the data flow. Indeed, if one adopts the array in Fig. 5.6(b) problems can be pipelined through the hardware. Unfortunately, and if we are not careful, different lists could collide and get mixed up because $-\infty$ values are used to flush out the previous list of the array. These values will break up the list following immediately behind, so some form of reset control is required if the problem is to be avoided. The odd–even scheme can also be pipelined provided that we are willing to add an input and output connection to each cell. (Note: If n is large this may not be practical.) The required array can be derived directly by noticing that Fig. 5.8(a) is just an array unrolling of the odd–even sorter. It follows that an array like that shown in Fig. 3.11 can be used as a pipelined sorter. Each row of the 2-D array computes one snapshot of the sort and then passes the list on to the next row. It follows that n rows of n cells or $\mathcal{A}=n^2$ cells are required to sort a single list. If we have m lists, list $p=1(1)m$ enters the array in the top row at time $t=p$ and leaves at time $t=n+p$. If $m \gg n$ lists are to be sorted the array becomes 100 per cent efficient, improves throughput significantly, and requires only $O(n)$ input–output connections. However, allowing this design into our working set of useful arrays admits many other problems. For example, if we can use an input and output connection for each cell we can load the original design for the odd–even sorter in a single step—this affects the choice of which sorting array should be preferred for sorting a single list. We will simply note this fact here and refer the reader to Chapter 6 which considers some of these practical issues.

5.2.3 Mergesort

Many other sorting methods exist. Indeed more systolic arrays for sorting can be produced by considering different projections of (5.11) and (5.14) and by extending the table format into higher dimensions. For example, designs based on preloading the list into a 2-D rather than 1-D array are also possible (see Thompson and Kung 1977). Perhaps the most surprising feature of our discussion is that the bubble-sort method produces an efficient array. It is well known that bubble sort is a very inefficient sequential algorithm. Our experiments here show that this inefficiency does not translate into inefficient systolic arrays. The important point is that novice designers coming from a sequential programming background tend to disregard these algorithms because they are dissuaded from using them in sequential programs. Of course very efficient sequential algorithms also have their dangers; in particular one tends to forget that a good sequential algorithm has been optimized for a sequential machine—that is what makes it efficient. To illustrate the danger we will consider one other parallel design which demonstrates that systolic design does not always pay dividends.

The mergesort algorithm was one of the first algorithms to show that sorting was an $O(n \log n)$ task and it still remains one of the fastest sequential sorting techniques. For this reason we would expect it to produce a good parallel algorithm (or would we?). From the historical point of view the pipelined version of mergesort that we consider appeared in Todd (1978) before the first real systolic algorithms. To demonstrate the method consider the following example for a list of size $n = 8$,

P_0:	[8]	[7]	[6]	[5]	[4]	[3]	[2]	[1]
P_1:	[7	8]	[5	6]	[3	4]	[1	2]
P_2:	[5	6	7	8]	[1	2	3	4]
P_3:	[1	2	3	4	5	6	7	8]

where [ ] is a sublist. The array consists of $k = \log_2 n$ cells connected as shown in Fig. 5.9. The idea behind the computation is to build up the sorted sublists generated by the mergesort technique, merging larger and larger lists as they move through the array. On emerging from the end of the array the list is fully sorted and requires just $O(n + \log n)$ steps. This time is already slower than the odd–even method but it is worthwhile examining the algorithm more closely. Although the design looks systolic it really is not; instead it just exhibits pipelined data flow. As the sublists get larger and larger a bottleneck at each processor next in line occurs and we must buffer successively larger lists of size $2^1, 2^2, 2^3, \ldots$. In general two lists of size 2^{k-1} must be buffered in the kth processor. The additional memory associated with each cell becomes dependent on n and the cell sizes are different along the array—thus the design contravenes some of the heuristics defined in Chapter 1. There is an important lesson to be learned here. Successful systolic design requires the correct choice of sequential algorithm (or recurrences) before the array is developed. Alternatively we must select the technique for computation that yields the most regular data dependencies. For example, so-called fast sequential sorters tend to make non-adjacent comparisons,

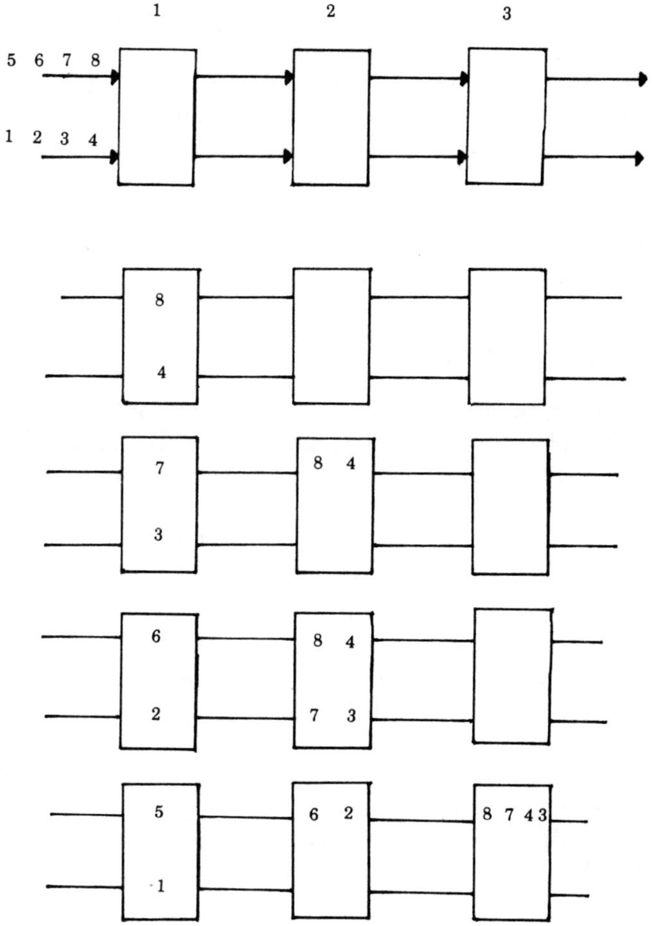

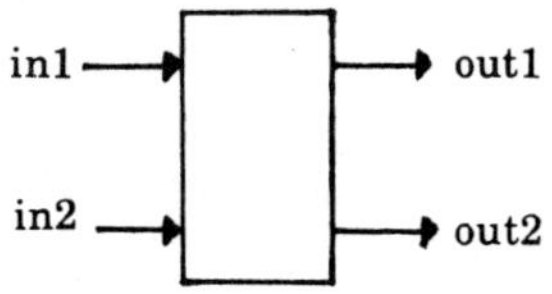


```
flag := *;

  For i := 1 TO p2 do
    Q1[i] := in1;
  For j := 1 TO p2 do
    Q2[j] := in2;

  IF flag = * THEN
    Merge(Out1, Q1, Q2, p)
  ELSE
    Merge(Out2, Q1, Q2, p)
```

where $p2 = 2^{p-1}$ and p is the cell number

Fig. 5.9 Pipelined mergesort (Redrawn from S. Todd, *IBM Journal of Research and Development*, © 1978, International Business Machines Corporation, with permission) which limits their use as effective systolic algorithms. This is not to say that locally connected topologies for these algorithms do not exist, but simply that the required retiming of the data flow to route the data through point-to-point connections requires overheads in time and area. For example, the mergesort algorithm described relies on buffering and the building up of longer and longer series of sequential computations, and as the merging increases this kills any benefits from pipelining. However, the method does have one redeeming feature—it only requires $\log n$ cells. If a more general processing element was available which incorporated a large enough memory to accommodate the buffered sublists the array would be highly attractive.

5.3 Systolic data structures

So far in this book we have developed systolic algorithms for both numerical and non-numerical applications by exploiting the loop structure of sequential programs. At this point it is useful to recall the famous phrase of Wirth (1976), namely

$$\text{programs} = \text{algorithms} + \text{data structures}$$

which asserts that any program depends upon two components: the algorithms for determining control flow, and the data structure for organizing data. A data structure can be defined as a set of data items together with a set of functions and a set of axioms which define the semantics of operations. In Chapter 1 we claimed that the appeal of systolic design was that algorithms and data structures combined could be used to determine architectures (or processor connection topologies for specific problems). For problems involving matrices or tables the justification of this statement is trivial because the data structure is static and assumes that elements of the structure can be randomly accessed using indices. The formulation of problems by recurrences follows naturally. In this section we briefly consider systolic solutions to some other common data structures such as stacks, queues, and trees in which the elements can only be accessed in certain orders. These structures can be defined recursively but the implementation in sequential (and procedural) programs is not normally in this form. Indeed we require a mapping of the data structures and their associated operations on to a recurrence structure which can be used to generate a systolic implementation.

5.3.1 Stacks

A stack is simply an ordered list where insertions (pushes) and deletions (pops) are made only at one end called the top. For example, a stack is used when procedure calls are being processed during the execution of a program. When a program calls a procedure the return address of the program counter is pushed on to a stack. When the procedure completes computation the address is popped off the stack and the program resumes from the site of the call. It follows that nested procedure calls can be processed easily by pushes and pops to a stack. A stack may be described by an abstract data type (see Horowitz and Sahni 1978) using just four operations,

IsEmpty(S), Create(S), Pop(S), Push(S,e)

where S is a stack that accepts elements e of some defined type (e.g. integers, reals, characters, etc.). The operation IsEmpty performs a test to see if the stack S contains any elements and returns a yes or no result. Create sets up and initializes an empty stack S. Pop removes the first element from the stack and Push adds element e on to the stack. This abstract definition makes no claims as to how it should be implemented and in particular places no restriction on the size of the stack. In sequential programs two methods of implementation are popular. The first method is static and uses the basic data structure array. The second approach is dynamic and makes use of indirection and pointers. Both these approaches are normally supported by a programming language.

Remark. An array in this context is a basic data structure, not a connection topology.

In a dynamic stack new locations are 'grabbed' from memory when a push is required and given back by a pop. A static stack is an array of fixed size where array locations act as the stack elements or pointers to a record of stack data, the ordering of data being implied by the adjacency of elements. In the former case the stack length is potentially infinite (within the bounds of available memory) and in the latter finite. Once a finite stack is full further pushes are not allowed until some pops are made to create an empty location.

The first thing to observe is that a systolic stack is targeted at a hardware implementation and as a result is inherently static in nature. However, if the cells are simple enough we should be able to build a very large array so that the probability of stack overflow is minimal. Suppose we denote the elements of the stack S by s_i for $i = 0(1)n$. Further we denote s_0 as the top of the stack and assume (for simplicity) that valid elements are positive integers. We derive the following recurrences

$$\left.\begin{aligned} s_0 &= -1 \\ s_i &= s_{i-1}, \quad i = 1(1)n \end{aligned}\right\} \tag{5.17a}$$

$$\left.\begin{aligned} s_i &= s_{i-1}, \quad i = n(-1)1 \\ s_0 &= e \end{aligned}\right\} \tag{5.17b}$$

and

$$\left.\begin{aligned} e &= s_0 \\ s_{i-1} &= s_i, \quad i = 1(1)n \\ s_n &= -1. \end{aligned}\right\} \tag{5.17c}$$

To Create a stack we use (5.17a) which flushes the stack S with negative values thus initializing an empty stack. IsEmpty is now trivially implemented by testing to see if s_0 is negative or not. A Push operation uses (5.17b) which first shifts all stack elements down the stack to leave an empty place at s_0; the element e is then inserted. Similarly a Pop operation reads the s_0 element and shifts all elements up one position, which overwrites s_0 (which is lost), and a negative element clears the last stack element. (Note: Implementing a stack in this manner in a sequential programming language is grossly inefficient and is not recommended.)

Notice that each stack operation requires $O(n)$ steps; if n is large the response time of the stack would be intolerable. In addition the recurrences only have a single index so that a loop unrolling produces a line in space–time with i representing time. The only possible projection is in the direction of this line so that a single point (a sequential processor) is demanded. Extending the equations to two indices produces

$$\left.\begin{aligned} &s_{0,0} = -1 \\ &s_{i,t} = \begin{cases} s_{i-1,t-1} & \text{if } i = t \\ s_{i,t-1} & \text{otherwise} \end{cases} \quad \text{for } i = 1(1)n,\ t = 1(1)n \end{aligned}\right\} \tag{5.18a}$$

$$\left.\begin{aligned} &s_{i,t} = \begin{cases} s_{i-1,t-1} & \text{if } i = n - t \\ s_{i,t-1} & \text{otherwise} \end{cases} \quad \text{for } i = 1(1)n,\ t = 1(1)n \\ &s_{0,n} = e \end{aligned}\right\} \tag{5.18b}$$

$$\left.\begin{aligned} &e = s_{0,0} \\ &s_{i-1,t} = \begin{cases} s_{i,t-1} & \text{if } i = t \\ s_{i-1,t-1} & \text{otherwise} \end{cases} \quad \text{for } i = 1(1)n,\ t = 1(1)n \\ &s_{n,t} = -1 \end{aligned}\right\} \tag{5.18c}$$

where t represents time. Laying out these computations in 2-D space–time illustrates that the updates to stack elements lay on lines with directions $(1, 1)^t$ or $(-1, +1)^t$. A projection in the $(0, -1)^t$ direction implies a linear array of $n + 1$ cells. For the Create and Push operations the cells are connected from left to right (i.e. in the direction of increasing i) and for the

Pop operation from right to left. Combining the two arrays produces a generic bidirectional array which computes all the required stack operations. A control tag must be added to the data so that cells can determine which operation is required. Four control states are needed, one for each operation Pop, Push, Create, and a Wait state where the cells do nothing except pass on the control information. Notice that the operation IsEmpty can be implemented by a Pop followed by a Push and requires no special control. Data falling off the end of the array are lost and the right end input always carries a negative value (i.e. supplies empty cell values).

Operating the array for multiple pops or pushes is shown in Fig. 5.10. In a Push operation we provide the array with an input element and the control tag is set for a Push operation. The first cell reads the data, decodes the tag, and stores the input. The control tag is then attached to the old stored data and output to the next cell. For a Pop operation we present an empty data element (-1) with an appropriate tag. The stored cell value is output to the left with the dummy and tag output right. The cell then waits for a reply from the right adjacent cell. Observe that the array requires one cell step for a Push but two steps to complete a Pop operation; if this were not the case it would be possible to perform a Pop operation and extract the wrong information. We conclude that a new operation can be performed every two cell cycles, which is independent of n, and exploits the pipelining of the updates in (5.18).

Another alternative, which results in a rather interesting systolic stack, is due to Guibas and Liang (1982) and based on extensions to the work of Leiserson (1981). We will consider how to develop this array using a number of intermediate designs. In the above example each of the cells has to be told what operations to perform by means of a control tag. Additional control translates to additional hardware in any implementation making it desirable to try and reduce the amount of control. One way to achieve this reduction is by making the cells 'state-less' so that they always compute the same operations independent of whether a push or a pop is occurring. One approach is to redefine the recurrence equations so that they have the form

$$\left.\begin{aligned} s_{i,t} = s_{i-1,t-1}, \quad & i = 1(1)n,\ t = 1(1)\ldots \\ s_{0,t} &= e_t \end{aligned}\right\} \tag{5.19a}$$

$$\left.\begin{aligned} e &= s_{0,t} \\ s_{i-1,t} = s_{i,t-1}, \quad & i = 1(1)n,\ t = 1(1)\ldots \\ s_n &= -1 \end{aligned}\right\} \tag{5.19b}$$

for a single push or pop at time t. Unrolling the equations in space–time shows that the direction vectors of the data movement are orthogonal (i.e. $(1,1)^t \times (-1,1)^t = 0$). Projecting out the time component of the space–time

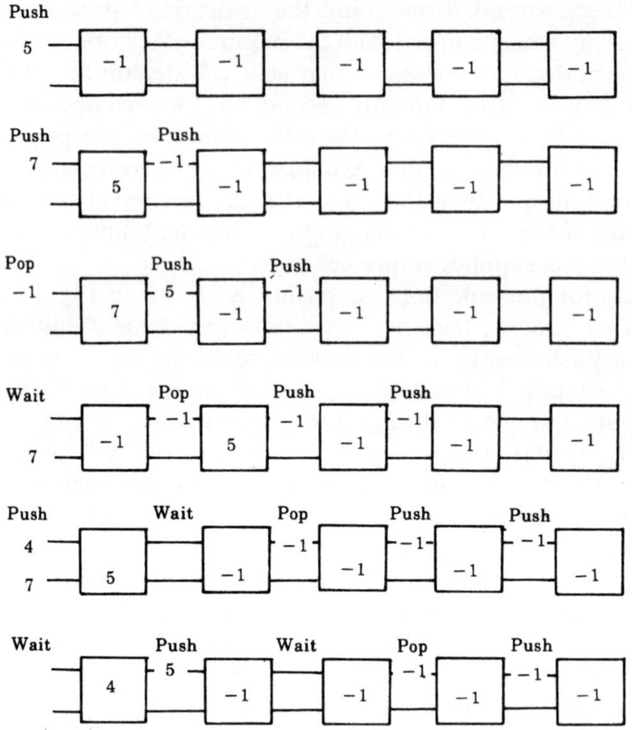

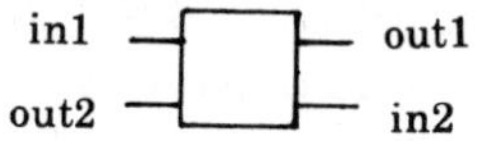


```
flag := *;

(a,b) = In1;
(c,d) = In2;

IF flag = * THEN { element := c; flag := # };
IF b = Push THEN { e:= element; element := a };
IF b = Pop  THEN { f := element; e := -1; flag := * };
IF b = Wait THEN { f := -1; e := -1 };

out1 = (e,b);
out2 = (f,-);
```

Fig. 5.10 Stack with control tags

representations produces unidirectional arrays. For (5.19a) the array has connections directed from left to right and the basic cells always compute pushes, while for (5.19b) connections are from right to left and cells compute pops. Adopting the wavefront approach for visualizing the data flow reveals that push and pop produce waves propagating in opposite directions.

So (5.19a) is really a global shift right operation while (5.19b) is a shift left operation. Next, consider what happens when we merge the two cell types to produce a single bidirectional array with cells computing a left followed by a right shift as the basic cycle. If we pop an element and then push it back on to the stack immediately the state of the stack is unchanged (i.e. a wait state). If we pop an element and push a negative value the element has truly been popped. Likewise, popping a dummy (negative) value and then pushing a real element mimics a true stack push. There is an obvious flaw in this array—it is impossible to push anything if the stack top is a non-negative element. Indeed, if by some chance the top element is negative it becomes impossible to make a pop. The important point is that the cells always compute the same function independent of what is popped or pushed at the stack top—they are essentially state-less.

To fix the array the cells need to be more intelligent and for this we need to introduce the idea of 'local' states. The simplest state a cell can detect is whether or not it contains a real stack element or is empty. If we allow cells to peek at the adjacent cells they can determine the local conditions surrounding them. For example, if a cell can look at the state of its neighbour to the right, (5.19a) can be simulated by the rewrite rule $xo \rightarrow ox$ where x denotes a full cell and o an empty one. The rule is equivalent to saying: if my cell is full and the next cell is empty then pass my value to the right. Similarly if a cell can sense the state of the left adjacent cell (5.19b) is simulated by the rule $ox \rightarrow xo$. The cells for the array above can now be implemented by sensing the right cell and applying the first rule in the first half cycle and sensing the left cell and applying the second rule in the second half cycle of a cell step. If the rules were not applied in this manner it would be possible for two full cells separated by an empty one to write to the empty cell and some information would be lost. Sensors for cells at the stack bottom are assumed to be given an occupied result and dummy cell values are always pumped left. Now suppose we start with an empty stack. To push an element we set the left sensor of the leftmost array cell (the stack top) for a full cycle and present the element to the left cell input. The first rule is applied shifting the element into the array, but the second rule is prevented from shifting it out because the left sensor is still set. On the next step, the first cell passes its element to the right. The second cell in the second half cycle will try to pass the value back unless the first cell received an element in the first half cycle. It follows that an element is moved right only if its current cell value is required by another cell. Conversely an element attempts to move itself left if a hole between it and other elements is created. Intuitively these rules are sensible. We want to keep all the stack elements in the correct order and close together, otherwise some elements could break away, move down the stack, and become difficult to retrieve. Unfortunately the stack can lock up quite easily. To demonstrate, suppose we attempt to insert three elements; the following happens

$$x\ x000$$
$$x\ 0x00$$

$$x\ xx00$$
$$x\ xx00$$

$$x\ x0x0$$
$$x\ xx00$$

where the element on the left is to be input and each pair of lines represents the two steps of each cell cycle. The state of the stack is the same in both the second and third steps and the third element has not been pushed on to the stack. The situation is cyclic and can only be broken by a pop operation.

The Guibas and Liang solution to the stack problem extends the idea of rewrite rules to allow the sensing of the neighbour and next-nearest-neighbour cells. The rule for simulating (5.19a) is $xxo \to oxo$ and the rule for (5.19b) is $oxx \to oxo$. The basic principle is to organize the stack elements so that cells are alternately full and empty and in the same order that they were input. Again rule (5.19a) is applied in the first half of a cycle and (5.19b) in the second half—thus avoiding any collision of elements. Pop and push elements can now be performed as shown in Fig. 5.11. Notice that when the stack is more than half full the empty cells are filled up from the bottom right of the array so that any free cells bubble towards the top making it easy to push elements continuously on to the stack in a time that is independent of n. Ultimately all the stack cells will be used, even though initially it looks as though the array works in an inefficient manner. Once the array is full the rewrite rule prevents any further pushes and no data is lost. Also observe that a push or a pop can only be made every four stack cycles. In fact the top of stack state can be used to determine an invariant condition which verifies that the array works correctly.

5.3.2 Queues

A queue is an ordered list in which all insertions take place at one end (the back or rear) and deletions at the other (or front). Queues arise naturally in many scheduling-type problems, for example the bank teller problem, where data or jobs must be buffered until they can be dealt with. For instance, a simple job scheduler must queue the jobs arriving so that none is lost and eventually all of them will be processed—this is trivially satisfied if a job arriving at the back of the queue will eventually become first. More sophisticated schedulers introduce priorities to jobs, so jobs with higher priorities will get processed quicker than lower-priority ones. A suitable choice of priorities and queue organizations minimizes the amount of time

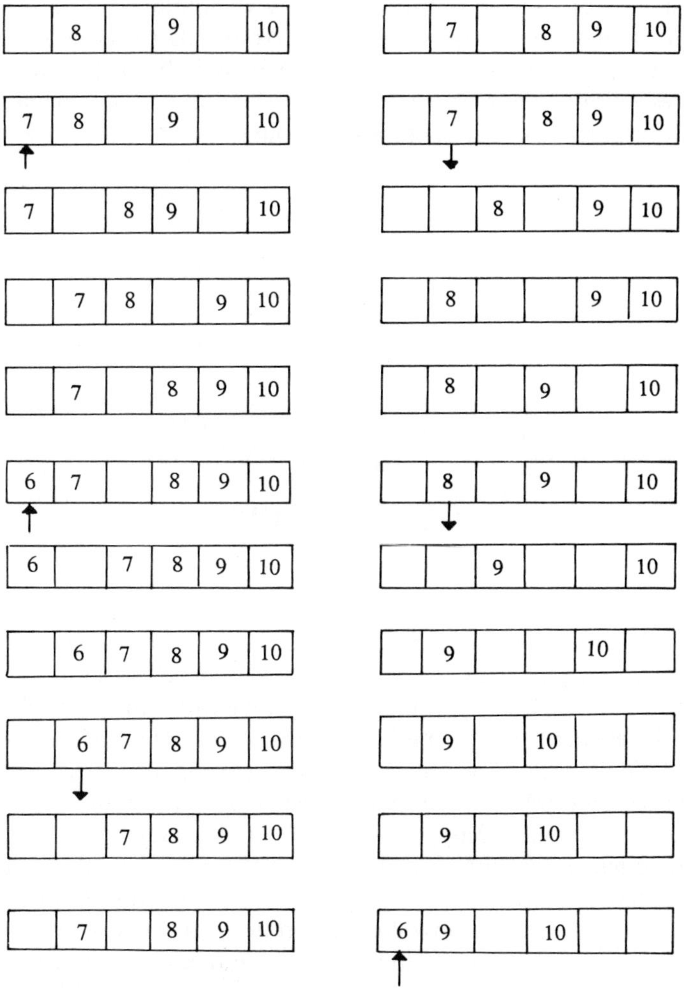

Fig. 5.11 Snapshots of a systolic stack

a job spends suspended in the queue. Below we will describe ways to implement these features on a systolic array. Extensions to multiple queues follow immediately.

Queues may be defined as abstract data types with the following operations

Create(Q), EnQueue(x,Q), DeQueue(Q), IsEmpty(Q)

which initialize an empty queue, insert element x on to the back of the queue Q, remove an element from the front of Q, and test for an empty Q respectively. In sequential programming queues are normally implemented by linked lists or arrays, the former being dynamic and the latter static. Although the dynamic implementation corresponds to the abstract idea of a queue we can only implement a fixed-size array in hardware so the systolic queue is essentially static. If we define Q to be a queue of n elements where q_i is the ith element, the EnQueue and DeQueue operations can be described as follows

$$\left.\begin{aligned} r_0 &= e \\ r_i = r_{i-1}, &\quad i = 1(1)j+1 \\ q_i &= q_i \\ q_{j+1} &= r_{j+1} \end{aligned}\right\} \tag{5.20a}$$

$$\left.\begin{aligned} e &= q_0 \\ q_{i-1} = q_i, &\quad i = 1(1)j \\ q_j &= -1 \end{aligned}\right\} \tag{5.20b}$$

where j is the current number of queue elements and r is a set of temporary variables used for pipelining the insertion. A DeQueue operation is essentially the same as a stack Pop operation in that we extract the front element and move all the elements up one position in the queue. The EnQueue operation is more difficult because we have to locate the end of the queue and then insert the element behind the others. In sequential programming the end of the queue can be marked by a cursor, which eliminates any searching and makes the queue operations independent of the queue length. Such features are prohibited in systolic design because the cursor implies random access to the cells and necessarily involves connections proportional to the length of the array. Instead we mark the front of the queue and keep a record of the number of queue items. The r_i values are then used to shift the element to the next free location and insert it. (Note: Implementing the queue operations this way in a sequential programming language is grossly inefficient and not recommended.)

Proceeding in the same manner as for the stack design we add a second subscript to produce

$$\left.\begin{aligned} r_{0,t-1} &= e_{t-1} \\ r_{i,t} = r_{i-1,t-1}, &\quad i = 1(1)j+1,\ t = 1(1)j+1 \\ q_{i,t} &= q_{i,t-1} \\ q_{j+1,t} &= r_{j+1,t} \end{aligned}\right\} \tag{5.21a}$$

and

$$\left.\begin{aligned} e_t &= q_{0,t} \\ q_{i-1,t} &= q_{i,t-1}, \quad i = 1(1)j,\ t = 1(1)j \\ q_{j,t} &= -1 \end{aligned}\right\} \tag{5.21b}$$

which can now be unrolled into space–time and the time component projected out to produce a bidirectional array. Each cell i contains q_i and r_i and cell 1 is the front. Control tags are required to switch between EnQueue and DeQueue operations with DeQueue implemented in exactly the same way as the stack Pop operation. For an EnQueue operation we use a mechanism similar to the stack Push operation except that an element passes through a cell if it is occupied. When the element in a cell is a dummy the end of the queue has been found and the r value can be inserted into the cell. The IsEmpty operation is implemented trivially by sensing the front queue element: if the cell is empty the queue must be empty. It follows that an empty queue can be created by n DeQueue operations. Notice that the actual value of j is not required explicitly in any of the operations and is purely for notational simplicity in (5.21).

A systolic queue such as that described above, although adequate, suffers from the same drawbacks as the systolic stack. Each array cell has to retain state information and decode control tags. All this extra activity must be paid for in terms of more complex hardware inside the basic cells, which in turn means more area for the whole design. As the dynamic feature of a queue has been lost by the physical constraints of implementation the cells need to be as simple as possible in order to allow more cells to be implemented in a given area. To help achieve this goal let us return to the idea of rewrite rules and exploit the similarity between the queue and stack operations. In fact the stack scheme of Guibas and Liang can be extended using the following two rules

$$nx \rightarrow xn, \qquad oon \rightarrow oox$$

where n is a new element to be inserted into the queue. The first rule obviously simulates the movement of the element along the array cells, while the second identifies the end of the queue allowing the new element to be inserted at the rear. An example of the queue operation is shown in Fig. 5.12. Each cell consists of the stack rules together with the new queue rules. The rules are applied sequentially using the queue rules first and then the stack rules.

A generalization of the stack and queue mechanisms which is particularly useful for job scheduling tasks or the maintenance of real-time order statistics is the *priority queue*. The priority queue allows elements to find their correct place in a queue according to their relative importance using a prioritizing

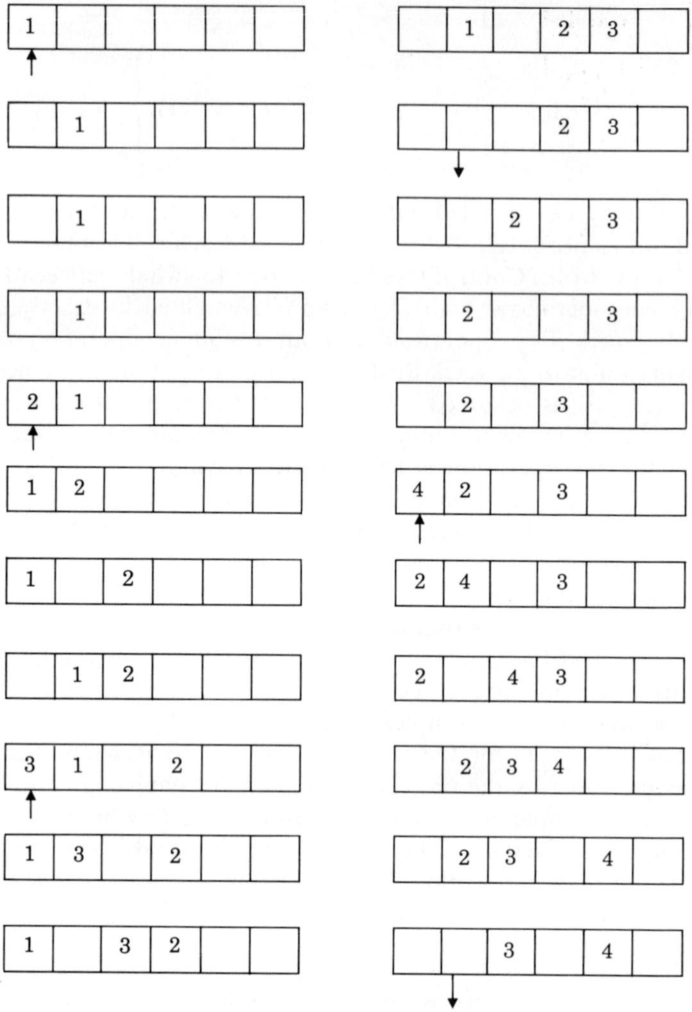

Fig. 5.12 Snapshots of a systolic queue

rule. This is best illustrated by modifying the queue rules as follows

$$n_p x_q \rightarrow x_q n_p \quad \text{if } p < q$$
$$n_p x_q \rightarrow x_p x_q \quad \text{if } p \geq q \qquad (5.22)$$
$$oon_p \rightarrow oox_p$$

where p and q are the priorities of the associated elements. A new element is inserted into the queue and filters through the cells until it finds an element of lesser priority in the next cell. The element then becomes an old element by being inserted into the queue. An element reaching the end of the queue simply becomes an old element and is placed at the end of the queue. Trivially, the rules implement a simple method of queue jumping.

Finally, observe that all these examples have used the four-cycle rule to reset the array between operations; these steps are necessary to allow the array to reset the host–array interface. To improve the efficiency of the stack or queue mechanisms we can try to reduce this interval by building safeguards into the cells which prevent data having to be moved forwards and backwards between cells unnecessarily. In this respect the work of Umeo and Nakatsaka (1987) has shown that three of the reset delay steps can be reduced to a single step, but unfortunately this requires three data registers in each cell to retain some of the old data. We also point out that the above rules require data from the nearest-neighbour cells and the next-nearest-neighbour cells, which implies that the cells must be capable of passing data through intermediate cells during the decision phase if non-planar connections are to be avoided. However, the state of a cell (full or empty) can be encoded in a single bit, so the direct connection of three consecutive cells is not unreasonable. Technically the designs must be classified as semi-systolic because next-nearest-neighbour connections are a limited form of broadcasting.

5.3.3 Trees

Trees are well-used data structures in many information-retrieval algorithms. Indeed work on implementing operations for relational databases and tree algorithms can be found in Kung and Lehman (1980) and Song (1981). The reader unfamiliar with these concepts is referred to Bonuccelli *et al.* (1989). The idea of tree architectures is not a new concept. Consequently we will only consider two very simple algorithms which show the general principle.

A tree is a collection of elements called nodes, one of which is distinguished as the *root*, together with a relation that places a hierarchical structure on the nodes. Formally a tree can be defined recursively as follows.

1. A single node itself is a tree, and is also the root.
2. Let n be a node and T_i be trees with roots denoted by n_i for $i = 1(1)k$. A new tree is constructed by making n the father of nodes n_i such that T_i are subtrees of the root.

General trees have an arbitrary value for k but cannot be easily translated into hardware designs in which the connections between nodes are constant (thus contradicting our design heuristics in Chapter 1). However, when $k = 2$ the useful class of binary trees is defined, which can be constructed with area-efficient layouts. Figure 1.4(e) illustrates the binary or H-tree (because

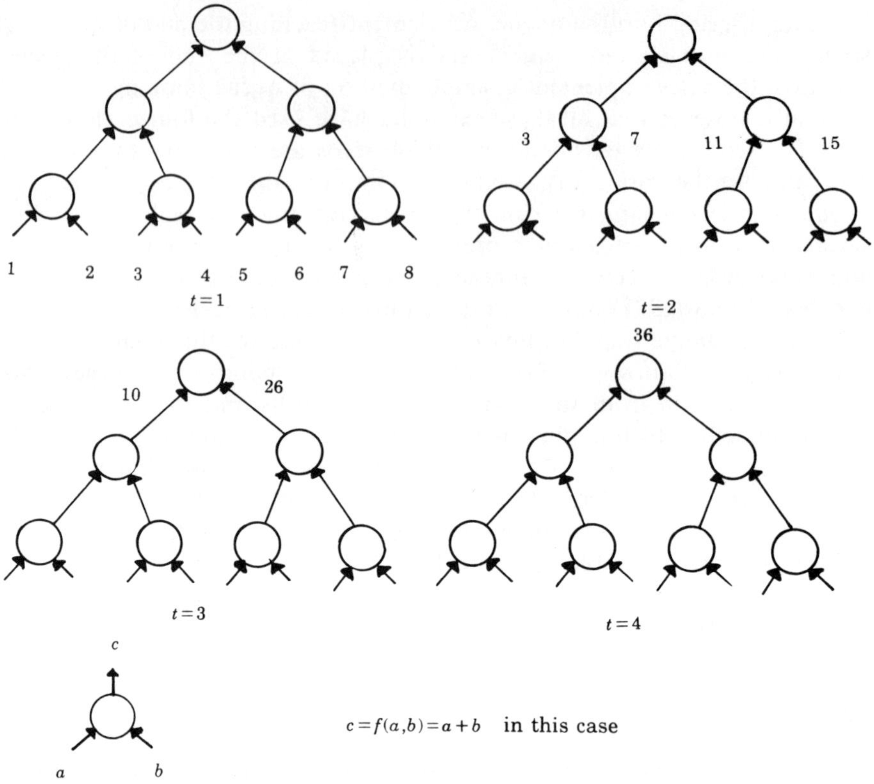

Fig. 5.13 Fan-in tree (expression evaluation)

of its appearance). Binary trees turn out to have wide applications in expression evaluation as well as searching.

First consider the computation of arithmetic operations. It is well known that the order in which subexpressions are computed can be represented by a binary tree. In sequential processing such trees are used in conjunction with tree-traversal algorithms to generate postfix or prefix notation which makes the expression easier to evaluate. This idea has been adopted for parallel processing by assigning the operations associated with an expression to the interior nodes of a tree, and inputting the data at the leaves. Figure 5.13 shows a simple example. At each step of the algorithm all the nodes perform the associated operation on data retrieved from the two sibling nodes and pass on a result to the father node. As computation progresses data are pipelined up the tree with data emerging at the tree root. This technique is useful for a wide range of computations and is essentially a data pipelining technique. The tree is often termed a fan-in tree for obvious reasons. A binary tree of height h requires $2^{(h+1)} - 1$ nodes and a tree with n leaf nodes requires a height of $h = \log_2 n$. It should be clear that h remains small even for large n, giving the fan-in network a very short latency. Unfortunately a large number of cell nodes are also required.

In search applications we are normally given a key (i.e. something to search for) and require to locate data items which match the key. Usually the search time is greatly diminished if the data are sorted into a certain order with respect to the search key. When data are sorted using the relations '<', '>', and '=' a binary tree can be used to partition the search space by a series of bisections that converge on to the required data items. In a parallel setting we adopt a binary tree as the architecture and distribute the key as shown in Fig. 5.14. Data are held in the tree leaves and the key is duplicated as it

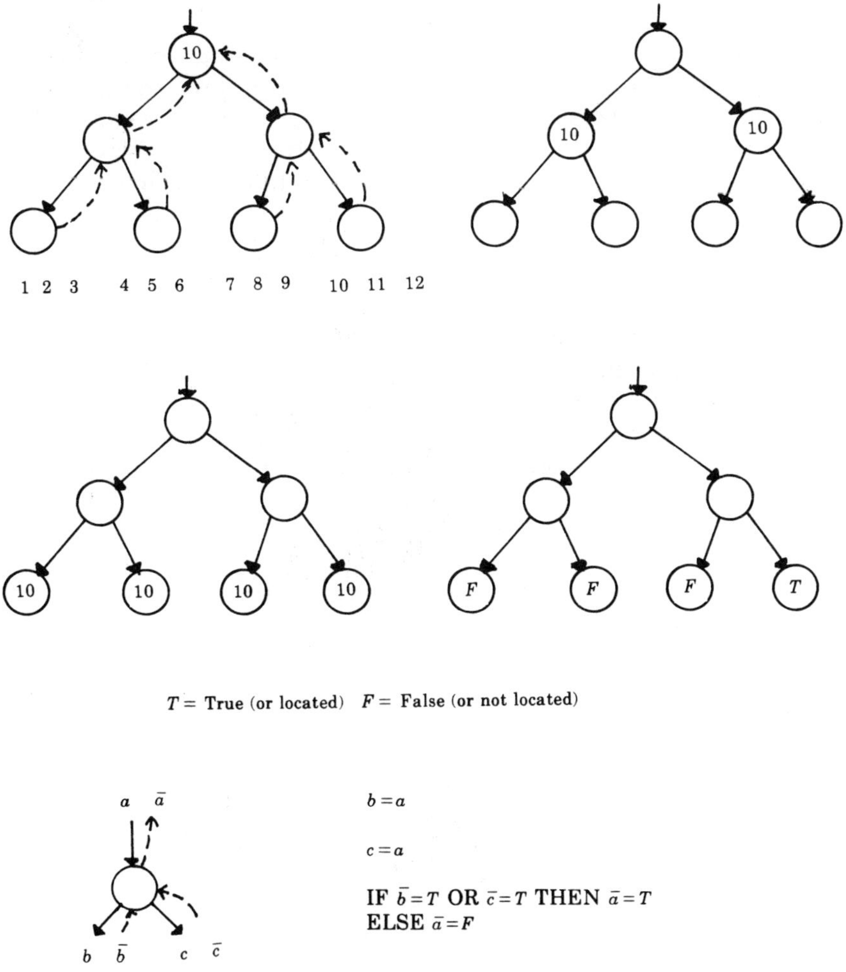

Fig. 5.14 Fan-out tree (for searching)

filters down the tree. On reaching the leaves the whole data space is searched simultaneously to locate the data item. The result is then propagated back up the tree to the root. Notice that the tree architecture is bidirectional and that different search keys can be pipelined. The forward distribution of a key is often known as a fan-out, and consequently the design is termed a fan-out tree. Many extensions to these basic array forms are possible, for example we can substitute queues for the leaves and reduce the number of levels in the tree. Alternatively more general trees can be adopted rather than binary trees, although in this case efficient layout of the tree and avoidance of long connections are more difficult.

5.4 Graph algorithms and semi-rings

We have already seen how graphs can be used to define a variety of different concepts such as data structures, algorithm control flow, and array topologies. In fact the generality of the graph concept makes it a universal tool for problem representation. Applications (see Horowitz and Sahni (1978) among others) include the analysis of electrical circuits, finding shortest routes, project planning (i.e. critical path analysis), identification of chemical structures, fingerprint matching, statistical analysis, genetics, cybernetics, linguistics (regular grammars etc.), and the social sciences. It is impossible to deal with all these applications individually. Fortunately graphs can be represented by matrices and operations on graphs can be interpreted as linear algebra or table manipulation problems. For example, suppose $G(V, E)$ is a graph with n vertices and e edges (see Chapter 2 for definition). An $n \times n$ matrix A is an adjacency matrix when $a_{ij} = 1$, if there is an edge between vertex i and j, and zero otherwise (see Fig. 5.15). A natural extension is the

(a)

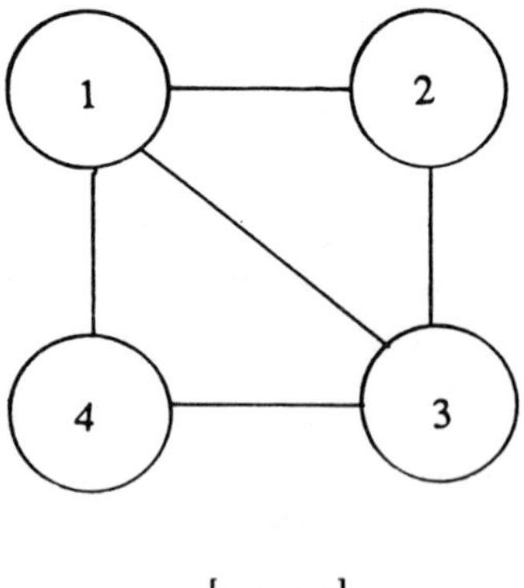

(b)

$$\begin{bmatrix} 0 & 1 & 1 & 1 \\ 1 & 0 & 1 & 0 \\ 1 & 1 & 0 & 1 \\ 1 & 0 & 1 & 0 \end{bmatrix}$$

Fig. 5.15 Graph (a) and (b) adjacency matrix

cost matrix C where c_{ij} is a real number representing some cost associated with the edge between i and j. The idea is trivially extended to digraphs.

One particular graph problem that arises frequently in networking and is associated with many practical applications is the so-called path problem. Given a cost matrix describing some graph G and an initial node S from G the following problems arise naturally:

1. Find a path p from S to a specified node T in G such that the cost of getting from S to T is minimized.
2. Find the shortest path from S to every other node in G.
3. Find the shortest paths between every pair of nodes in G.

Of these problems 3 is the most difficult.

Now suppose that A is the $(n \times n)$ adjacency matrix of a digraph, and $p > 0$ is some integer. The entries of the matrix A^p give the number of paths of length p from each node to every other (this can be proved by induction on p). It follows that

$$P = \bar{A} = I + A + A^2 + \cdots + A^n \tag{5.23}$$

with the element $p_{ij} = 1$ if $\bar{a}_{ij} > 0$ and zero otherwise. Clearly this matrix shows whether a path exists between node i and j, and if such a path is to exist it must be less than or equal to n in length. We conclude that the path problem reduces to computing the first n powers of the matrix A and forming the summation (5.23). In general $A^r = A \times A^{r-1}$ for $r > 1$ so that $O(n^3)$ sequential operations are required per multiplication, yielding $O(n^4)$ operations in total. Using the matrix product arrays in Chapter 2 implies that (5.23) can be solved in $O(n^2)$ time using an array of $O(n^2)$ cells. Unfortunately this approach is rather naive and not very efficient because the matrices must be fetched repeatedly from the host to the array. However, the path problem can be reformulated by defining a cost matrix C as follows

$$C = (c_{ij}) = \begin{cases} c_{ij} & \text{cost of moving from } i \text{ to } j \\ 0 & \text{staying at the same place} \\ \infty & \text{no arcs from } i \text{ to } j \end{cases} \tag{5.24}$$

and using the recurrence

$$\begin{aligned} C^{(0)} &= C \\ C^{(k)} = c_{ij}^{(k)} &= \min(c_{ij}^{(k-1)}, c_{ik}^{(k-1)} + c_{kj}^{(k-1)}), \quad i, j = (1)n \end{aligned} \tag{5.25}$$

for $k = 1(1)n$. The matrix $C^{(n)}$ contains the shortest (or minimum cost) path between each node and every other. The method works as follows. At the kth stage $C^{(k)}$ contains entries recording the number of paths between every pair of nodes using only the nodes $1, \ldots, k$ as intermediate steps. We could proceed to a space–time diagram and project out possible arrays but it is simpler to notice that (5.25) has an inner product appearance (i.e. interpret min as $+$ and $+$ as $\times$) so that the arrays in Chapters 2 and 3 can be used to construct a composite array using the building block approach.

The correspondence between graph and matrix computations is no coincidence and is discussed at great length by Carré (1979). Informally Carré's work amounts to the exploitation of algebraic structures known as semi-rings. A semi-ring may be defined as a quadruple

$$S_r = (S, R, `+', `*') \tag{5.26}$$

where S is a set of elements, '+' and '*' are two binary operations which are closed on S, and R is a list of axioms of the form:

R[0]: For any a, b, c in S, $(a + b) + c = a + (b + c)$.

R[1]: There is an element 0 in S called the zero element and

$$a + 0 = 0 + a = a.$$

R[2]: For each a in S there is an element called the negative of a denoted $-a$ such that $a + (-a) = (-a) + a = 0$.

R[3]: For any a, b in S, $a + b = b + a$.

R[4]: For any a, b in S, $(a * b) * c = a * (b * c)$.

R[5]: For any a, b, c in S, $a * (b + c) = a * b + a * c$ and $(b + c) * a = b * a + c * a$.

The ring is commutative if $a * b = b * a$ for all a, b in S and a ring with a unit element satisfies $a * 1 = 1 * a = a$ for all a, b in S. Some examples of semi-rings are given below

1. Real arithmetic, where S is the set of real numbers, '+' is addition and '*' is multiplication, the unit element is the one, and the null element is zero (i.e. numerical algorithms).

2. A comparison algebra, with the real numbers augmented with the elements $+\infty$ and $-\infty$, unit element zero, and null element ∞. This semi-ring also obeys the rules $\infty + a = \infty$ and $(-\infty) + 1 = -\infty$ (sorting).

3. Boolean arithmetic, where $S = \{0, 1\}$, '+' = logical 'OR' and '*' = logical 'AND', and the unity and null elements are zero and one respectively (bit serial algorithms).

4. Matrix arithmetic, with S the set of $n \times n$ real matrices, and '+' = matrix addition, '*' matrix multiplication (linear algebra). The unit element is the $n \times n$ identity matrix, and the null element is the null matrix.

Now semi-rings define algebras for certain types of applications, the practical significance of which is that seemingly different problems yield the same data flow and data dependencies but interpret the basic elements and operations differently. As systolic arrays place emphasis on data dependencies and not the cell operations, designs produced in one semi-ring can be transported to other semi-rings. It follows that the inner product step which is a basis for all the semi-rings defines generic cells which simply require a reinterpretation of the basic computations. Thus the designs we developed in this and previous chapters such as real arithmetic for numerical problems can be applied readily to problems such as sorting, searching, and graph algorithms by formulating them in terms of appropriate semi-ring algorithms. A particularly useful application of this relationship is to notice (Rote 1985) that

$$(I - A)^{-1} = I + A + A^2 + A^3 + \cdots . \tag{5.27}$$

It follows that the algebraic path problem (5.23) is equivalent to matrix inversion. Figure 3.13 shows a systolic array for matrix inversion. It is now clear that the path problem can be solved in $O(n)$ steps with $O(n^2)$ processors. In general all we need to do is allow the inner product cell to be programmable so that arrays can switch their character to match any of the semi-rings we want to implement. Systolic algorithms which exploit generic or programmable cells are considered in Chapter 7. The concept of a Boolean semi-ring is also used for bit serial design in Chapter 6.

5.5 Design principles

In this chapter we have considered systolic designs for a range of non-numerical problems. Although we do not claim to have covered the area in detail the examples presented illustrate the major problems likely to be encountered with such applications. In particular the reader should be aware of two design features: first, the gradual movement away from algorithms dictating program control flow to algorithms defining data structure operations; second, the effects of conditional statements on the design methodology and the limitations they place on the applicability of systolic concepts. We summarize the main design principles below.

Problem duality

This was introduced in the previous chapter to link matrix and table generation problems thus allowing the reuse of previously developed arrays. In Section 5.1 this theme was continued to develop designs for systolic pattern matchers using a linear algebra interpretation and a table specification of the problem. Both mechanisms lead to for-loop programs but the table method leads to a more geometric form which has a natural interpretation in space–time. In particular a 2-D table together with its generation rule can be used as a data dependency graph to project a 1-D array or as a 2-D array projected from higher dimensions. Applying the principle of array unrolling then allows the recovery of the original higher-dimensional data dependency graph. The unrolled graphs can be used to develop arrays with high throughput by pipelining multiple wavefronts of data.

Conditional statements

Problems with the design methodology arise when the loops of an algorithm can be conditional. In Chapter 4 we briefly considered the problem of potentially unbounded (i.e. while and repeat) loops for semi-infinite and infinite tables. The solution proposed was to partition the table into finite-sized blocks and to compute the blocks on a fixed-size array using multiple passes of data. This approach is fine provided that the body of the loop consists only of assignments, because a block of computation produces a finite-sized data dependency graph. When the loop body of an algorithm contains conditionals as well as assignments further difficulties arise. Section 5.2 considered the problem of systolic sorting. In sorting, conditional statements are an integral part of the algorithm because the decision of whether or not to exchange elements imposes the ordering relationship on the given list. Unrolling a loop program with conditional statements leads to different loop-less programs depending upon the result of the conditionals. As unrolled loops are mapped into space–time by our design methodology it follows that we associate one data dependency graph with each problem instance. Even allowing for instances that produce the same path through the program, the number of different graphs could be enormous. Although systolic design is geared towards algorithmically specialized devices one array for each problem instance is not practical. Specialized, in this context, means solving a class of problems, for example producing a design for sorting *all* lists of size n. The solution is to impose a single, global set of data dependencies. Such a set of dependencies could obviously be produced by unifying the dependency graphs for each instance—but this amounts to performing the worst-case number of comparisons. The more inefficient sequential sorting algorithms meet this criteria and result in quite useful systolic arrays. More sophisticated and faster sequential programs such as mergesort and quicksort take advantage of conditionals to reduce the number of comparisons required to sort a list and cannot be used for effective array designs. This is because the most efficient sorting algorithms tend to make comparisons between non-adjacent list elements forcing irregularities in the unrolled data dependency representation. Smoothing out these irregularities (say by retiming) is possible but introduces unacceptable delay overheads.

Remark Note that the edit distance array includes a conditional in the loop body but always results in an assignment; only the right-hand side of this assignment is affected by the conditional result so that the worst-case criterion is satisfied.

Systolic data structures

Section 5.3 considered the mapping of basic operations associated with common data structures on to systolic arrays. Applying the design methodology requires a change in perspective. In particular the recurrences examined are related to individual operations on data and not the driving or control algorithm applying the operation to the data. Obviously if the control algorithm was unrolled in space–time the occurrence of data structure operations would be intermingled with other operations. As a result the data dependencies of the required operation would be obscured. Another problem is that the application of data structure operations may be dependent on conditionals so that the order in which operations are applied to the data structure and the period between their application are not generally known until run time. Unfortunately deriving systolic algorithms for each data structure operation is only a part of the solution. The interaction between the data structure and the control algorithm is also important. For this reason unified or generic arrays which provide all the required operations of the data structure are required. For data structures with many operations the potential arbitrary interleaving of operations makes the design of compatible operations extremely difficult. As a result efficiency is often sacrificed in favour of correctness. In many cases the design task is largely *ad hoc* and relies heavily on the intuitive use of control tags to switch between operations. Notable exceptions are the stacks and queues based on local rewrite rules. Indeed, the reader is referred to the work of Probst and Li (1988) which develops the idea of specification axioms and transformation rules for the verification of systolic networks including stacks and queues. Because the operations with data structures are mapped on to a generic array it is not surprising that the connection topology tends to model the conceptual view of the data structuring. For example, matrix operations produce 1-D (vector) and 2-D (matrix) arrays while stacks and queues resemble linked lists, and tree architectures are physical realizations of trees.

Semi-rings

The changes in perspectives offered by duality and the interpretation of non-matrix problems as linear algebra problems is useful in reducing design time. The logical conclusion of this principle is the use of similarities in algebraic structures such as semi-rings. The mapping of algorithms with identical control flow in different instances of semi-rings is much more general than allowing graph algorithms to be converted into matrix problems. Indeed, any algorithm which is composed of operations which obey the rules of a semi-ring may result in a well-studied systolic solution. It follows that one of the first tasks of a designer is to consider whether a problem can be reformulated in a manner that produces data dependencies similar to other designs. To realize such correspondences requires the working knowledge of a number of systolic algorithms—*a working set*. In this and the previous two chapters we have provided such a set of algorithms. Many other systolic algorithms have appeared in the literature, and the designs presented here together with the exercises provide examples of most types of data flow. Use of techniques such as semi-rings, tables, or linear algebra formulations together with the transformation and projection methodology allow the extension of these basic data flow templates to new algorithms.

Exercises

1. Derive column and row stationary systolic arrays for the edit distance computation. Comment on the efficiency and indicate the circumstances in which the arrays might be used.
2. Explain how the edit distance array would have to be modified if the whole table was required. In particular discuss the number of input–output connections and the loading–unloading of the design.
3. Show how the edit distance table could be computed on a fixed-size array of $k > 0$ processors.
   [Hint: Partition the table into $k \times k$ blocks.]
4. The dynamic programming problem for determining optimal binary search trees for n items can be given the form

$$c_{ij} = w_{ij} + \min_{i<k<j} (c_{ik} + c_{kj}), \quad i = 1(1)n,\ i < j$$

   where w_{ij} is the weight, c_{ij} is the cost of the optimal tree for items i to j, and c_{1n} is the cost of the full tree. Derive systolic arrays for evaluating the recurrence.
5. Discuss the problems of implementing a systolic sorter when the elements to be sorted are records of information. Repeat the exercise for stacks and queues.
6. Show that a priority queue can be used to simulate a sorting network and explain how the maintenance of statistics such as max and min could be implemented on a single array.
7. Prove that a systolic stack will always be ready for a new Push or Pop operation after four steps. Repeat the question for queues.
   [Hint: Derive an invariant condition on the array cells.]
8. By using extra cell values show that the number of cycles between each

operation on a stack can be reduced. What is the optimal number of cycles?

9. Using the concept of a semi-ring discuss the construction of generic hexagonal and rectangular arrays with respect to (a) compatibility of problems, (b) the basic cell complexity, (c) flexibility of the communication network.
10. The join operation in relational databases can be defined as follows: for two relations R and S on attributes A in R and B in S, a result relation T is defined by concatenating each tuple in R with each tuple in S where $A(\mathrm{Op})B$ is one of the operators $=$, $<$, $>$, $\leq$, $\geq$ and $\neq$. Derive a generic systolic array for computing the join operation.
[Hint: Output the result as a matrix R in which r_{ij} is one if the relation is valid and zero otherwise.]
11. Show how a fan-in tree can be used to compute (a) the inner product of two vectors, (b) the matrix–vector computation, (c) the comparison of two strings.
12. By treating a binary fan-in tree as a data dependency graph show how the mergesort array in Fig. 5.9 can be derived using a suitable projection.
13. Using fan-in and fan-out trees discuss ways of loading and unloading linear arrays with data. Comment on the efficiency and any limitations of such methods.

6
IMPROVING ARRAY PERFORMANCE

The previous chapters have defined a methodology for producing systolic designs and developed a collection of useful algorithms and connection topologies using this methodology as a guiding principle. Consequently the value of systolic design may seem to have been demonstrated. However, transformation methods do not tell us directly if one design will be better or worse than another. We must search through the possible transformations to find better efficiency, reduced area, or improved time properties. The design methodology does not place emphasis on the operations associated with nodes in a data dependency graph—only on the data flow. Consequently different designs can only be compared according to a standard notion of unit area (for a cell) and unit time (for a single cell step). In practice different designs may require more complex operations than others which cause increases in cell area and the basic cell cycle time. It follows that comparing different systolic algorithms with respect to area and time is only a first pass in eliminating some of the possible designs. Surviving designs must then be considered with respect to the implementation heuristics defined in Chapter 1. In particular problems such as input bandwidth, wire length, and the construction of basic components become important.

The design heuristics are mutable—they embody what is practical—and depend upon the technological capabilities prevailing at the time. Thus as time passes and manufacturing processes improve what we consider to be the best design (i.e. the one to implement) will change. Indeed it may not be practical to implement the design which the designer considers to be the first choice. For example, many scientific problems require matrices with thousands of elements. With current technology (*circa* 1990) it is not practical to build systolic arrays with thousands or millions of processors. This restriction does not devalue the concept of systolic computation but in fact strengthens its position. We can generate feasible designs which help to define the direction of movement, and create an impetus for technological change, which will make such designs practical. Unfortunately, for designers who need to implement algorithms today these arguments are rather academic. Indeed, given that the best design, on paper, cannot be implemented economically a different design must be developed and used in its place. We conclude that it is desirable to consider ways in which to improve the design performance in terms of area, time, and cell utilization.

The design methodology ensures only that the data dependencies of a problem are satisfied and obey certain axioms which characterize the design as systolic. In this and the next chapter we will consider some of the practical issues associated with the implementation of systolic designs and how to overcome them. For example, the designs considered in previous chapters have made some rather naive assumptions, which may be enumerated as follows:

1. The data can be presented and retrieved from the array on a very large number of input and output connections.
2. The number of processing elements available is unlimited.
3. Very little attention has been given to how cells will finally be implemented.
4. Once a design is implemented the cells will always function correctly and never become faulty.

Consideration of such problems leads to additional criteria for choosing the design to implement. Below we will introduce some techniques for improving designs. Among these topics are *multipass*, *interleaving* and *folding*, *block partitioning*, and ways to remove feedback from designs. On the more practical side we consider briefly the problem of *bit serial* versus *bit parallel* design and its effect on cell area and input–output connections. In addition, some ideas on *fault tolerance* for coping with permanent and transient errors once the array has been constructed are outlined. Although expressed informally these techniques have wide applicability and can be employed in a considerable number of designs.

6.1 Multipass algorithms

Hwang and Cheng (1982) considered the idea of partitioning matrices to solve arbitrarily large linear systems on fixed-size arrays. They employed a direct technique using an iteration to solve subproblems which build up the whole problem solution. More recently Heller (1985) has considered a similar partitioning for solving large matrix problems on small fixed-size systolic arrays. The technique utilized in both schemes is known as multipass, and can be summarized by using a simple analogy with sequential sorting techniques. Sorting can be divided roughly into two categories, external and internal. Internal sorting occurs when the whole list of elements to be sorted can be loaded into the main memory of a machine and processed without access to external storage devices. External sorting applies to lists which are too large to be accommodated in the memory at one go. In the former case algorithms will run very quickly. In the latter we must repeatedly load chunks of data into the available memory and employ algorithms to sort the whole list in a series of passes separated by the loading and unloading of data. The two problems lead to very different algorithms and as one might imagine internal techniques are simpler to construct. In systolic schemes the fixed internal memory size corresponds to fixed-size arrays and consequently fixed numbers of input–output connections. Intuitively this limiting of the number of cells implies that not all the required data sequences can be pumped into the array simultaneously.

We have already seen an example of a multipass algorithm in the form of a systolic ring (see Chapter 4). Essentially the cell efficiency is improved by limiting the size of the array and wrapping the output back to the input. Each cycle around the ring is a pass of the data through the array. The idea works because the cell latency is sufficient to allow all the input data to be input before any output occurs. It follows that unused cells at the end of the array can be removed. In a systolic ring the timing of the data is critical to success. In the example of Chapter 4 no time is lost and no buffering of data values is required—this is the ideal situation. Clearly, if data on the current pass begin output before the original input is finished buffers must be added to delay and resynchronize the data. Conversely when there is a delay between the last input entering the array and the start of the output no resynchronization is required and the delay between input and output can be used to derive an upper bound on the array size.

Unfortunately the size of the systolic ring described is still dependent on the problem size. Ideally, and to cope with cases 1 and 2 above, the array should be independent of problem size, especially if the problem bounds can become very large. A true multipass design is illustrated by the cascaded iteration array for the Jacobi iterative method (see Figs 3.9 and 3.10). The number of iterations in the Jacobi method is variable and dependent upon the convergence rate of the iteration matrix. It follows that a very large number of iterations may be required (although usually they are bounded and of reasonable size). Clearly it is not practical to build an array with an infinite number or even a large number of linear arrays. Even with a bound on the number of iterations (say $k > 0$) the fixed-size array may still be significantly large. For a multipass scheme k passes of the data on a single linear array such as the one in Fig. 3.10 yield a time complexity $O(nk)$. For k arrays the delay is proportional to k and $O(2n - k)$ delay cycles will be required for buffering the output data leaving the array before the next iteration of the method (second pass) can be started. Between these two extremes lie a number of designs with $0 < r \leq k$. The choice of r is arbitrary and can be made to satisfy practical limitations. Also, note that because r can be constant the architecture is independent of the matrix size (provided the matrix is banded). Thus in a multipass design we trade off the reduction in cells against the increase in computation time and the degree of data buffering.

6.1.1 Additive splitting

The idea of multipass computation can be generalized for matrix computations by using an additive splitting of the form

$$A = A_1 + A_2 + \cdots + A_i + \cdots + A_m, \quad i = 1(1)m \tag{6.1}$$

for an $n \times n$ matrix A. When A is a band matrix with bandwidth w the size of a systolic array is usually proportional to the bandwidth and requires $O(w)$ cells. Consequently a fixed-size systolic array implies $O(\bar{w})$ cells where $\bar{w} \leq w$. A simple multipass scheme is produced by choosing the A_i to have bandwidths $\bar{w}_i \leq \bar{w}$, $i = 1(1)m$. As an example consider the band matrix–vector problem

$$Ax = y. \tag{6.2}$$

This is solved for $\bar{w} \geq 1$ using the above splitting and the recurrence

$$\begin{aligned} y &:= 0 \\ y &:= y + A_i x, \quad i = 1(1)m \end{aligned} \tag{6.3}$$

where each basic operation is a matrix–vector computation. Referring back to Fig. 2.8 shows that (6.3) can be solved using m passes of data through the array, one for each A_i. The y and x values need to be brought from the external (or host) device m times. Note that an unrolling of (6.3) to produce an array similar to the iterative array considered above is not permitted because the matrix A_i changes from one iteration to the next. However, we can replace the matrix–vector equations by the recurrence form used for Fig. 2.8 thus deriving the multipass array directly from space–time data dependencies. There is little motivation for this latter approach because the matrix–vector array is already known. It is trivial to observe that (6.3) can be evaluated by repeated use of this design.

When the matrix bandwidth is $\bar{w}$ the array has $\bar{w}$ cells. For matrices of order n the computation of a single pass is $2n + \bar{w}$ inner product steps so that the total computation time is $\mathcal{T} = m(2n + \bar{w})$ steps. It follows that in order to minimize the time and area we should try to minimize m and $\bar{w}$ (the order of the matrix will be considered later). When $\bar{w} = 1$, $m = w$ and the solution is achieved using single elemental 'diagonal'-type matrices and a single inner product cell. Alternatively when $\bar{w} = n$ and $m = 2$ a dense matrix product can be computed on just n cells rather than $2n - 1$ using two passes, one for the lower triangular multiplication ($y_1 = Lx$) and the second for the upper triangular multiplication ($y_2 = Ux$). The product (6.2) is then given by $y = y_1 + y_2$ where $A = L + U$. Finally, when $\bar{w} = w$ and $m = 1$ we have the normal one-pass systolic array.

It should be clear that multipass admits a wide range of area/time trade-offs which can be used to meet practical design constraints. Unfortunately this flexibility does not come for free. In a single-pass scheme the data are only brought from the external device once. In a multipass scheme repeated accesses to the data are required which can adversely affect the performance of the array, especially if the controlling device is itself slow.

For more complex multipass strategies the overhead associated with this external access can destroy any advantages gained by using the reduced array in the first place.

6.1.2 Block splittings

Now, (6.1) can be termed a linear splitting because it splits whole matrices into simple linear combinations of sparser matrices. Additive splittings also apply to matrices and can be extended to 2-D table generation. For example, let

$$A = \begin{bmatrix} A_{11} & A_{12} & \cdots & A_{m1} \\ A_{21} & & & \vdots \\ \vdots & & & \vdots \\ A_{m1} & \cdots & \cdots & A_{mm} \end{bmatrix} \tag{6.4}$$

where $k \times m = n$ determines the block size for k, a positive constant. The matrix–vector computation (6.2) can be reformulated as

$$y_i := y_i + A_{ij}x_j, \quad i = 1(1)m, \quad j = 1(1)m \tag{6.5}$$

so that y_i and x_j represent the partitions $(y_{(i-1)k+1}, \ldots, y_{(ik)})^t$ and $(x_{(j-1)k+1}, \ldots, x_{(jk)})^t$ respectively. It should be clear that we can process $m \times m$ subproblems on a fixed-size array with maximum bandwidth $w \leq 2m - 1$. A simple matrix–vector array requires at most $\mathscr{T} = 2m + (2m - 1) = 4m - 1$ steps and $\mathscr{A} = 2m - 1$ cells, giving a total time of $\mathscr{T} = m(4m - 1)$ steps with $m = n/k$. Note that this block splitting can be applied to dense as well as banded matrices and could also be applied to (6.3) to derive even smaller arrays.

The principle extends readily to more complex splittings such as matrix product and can also be used to produce multipass table-generating algorithms. For example, in the edit distance table generation defined by (5.7) and (5.3) the table can be partitioned into blocks P_{ij} and the blocks generated in the order $t = i + j - 1$ where the tth pass produces block P_{ij}. If $m \times m$ blocks are used the 2-D array reduces to an $m \times m$ mesh, and by collecting the row and column data of different partitions we can overlap successive computations using multiple wavefronts of data on the mesh to reduce the computation time still further. The same principle applies to the 1-D array in Fig. 5.4. Note that because m can be chosen arbitrarily the arrays can be considered as practical possibilities (indeed a silicon chip version of the edit distance array has been proposed). Again nothing is for free and additive splittings for multipass computations have to be optimized by finding a balance between the number of passes and the time for a single pass. We point out that in our example the number of passes is reduced only by increasing $\bar{w}$, while the duration of a pass is affected by modifying the array design.

6.2 Interleaving, folding, and double pipes

Multipass computation improves efficiency by reducing cell count and pipelining subproblems on the resulting small array. Often it is the computation time which is the key problem (and is usually the motivation for parallel processing in the first place). For example, changing the number of cells in a matrix–vector scheme does not reduce the $2n$ term in the timing equation. Consequently we are usually more interested in improving efficiency without lengthening, and if possible reducing, the total input length. A common trait of many systolic designs is that some cycles are wasted by neutral elements that are used solely for achieving computation synchronization. These elements are often introduced as a result of retiming and pipelining of variables in order to remove broadcasting and thus achieve nearest-neighbour connections. It follows that if a method for filling these neutral elements could be found the design efficiency would increase automatically. Interleaving, folding, and double pipes are ways to produce this increased efficiency.

6.2.1 Interleaving

Interleaving exploits the fact that input data patterns incorporating neutral elements can often be decomposed into mutually disjoint data sets. For example, in the matrix-vector example of Chapter 2, the diagonally ordered input pattern consists of a real matrix element followed by a synchronizing element. Placing spurious non-zeros into one of the 'holes' will not affect the computation (try an example to prove this is correct). It follows that the array input can be treated as two disjoint matrix–vector computations out of phase with each other. Similarly the hexagonal arrays in Chapters 2 and 3 allow three disjoint problems to be overlapped. It follows that three matrix products, *LU* decompositions, or two matrix–vector computations can be solved simultaneously on the same array. Normally this result would only be of significance if we had a sequence of independent problem instances to solve so that each instance could be pipelined or overlapped with the others. Unfortunately the results of one problem will often influence the computations later on in the algorithm so the result is not very useful in general. But, if we use interleaving in conjunction with multipass schemes, sequences of virtually identical problems and arrays which do benefit from interleaving can be generated. For example, we could compute the odd and even pairs y_{2i-1} and y_{2i} of (6.3) by interleaving techniques and then sum the disjoint partial results. This is a non-trivial problem for the design method because the summation has a less regular data dependency structure than the original scheme and is complicated by the overlapping of array operation and the sum. Interleaving as described is a fairly obvious way of improving cell efficiency and also improves computation time by running passes in a parallel overlapped manner. Observe that the time improvement due to interleaving is offset against the extra work to sum up the partial results.

6.2.2 Folding

To improve efficiency without multipass arrangements requires arguments based on folding mechanisms. Consider the diamond shapes shown in Fig. 6.1. These could represent the bounding polygon describing the input pattern for a matrix–vector or hexagonal array input belonging to dense and banded matrix problems. To apply a folding technique we have three basic options.

1. Space folding, that is fold the data along the line DB.
2. Time folding, that is fold the data along AC (or A″C″).
3. Space–time folding, that is fold the data along lines S_1 or S_2.

The essential motivation behind folding is to observe that the axes BD and AC represent time and space respectively. Consequently option 1 implies savings in area, 2 savings in time, and 3 reduction in both area and time. From the viewpoint of efficiency category 3 is most interesting and as would be expected more difficult to produce.

In space folding the size of the array is reduced but maps two data elements on to the same space location. Thus we must retime computations in the triangle ABD to skew them relative to BDC so that folding allows the skewed data elements to slot into the dummy element pattern of ADB. Intuitively this yields a 100 per cent cell utilization, the same as an interleaving scheme, but in addition also reduces the cell count for the same computation time.

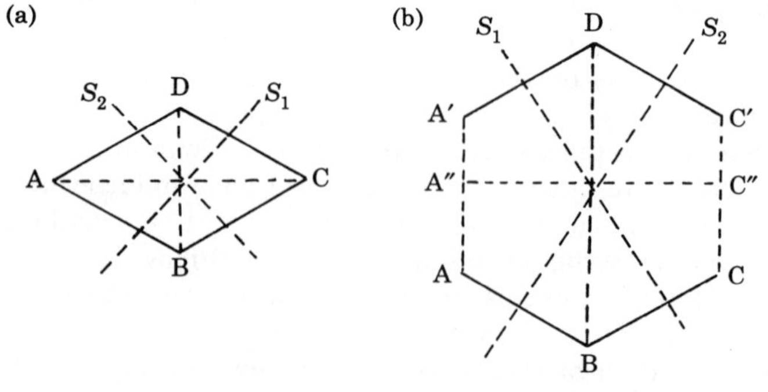

Fig. 6.1 Folding mechanism: (a) dense case ($w = 2n - 1$); (b) banded case ($w \ll n$)

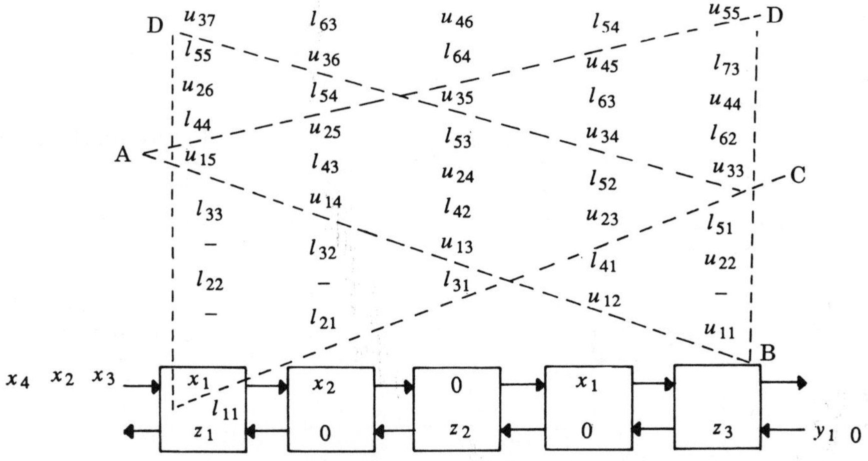

Fig. 6.2 Space fold

Figure 6.2 illustrates folding for the matrix–vector scheme. The ordering of the input data is easily determined by considering the matrix to be split into the lower and upper triangular forms $A = L + U$ so that the product is $Lx + Ux = y$. Consequently in this case the fold is equivalent to an additive splitting in which the passes for $Lx = y^{(1)}$ and $Ux = y^{(2)} = z$ are interleaved on the smaller array. If the maximum bandwidth of A is $w = p + q - 1$, where p and q are the bandwidths of U and L respectively, the array size is $\max(p, q)$. The computation time of $Lx = y$ is $\mathscr{T}_1 = 2n + q$ inner product steps. Likewise $Ux = z$ requires $\mathscr{T}_2 = 2n + p$ steps. It follows that the resultant computation time is $\mathscr{T} = \max(\mathscr{T}_1, \mathscr{T}_2) = 2n + \max(p, q)$. Note that this is not the total computation time because we still have to evaluate the sum $y^{(1)} + y^{(2)}$. In the example components of z lead the components of y so that delays must be inserted to resynchronize the two sequences before the addition can occur. It should be clear that one must consider very carefully the implications of folding. Any saving in cells must be weighed against the additional costs in time and offset against additional cells required for combining partial results.

Time folding leaves the number of cells unchanged but modifies the length of the time axis. By retiming the computations in ADC so that they fill dummy elements in ABC, the computation time is reduced and the efficiency improved but the array area is unchanged. Figure 6.3 illustrates the method for the matrix–vector problem. In this scheme the elements y_i and y_{n-i+1} of $Ax = y$ are computed simultaneously. The motivation is as follows. Suppose A has bandwidth w and the special form

$$\begin{bmatrix} A_{11} & 0 \\ 0 & A_{22} \end{bmatrix}$$

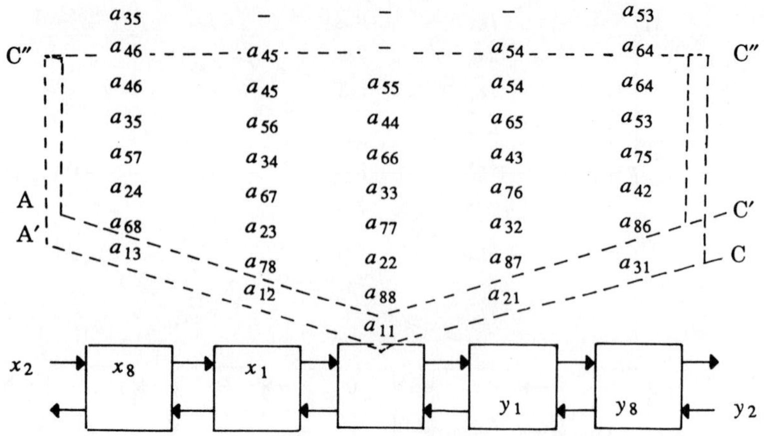

Fig. 6.3 Time fold

then the matrix–vector product can be replaced by two decoupled problems of the form

$$A_{11}x^{(1)} = y^{(1)} \tag{6.6a}$$

$$A_{22}x^{(2)} = y^{(2)} \tag{6.6b}$$

where $y = (y^{(1)}, y^{(2)})$ and $x = (x^{(1)}, x^{(2)})$ with $y^{(i)}$ and $x^{(i)}$ simple partitions of the vector elements. Now A_{11} and A_{22} are matrices of order $n/2$ so that a standard matrix–vector array for (6.6a) or (6.6b) requires $\mathscr{T} = 2(n/2) + w$ steps and w cells. As (6.6a) and (6.6b) are decoupled they can be interleaved on the same array so that (6.6) can be evaluated in $\mathscr{T} = n + w$ steps. Interleaving produces 100 per cent efficiency once the array is full. The scheme works because the computations of the individual components of the matrix–vector problem are independent of one another. It follows that we can compute the components in any order so that reversing the order of evaluation does not affect the result. Hence evaluation of y_i and y_{n-i+1} can proceed simultaneously. The same strategy can be used for the more general matrix–vector problem using a partitioning of the form

$$\begin{bmatrix} A_{11} & A_{12} \\ A_{21} & A_{22} \end{bmatrix} \tag{6.7}$$

and noticing that A_{12} and A_{21} are null apart from $q \times q$ and $p \times p$ triangles of elements. These non-zero elements produce a zone of overlap between the two subproblems and demand some duplication of the a_{ij} entries to prevent computations being lost. These elements are easily derived by folding the matrix along the antidiagonal. The amount of duplication is proportional only to the bandwidth of A so that when the matrix is really banded the saving in time outweighs the additional input.

Finally, consider option 3, space–time folding. Folding along S_1 or S_2 requires some retiming to fill neutral elements, but will intuitively reduce cells and computation time simultaneously. The idea is to average the effects of options 1 and 2, to produce a trade-off of reduced cells, improved efficiency, and computation time. Such changes are simple when either space or time, but not both, are considered because the design goal is more intuitive. For combined space–time folding the preservation of data dependencies becomes non-trivial. As an example consider the matrix–vector problem and the matrix partition in (6.7). Clearly,

$$A_{11}x^{(1)} = y^{(1)}, \qquad A_{12}x^{(2)} = y^{(2)}$$
$$A_{21}x^{(1)} = y^{(3)}, \qquad A_{22}x^{(2)} = y^{(4)}$$

and $y = (y^{(1)} + y^{(2)}, y^{(3)} + y^{(4)})$ with $y^{(i)}$ suitable vector partitions. Each partition corresponds to a quadrant of the input polygon in Fig. 6.1(a) or (b). A space–time fold about the line S_2 in Fig. 6.1(a) produces the array format shown in Fig. 6.4 from which it is clear that the subproblems involving A_{12} and A_{22} (likewise A_{11} and A_{21}) can be interleaved. When the matrix is dense and of order n, the design saves $n/2$ cells and approximately $n/2$ steps. The same folding applies to the banded case but the savings are less dramatic. Indeed for systems of narrow bandwidth and larger orders the cell count can actually increase. This latter observation is one of the reasons why space–time folds appear not to have been utilized effectively in the literature (an exception is the matrix product discussed in Robert and Tcheunte (1985)).

6.2.3 Double pipes

The method behind folding and interleaving is to preserve the global array structure while modifying data flow. The restriction on array structure allows

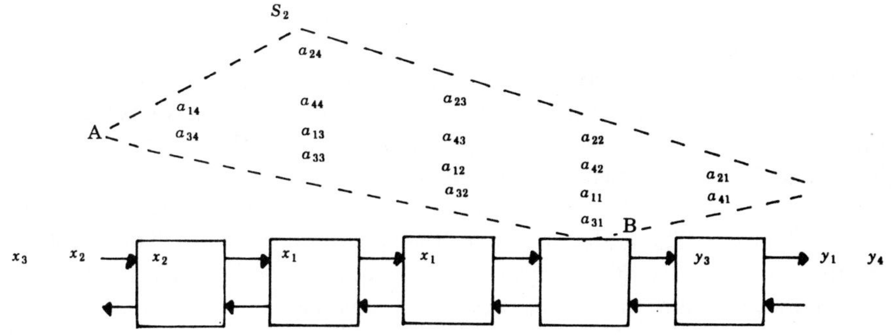

Fig. 6.4 Space–time fold

only simple partitions and splittings of the recurrence equations. A useful technique which avoids this constraint and allows modification to the array itself is known as double piping (see Megson and Evans 1985). As implied by the name, double piping increases the degree of pipelining at the array level. We distinguish it from the so-called two-level pipelining introduced by Kung and Lam (1984) which occurs internal to an array at the cell level.

To illustrate the technique consider the problem of lower triangular matrix–vector product

$$Lx = d \tag{6.8}$$

where L is an $n \times n$ matrix, x is a known $1 \times n$ vector, and d is an $n \times 1$ result. First we define an additive splitting of the form

$$L = L_1 + L_2 \tag{6.9}$$

where L_1 and L_2 have the forms

$$L = \begin{bmatrix} l_{11} & & & & \\ 0 & l_{22} & & & \\ l_{31} & 0 & l_{33} & & \\ 0 & l_{42} & 0 & l_{44} & \\ l_{51} & 0 & l_{53} & 0 & l_{55} \end{bmatrix}, \quad L_2 = \begin{bmatrix} 0 & & & & \\ l_{21} & 0 & & & \\ 0 & l_{32} & 0 & & \\ l_{41} & 0 & l_{43} & 0 & \\ 0 & l_{52} & 0 & l_{54} & 0 \end{bmatrix}. \tag{6.10a}$$

Then (6.8) is written in the form

$$L_1x = y_1, \quad L_2x = y_2, \quad d = y_1 + y_2. \tag{6.10b}$$

Now it is easily deduced that application of multipass and interleaving allows (6.10) to be computed as shown in Fig. 6.5(a) where q is the bandwidth and $\mathscr{T} = n + (q/2) + 1$ steps are required. The array uses the same number of inner product cells as the normal matrix–vector array plus an additional adder and delay cell.

Referring back to the axioms and heuristics in Chapter 1 one might try to disqualify this design from being a systolic array on the grounds that (a) it involves non-planarities, (b) it requires broadcast of the x values between pipes. The first case is easily dismissed: simply unfold the design so that the cells numbered 4 and 5 form the left wing of the design and cells 1, 2, and 3 the right wing. The adder is now in the centre of the array. The unfolded design is completely planar and the x values are sent only to nearest-neighbour cells. We have to concede that x values are duplicated in both wings of the array but duplication occurs only inside the array and does not contribute to broadcast or additional accesses to the host device. Applying

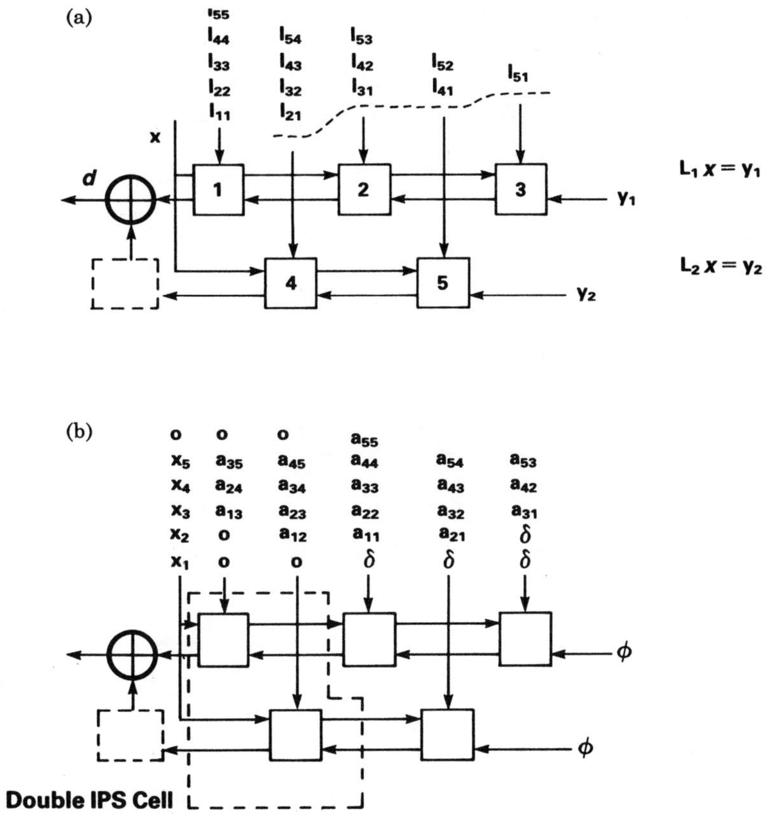

Fig. 6.5 Double-pipe matrix–vector arrays: (a) $Lx = d$, $q = 5$; (b) $Ax = d$

the same splitting technique to the more general banded matrix–vector problem produces the array in Fig. 6.5(b) and yields a time of $\mathscr{T} = n + w + 1$, efficiency $e = 1$, and $\mathscr{A} = w + 1$. The slight increase in hardware (i.e. one cell equivalent) is negligible compared with the improved performance.

Double-pipe splittings extend in a straightforward manner to matrix–matrix product as follows. First make the additive splitting

$$c = \sum_{i=1}^{m} A_i B_j, \quad j = 1(1)m \tag{6.11}$$

for two matrices of bandwidths w_1 and w_2 respectively. The double pipe has the algebraic form

$$AB = (A_1 + A_2)(B_1 + B_2) \tag{6.12}$$

where A_i and B_j for $n = 6$ have the forms

$$A_1 = \begin{bmatrix} a_{11} & 0 & a_{13} & 0 & a_{15} & 0 \\ 0 & a_{22} & 0 & a_{24} & 0 & a_{26} \\ a_{31} & 0 & a_{33} & 0 & a_{35} & 0 \\ 0 & a_{42} & 0 & a_{44} & 0 & a_{46} \\ a_{51} & 0 & a_{53} & 0 & a_{55} & 0 \\ 0 & a_{62} & 0 & a_{64} & 0 & a_{66} \end{bmatrix} \quad A_2 = \begin{bmatrix} 0 & a_{12} & 0 & a_{14} & 0 & a_{16} \\ a_{21} & 0 & a_{23} & 0 & a_{25} & 0 \\ 0 & a_{32} & 0 & a_{34} & 0 & a_{36} \\ a_{41} & 0 & a_{43} & 0 & a_{45} & 0 \\ 0 & a_{52} & 0 & a_{54} & 0 & a_{56} \\ a_{61} & 0 & a_{63} & 0 & a_{65} & 0 \end{bmatrix} \tag{6.13}$$

and

$$B_1 = \begin{bmatrix} b_{11} & 0 & b_{13} & 0 & b_{15} & 0 \\ 0 & b_{22} & 0 & b_{24} & 0 & b_{26} \\ b_{31} & 0 & b_{33} & 0 & b_{35} & 0 \\ 0 & b_{42} & 0 & b_{44} & 0 & b_{46} \\ b_{51} & 0 & b_{53} & 0 & b_{55} & 0 \\ 0 & b_{62} & 0 & b_{64} & 0 & b_{66} \end{bmatrix} \quad B_2 = \begin{bmatrix} 0 & b_{12} & 0 & b_{14} & 0 & b_{16} \\ b_{21} & 0 & b_{23} & 0 & b_{25} & 0 \\ 0 & b_{32} & 0 & b_{34} & 0 & b_{36} \\ b_{41} & 0 & b_{43} & 0 & b_{45} & 0 \\ 0 & b_{52} & 0 & b_{54} & 0 & b_{56} \\ b_{61} & 0 & b_{63} & 0 & b_{56} & 0 \end{bmatrix} \tag{6.14}$$

where the result is

$$C = C_1 + C_2 + C_3 + C_4 \tag{6.15}$$

when

$$\text{(a) } C_1 = A_1 B_1, \quad \text{(b) } C_2 = A_1 B_2, \quad \text{(c) } C_3 = A_2 B_1, \quad \text{(d) } C_4 = A_2 B_2 \tag{6.16}$$

and C_1 has the form

$$C_1 = \begin{bmatrix} c_{11} & 0 & c_{13} & 0 & c_{15} & 0 \\ 0 & c_{22} & 0 & c_{24} & 0 & c_{26} \\ c_{31} & 0 & c_{33} & 0 & c_{35} & 0 \\ 0 & c_{42} & 0 & c_{44} & 0 & c_{46} \\ c_{51} & 0 & c_{53} & 0 & c_{55} & 0 \\ 0 & c_{62} & 0 & c_{64} & 0 & c_{66} \end{bmatrix}. \tag{6.17}$$

Taking advantage of the zero patterns in A_1, B_1, and C_1 produces a reduced hexagonal array with retimed data flow (see Fig. 6.6). This reduced design requires $\mathcal{T} = (3n/2) + \min(w_1/2, w_2/2)$ steps and approximately $w_1 w_2/4$ cells, which is one-quarter the cells of the normal hexagonal array. The new array also improves efficiency from $e = 0.33$ to $e = 0.66$.

Next, apply the following computation-preserving row and column interchanges:

(1) with C_2 and B_2 interchange row i and $i+1$ for $i = 1(2)n-1$ to yield $\bar{C}_2$ and $\bar{B}_2$;

(2) with C_3 and A_2 produce $\bar{C}_3$ and $\bar{A}_2$ by interchanging row i and $i+1$ for $i = 1(2)n-1$;

(3) for A_2, B_2, and C_4 interchange first rows i and $i+1$ of A_2 and C_4 and second columns i and $i+1$ of B_2 and C_4 to produce $\hat{C}_4$, $\hat{A}_4$, $\hat{B}_4$.

Now replace (6.16) by the expressions

$$\text{(a) } C_1 = A_1 B_1, \quad \text{(b) } \bar{C}_2 = A_1 \bar{B}_2, \quad \text{(c) } \bar{C}_3 = \bar{A}_2 B_1, \quad \text{(d) } \hat{C}_4 = \hat{A}_2 \hat{B}_2. \tag{6.18}$$

The reduced array can be used to compute the four partial products in four passes to derive the time $\mathcal{T} = 2(3n + 2\min(w_1/2, w_2/2))$ which is twice that of the original array. Note that we have neglected the time for the summation of the four products; we will deal with this later. A double pipe is constructed by using two reduced arrays and noticing that C_1 and C_4 (likewise C_2 and C_3) have the same structures to that a final result can be computed by evaluating C_1 and C_4 on separate arrays and forming $C_1 + C_4$ and $C_2 + C_3$. Now, because the arrays compute using the normal (or transformed) form of the matrices we must permute them back to the correct form before the addition. Fortunately this permutation can be carried out 'on-the-fly' using

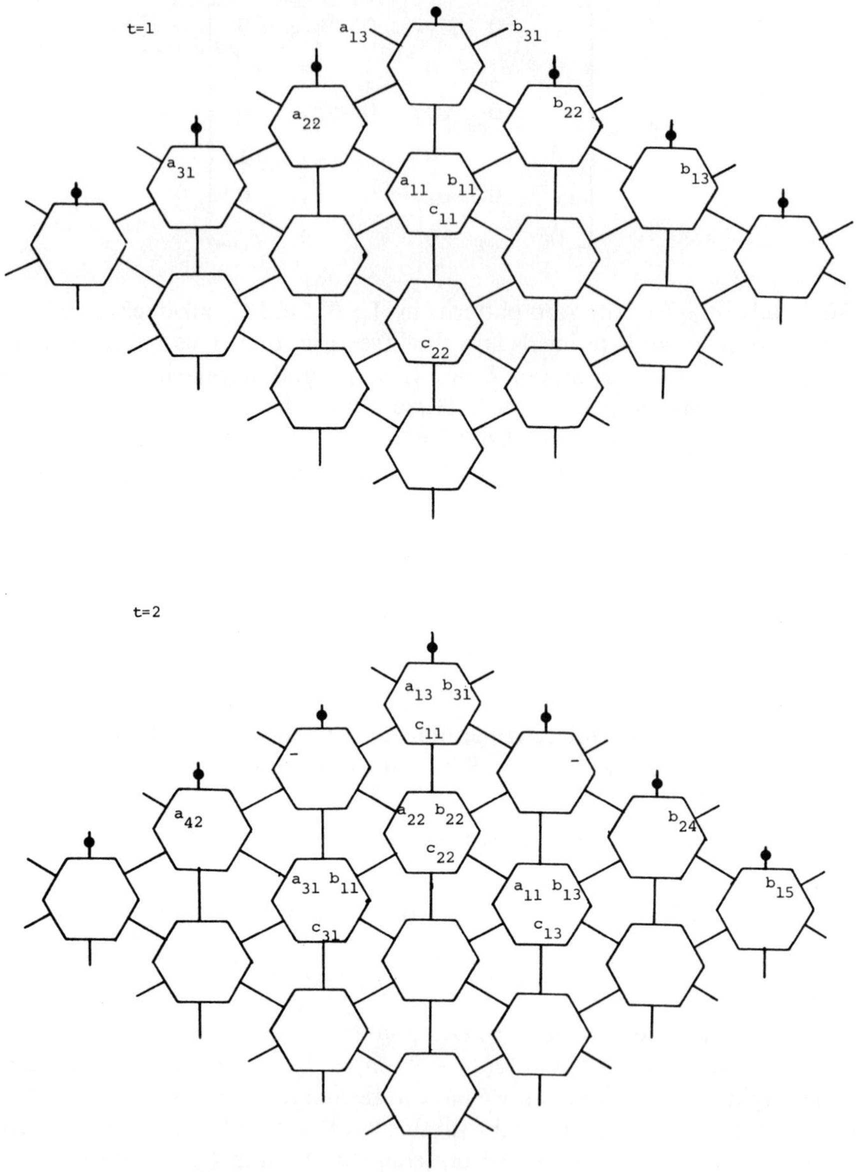

Fig. 6.6 Double-pipe matrix product arrays

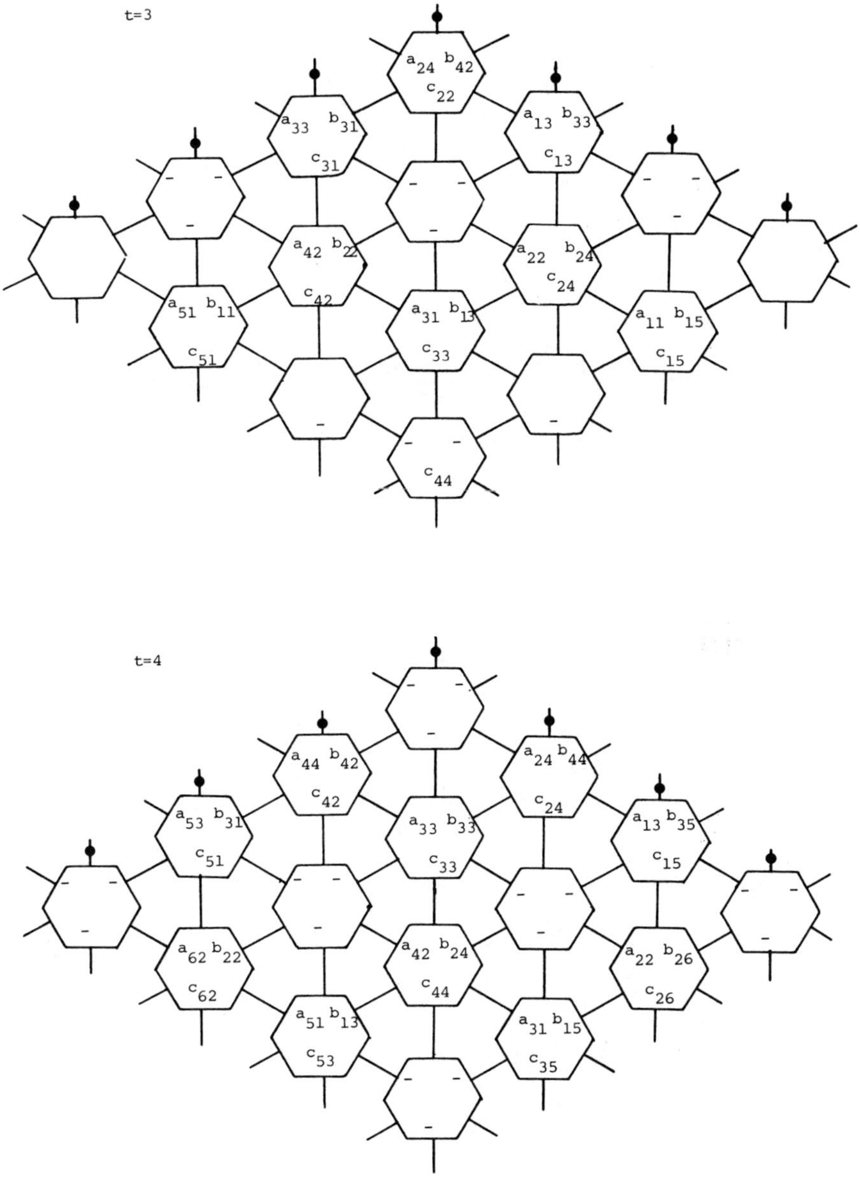
t=3
a24 b42
c22
a33 b31
c31
a13 b33
c13
a42 b22
c42
a22 b24
c24
a51 b11
c51
a31 b13
c33
a11 b15
c15
c44
t=4
a44 b42
c42
a24 b44
c24
a53 b31
c51
a33 b33
c33
a13 b35
c15
a62 b22
c62
a42 b24
c44
a22 b26
c26
a51 b13
c53
a31 b15
c35

Fig. 6.6 (*cont.*)

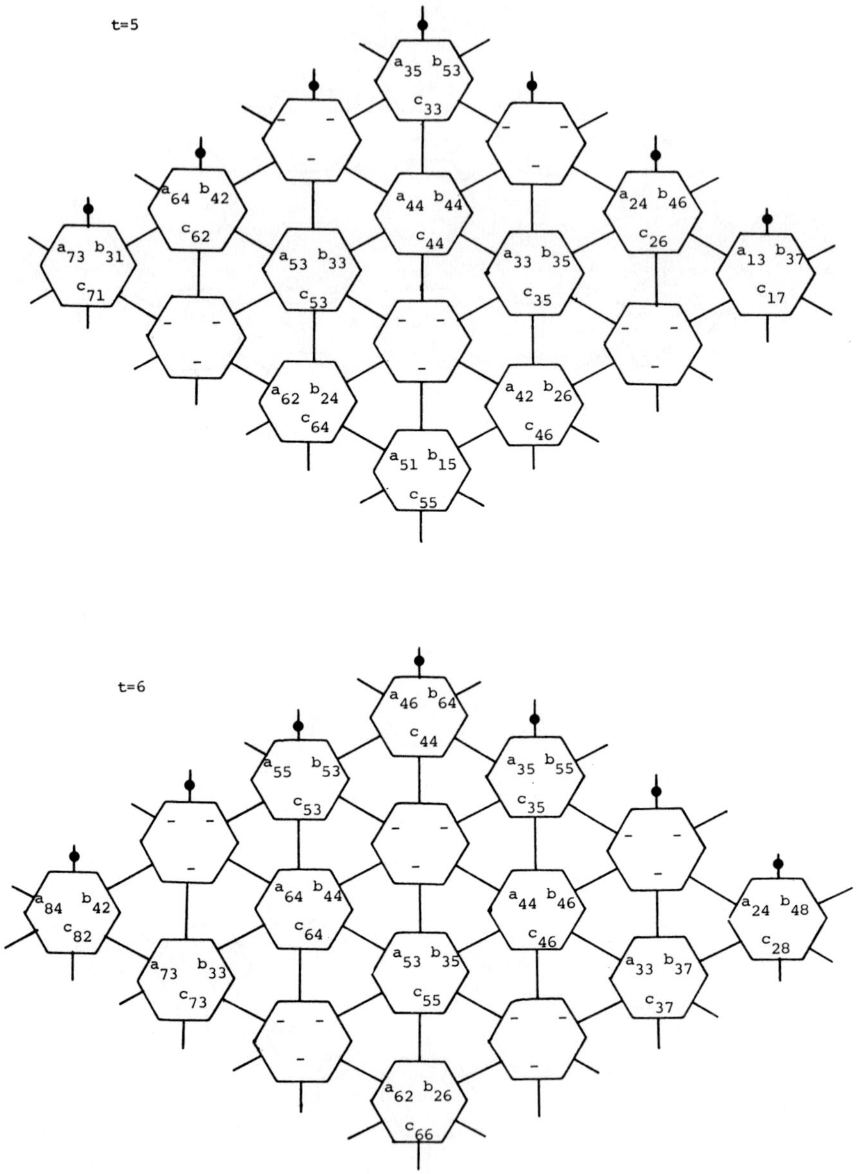

Fig. 6.6 (*cont.*)

localized permutations of the 2 × 2 block matrices with the forms

$$C_2 = \begin{bmatrix} c_{12} & 0 & c_{14} & 0 & c_{16} & 0 \\ 0 & c_{21} & 0 & c_{23} & 0 & c_{25} \\ c_{31} & 0 & c_{34} & 0 & c_{36} & 0 \\ 0 & c_{41} & 0 & c_{43} & 0 & c_{45} \\ c_{52} & 0 & c_{54} & 0 & c_{56} & 0 \\ 0 & c_{61} & 0 & c_{63} & 0 & c_{65} \end{bmatrix}$$

$$C_3 = \begin{bmatrix} c_{21} & 0 & c_{23} & 0 & c_{25} & 0 \\ 0 & c_{12} & 0 & c_{14} & 0 & c_{16} \\ c_{41} & 0 & c_{43} & 0 & c_{45} & 0 \\ 0 & c_{32} & 0 & c_{34} & 0 & c_{36} \\ c_{61} & 0 & c_{63} & 0 & c_{65} & 0 \\ 0 & c_{52} & 0 & c_{54} & 0 & c_{56} \end{bmatrix} \qquad (6.19)$$

$$C_4 = \begin{bmatrix} c_{22} & 0 & c_{24} & 0 & c_{26} & 0 \\ 0 & c_{11} & 0 & c_{13} & 0 & c_{15} \\ c_{42} & 0 & c_{44} & 0 & c_{46} & 0 \\ 0 & c_{31} & 0 & c_{33} & 0 & c_{35} \\ c_{62} & 0 & c_{64} & 0 & c_{66} & 0 \\ 0 & c_{51} & 0 & c_{53} & 0 & c_{55} \end{bmatrix}$$

by swapping diagonal elements of the blocks. Thus the output of the two reduced arrays can be pipelined directly into a bank of adders attached to the upper boundary (shown as full circles in the diagram) to form the complete product. As two passes are made on the double-pipe array the final design computes the complete product (including summation) in the same time as the original hexagonal array in Chapter 2, but with improved efficiency and approximately half the number of cells. Note that in this scheme inputs and outputs to the array occur only at the boundary so that the array can be unfolded to produce a planar array. The data flow demands that some of the matrices are retrieved from the external controlling device more than once—a factor which could degrade performance appreciably.

Remark A similar splitting technique combined with interleaving can reduce computation time and area simultaneously (see exercises).

In this section we have introduced a number of methods for improving the area, time, and efficiency properties of an existing design. The main objective is to reuse or eliminate the dummy elements introduced to data flow sequences for synchronization purposes. Of course there are some limitations to the methods. For example, one cannot continue folding or interleaving indefinitely. Clearly, once all the dummy spaces are full, or sufficiently full that more subproblems cannot be accommodated, the process reaches a natural conclusion. What the limits of folding or interleaving are depends upon the exact structure of the array and the input data sequences. Conversely, it is pointless to consider interleaving or folding for designs which contain no synchronizing elements because there are no spare elements to use. In general the more folds that are made the more contorted the data flow patterns become. In these circumstances fixing the result, by adding together partial results or generating duplicated inputs, becomes increasingly complex and erodes the possible savings by demanding more hardware and external interfacing. Double pipes can be used to reduce the time and area of a design but are not strictly space–time fold combinations. The intention is to reformulate the basic recurrence so that synchronizing spaces are removed rather than filled explicitly. For example, compare the matrix–vector designs above with those in Chapter 2. Notice that the original recurrence formula leads to arrays with row-, column-, and diagonal-ordered input. The diagonal-ordered array required synchronizing spaces but the design in this chapter does not. One significant advantage of the double-pipe technique is that it can be applied to designs that do not contain synchronizing delays in their input data sequences (see exercises).

6.3 Feedback and block schemes

Interleaving, folding, and double pipes rely on the fact that a problem can be broken down into a number of subtasks which themselves can be solved on smaller and faster arrays. This approach is easy to apply provided the problem involves no feedback. For arrays that do require feedback, such as the *LU* factorization and back-substitution, folding disturbs the feedback causing data to 'thrash' around the cells in a complex manner. Thrashing has two effects: first it demands more control inside basic cells because of the more complicated data flow; and second it can lead to cyclic data dependency graphs and breakdown of the design method. Indeed, the *LU* hexagonal array is not directly decomposable into smaller identical and independent subproblems so that interleaved, multipass, or double-pipe designs are not so obvious. Of course this does not mean that the problem cannot be decomposed—simply that the resulting subtasks are coupled in some way. Coupling implies more restrictions on the permissible partial orderings and hence schedules for the computation.

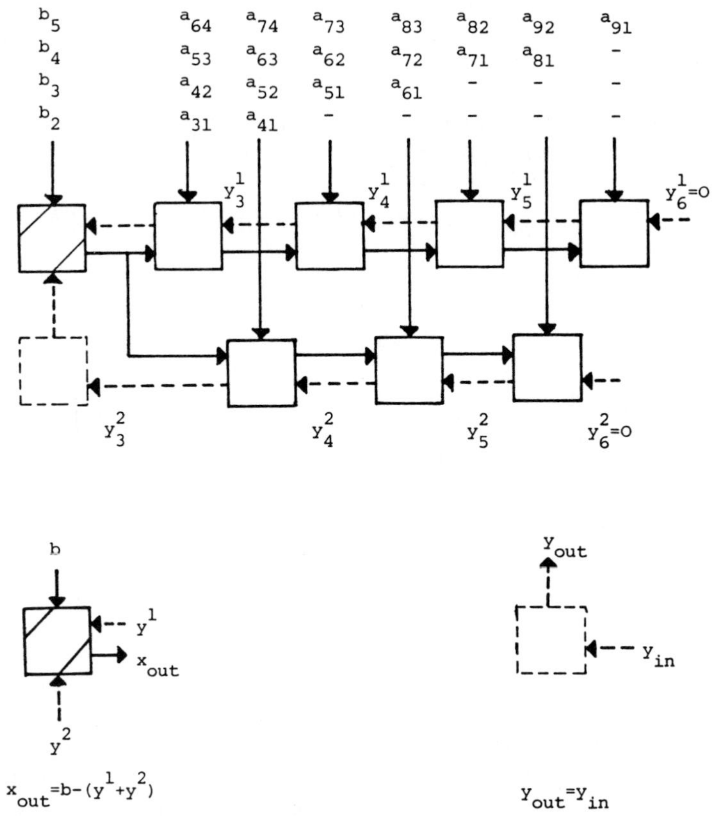

Fig. 6.7 Double-pipe back-substitution array

6.3.1 Feedback and double pipes

Where the feedback involves data sequences that remain constant the double-pipe technique can yield some improvements. To illustrate this idea we will consider the back-substitution network in Fig. 3.1 and produce the design in Fig. 6.7 due to Robert and Tcheunte (1984) which is a double pipe. To start we must be willing to allow some manipulation of the original problem. For example, when

$$Lx = b \tag{6.20}$$

where x is unknown, b is known, and L is a banded lower triangular matrix, letting

$$x = D^{-1}y \tag{6.21}$$

produces

$$By = LD^{-1}y = b \tag{6.22}$$

and essentially divides the columns by their corresponding diagonal value, thus normalizing L. Now put

$$y = Pz \tag{6.23}$$

so that

$$Cz = BPz = b \tag{6.24}$$

where

$$P = \begin{bmatrix} 1 & & & & & \\ -b_{21} & 1 & & 0 & & \\ & -b_{32} & 1 & & & \\ & & -b_{43} & 1 & & \\ & 0 & & -b_{54} & 1 & \\ & & & & -b_{65} & 1 \end{bmatrix} \tag{6.25}$$

(for the case $n = 6$) such that C has a unit diagonal and a null first diagonal. The null diagonal effectively breaks the restriction imposed by the feedback loop and produces the array in Fig. 6.7 directly. Also notice that the values being fed back along the array are constant, which is why the partitioning works. If the result of the next cell on the feedback connection was dependent on the previous one it would not be as straightforward to partition the cells. Again the design is 100 per cent efficient and can be unfolded to produce a planar array. The next computation involved with producing C is an overhead which must be accepted as a means of reducing the problem to two coupled subproblems each of which is solved on a separate pipe. Clearly, producing C requires additional cells which affect the area–time trade-off. More complicated designs can also benefit from a double-pipe approach; for example, the Gaussian elimination and Faddeev design in Chapter 3 can be accelerated for only a modest addition of extra delay cells (see Megson and Gaston 1990; Megson 1990d). Unfortunately the same technique is not easily applied to hexagonal arrays with feedback such as the LU decomposition design.

6.3.2 Block computations

In Section 6.1.2 it was indicated that block partitionings could be used to reduce the area of a design thus making it more practical to implement. The emphasis was on producing an array which could process individual blocks of data as quickly and as efficiently as possible. In contrast this section considers the problem of changing the granularity of the array cells. For example, we could increase the granularity of the inner product cell by interpreting $y = y + (a \times x)$ as a block matrix operation rather than a computation involving scalars. For many computations an algorithm based on scalar arithmetic has an alternative method based on block computations (e.g. 2×2 and 3×3 matrix product and triangularization). To illustrate this idea consider the hexagonal array in Fig. 2.10. Interpreting the input elements as 2×2 matrices and performing 2×2 matrix product and matrix–vector operations in each cell produces a 2×2 block matrix array. Now because each data element is a 2×2 block the input length is $3n/2$ for a matrix of order n. Likewise the block bandwidth of the matrices is approximately half the original bandwidth so that approximately $w_1 w_2/4$ block cells are required for matrices of bandwidth w_1 and w_2 respectively. It follows that for $k \times k$ blocks we require roughly $w_1 w_2/(k^2)$ cells, $\mathscr{T} = 3n/k + \min(w_1/k, w_2/k)$ block steps, and efficiency $e = 0.33$ to compute a $k \times k$ block matrix product. If we assume that each block cell performs its computation sequentially, then a $k \times k$ block requires $O(k^2 + k^3)$ operations (i.e. $O(k^2)$ operations for a matrix–vector product and $O(k^3)$ operations for a matrix product). Consequently the time of the array in scalar inner products is $\mathscr{T} = 3nk^2 + k^2 \min(w_1, w_2)$ steps. The apparent reduction in cells is offset by an increase in computation time. In addition, the cells must compute a $k \times k$ block computation which requires additional hardware and more complex cells, so the trade-off is not very attractive unless the basic cell is already quite sophisticated. A real saving would be made only if the basic cell was already a programmable or general-purpose microprocessor (see Chapter 7).

The above discussion raises a number of questions. For example, how can we modify the internal arrangement of the basic cell to perform a block computation? Can we use blocks to improve the efficiency of the design and hence the number of steps required? The motivation for the latter is that any reductions in the total number of steps can be used to offset the additional complexity of block computations. To answer some of these queries we consider the 2×2 block hexagonal array due to Robert (1985). This array, shown in Fig. 6.8, uses $\mathscr{T} = 2n + \min(p, q)$ scalar inner product steps and has efficiency $e = 0.5$. The array is virtually identical to the original design in Fig. 3.8 except that the calculation has the form

$$A_{ij} = A_{ij} - L_{ik}(-U_{kj}). \tag{6.26}$$

For example, a 4×4 system can be represented as

$$A = \begin{bmatrix} A_{11} & A_{12} \\ A_{21} & A_{22} \end{bmatrix} \tag{6.27}$$

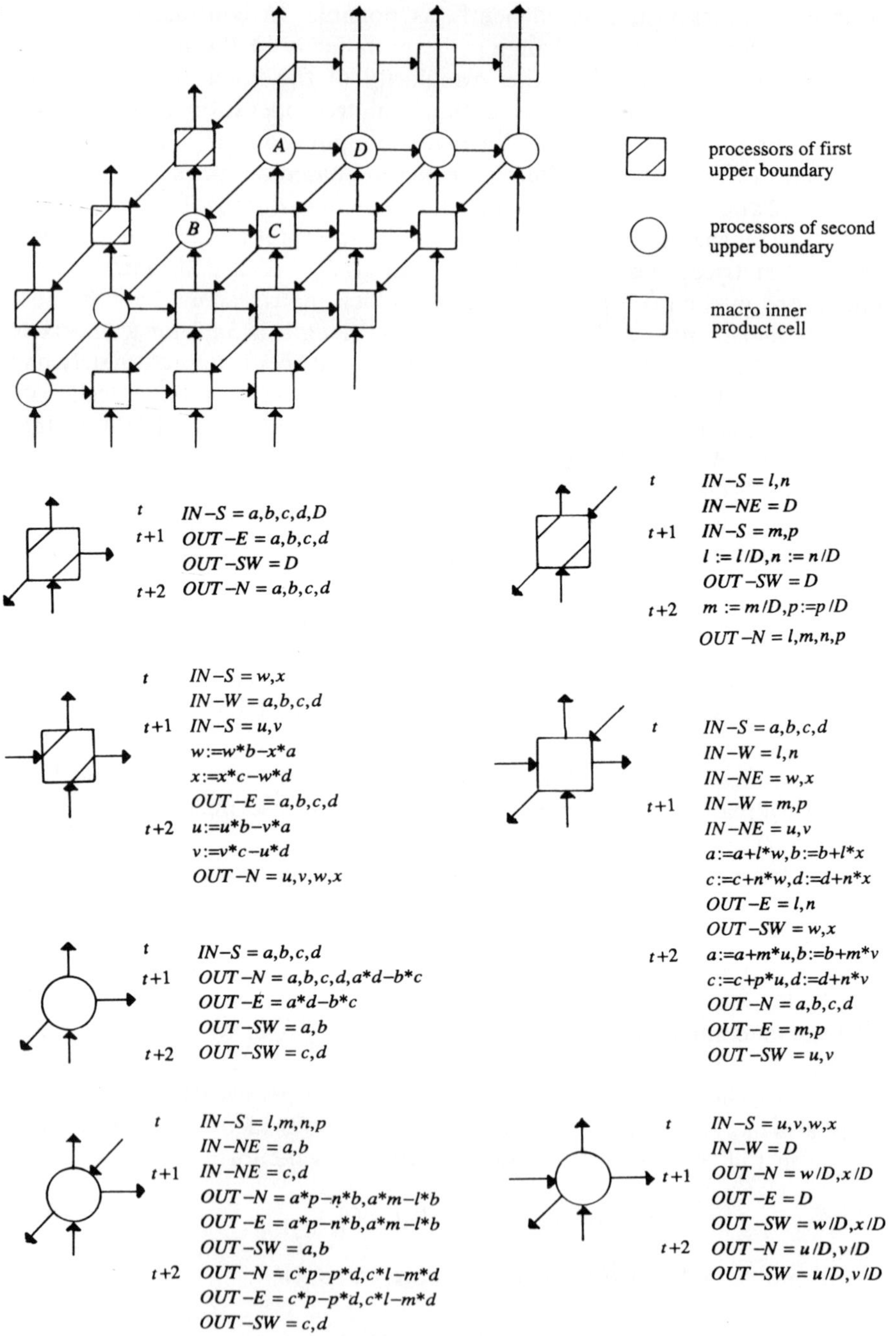

Fig. 6.8 Block *LU* decomposition array. (Source Y. Robert, *International Journal of Computer Mathematics*, Vol. 17, 1985, Gordon & Breach Science Publishers Inc.)

where the A_{ij} are 2×2 blocks, and

$$\begin{bmatrix} I & 0 \\ L_{21} & I \end{bmatrix}\begin{bmatrix} U_{11} & U_{12} \\ 0 & U_{22} \end{bmatrix} = \begin{bmatrix} A_{11} & A_{12} \\ A_{21} & A_{22} \end{bmatrix}. \tag{6.28}$$

Thus, putting $\Delta = a_{11}a_{22} - a_{12}a_{21}$, we get

$$L_{21} = A_{21}U_{11}^{-1} \tag{6.29}$$

or

$$\Delta \cdot L_{21} = \begin{bmatrix} a_{31} & a_{32} \\ a_{41} & a_{42} \end{bmatrix}\begin{bmatrix} a_{22} & -a_{12} \\ -a_{21} & a_{11} \end{bmatrix} = \begin{bmatrix} \Delta \cdot l_{31} & \Delta \cdot l_{32} \\ \Delta \cdot l_{41} & \Delta \cdot l_{42} \end{bmatrix} \tag{6.30}$$

and

$$U_{22} = A_{22} - (\Delta \cdot L_{21})(A_{22}) \tag{6.31}$$

which is evaluated easily in just four steps:

t1: $\Delta = a_{11}a_{22} - a_{12}a_{21}$

t2: $\Delta \cdot l_{31}$, a_{13}/Δ, a_{14}/Δ

t3: $\Delta \cdot l_{32}$, a_{23}/Δ, a_{24}/Δ, $a_{33} = a_{33} + (\Delta \cdot l_{31})(a_{13}/\Delta)$,
$a_{34} = a_{34} + (\Delta \cdot l_{31})(a_{14}/\Delta)$

t4: update a_{33} and a_{34} again to complete the modification.

Likewise a computation to find a_{43} and a_{44} must be done simultaneously. Steps t1–t4 describe the feedback loop marked by the cells A, B, C, and D in Fig. 6.8 and so determine the four-step gap between block computations. As the total data length is $m = n/2$ and the initial synchronization delay is $O(w)$ cycles the timing is $\mathcal{T} = 4m + \min(p, q) = 2n + O(w)$. The dimensions of the array are half that of the original array, apparently reducing the cells by half. However, in order to calculate the steps outlined above we need four inner product cell equivalents in each of the block cells so that approximately the same hardware is required. The efficiency is $e = 0.5$ due to the fact that these 2×2 block cells utilize hardware more efficiently. They compute two out of every four cycles.

Remark The area of the block cells may still increase when compared with a scalar cell because of the additional routing and control wires needed to realize the computations described above.

Clearly we could repeat the design process for different block sizes—which size produces the best efficiency? It can be shown (Megson and Evans 1990*c*) that a 3×3 block scheme using nine inner products per block cell can also compute LU decomposition in a time of $\mathcal{T} = 2n + O(w)$ scalar inner product steps and with efficiency $e = 0.5$. Indeed a simple argument involving the time to traverse the feedback loop ABC of Fig. 6.8 is sufficient to show that 3×3 blocks yield the same efficiency and time as 2×2 blocks and that 4×4 blocks must yield a slower computation time. As the complexity of block cells increases with block size it follows that 2×2 blocks produce the optimal systolic design with respect to time, cells (not area), and efficiency.

6.4 Two-level pipelining and bit serial arrays

The techniques in the previous sections modify the basic properties of area, time, and efficiency for a given design but place no emphasis on the way a design will finally be implemented. As the last example shows, neglecting these considerations can lead to misleading designs and to arrays with little practical value. In this section we consider methods that are geared towards the practical problem of cell construction.

6.4.1 Two-level pipelining

Chapter 4 introduced the main features of two-level pipelining and showed how these properties could be used to improve throughput and derive systolic rings. In a two-level design an array exhibits pipelining at two separate levels of granularity. For example, in the Romberg array (Fig. 4.9) data are pipelined not only between cells, but also between the components of each cell. This organization or two-level pipe improves throughput because data can be input as soon as the first subcells have finished computation rather than having to wait for the data to propagate all the way through the cell. The level of granularity in a design depends upon the complexity of the basic operations in the defining recurrence equations. For example, the basic cells of the Romberg array define the rules for generating the Romberg table and these rules are themselves made up of simpler operations such as addition, multiplication, division, etc. which can be considered easier to implement. Indeed adders and multipliers are available as off-the-shelf components. It follows that a basic cell of the Romberg array can be built at the board level using current technology.

Two-level pipelining can also be applied at lower levels of granularity by decomposing basic arithmetic operations into simpler computations. For example, consider the convolution array in Chapter 1, Fig. 1.1(c). The basic cell consists of simple inner products constructed from an adder and multiplier plus some delays. There appears to be little scope for pipelining but it can be introduced as follows. Suppose we want to multiply two three-digit numbers $A = a_2a_1a_0$ and $B = b_2b_1b_0$. The product may be written as shown in Fig. 6.9(a) where the c values are found by summing the entries in the appropriate column and taking into account any carries. A pipelined multiplier can be constructed by accumulating the first partial product on the first step, the second partial product on the second step, and so on.

(a)

		a_2	a_1	a_0
		b_2	b_1	b_0
b_2a_2	b_2a_1	b_2a_0	0	0
	b_1a_2	b_1a_1	b_1a_0	0
		b_1a_2	b_1a_0	b_0a_0
c_4	c_3	c_2	c_1	c_0

(b)

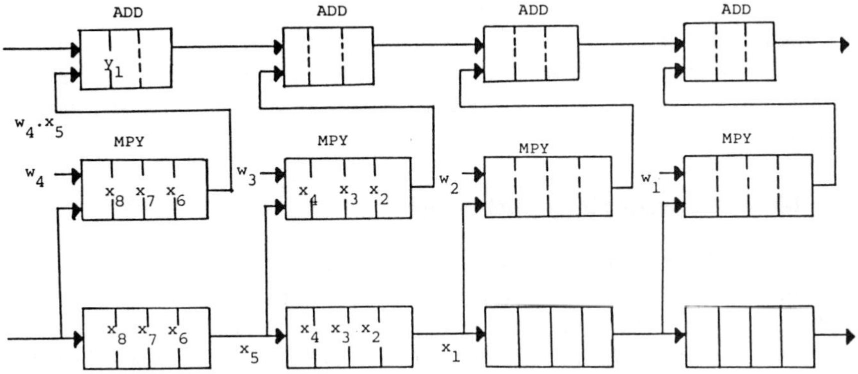

Fig. 6.9 Two-level pipelining of basic arithmetic units: (a) partial products for bit serial multiplication; (b) two-level pipelined convolution. (Source H. T. Kung and M. S. Lam, *Journal of Parallel and Distributed Computing*, Academic Press Inc., 1984.)

Pipelined devices with this form can be found in many textbooks on digital design. The computation of the second partial product and the first partial product of the next multiplication can be pipelined. Applying the same principle to the adder produces a two-level pipelined design for convolution as shown in Fig. 6.9(b). To emphasize the change in granularity we have dispensed with the bounding box used to denote inner product cells. Notice how the delay, multiplier (MPY), and adder (ADD) are skewed relative to each other in time so that the correct data synchronize. Skewing is necessary because of the delay associated with the extra pipeline stages introduced to the arithmetic units. Kung and Lam (1984) suggest that the required timing can be produced by applying the cut theorem (Chapter 2) to introduce additional delays for each pipelined segment in the final design. These delays can then be replaced by the appropriate pipeline hardware.

Remark We assume in this example that four stages are sufficient to compute multiplications. In general the number of stages in the multiplier pipe is proportional to the maximum number of bits used to represent the values *w*, *x*, *y*.

Fast arithmetic components such as Weitex floating-point chips are available for many tasks and demonstrate that speed-ups using these techniques are possible. The essential difference between the Romberg table and convolution-type pipelining is the complexity (or granularity of the pipeline segments). In fact we could argue that by redefining the bounding polygons—used to demark cell definitions—one level of pipelining apparently disappears. That is, changing granularity is equivalent to levels of abstraction in the design process. Finally, it should be pointed out that the improved throughput is paid for by increased array and design latency. Pipelined arithmetic units require more area than sequential ones and the different pipelined stages should be latched so that the values of the previous segment do not get overwritten by new values until they have been used by the next segment. For large designs this extra hardware can lead to significantly increased area and power requirements.

6.4.2 Bit serial versus bit parallel design

So far in this text we have ignored the physical representation of data. For example, in the matrix and table designs of Chapters 3 and 4 we assume implicitly that a single value can be input or output to a cell easily. In practice the representation of data determines the number of physical wires that must be used to carry data from one cell to another and between the array and external device. The total number of connections, particularly in the latter case, has great bearing on whether a design is practical or not. In computer systems data is usually represented as a sequence of binary digits (or bits). This preference is largely due to the fact that binary arithmetic is simpler to implement in hardware than other forms of encoding and so leads to fast and efficient hardware. Data are normally divided into bytes (i.e. sequences of 8 bits) and bytes are collected into words. How we present bytes and words of data to the underlying architecture defines the structure of the hardware and to some extent its performance. For instance, we could present all the bits to the hardware simultaneously (i.e. bit parallel) or in a given order (bit serial). For a single byte each input and output connection for a data item demands eight physical connections in bit parallel mode and only one connection in bit serial mode. Take a few moments to refer back to the examples given in the previous chapters and calculate the number of external inputs and outputs. It is surprising how many physical connections are required even for these small examples. In addition examine the internal arrangements of the two-level cells in Chapter 4 and consider the effect of the extra space needed for routing using bit parallel methods. In some cases the amount of routing area could be larger than that required for the computation hardware. It follows that arithmetic complexity is not always a good measure of cell complexity. It appears that serialization of basic cell computations has a lot to offer in terms of reducing array inputs and cell area.

Serialization reduces the area of arithmetic units by replacing parallel logic with smaller pieces of logic performing the same task sequentially. Unfortunately there are a number of difficulties. First, additional circuitry is required for registers to hold data and for logic to control the serialized computation; this offsets initial reductions. Second, serialization also affects the cycle time of a cell due to the increased number of steps; this must be offset by a reduction in the circuit clock period resulting from smaller propagation delays through the simplified cell logic. It should be clear that serialization is related to pipelining. In pipelining we break up the computation into a number of not necessarily identical steps with the same delay. All the original logic is used with the addition of registers (latches) between each stage to allow successive problems to be overlapped. If the segments of the pipe are identical a sequential loop can be produced by rolling up the pipeline and using only a single segment of hardware. The area of the cell is reduced but no pipelining occurs, so the reduction is offset by the increased cycle time of the array.

To illustrate the general principles behind bit serial design we will examine two familiar examples from Chapters 2 and 5. To start, briefly reconsider the systolic pattern matching algorithm of Foster and Kung (1980) given in Fig. 5.1. The design is implicitly bit parallel because we expect to read in all the bits associated with a string symbol and process it in unit time. The cells pass whole symbols around as the basic data unit. To adopt a bit serial approach observe that each symbol is just a bit string encoding. For example, strings made up from an alphabet of eight symbols can be encoded by 3 bits. Thus a string like 'abc' could be encoded as '000001010' where 'a = 000', 'b = 001', and 'c = 010'. For our first draft design we change the granularity of the problem so that a pattern of length m with k bits per symbol is encoded as a bit string of length mk. The pattern match array described previously can now be used directly to form the match on the much longer string. The number of cells required to match the string has increased because both the string and the pattern are much longer at this lower level of granularity, but the cells themselves are simpler single-bit processors which require only single-bit input–output connections. Consequently the speed-up and area reduction resulting from the bit serial cell hardware is offset by the increased array latency and cell count. VLSI techniques can be used directly to provide a large number of bit cells on a single chip so the design may be considered practical. However, the bit parallel design implied by Fig. 5.1 and the bit serial design above represent two extremes. What is normally required in design is a trade-off that attempts to maximize the advantages and minimize the disadvantages of different approaches to the same problem. For bit serial design this means balancing the degree of bit parallel and bit serial computation. We can do much better by applying our design methodology.

The first thing to do is to find a recurrence formulation which includes bit level operations explicitly. Such an equation can be derived easily from eqn (5.2) by adding a third iteration in (5.3). This produces the recurrence

$$m_{i,j,0} = 0, \quad M_{0,-1,nb} = 0 \tag{6.32a}$$

$$m_{i,j,k} = m_{i,j,k-1} + P_{j,k-1}S_{i+j,k-1}, \quad i = 0(1)m - n, j = 0(1)n - 1, k = 1(1)nb \tag{6.32b}$$

$$M_{i,j,nb} = M_{i,j-1,nb} + m_{i,j,nb}. \tag{6.32c}$$

The value nb represents the number of bits in a string symbol. $P_{j,k-1}$ is the kth bit of symbol P_j and $S_{i+j,k-1}$ is the kth bit of symbol S_{i+j}. Thus lower-case variable m accumulates the result of a bit-wise comparison of symbols while the upper-case M accumulates the result of matching symbols and consequently the pattern P with a substring of S. Now, the variables in (6.32) must be fully indexed. By pipelining the variables the alternative form

$$m_{i,j,k} = m_{i,j,k-1} + P_{i-1,j,k-1}S_{i+1,j,k-1}$$

can be used instead of (6.32b) and it is clear that the bit level computation is a three-loop program which can be mapped into 3-D Euclidean space. Next observe that j is constant in the revised equation so that for a particular value of j we get the array in Fig. 6.10(a) for a single-bit-wise comparison of two symbols. A rectangular region of size $nb \times (m + n - 1)$ is defined by replicating Fig. 6.10(a) between the extreme values of k and i for each j. Similarly, for $k = nb$ eqn (6.32c) defines a path for accumulating substring accumulations pipelined in the j direction. It follows that projecting out the j axis will produce the bit serial array in Fig. 6.10(b) which requires $m - n + 1$ columns and $nb + 1$ rows. The M values are stationary (because they move only in the j direction and are parallel to the direction of projection) so that the different matches of P with each substring remain stationary in the last row of the cells. A simple comparison with the design in Fig. 5.1 shows that all these conclusions are consistent. It remains only to move the match data out of the array—as discussed previously this is achieved by the addition of a simple control tag which makes the accumulated M values non-stationary.

The second example we consider is that of producing a bit serial version of the matrix–vector array first introduced in Chapter 2. The problem is interesting because many problems can be reformulated as special cases of matrix–vector computation (e.g. convolution and filtering). In addition it also involves the formulation of a single inner product step as a bit level computation. To start, consider two sign-extended binary numbers, that is numbers suitably padded with zeros so that any operation is guaranteed to result in m bit values. For example, Fig. 6.9(a) shows the required partial products for two extended 5 bit values. Accumulating each column can be formulated as an inner product step involving only single-bit operations. As a single-bit product is equivalent to logical AND a bit inner product is

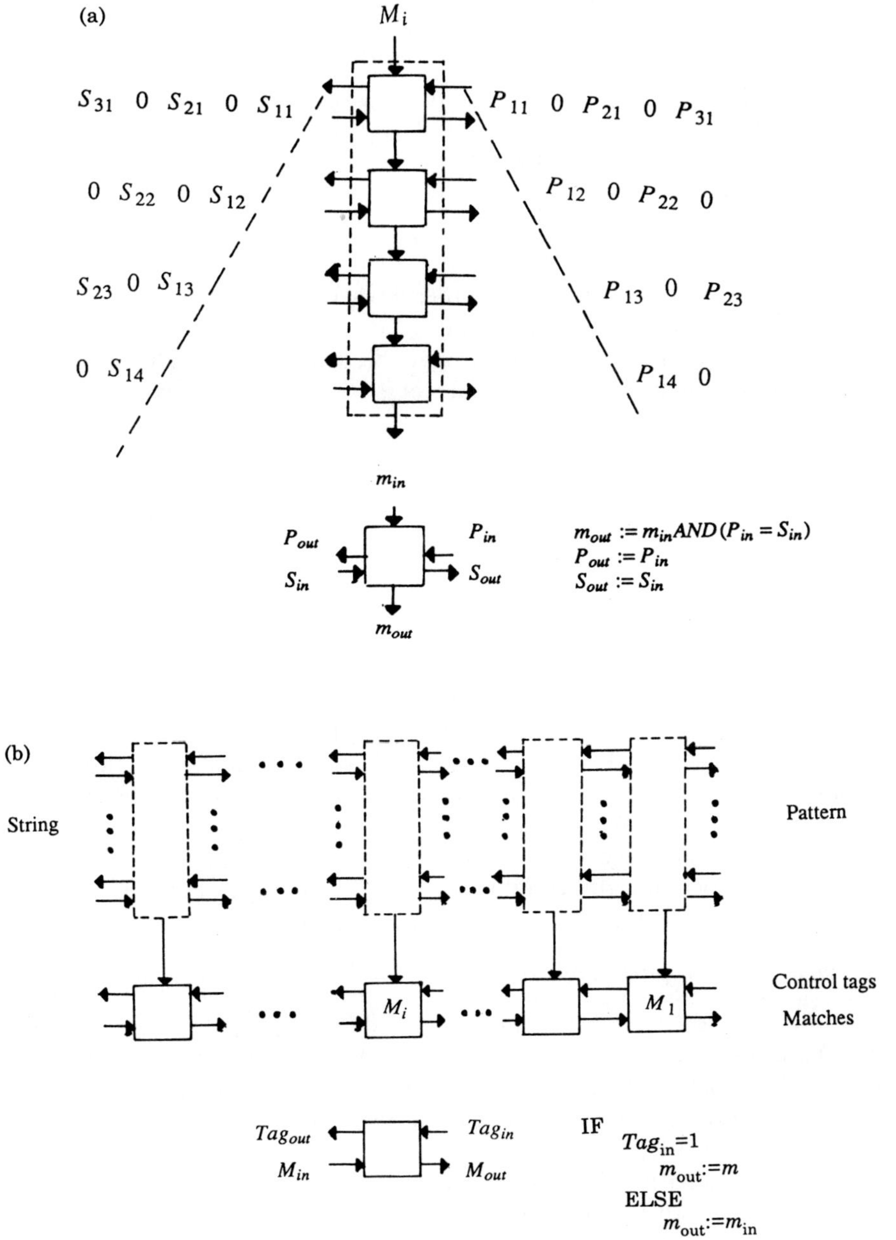

Fig. 6.10 Bit-serial pattern matcher. (Source M. J. Foster and H. T. Kung, © *IEEE Computer*, 1980.)

equivalent to a single-bit addition, and we can write

$$s_{k,l} = s_{k,l-1} \oplus b_l a_{k-l+1} \oplus c_{k-1,l}$$

$$c_{k,l} = b_l a_{k-l+1} s_{k,l-1} + b_l a_{k-1+1} c_{k-1,l} + s_{k,l-1} c_{k-1,l}$$

for k, $l = 1(1)m$, where $s_{k,l}$ and $c_{k,l}$ are the single-bit sum and carry of the lth term of bit k. Also $\oplus$ is exclusive OR, $+$ is logical OR, and juxtaposition is AND. Now we already know from previous results that the matrix–vector product can be expressed as

$$y_{i,j-1} = y_{i,j} + a_{ij} x_j, \quad i = 1(1)n, j = 1(1)n$$

for some matrix A and vector x of order n when the operations are addition and multiplication of multibit numbers. For a bit serial design we have to replace the multibit computation by single-bit computations. This is achieved by combining the previous two recurrences to yield the following

$$y_{ijk0} = y_{i,j-1,k,m} \tag{6.33a}$$

$$y_{ijkl} = y_{i,j,k,l-1} \oplus a_{i,j,0,k-l+1} x_{i,j,0,l} \oplus c_{i,j,k-1,l} \tag{6.33b}$$

$$c_{ijkl} = a_{i,j,0,k-l+1} x_{i,j,0,l} y_{i,j,k,l-1} + a_{i,j,0,k-l+1} x_{i,j,0,l} c_{i,j,k-1,l} + y_{i,j,k,l-1} c_{i,j,k-1,l} \tag{6.33c}$$

$$c_{i,j,0,l} = 0, \quad y_{i,0,k,0} = 0, \quad x_{i,j,0,l} = x_{j,l}, \quad a_{i,j,0,k-1+1} = a_{i,j,k-l+1} \tag{6.33d}$$

for $i, j = 1(1)n$, $k, l = 1(1)m$. These recurrences look complicated but are really quite straightforward. For example, x_{jl} means the lth bit of x_j, and $a_{i,j,0,k-1+1}$ means bit $k - l + 1$ of a_{ij}. Thus, y_{ijkl} represents the lth term to be added to the kth bit belonging to the jth accumulation of the y_i value. Some indices have been added to index the system fully so that it can be mapped into 4-D space—this implies a four-loop program. Applying the principle of pipelining the variables $a_{i,j,0,k-l+1}$ and $x_{i,j,0,l}$ can be replaced by the equivalent values $a_{i,j,k+1,l}$ and $x_{i,j,k-1,l}$.

Remark Choose pipelining vectors $(0, 0, 1, 0)^t$ and $(0, 0, -1, 0)^t$ respectively.

In addition i and j are constant in (6.33b) and (6.33c) so that we can consider a 2-D plot of the data dependency graph in the k–l plane; this produces Fig. 6.11(a). The graph can be interpreted as a 2-D array for computing the term y_{ij} in the matrix–vector recurrence using the cell definition in Fig. 6.11(b). Now, eqn (6.33a) tells us how to connect copies of the 2-D array into a pipeline for evaluating the matrix–vector computation as i and j vary. The final array is shown in Fig. 6.11(c). For an $n \times n$ matrix and m bit numbers. We require n major cells consisting of an $m \times m$ 2-D bit serial array. The global array data flow is the same as the array described in Fig. 2.8(b) but we use nm^2 single-bit adder cells.

6.4.3 Numerical accuracy and performance

Exploitation of the bit serial design concept can be largely attributed to McCanny and McWhirter (1982a and b) who have used it extensively for 1-D and 2-D (hexagonal) arrays. Indeed most of the successfully implemented designs to date have exploited bit serial computations in one form or another, sometimes for quite complicated operations. In this last section we briefly consider some of the performance claims for bit serial designs. McCanny *et al.* (1982) estimate that a 20 times 30 array of bit cells can be implemented on a single chip using CMOS technology with a 3 μm feature size and clock rate in excess of 20 MHz. For 16 bit numbers a systolic device could perform convolutions of 32 points at a rate of 0.5 per megahertz. Similarly a matrix–vector product using bit level cells and 4 μm in CMOS/SOS technology claims a 40 MHz clock rate and a data rate of 20 MHz. A more complex example is the pipelined lattice processor (PLP) which solves Topelitz matrices (see Kung and Hu 1983). The PLP was a joint venture between Hughes Research Laboratory and the University of Southern California. The device implements 16 processors incorporating 28 bit ALUs with 8 bit data and achieves a 4 MHz clock rate using 6 μm feature size and NMOS technology. A 16×16 system of equations can be solved in 0.6 ms on a chip with dimensions $230 \times 300\ \mathrm{mm}^2$. Finally, a one-stage fast Fourier transform (FFT) has been implemented at the board level using an 18×15 inch circuit board and 22 bit floating-point format (see Swartzlander 1986). The board uses 22 floating-point adders and 12 floating-point multipliers and performs approximately 320 million floating-point operations per second. These examples give some idea of the scale of computation that can be achieved. Many other examples are documented in the literature. Indeed it is possible to outperform these arrays by reducing the feature size, improving the clock speeds, or reducing multichip design into single chips. However, the value of bit serial techniques for high-performance computing has been demonstrated.

An interesting feature of bit serial designs is the way that one can trade off cell area with accuracy. In the pattern matcher the number of bits used to represent a symbol is static. That is, 8 bits can be used to represent all the ASCII symbols used by modern computers (e.g., alphabetic, numeric, punctuation, etc.). There is no need to use more than 8 bits for a symbol, which gives an upper bound for the number of bit level cells used for symbol comparison. In the numerical examples such as convolution the number of bits used to represent data affects the numerical accuracy. For most practical applications real numbers will be required so that bit level circuitry needs to evaluate at least fixed-point arithmetic. This means that a certain number of bits will be used to represent fractional parts of numbers. Depending upon the accuracy required in the calculations we can vary the bit length of

(a)

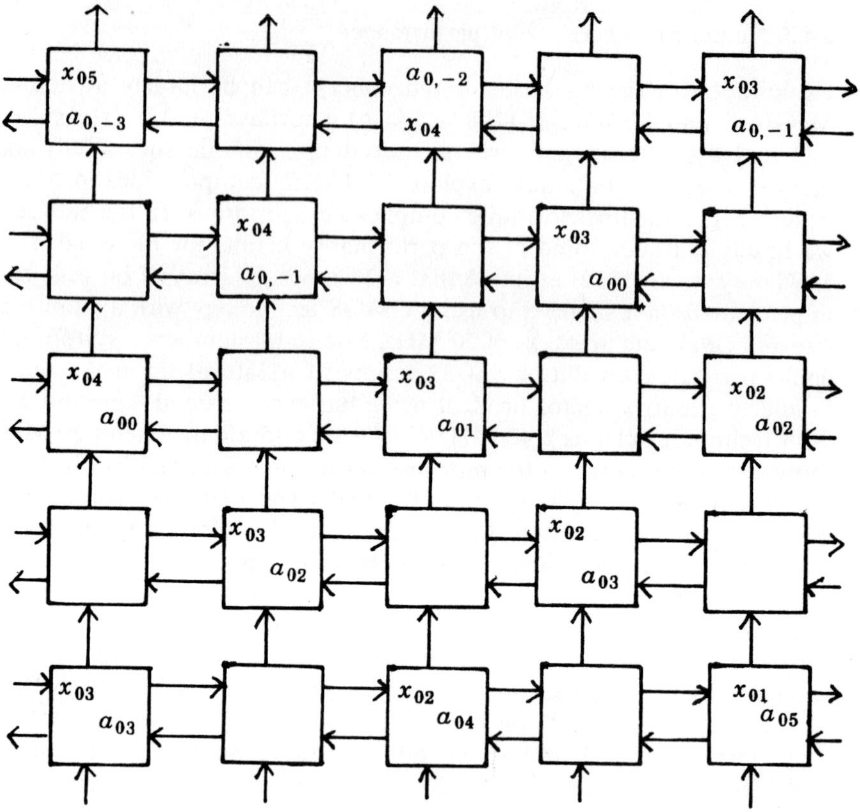

(b)

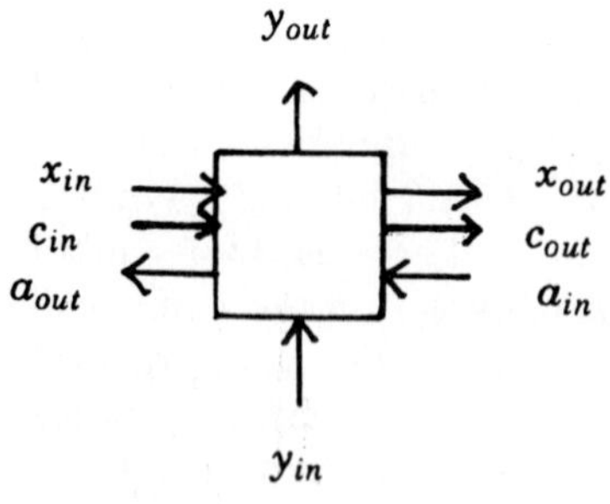

$$y_{out} = y_{in} \oplus (a_{in}x_{in}) \oplus c_{in}$$

$$c_{out} = (a_{in}x_{in})s_{in} + (a_{in}x_{in})c_{in} + s_{in}c_{in}$$

$$a_{out} = a_{in}$$

$$x_{out} = x_{in}$$

Fig. 6.11 Bit serial matrix–vector: (a) 2-D bit level inner product ($x_{kl} = x_{ijkl}$); (b) bit cell definition.

(c)

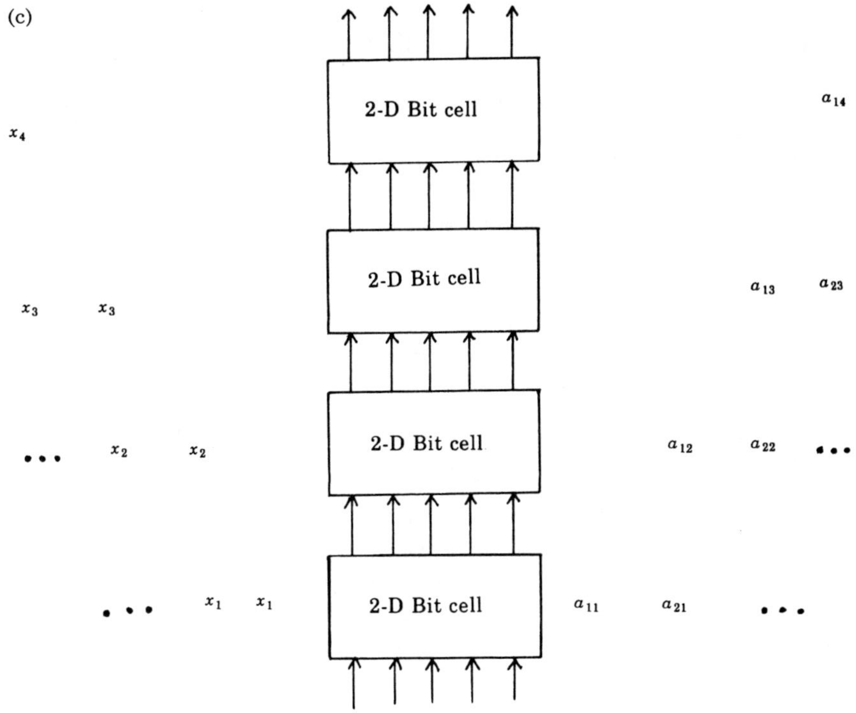

Fig. 6.11 (*cont.*) (c) pipelined array ($n = 4$, x_j and a_{ij} are multibit values.)

numbers to deliver the minimum degree of accuracy acceptable. Now because bit level arrays have a size dependent upon the bit length this means that a trade-off exists between accuracy and area. The convolution example above uses 16 bit numbers while the PLP suggests 8 bit numbers, and the FFT 22 bits. In the latter a 16 bit fraction and a 6 bit exponent are used, which improves the dynamic range of the numbers and so provides better precision than fixed-point representation. How many bits you use depends upon the accuracy you need. It must be emphasized that reducing hardware in this way, albeit legitimate, is a dangerous game to play and requires great familiarity with the application domain. In particular it should be noted that restricting the bit length of numbers involves truncation or rounding errors in the arithmetic. Where results are used repeatedly, for example in a pipelined accumulation of partial products, an error is made at each step. As these errors accumulate the numerical accuracy (and in some cases stability) of the numerical technique being implemented can be affected.

6.5 Unidirectional arrays and fault tolerance

As the data flow of a systolic algorithm becomes more complex it becomes increasingly difficult to modify the associated architecture. This is because the data dependencies impose a more restrictive order on the required operations. In particular the occurrence of feedback or opposing directions of flow often leads to the introduction of dummy values into the data to achieve synchronization. These dummy values add extra computation time to the design and reduce the efficiency. In Section 6.1 we introduced some methods for alleviating these problems but it would be better if arrays could be modified to avoid such problems. As we will see below such techniques are possible in certain circumstances.

6.5.1 Systolic rings revisited

Let us first return to the concept of systolic rings discussed in Chapter 4. We have used systolic rings as a convenient method for reducing the cell count of a design but the same concept can be extended to remove feedback from arrays. To illustrate the technique consider another table-generating algorithm which can be defined by the following generating rule

$$\begin{aligned} r_{ij} &= r_{i-1,j+1} - m_i r_{i-1,j+1} \\ m_i &= r_{i-2,1}/r_{i-1,1} \end{aligned} \tag{6.34}$$

with the starting values

$$\begin{aligned} r_{01}, r_{02}, r_{03}, \ldots &= 1, a_2, a_4, \ldots \\ r_{11}, r_{12}, r_{13}, \ldots &= a_1, a_3, a_5, \ldots \end{aligned} \tag{6.35}$$

where the a_i are known values. In fact they are usually the coefficients of the so-called characteristic polynomial describing a control system, but any polynomial could be used. Once the table has been constructed the number of sign changes indicates the number of polynomial roots which lie in the positive half of the complex plane. Thus the array can be used to give some information about the root distribution of a given polynomial. In control theory, if any roots with positive real parts exist the associated control system is unstable—the table construction is known as the Routh–Hurvitz test for absolute stability.

When the table is of size n, applying the design methodology and mapping the data dependencies into space–time produces a bidirectional array of $n/2$ cells as shown in Fig. 6.12. The boundary (circular) cell computes the value of m_i, while the square cell is an inner product cell augmented with delay registers and simple control. The exact details are not important here but the array computes as shown in Fig. 6.12(a) so that the cells in Fig. 6.12(b) are easily derived. The initial polynomial coefficients are fed from right to left through the array until they reach the boundary cell where the appropriate m_i is produced and fed back along the array thus demanding a spacing element between each input value if it is to meet all the values in a given row. Because each row of the table contributes to the construction of two other rows the data must be continually realigned. This realignment is achieved by a control tag (shown by the asterisk) which filters from left to right along the array. Tracing out the snapshots to completion demonstrates that $\mathscr{T} = 3n - 2$ steps are required to generate the whole table and that the array computes with efficiency $e = 0.5$ (50 per cent).

Next we show that the above feedback array can be retimed to produce a unidirectional array. The essential idea is to use an array unrolling (see Chapter 2) to produce a space–time diagram. The required diagrams are shown in Fig. 6.13. Fig. 6.13(a) corresponds to the array in Fig. 6.12 and it is simple to notice that r_{i1} values are produced every two cycles (for simplicity the nodes have been numbered according to the time cycle when they are computed). Now Fig. 6.13(b) is isomorphic to Fig. 6.13(a) and represents an alternative array unrolling. It is apparent that by rolling up (or projecting out the vertical axis) a unidirectional array is defined. This array is shown in Fig. 6.14. The graphs in Fig. 6.13 are labelled as non-stationary and stationary respectively, because the former array is stationary with respect to columns while the latter is non-stationary. In the unidirectional design we require n cells each of which can perform either the evaluation of an m_i value or the inner product operation. In general a basic cell waits until it receives the first two real entries and computes an m_i value loading it into the cell. On subsequent computations the m value is used to update the table rows using the inner product rule. Selection of the correct computation is controlled by a simple tag that is pumped along with the first input elements using the natural delay of the pipeline. Finally a systolic ring is produced by observing that sides A and B in Fig. 6.13(b) can be connected together. The resulting projection or rolling-up of the array produces the ring and limits the number of processors to $n/2$.

The above example shows that bidirectional arrays with feedback can be converted to unidirectional arrays. A more difficult problem is encountered when direct feedback to non-boundary cells are permitted. One such design is the back-substitution array (Fig. 3.1). Unrolling the array in the same manner as above produces a space–time diagram similar to that shown in Fig. 2.11; this diagram is also isomorphic to Fig. 6.13(b) so that a unidirectional array is possible. Again connecting opposite sides of the diagram together produces a ring—rolling up the diagram produces the array as shown in Fig. 6.15. The a_{ii}^{-1} values arriving at the cells determine a new x_i value which is then loaded into the cell. Subsequent matrix inputs use this value, accumulating a single term of the substitution process and

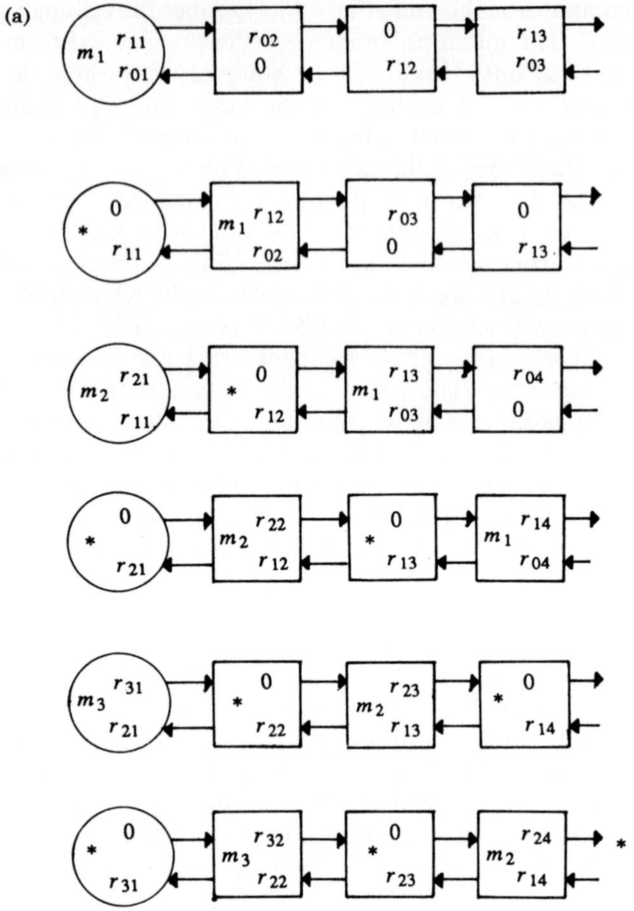

Fig. 6.12 Bidirectional Routh–Hurvitz array: (a) array snapshots

shifting it right. In the example the matrix is lower triangular and has bandwidth $q = 6$, and the first three values x_1, x_2, and x_3 get loaded into the cells when the corresponding a_{ii}^{-1} value arrives, the value emerging on the feedback loop is the accumulation of the first three terms in row 4 of the matrix which must meet with a_{44}^{-1} and b_4 to produce x_4. The data for a_{44}^{-1} and a_{55}^{-1} etc. would normally require extra cells to the right of the cell but by connecting the two sides of the space–time diagram the spare trailing spaces can be filled and cells are reused. As all the matrix elements in column 1 have been input by the time a_{44}^{-1} arrives the stored value of x_1 can be replaced by x_4. In general the idea is to cycle $q/2$ unknowns around the ring with the $q/2$ most recently computed results stored in each of the $q/2$ cells (one per cell). The $q/2$ partial sums travel around the ring and meet each of

(b)

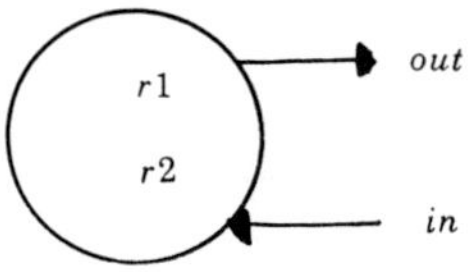


```
IF NOT * THEN
 { out := r1/r2;
   r1 := r2;
   r2 := in
 } ELSE
 {
   out := 0;
   r2 := in
 }
```

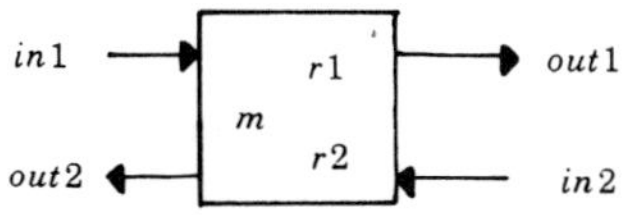


```
IF NOT * THEN
 { out2 := r2 - m*r1;
   out1 := m;
   r1 := r2;
   r2 := in1;
   m := in2;
 } ELSE
 { out2 := 0;
   out1 := 0;
   r2 := in2;
   m := in1;
 }
```

Fig. 6.12 (*cont.*) (b) cell definitions

the stored values. Thus every two cycles a new unknown is obtained; this new value is then made stationary by loading it into a cell and overwriting the oldest $q/2$ value. Observe that the original non-stationary data eventually become stationary and that data are left in places where the cycling values will eventually find them. It follows that a systolic ring with just $q/2$ processors can compute the back-substitution in $\mathcal{T} = 2n + q$ steps with 100 per cent efficiency. The cost of the cell reduction and the improvement in efficiency compared with the design in Chapter 3 are offset by the more complex control required to switch data between stationary and non-stationary states. Also notice that we input a_{ii}^{-1} rather than a_{ii} in the original scheme. This change implies that the reciprocal of the diagonal entries are precomputed before starting the array. The cost is not included in the timing calculation because reciprocal evaluation and array operation can proceed simultaneously. Clearly, if the reciprocals are not computed the cells must be capable of performing division as well as inner product computation, which would increase the cell area and the cycle time dramatically.

Removing feedback to create unidirectional arrays and systolic rings is not confined to simple 1-D designs—it can also be applied to more complex 2-D structures such as LU decomposition and triangularization. In the former, an array with bandwidth $2q - 1$ requires just $q/3$ rows of cells with

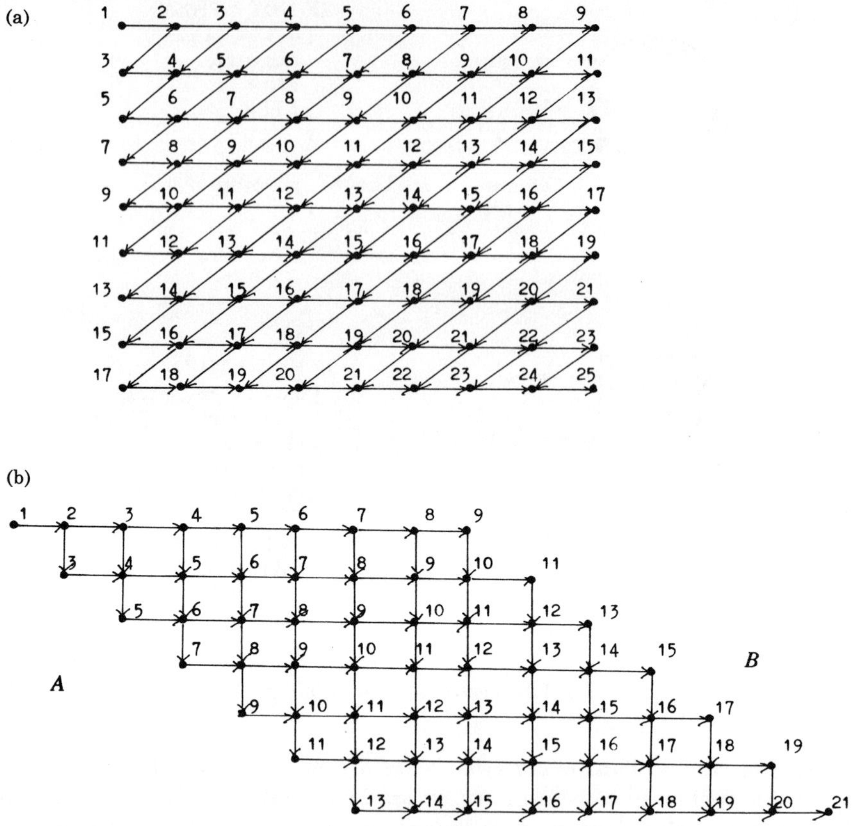

Fig. 6.13 Array unrollings: (a) stationary case; (b) non-stationary case

q cells in each row as shown in Fig. 6.16. The $q/3$ most recent computed rows of the u_{ij} are stored in the cells as they are generated, while the l_{ij} are passed down the rows. The resulting design is simply an array of rings which can be connected to form a cylinder. The reader is referred to Kung and Lam (1984) for detailed descriptions.

6.5.2 Error recovery

One of the reasons for trying to limit the area and complexity of basic cells in a systolic design is the problem of fault tolerance. If we confine our attention to the problems of manufacturing VLSI chips there is a trade-off between chip area and the yield (or the number of working chips produced from a single wafer of silicon). The higher the yield the more cost effective the design becomes. Unfortunately, during the fabrication process many opportunities arise for a flaw to appear and make a chip completely useless.

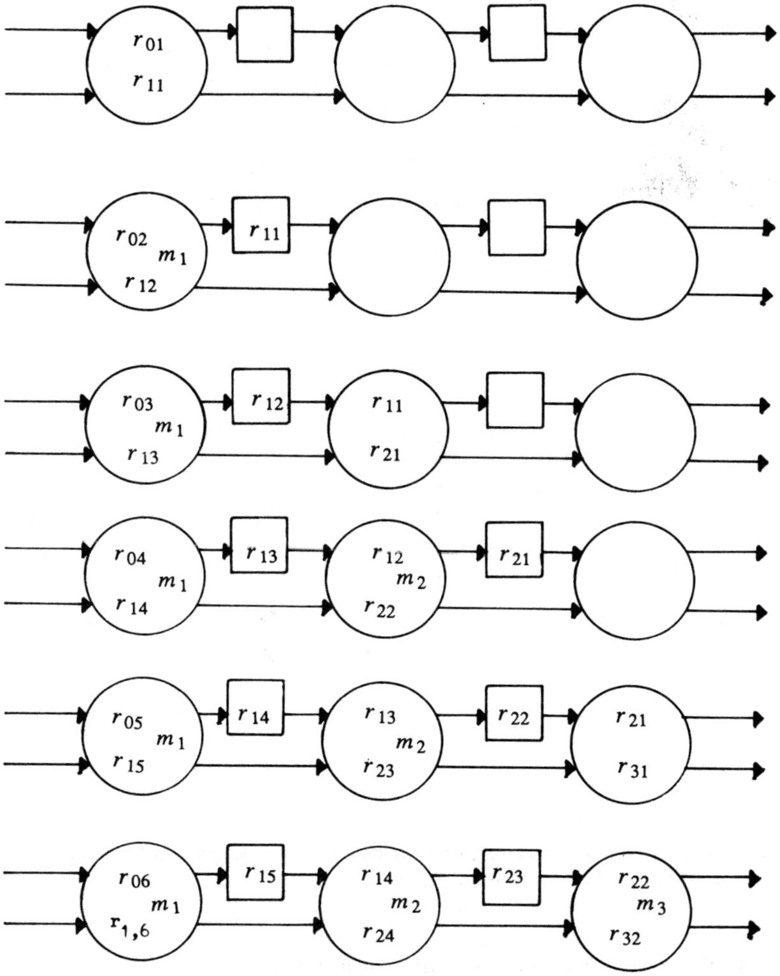

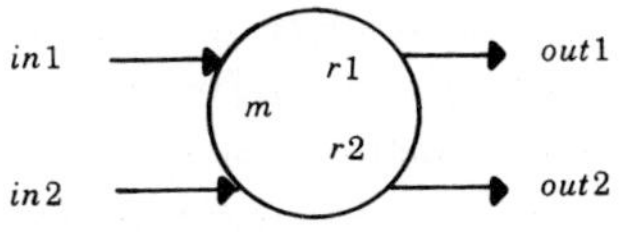


```
IF * THEN
 { r1 := in1;
   r2 := in2;
   m := r1/r2;
   out1 := r2;
   out2 := 0;
 } ELSE
  { r1 := in1;
    r2 := in2;
    out1 := r2;
    out2 := r1 - m*r2
  }
```

Fig. 6.14 Unidirectional Routh–Hurvitz array

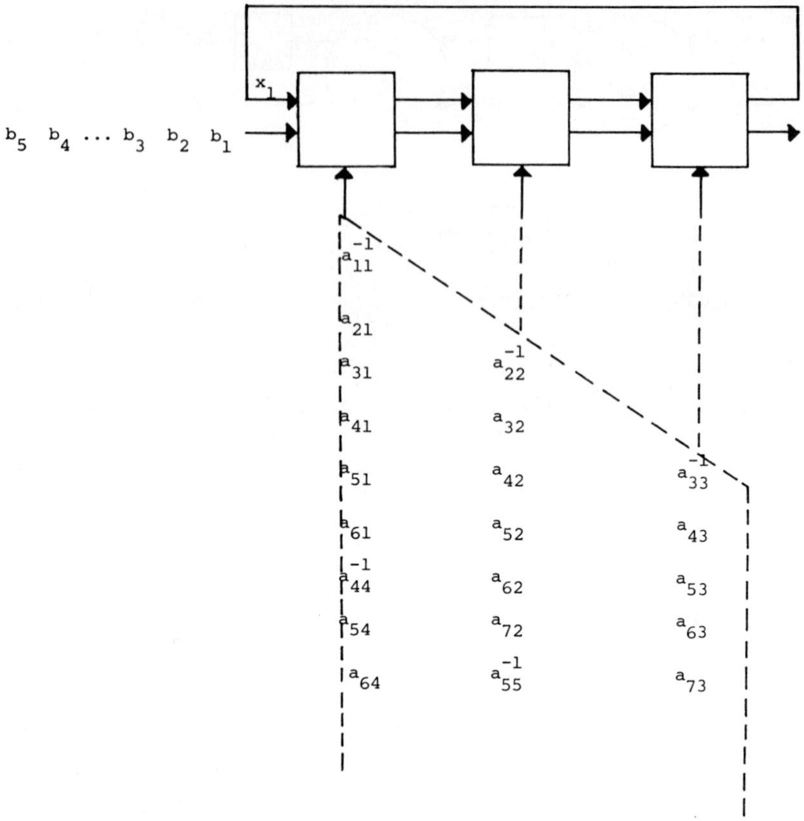

Fig. 6.15 Systolic ring for back-substitution. (Source H. T. Kung and M. S. Lam, *Journal of Parallel and Distributed Computing*, Academic Press Inc., 1984.)

In fact the largest feasible circuits (manufactured today) have a very low probability (10 per cent) of being error free. The total cost of manufacture must be spread over all the unflawed chips making the cost inversely proportional to the yield. For example, if we multiply chip area by a constant $c > 1$ the probability of a good chip is 0.1^c with cost increasing according to 10^c (Ullman 1984). It follows that designs with small area have economic advantages, and conversely designs with large and complex basic cells are a disadvantage. The area of a chip must be kept low to improve the probability of producing a working device, but small area implies a small perimeter and a bounded space from which connections to the outside world (pins) can be made. It should be clear that bit serial design has attractive properties for dealing with area/yield problems.

Another argument is that a more complex design can be 'stuffed' into the same area by reducing the feature size of basic components (which defines

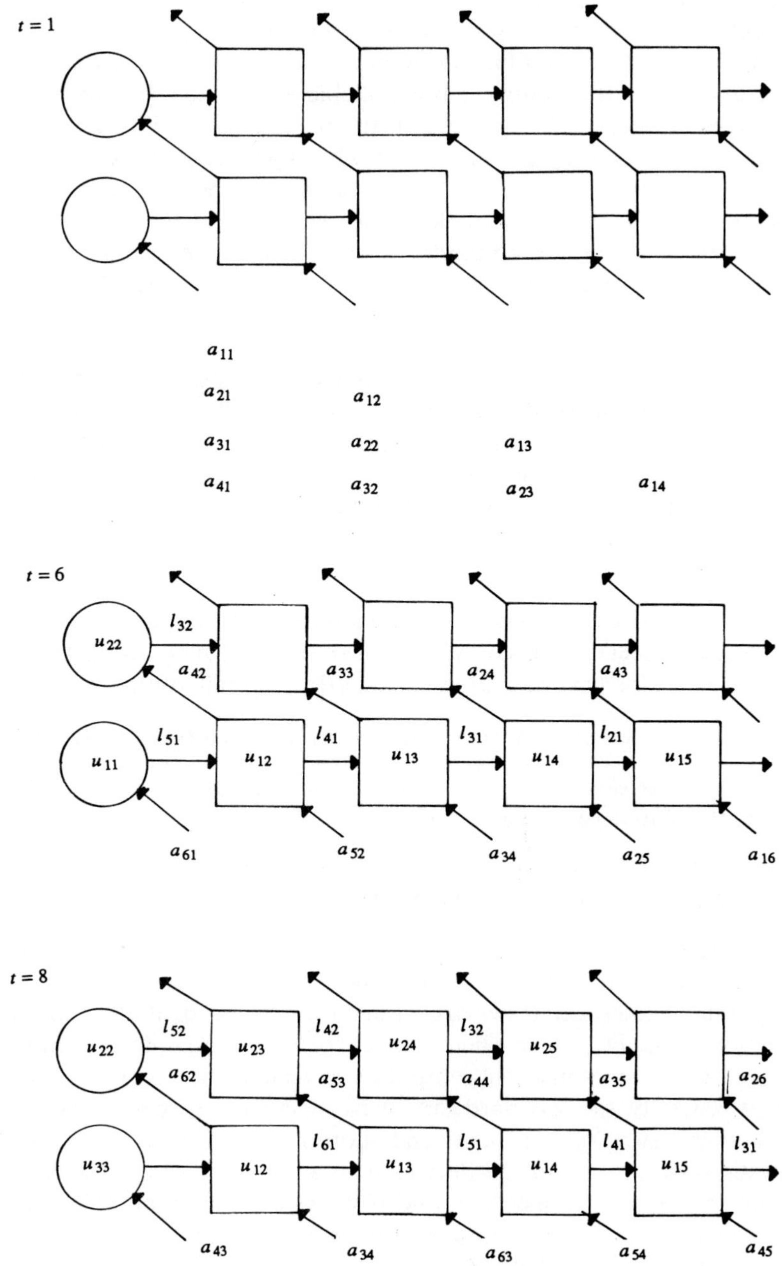

Fig. 6.16 Systolic ring for *LU* decomposition. (Source H. T. Kung and M. S. Lam, *Journal of Parallel and Distributed Computing*, Academic Press Inc., 1984.)

the basic dimensions of wires and logic elements). Indeed this process of miniaturization has worked very successfully in the past. Unfortunately, manufacturing techniques are reaching the limits of resolution in the manufacturing process and further miniaturization without radically changing the underlying technology is not possible. Consequently more complex cell designs have no alternative but to increase area. Further practical problems are also emerging. The electrical properties of wires and components are beginning to limit the performance of devices. For example, propagation delays through smaller logic elements can be reduced but the propagation delay on interconnections remains the same—this means that eventually transmission speed dictates the switching time (and hence cycle time) of cells. This is one of the reasons why systolic designs attempt to limit the length of wires by nearest-neighbour connections.

Another (perhaps more devious) approach to solving area/yield problems is to increase yield dramatically so that area is no longer a good measure for cost. For example, if yield (i.e. the probability of an unflawed chip) was around 0.9 (90 per cent) then increasing area by a constant would produce a yield which decreases slowly thus making the cost rise slowly—hence less sensitivity to chip area.

Remark Of course cost is not the only justification for fault tolerance. Many applications, especially in safety-critical systems, demand robustness and reliability as an integral part of the design (e.g. aircraft control systems).

In general we can classify errors in devices into two broad categories:

(1) *production defects*, which occur during manufacture and are high with current manufacturing techniques;

(2) *operational defects*, which occur while the device is embedded and working in the external environment.

The corresponding fault-tolerant strategies are termed static and dynamic respectively. In static schemes we test and fix defects before the device is packaged; fault tolerance is performed just once and contributes only to the production costs. Dynamic schemes cater for operational defects and must be applied many times in a real computing environment. Consequently static schemes generally use less hardware than dynamic schemes which require programmable switching elements and additional control networks to allow automatic restructuring of the device. Where the complexity of a basic cell is similar to the extra connections and switches to implement fault tolerance dynamic schemes are questionable. This is because the probability of the fault-detecting equipment itself being fault increases (Sami and Steffanalli 1986). We consider below one static and one dynamic error recovery scheme.

Fault tolerance techniques can be tailored to systolic arrays by using

(a)

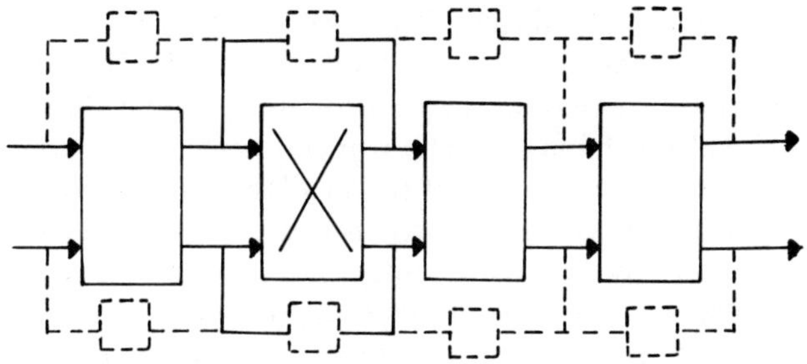

(b)

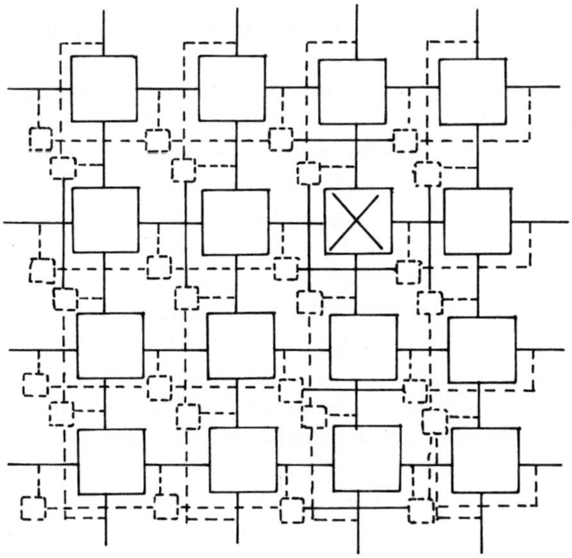

Fig. 6.17 Rerouting in fault arrays: (a) 1-D fault tolerance; (b) 2-D fault tolerance

additional information about the regularity of data flow to produce effective low-overhead error recovery schemes. When attention is restricted to static error recovery the cells of unidirectional arrays can be augmented with simple bypass registers and switches (see Fig. 6.17). When a faulty cell is detected it is switched out using these extra connections and registers to maintain data flow and throughput. The range of problems that can be solved is reduced because of the smaller number of working cells. For example, in the convolution array of Fig. 1.1(c) a fault in a single cell would mean that only three coefficients could be used instead of four. Notice that nearest-neighbour connections are maintained by feeding data from bypass register to bypass register in sequences of adjacent faulty cells so that regularity of data flow is preserved and data skewing problems avoided. The amount of extra hardware is trivial so that we can reasonably assume that the extra wires and registers will not be faulty. The principle extends readily to 2-D arrays with unidirectional flow in each of the available directions; for example, try to augment the matrix product array in Fig. 2.10(a). One can determine the additional registers by removing faulty cells and replacing them with delay registers to preserve data flow and then augmenting the original design with a generalized pattern of bypass registers. It is important to make sure that the faulty design with bad cells replaced is a valid retiming of the original design by using the cut theorem. During this checking process data flow can only be preserved if some working cells are also bypassed, for example a row or column of cells in the product array. This redundancy is an overhead and the price of coping with faults—provided the number of faulty cells is small it is acceptable.

For arrays involving more complex data movement such as bidirectional flow and feedback the problem is more complex and throughput is reduced rapidly as faults occur. The reason for this behaviour is easily demonstrated by trying to retime a bidirectional array with faulty cells using the cut theorem—we are forced to add many additional delay registers between cells to retain the original data dependencies. A solution to the feedback problem is to convert feedback arrays into unidirectional ones using the method described above or from first principles using retiming.

An alternative approach to reliability is algorithmic fault tolerance (Huang and Abraham 1984). This technique is used to detect and correct errors resulting from permanent and transient errors and can be classed as dynamic. The technique is not generally applicable but for specific cases involving matrix computations it can be performed with a very low overhead. The general idea is to try and mask the error resulting from fault hardware. The technique is to augment the algorithm with extra computations as follows:

1. Encode the input data.
2. Redesign the algorithm to operate on the encoded data.
3. Distribute the new computation on to the architecture.

For a low-overhead scheme the unencoded result (or information part) must be easy to recover, and enough redundancy must be available for the detection and correction of errors. One particular encoding which is applicable to many common matrix operations and has been used successfully for communication protocols in distributed systems is the checksum method.

Definition The row, column, and checksum matrices for an $n \times m$ matrix $A = (a_{ij})$ are defined as follows.

1. The column checksum matrix A_c of A is an $(n+1) \times m$ matrix consisting of A and the extra row

$$a_{n+1,j} = \sum_{i=1}^{n} a_{ij}, \quad j = 1(1)m.$$

2. The row checksum matrix A_r of A is an $n \times (m+1)$ matrix consisting of A and the extra column

$$a_{i,m+1} = \sum_{j=1}^{n} a_{ij}, \quad i = 1(1)n.$$

3. The full checksum matrix A_f of A is the $(n+1) \times (n+1)$ matrix which is the column checksum of the row checksum matrix of A.

Each column of A_f is an encoded vector, and the following results hold for $n \times n$ matrices:

$$\begin{aligned} C_f &= A_c B_r \quad &&\text{(matrix product)} \\ C_f &= L_c U_r \quad &&\text{(matrix factorization)} \\ C_f &= A_f + B_f \quad &&\text{(matrix addition).} \end{aligned} \tag{6.36}$$

Using these relations fault tolerance is conducted by first computing the result and then checking for errors as follows. (i) *Detect the error* by (a) computing the sum of each row and column, (b) comparing the results with corresponding checksums in the last row and column, (c) noting that errors are indicated by inconsistent values. (ii) *Locate the error* by finding the intersection of inconsistent rows and columns. (iii) *Correct the error* by (a) adding the difference between the computed row or column sum and its corresponding checksum value to the element at the intersection, or (b) replacing the checksum by its computed value.

Remark In general a small tolerance is added to the calculations to allow for the finite arithmetic of computers thus avoiding the false detection of errors.

Figure 6.18 illustrates the method for a small example. In a systolic implementation additional cells are required to compute the checksum part, but there is no need to route around faulty cells. Thus problems can be solved in the presence of errors using the full array size and then fixed up afterwards. Unfortunately the scheme has only a limited correction capability, and for certain configurations of errors the technique can be fooled. For example, if the errors can be connected into cycles it becomes impossible to determine the correction for the error. A more powerful method is the weighted checksum scheme reported by Jou and Abraham (1986) and extended by Luk (1988).

$$\begin{bmatrix} 1 & 4 & 2 & 1 \\ 3 & 1 & 2 & 0 \\ 0 & 1 & 2 & 3 \\ 3 & 0 & 1 & 2 \end{bmatrix} \begin{bmatrix} 1 & 0 & 1 & 2 \\ 3 & 4 & 1 & 2 \\ 5 & 6 & 1 & 2 \\ 1 & 5 & 7 & 8 \end{bmatrix} = \begin{bmatrix} 24 & 33 & 14 & 22 \\ 16 & 16 & 6 & 12 \\ 16 & 31 & 24 & 30 \\ 10 & 16 & 18 & 24 \end{bmatrix}$$

Original problem

$$\left[\begin{array}{cccc} 1 & 4 & 2 & 1 \\ 3 & 1 & 2 & 0 \\ 0 & 1 & 2 & 3 \\ 3 & 0 & 1 & 2 \\ \hline 7 & 6 & 7 & 6 \end{array}\right] \left[\begin{array}{cccc|c} 1 & 0 & 1 & 2 & 4 \\ 3 & 4 & 1 & 2 & 10 \\ 5 & 6 & 1 & 2 & 14 \\ 1 & 5 & 7 & 8 & 21 \end{array}\right] = \left[\begin{array}{cccc|c} 24 & 33 & 14 & 22 & 93 \\ 16 & 16 & 6 & 12 & 50 \\ 16 & 31 & 24 & 30 & 101 \\ 10 & 16 & 18 & 24 & 68 \\ \hline 66 & 96 & 62 & 88 & - \end{array}\right]$$

Encode problem

$$\left[\begin{array}{cccc|c} 24 & 33 & 14 & 22 & 93 \\ 16 & 16 & 6 & 12 & 50 \\ \textcircled{19} & 31 & 24 & \textcircled{28} & 102 \\ 10 & \textcircled{30} & 18 & 24 & 92 \\ \hline 69 & 110 & 62 & 86 & - \end{array}\right]$$

Detect errors (in cols 1,2 and rows 3 and 4)

$$\left[\begin{array}{cccc|c} 24 & 33 & 14 & 22 & 93 \\ 16 & 16 & 6 & 12 & 50 \\ 16 & 31 & 24 & \textcircled{28} & 99 \\ 10 & \textcircled{30} & 18 & 24 & 82 \\ \hline 66 & 110 & 62 & 86 & - \end{array}\right]$$

Correct error (66–69=–3, 101–102=–1)

$$\left[\begin{array}{cccc|c} 24 & 33 & 14 & 22 & 93 \\ 16 & 16 & 6 & 12 & 50 \\ 16 & 31 & 24 & \textcircled{28} & 99 \\ 10 & 16 & 18 & 24 & 68 \\ \hline 66 & 96 & 62 & 86 & - \end{array}\right]$$

Correct error (88–86=2, 101–99=2)

$$\left[\begin{array}{cccc|c} 24 & 33 & 14 & 22 & 93 \\ 16 & 16 & 6 & 12 & 50 \\ 16 & 31 & 24 & 30 & 101 \\ 10 & 16 & 18 & 24 & 68 \\ \hline 66 & 96 & 62 & 88 & - \end{array}\right]$$

Fig. 6.18 Error correction with checksums

6.6 Incomplete arrays

Finally, and to complete the set of techniques introduced in this chapter, we consider a relatively new approach to improving array designs. The previous methods are all based on the idea of preserving computation and correctness while also improving the area, time, or efficiency of the design;

that is, the array must eventually produce the correct solution to the problem it was designed for. In contrast incomplete arrays, as the name suggests, are based on the premise that some of the algorithm 'correctness' can be sacrificed to produce improved area–time trade-offs. Put another way, we design an array to perform an incomplete or 'incorrect' computation which can be fixed or corrected later by additional cells or the external controlling device with very little overhead. Consequently to be effective an incomplete scheme must be capable of measuring the degree of correctness that the array produces. Intuitively incomplete methods are similar to error recovery schemes. If it is assumed that an array can be manufactured without faults then we can choose some cells to be removed from the design. These missing cells cause errors because their associated computations are not included in the design. Thus area is saved but the computation is incomplete.

To illustrate the technique consider the special case of an array design for a fast tridiagonal matrix solver as shown in Fig. 6.19. The array is a simple Gaussian elimination array derived from Fig. 3.7 except that it adopts a standard matrix–vector input format and consists of three cells: a boundary cell to the left and two simple inner product cells to the right. Simple (nearest-neighbour-pivoting) row interchange facilities are assumed.

Remark The usefulness of a three-cell array is somewhat dubious. The cost of fetching the data from the external device would probably outweigh any improvement in computation speed. However, the design illustrates the principle of incomplete computation.

The boundary cell selects the next pivot row, setting a control tag (c) to indicate interchanges, and computes a multiplier (m) to update adjacent (non-pivot) rows. Snapshots of the array operation are depicted in Fig. 6.20. From the boundary cell definition it is easily shown that

$$(F < 0) \text{ and } (\text{sign}(P_1) \text{ xor sign}(P_1)) = 1 \text{ for } m = \frac{P_2}{P_1} \text{ and } c = 0 \quad (6.37)$$

and

$$(F < 0) \text{ and } (\text{sign}(P_1) \text{ xand sign}(P_2)) = 1 \text{ for } m = \frac{P_1}{P_2} \text{ and } c = 1 \quad (6.38)$$

ensuring that the boundary and modifying cells both have a basic cycle time equivalent to a single inner product step. When no interchanges occur the array generates two output data sequences, one for each of the two bidiagonals. When interchanges are allowed three output sequences are used to accommodate the fill-in of the second superdiagonal. In general the output

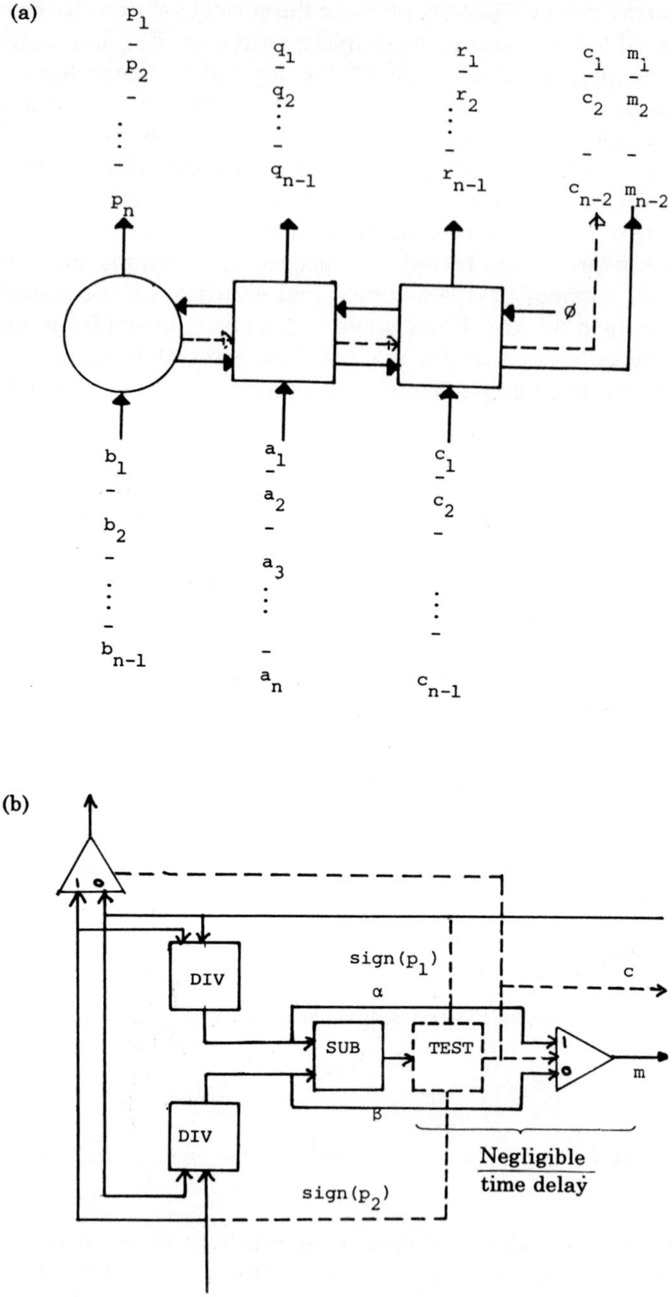

Fig. 6.19 Incomplete arrays for tridiagonal Gaussian elimination: (a) modified triangularization array; (b) boundary cell definition

has the triangular form

$$U = \begin{bmatrix} p_1 & q_1 & r_1 & & & \\ & p_2 & q_2 & r_2 & & \\ & & p_3 & q_3 & r_3 & \\ & & & p_4 & q_4 & r_4 \\ & & & & p_5 & q_5 \\ & & & & & p_6 \end{bmatrix}. \tag{6.39}$$

The c_i and m_i, for $i = 1(1)n - 1$, move from left to right, eventually leaving the array to be stored for later retrieval of the row interchanges. If the computation involves multiple right-hand sides additional cells can be added to the right of the array (one for each RHS). The array timing is trivially derived from the array snapshots as $\mathscr{T} = 2n + k$ where $k > 0$ is a constant derived from the delay of the first output (i.e. $k = 2$).

Next, apply a simple permutation (a QI permutation; see Evans and Hadjidimos 1980) to produce an implicit 2×2 block structure which for odd and even matrix orders produces

$$\begin{bmatrix} a_1 & 0 & b_1 & 0 & & & & \\ 0 & a_8 & 0 & b_7 & & & & \\ b_1 & 0 & a_2 & 0 & b_2 & 0 & & \\ 0 & b_7 & 0 & a_7 & 0 & b_6 & & \\ & & b_2 & 0 & a_3 & 0 & b_3 & 0 \\ & & 0 & b_6 & 0 & a_6 & 0 & b_5 \\ & & & & b_3 & 0 & a_4 & b_4 \\ & & & & & b_5 & b_4 & a_5 \end{bmatrix}$$

when $n = 8$ and

$$\begin{bmatrix} a_1 & 0 & b_1 & 0 & & & \\ 0 & a_7 & 0 & b_6 & & & \\ b_1 & 0 & a_2 & 0 & b_2 & 0 & \\ 0 & b_6 & 0 & a_6 & 0 & b_5 & \\ & & b_2 & 0 & a_3 & 0 & b_3 \\ & & 0 & b_5 & 0 & a_5 & b_4 \\ & & & & b_3 & b_4 & a_4 \end{bmatrix}$$

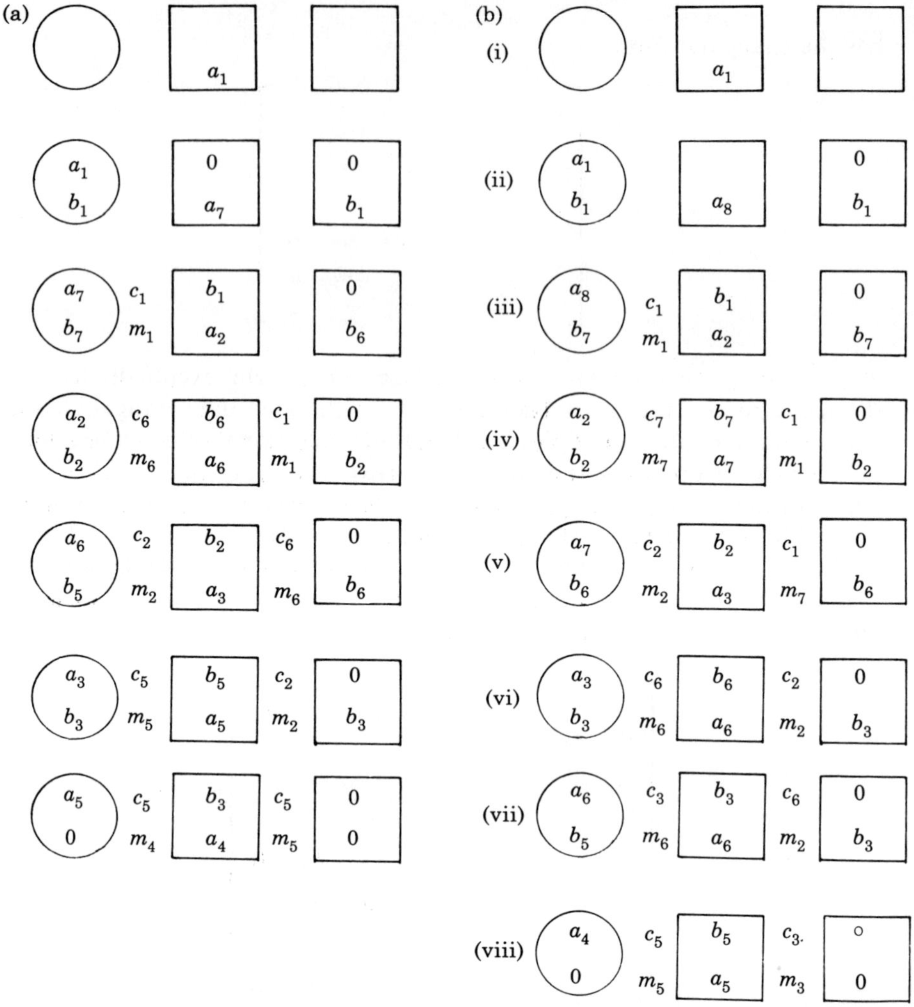

Fig. 6.20 Snapshots for tridiagonal array: (a) odd case; (b) even case

when $n = 7$. Notice that the input format is similar to a double-pipe splitting except that the rightmost bottom 2×2 block fills in. With a double-pipe splitting the feedback of the array would be weakened and we could easily derive a fast array by filling the dummy elements. Unfortunately the design requires six cells instead of three (because of the increased bandwidth). Next fold the design using option 2 in Section 6.2 so that the array is reduced back to three cells. Observe that splitting and folding are equivalent to triangularizing simultaneously from the bottom and top of the matrix. Drawing out a series of snapshots demonstrates that the computation is

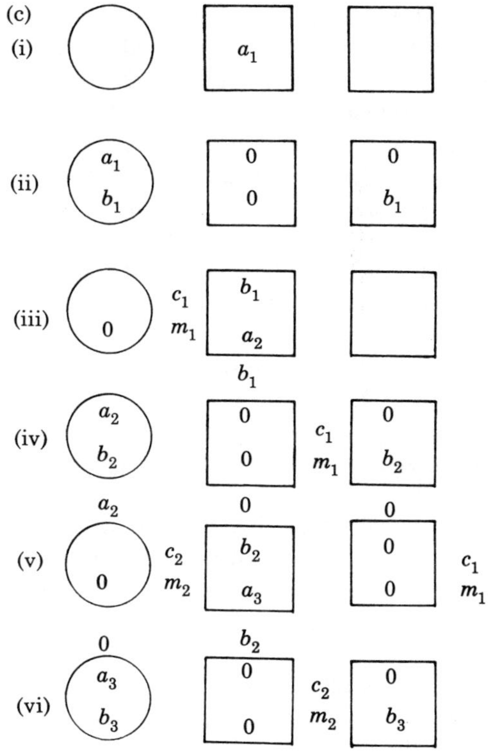

Fig. 6.20 (c) snapshots

correct until the bottom 2 × 2 block is encountered. The array is incomplete, it will compute with just $\mathscr{T} = n + k$ steps and 100 per cent efficiency, but it makes mistakes for a single 2 × 2 block of elements (or a scalar if n is odd). Ordinarily the design would be abandoned at this stage but let us continue. By considering the missing computations we can determine that approximately five inner product operations are required to fix the calculation (which is independent of n). The original array required $\mathscr{T} = 2n + k$ steps, three cells, and 50 per cent efficiency. The incomplete design requires $\mathscr{T} = n + k$ steps, three cells, has 100 per cent efficiency, and is twice as fast as the original. For sufficiently large n the cost of fixing the computation can be offset against the speed-up.

Incomplete arrays arise in many situations which result from the use of heuristics or approximations instead of actual computations. To illustrate, recall the edit distance problem discussed in Chapter 5. Lipton and Lopresti (1986) showed that a simple heuristic could be used to reduce the size of the edit distance array. The key observation is this: when two strings are similar the edit distance is quite small. Now if we impose the restriction that the strings to be compared will all have an edit distance less than or equal to d, where d is some positive integer, all the required changes can be determined from the table entries enclosed by the first d sub(super)diagonals of the edit distance table. It seems sensible to compute only the entries within this band of size $2d - 1$ around the main diagonal of the table and forget about the others. The remaining elements are neglected so the computation is incomplete. The array in Fig. 5.4 can be reduced from $m + n - 1$ to $2d - 1$ cells, and as m and n can be quite large and d will generally be small a significant saving in area is produced. Of course if two strings have an edit distance greater than d the array computes the incorrect answer, but generally good results can be obtained. In this case there is no need for additional computation after the result has been produced so the design is particularly attractive.

6.7 Design principles

The design methodology used in this book places emphasis on the data dependencies of a problem and ignores the computations actually being performed. This approach is useful because it allows the designer to concentrate on data flow and establishes common forms for array topologies that can be reused. The methodology deals with the axioms of systolic computation ensuring regular and nearest-neighbour data flow. For practical implementations this abstract model of systolic computation must be distorted to deal with the problem of implementation as embodied by a set of heuristics defining technical capabilities. In a practical design certain design constraints must be met and consequently define the design objectives. In engineering, design objectives are traditionally formulated as objective (or cost) functions which have to be maximized or minimized. For each design we evaluate the cost function and use the results to grade the design against other possibilities. A particular design may be improved iteratively by applying different design techniques geared towards improving different design properties and hence constraints. An experienced designer chooses a technique which will improve a constraint without causing severe or adverse effects in other constraints. Consequently the iterative process converges to a satisfactory design.

In previous chapters we have used three constraints to grade designs—area, time, and efficiency; indeed we suggested grading designs by evaluating the cost functions $\mathcal{AT}$ or $\mathcal{AT}^2$. Intuitively the best design is the one that minimizes the area–time function but maximizes efficiency. This chapter suggests many other cost functions such as minimizing array latency, maximizing throughput, minimizing cell area and routing complexity, maximizing fault tolerance capability, minimizing array bandwidth (i.e. number of connections with outside world). Clearly some objectives are more important than others depending upon the operating environment of the final implementation. It is also clear that many constraints have conflicting requirements. For example, a device designed for a space probe will place emphasis on maximizing fault-tolerant capability and minimizing area. This is because the device must be light and compact and once launched cannot be fixed manually. Unfortunately fault tolerance implies extra hardware and more space. It is clear that in this example fault tolerance is the primary concern with hardware secondary—note that if the final design is very robust but too bulky it will be useless. It follows that the final design may allow some constraints to be non-optimal. Which constraints are given priority is very subjective and depends upon familiarity with the problem domain.

In the context of systolic algorithm design, a possible array is first developed using the space–time representation and projection technique. A collection of objective functions is then selected and evaluated to give an initial measure of the design effectiveness. Next, apply the appropriate design technique (or if in doubt each one in turn). For each new design compute the objective function and discard designs which produce no improvements. If none of the designs gives an improvement then repeat the process using another projection of the space–time representation. When no more projections are possible we are done. The design that 'best fits' the constraints is the one to implement. Observe that the phrases 'improvement' and 'best fit' are relative terms and depend upon the designer's judgement and can only be learned by experience. It should also be appreciated that the design space is very large so a potentially infinite sequence of designs is possible. An experienced designer can cut down the search by neglecting dead-end possibilities. The examples in this text have been selected to give some help in choosing useful decision paths through the design space.

Exercises

1. Use folding to derive triangular arrays for (a) matrix product, (b) LU factorization. By exploiting symmetry construct a similar array for the Cholesky factorization of the form $A = LL^{\mathrm{T}}$ and compare the designs with the designs given in previous chapters and comment on the efficiency, area, and time.
2. By use of interleaving extend the arrays described in Chapters 2 and 3 so that they compute with complex rather than real numbers.
3. Make block-partitioned arrays for (a) matrix–vector, (b) matrix product, (c) matrix triangularization. Comment on the efficiency and timing of the designs.
4. Show that a 3×3 block LU array has a time $O(2n)$ and $e = 0.5$. Use the result to show that 2×2 block arrays are optimal.
5. Using permutation matrices show that quadrant interlocking (QI) schemes are forms of 2×2 block computations. Show how such

permutations can be used to derive arrays for (a) dense, (b) banded, and (c) periodic matrices.

6. Derive preprocessor arrays for generating block input formats from standard array inputs. Discuss how such devices might be used to control the input–output bandwidths of designs.
7. Derive double-pipe splittings for the Faddeev algorithm using (a) row- and (b) column-orientated input. Show that the arrays can be unfolded to produce a planar systolic array with reduced computation time. Use the above result to demonstrate that matrix inversion can be computed on a systolic array in $O(4n)$ steps.
8. If two n-digit numbers are given by $A = a_n a_{n-1} \cdots a_1$ and $B = b_n b_{n-1} \cdots b_1$ show that all the terms of the partial products can be generated by the outer product AB^t. Hence define a systolic algorithm for multiplying two numbers, extending the method to produce a bit serial array for binary multiplication. Using the previous design as a building block construct a bit serial array for the convolution problem.
9. Extend the method in Exercise 8 to produce a bit serial matrix product array.
10. Distinguish between static and dynamic fault tolerance and discuss the advantages and disadvantages of fault-tolerant schemes with respect to systolic design. In what situations would fault tolerance be a principle design objective and why?
11. By applying the cut theorem derive a fault-tolerant scheme for the orthogonally connected matrix product scheme in Chapter 2. Attempt to apply this principle to the hexagonally connected matrix product array and comment on any difficulties that arise.
12. Design systolic arrays for computing the checksum values necessary for error detection. Hence or otherwise modify designs for the matrix product computation so that they are algorithmically fault tolerant.
13. Develop incomplete arrays for (a) LU decomposition and (b) Gaussian elimination. What can you say about the correctness of the results and how might this control the cost effectiveness of the design?
    [Hint: Use a sparse matrix form with a striped banded structure and ignore fill-in below a certain tolerance.]

7

PROGRAMMABLE SYSTOLIC ARRAYS

A common criticism of systolic computation is that it leads only to algorithmically specialized devices, that is a device for sorting numbers cannot perform a matrix triangularization and vice versa. Furthermore an array—being of fixed size once manufactured—can only solve a restricted range of instances in the problem domain. The advantage of this approach is that physical implementations of arrays are well suited to VLSI techniques. In fact the few algorithms which have been implemented in silicon have been shown to be very cost effective (see Moore *et al.* 1987). It is clear that the application of systolic computation will be very limited if methods for coping with more general problem ranges cannot be found. Some *ad hoc* techniques such as multipass (see Chapter 6) can be used to cope with this problem but a satisfactory and general solution is still some way off. An alternative approach, and the subject of this chapter, is to move away from dedicated VLSI implementation and to use 'off-the-shelf' components such as programmable processors for basic cells. Connecting groups of processors into arrays with flexible communication has great appeal because a range of systolic designs can be implemented by reconfiguration of the connection network and the loading of different cell codes.

Now, for the purpose of discussion let us introduce the idea of a 'systolic program'. Following Wirth (1976) we will use the definition

$$\text{program} = \text{algorithm} + \text{array}$$

to indicate that a systolic program is a combination of a systolic algorithm and a systolic array. The algorithm specifies control and data flow while the array determines realistic topologies which can perform the computation. In Chapter 1 we gave a list of axioms and heuristics for systolic design. The axioms can be interpreted as restricting the type of algorithm considered while the heuristics define the type of arrays that can be implemented. Chapter 6 considered various methods for redesigning the algorithm once the array structure was restricted. In this chapter the converse situation is considered with the algorithm restricted by the design methodology but with the array being flexible. We can consider any design produced by the mapping technique as practical—all that is required is an additional mapping of the algorithm on to programmable processors and the topology supplied. The idea of projection in our design method exploits the regularity of systolic data flow to determine practical array topologies. Whether these topologies are implemented directly in hardware or on an existing multiprocessor architecture is up to the designer. Of course the penalty for this flexibility is extra overheads in communication and basic cell cycle time plus additional costs for the more complex processors.

In Chapter 1 we defined three loose classes of algorithm, hard-, hybrid-, and soft-*systolic* respectively. Hard-systolic algorithms were characterized by a low degree of programmability, were inherently special purpose, and suited to VLSI implementation. Hybrid-systolic algorithms allowed limited flexibility by introducing a medium degree of programming but with the connection topology constrained to be essentially systolic. Finally, soft-systolic designs allowed a high degree of programmability using the connection topology defined by the array part of a systolic program as a 'harness' or data structure expressing the amount of parallelism available. Most of the designs presented in this text can be intepreted directly as hard-systolic designs by constructing basic cells at the board level or applying bit serial techniques to produce true VLSI (silicon chip) devices. In this chapter we briefly explore the possibilities of hybrid- and soft-systolic implementation.

7.1 Generic architectures

Dedicated implementations achieve high performance and efficiency by considering a very restricted class of problem. Consequently to recoup the design cost large numbers of devices must be sold. However, the narrow application of each systolic device limits sales of devices to only a small market area. A more economic solution is to implement arrays that incorporate features for a number of systolic algorithms. We have seen that many different systolic schemes result in similar data flow and array topologies. Indeed the concept of a semi-ring was introduced in Chapter 5 to give a generic description to a number of similar algorithms. Hybrid-systolic algorithms arise from an extension of these principles and have resulted in several popular array architectures. We call them generic architectures because they solve a number of systolic tasks but are not intended as general-purpose parallel processors.

7.1.1 The WARP architecture

The WARP architecture, developed at Carnegie Mellon University (CMU) by H. T. Kung and his associates, is the most advanced generic design for purely systolic algorithms. The project began with a study to identify architectures of general-purpose microprocessors which could implement a variety of systolic algorithms effectively. The study resulted in the design of the programmable systolic chip (PSC) discussed in Fisher (1984) and Fisher *et al.* (1984), whose work prompted research into cell structures for high-performance systolic arrays in particular areas (i.e. signal processing). The result was the WARP architecture, a 1-D linear systolic array supporting data and control sequence flow in one direction, and with input at one end of the array and output at the other. The design promotes easy implementation by using a simple global clock mechanism, minimum input/output requirements, and the use of efficient fault tolerance techniques. The basic WARP cell is constructed from a collection of chips as illustrated in Fig. 7.1, the main characteristics being the pipelining of data and control. A Weitek 32 bit floating-point multiplier (MPY) and arithmetic logic unit (ALU) perform operations and can be used in pipeline mode to improve throughput by two-level pipelining. The MPY and ALU use Weitek register file chips to compute approximate functions like inverse and square root problems by table look-up methods. The x, y, and addr values indicated are also register files but are used to implement delays for synchronizing data paths, or for book-keeping (temporary result) operations. Data memory is used to reduce the input/output bandwidth requirements of arrays by implementing tables of data and storing intermediate results. The memory can also be used to implement multiple cells on the same processor and hence simulate 2-D arrays. The crossbar and input multiplexers (muxs) provide communication between the individual elements and can be reconfigured by control signals. The muxs allow bidirectional data flow and rings (using wraparound). A 10 cell prototype has been built at CMU and tested on a number of example arrays discussed in Kung (1984*a*). Programming is achieved using the language W2 designed specifically for programming the WARP machine, the user specifies code for the different processors, and the compiler automatically generates the necessary interfacing code to run the problem. Benchmarking for standard algorithms is discussed in Deutsch *et al.* (1988) but the mean performance is in the region of 28 Mflops (million floating-point operations per second). The WARP cell has been reduced to VLSI to provide a single-chip version. The WARP chip developed by Intel and CMU requires approximately 600 000 transistors and is capable of 100 Mflops.

7.1.2 The wavefront array processor (WAP)

The WAP architecture was introduced by Kung (1984) and consists of an $n \times n$ mesh of processing elements with a regular connection structure, a program store, and memory modules as shown in Fig. 7.2. The processor grid acts as a wave propagating medium, the timing is asynchronous and uses two-way handshaking protocols so that no global clock is needed, that is the algorithm is self-timed and data driven. Each processor implements a limited number of operations which can be performed in a single processor cycle, and is controlled by a program loaded from the program store. Data paths are 32 bits wide and arithmetic is implemented in fixed-point format. Interprocessor communication can be performed simultaneously for each of

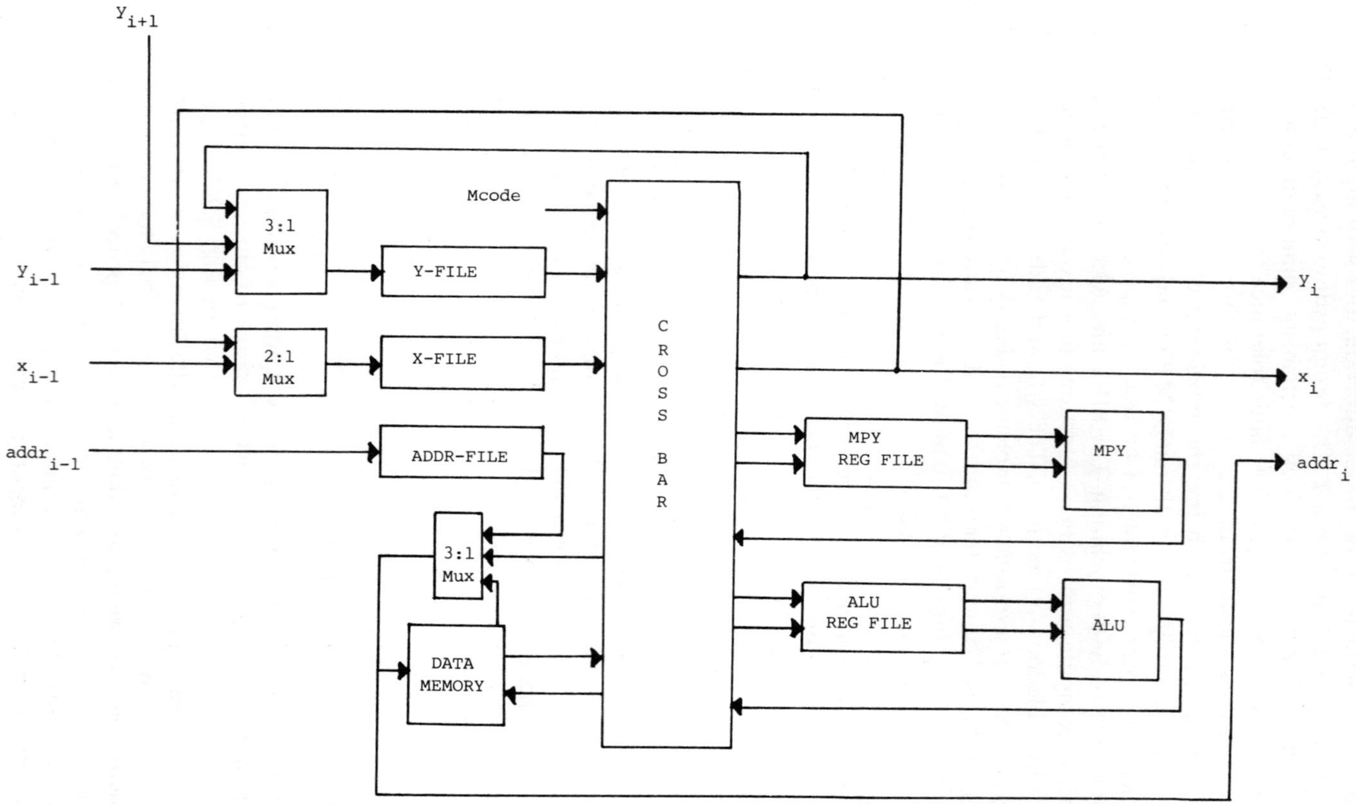

Fig. 7.1 WARP cell

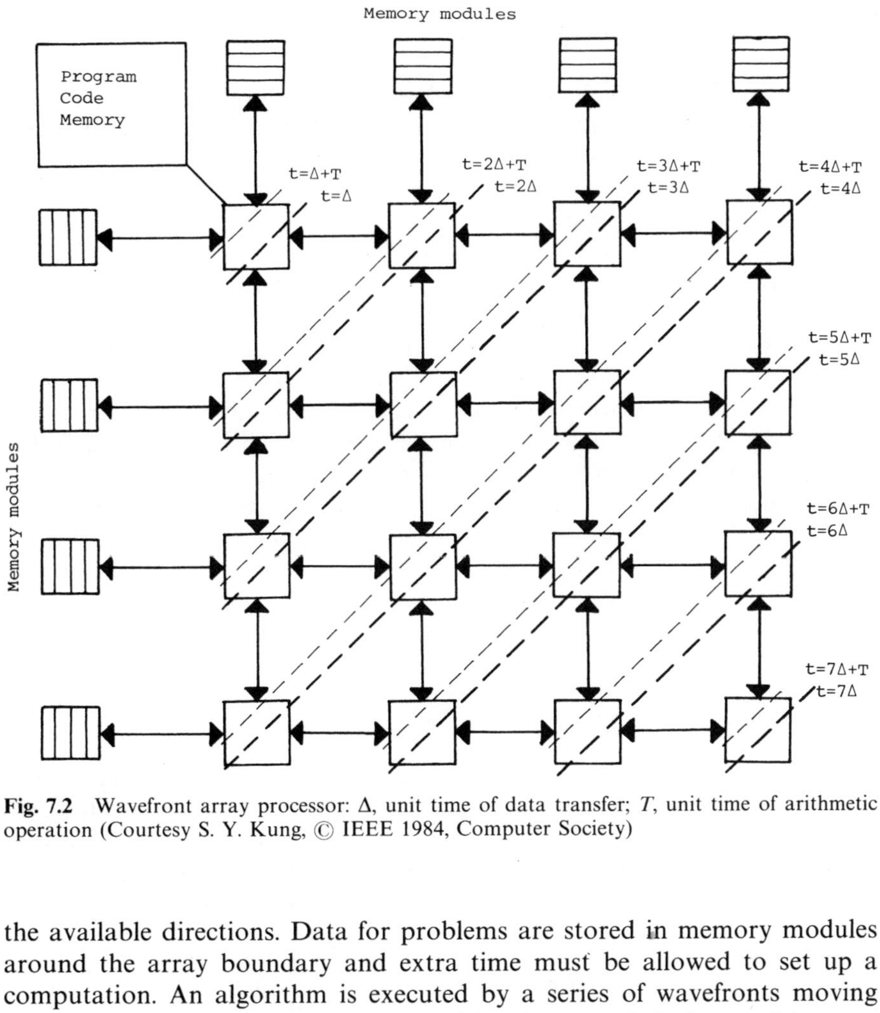

Fig. 7.2 Wavefront array processor: Δ, unit time of data transfer; *T*, unit time of arithmetic operation (Courtesy S. Y. Kung, © IEEE 1984, Computer Society)

the available directions. Data for problems are stored in memory modules around the array boundary and extra time must be allowed to set up a computation. An algorithm is executed by a series of wavefronts moving across the grid with processors computing whenever their data and instructions are available. Processors are assumed to support pipelining of waves and the spacing of waves (T) is determined by the availability of data and the execution of the basic operations. The speed of the wavefront Δ is equivalent to the data transfer time. Different algorithms are computed by changing the control program which is written using special matrix data flow language (MDFL) (see Kung *et al.* 1981) and exploits the principles of waves acting according to Huygen's principle. Non-wavefront algorithms can be converted (or systolized) to produce wavefront versions using retiming and cut theorems similar to those in Chapter 2. Simple illustrations of the WAP mechanism can be produced by tracing out a sequence of snapshots for the arrays shown in Figs 2.10 and 5.3 respectively.

7.1.3 The instruction systolic array (ISA)

The previous two examples place emphasis on data flow rather than control flow; to overcome this problem Lang (1986) has proposed the instruction systolic array (ISA). Contrasting with the conventional notion of systolic arrays the ISA pumps instructions rather than data through a mesh-connected array of processors. Consequently while a systolic array realizes only a special algorithm (or at best a collection of related problems in a generic array), the ISA can implement a wide range of parallel algorithms provided they are specified as ISA programs. The ISA can be derived by retiming the execution of instructions on a mesh-connected array processor. For example, in a multiple instruction multiple data (MIMD) array all the processors of a given array (denoted PA) can execute different instructions. If the array consists of n^2 independent processors each containing a central store, a PA program consists of up to n^2 different programs. These programs must be distributed over the array before the PA program can be executed. In an ISA the program executes as it filters through the array, making it easy to execute a pipelined sequence of programs using an ISA instead of a PA. Three types of parallel machines which differ only in the way control information reaches processors are now easily defined (see Fig. 7.3).

1. *The processor array* (*PA*): as defined above where each processor has its own control store (MIMD).

2. *Instruction broadcast array* (*IBA*): where processors use a simple control unit but no control store, and instructions are broadcast to all the cells in the same column and selector information (0, 1) is broadcast to processor rows. If I_j is the instruction in column j and S_i is the selector in row i, processor p_{ij} performs operations according to

$$p_{ij} = \begin{cases} I_j & \text{iff } S_i = 1 \\ \text{no-op} & \text{iff } S_i = 0 \end{cases}$$

   where 'no-op' is a null or mask operation.

3. *Instruction systolic array* (*ISA*): which is identical to the IBA except that instructions and selectors are retimed to avoid broadcasting. Instructions move row-wise and selectors columnwise.

For a processor array of side n a program is now defined as a sequence $p^{(1)} \ldots p^{(r)}$ of n-tuples over I and sequences $s^{(1)} \ldots s^{(r)}$ of n-tuples over selectors. For $i, j \leq n$ and $t \leq r$, $p^{(t)}$ is the row of instructions entering the jth row of the ISA at time $t + i - 1$, and $s^{(t)}$ is the column of selector information entering the jth column of the ISA at time $t + j - 1$, that is

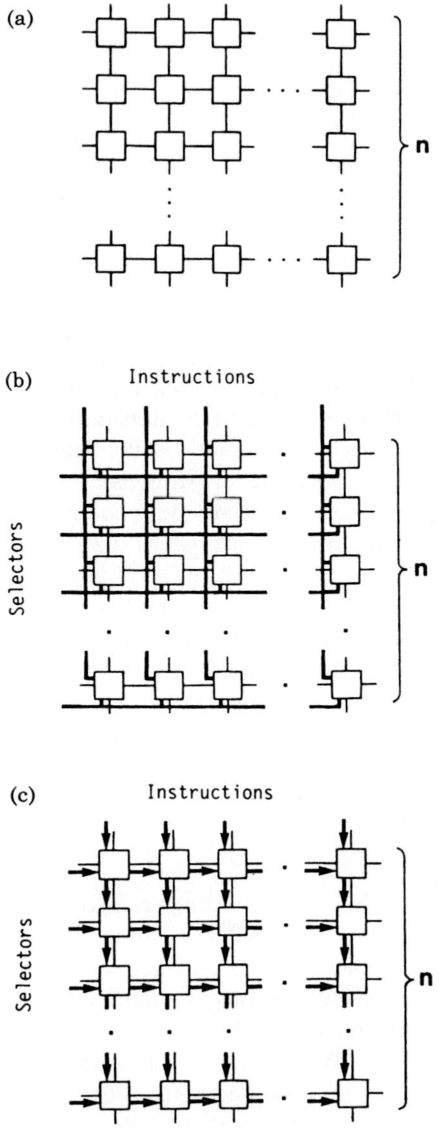

Fig. 7.3 Instruction flow machines: (a) processor array (PA_n); (b) instruction broadcast array (IBA); (c) instruction systolic array (ISA). (Source M. Kunde *et al. Parallel Computing 85*, North-Holland, Elsevier Science Publishers.)

processor (i, j) performs

$$p(i,j) = \begin{cases} p_j^{(t+i-1)} & \text{iff } s_i^{(t-j+1)} = 1 \\ \text{no-op} & \text{otherwise.} \end{cases}$$

The program terminates when the last row of instructions $p^{(r)}$ has entered the first row of the ISA. If $p^{(r)}$ must filter through to the last row, $n - 1$ rows of no-ops must be appended to the program. Input and output to the grid occurs whenever processors read or write to non-existent processors around the mesh boundary. The input program (P) is then defined as a sequence of $4n$-tuples (an n-tuple) for each boundary which can read during the execution of P. Likewise the output of P is a sequence of $(4n - 1)$-tuples from the border of the array. A simple example for multiplying two matrices is given in Fig. 7.4 where the similarity between the ISA and WAP should be obvious.

Properties of the ISA have been outlined in Kunde *et al.* (1985) where it is noted that the design is well suited to non-numerical problems such as sorting and searching, matrix transposition, etc. The ISA also generalizes in a straightforward manner to higher dimensions and to more general instruction sequences, for example redefining the instructions and selectors to be sets of composite instructions such that whenever they meet in processors a full instruction is produced and executed. Using composite no-op elements increases the masking capability of the machine and yields greater control over the type of computation that can be performed. The ISA is the first systolic architecture which explicitly deals with the systolic movement of instructions rather than data. Clearly the processing element required to implement the control kernel of the ISA instruction set needs to be quite sophisticated.

7.1.4 Comparison

The WARP, WAP, and ISA are geared towards different aspects of systolic computation. For example, the WARP machine is one dimensional and so well disposed to solve problems involving linear arrays efficiently. The WAP, being two dimensional, solves problems such as matrix product and 2-D table generation efficiently, especially when multiple wavefronts can be pipelined across the array. WARP can be used to solve 2-D problems but requires an additional mapping of the problem into one dimension resulting in extra overheads for communication and data movement. Likewise the WAP array can solve 1-D problems but involves a large overhead in terms of processor redundancy. For example, we could run a 1-D array of n cells on an $n \times n$ WAP by using only the first row or first column of cells. The remaining $n(n - 1)$ cells would be wasted. In contrast it is easy to show that the ISA can simulate both 1-D and 2-D arrays quite efficiently by using more complex wavefront patterns (see Megson and Evans 1990b).

(a)

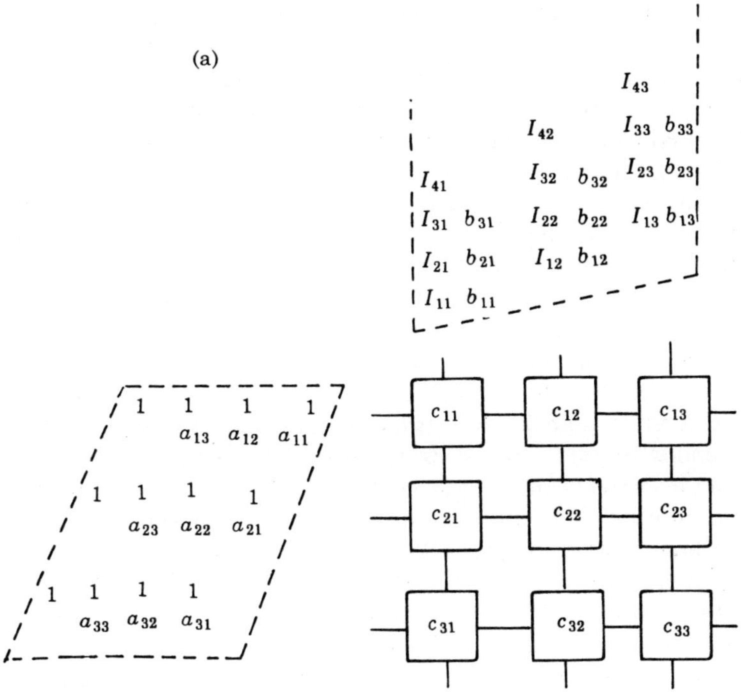

(b)

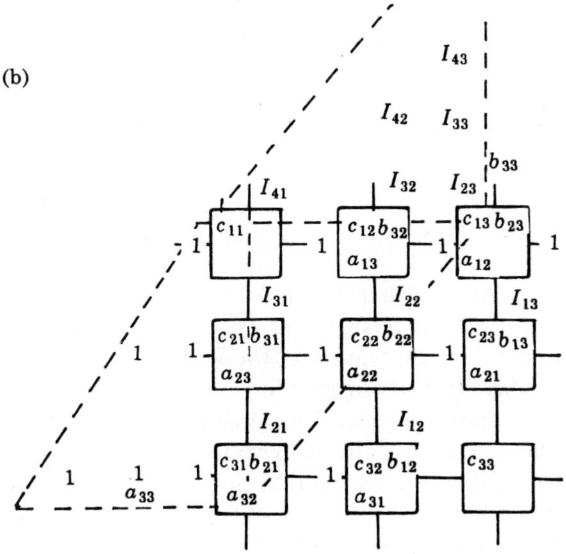

Fig. 7.4 ISA for matrix product: (a) starting input; (b) position after four steps; I_{ij} = inner product step

The mismatch between problem types makes any direct comparison between architectures difficult but there are some common features, namely pipelining ability, architectural extendability, programming simplicity, and fault tolerance. Observe that, apart from interpreting data sequences as instruction sequences, the operation of the WAP and ISA are very similar; thus for the remainder of this section we will only compare the WARP and WAP designs. The WARP is essentially a synchronous pipelined architecture and can use two-level pipelining to improve throughput, as well as having the ability to perform stationary and non-stationary algorithms with special control requirements such as the table-generating problems. On the other hand the WAP, being asynchronous, can take advantage of data dependencies in problems which may result in significant speed-ups due to the differing complexity of instruction procedures in different cells. In terms of extendability the WAP is quite flexible. Its lack of global clock allows the array size to be extended to very large sizes, whereas the synchronous WARP must use folding arguments on the layout to bound clock skew which requires reconfiguration on each upgrade of cells. The WAP is simpler to program, having an architecture already well studied in SIMD and MIMD machines and being supported by the MDFL language. The WARP on the other hand requires the pipelining of control and the choice of a suitable language for performing computations (a compiler called W2 is available). In fault tolerance the WARP processor has an advantage as it can cope with faults quite easily by exploiting unidirectional data flow and data files. Hardware recovery is quite difficult on the WAP without additional processors. A neat solution would be to modify wavefront algorithms to use algorithmic fault tolerance like checksums, which would require the addition of an extra row and column of processors to detect, correct, and fix the errors.

7.2 General-purpose processors and simulation

Generic designs such as the WARP, WAP, and ISA are not general purpose. The processors are designed to exploit specific features of pipelined data and instruction flow. For example, the WARP allows two-level pipelining of data and the ISA pipelines instructions. An alternative method of implementation is to use an existing general-purpose processor and construct approximations to the generic architectures or to force the array topology to fit an existing parallel architecture by use of a suitable mapping. The implementation is an approximation because the general-purpose nature of the processing element must pay some penalty in performance over a dedicated network. Of course not just any processor will do—we want a device that can execute potentially aribtrary programs but also allow communication between other processors. One particular processor which has received much publicity lately is the Inmos transputer.

7.2.1 Transputers and OCCAM†

The Inmos transputer is a single-chip microprocessor containing a memory, processor, and communication links (for connection to other transputers), which provides direct hardware support for the parallel language OCCAM. The structure of a transputer is given in Fig. 7.5. The transputer and OCCAM were designed in conjunction and all transputers include special instructions and hardware which provide optimal implementations of the OCCAM model of concurrency and communication. Different types of transputers can have different instruction sets depending on the required balance between cost, performance, internal concurrency, and hardware, without altering the user's view of OCCAM. Hence the transputer is a reduced instruction set

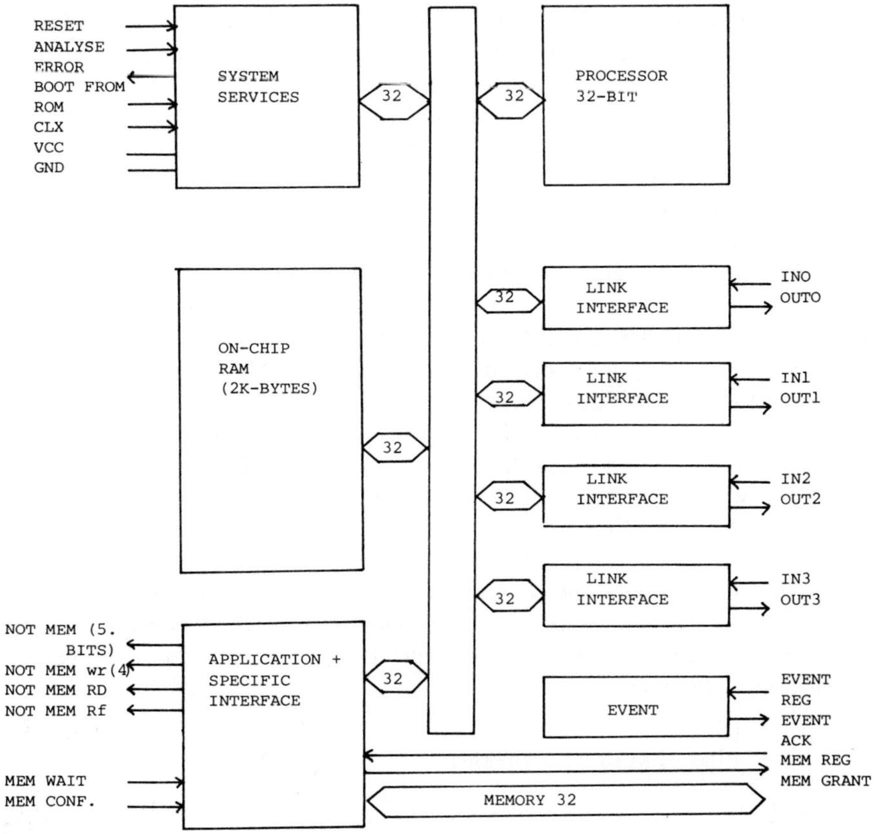

Fig. 7.5 Inmos transputer. (Reproduced with permission, Inmos Ltd.)

† Transputer and OCCAM are trademarks of Inmos.

computer (RISC). The processor contains a scheduler which enables any number of processes to run on a single transputer sharing processor time and each link provides two unidirectional channels for point-to-point communication synchronized by a handshaking protocol. Communication can occur concurrently with communication on other links and with process execution.

OCCAM itself is based on communicating sequential processes (Hoare 1978) where parallel activities are viewed as black boxes with internal sequential programs called processes that communicate with each other using a one-way channel. Communication is achieved by sending a message down a channel between two processes: one process sends a message and the other reads it from the channel. It is up to the programmer to ensure that each processor knows when to read or write. As every transputer implements OCCAM, an OCCAM program can be executed on a single transputer or a network. In the former case, parallel processes share the processor time and channel communication is simulated by moving data in memory. For a transputer network processes are distributed among transputers and some (possibly all) channels allocated to links. Thus the OCCAM program can be implemented in a variety of ways which reflect different trade-offs of speed, efficiency, and cost.

It should be clear that an approximation to the WARP, WAP, and ISA designs can be made using transputers. Of course the performance characteristics of the device will be different. Where one is interested in the rapid prototyping of many trial algorithms the flexibility makes the approach quite attractive. In the case of the WAP, OCCAM is particularly useful for implementing wavefronts, but for WARP simulations we lose the special features, such as two-level pipelining, which are often useful in improving design performance. A transputer also has a fixed number of links to other transputers so that designs which require more communications than the available links must be recoded to multiplex the data. For example, a transputer with four links cannot be used directly to simulate a hexagonally connected array (see Fig. 2.10) which uses six links per cell. Instead we have to adopt an orthogonally connected mesh, embed the hexagonal array into the mesh, and simulate the diagonal connection by routing it through an adjacent processor (horizontally and vertically). Clearly this requires extra programming (and processes) for each transputer and the overhead of intermediate communications.

7.2.2 Simulation of systolic algorithms

One of the main advantages of OCCAM and the transputer is the logical distinction between the idea of a process and a processor. A single OCCAM program can be written to simulate an (almost) arbitrary connection topology. Thus algorithms can be debugged and tested with little regard for the final physical topology available. In the case of a systolic program, the algorithm can be realized by defining a single process for each cell type and connecting them together as described by the array topology.

To elaborate, consider the following simple example for the banded matrix–vector array shown in Fig. 2.8. A representation of this array is shown in Fig. 7.6(a), where the square cells are the inner product cells and the circles represent data sequences. A circle with an outgoing edge is a source and a circle with an incoming edge is a sink. Sources are responsible for pumping the data for a particular sequence into the array suitably delayed and augmented with any synchronizing spaces. Likewise the sinks are responsible for collecting any output from the array and removing leading and synchronizing dummy values from the output sequence. An implementation of the array in (Loughborough) OCCAM is shown in Fig. 7.7. The setup procedure uses a bandwidth of $w = p + q - 1$ to compute the initial delays of the x, y,

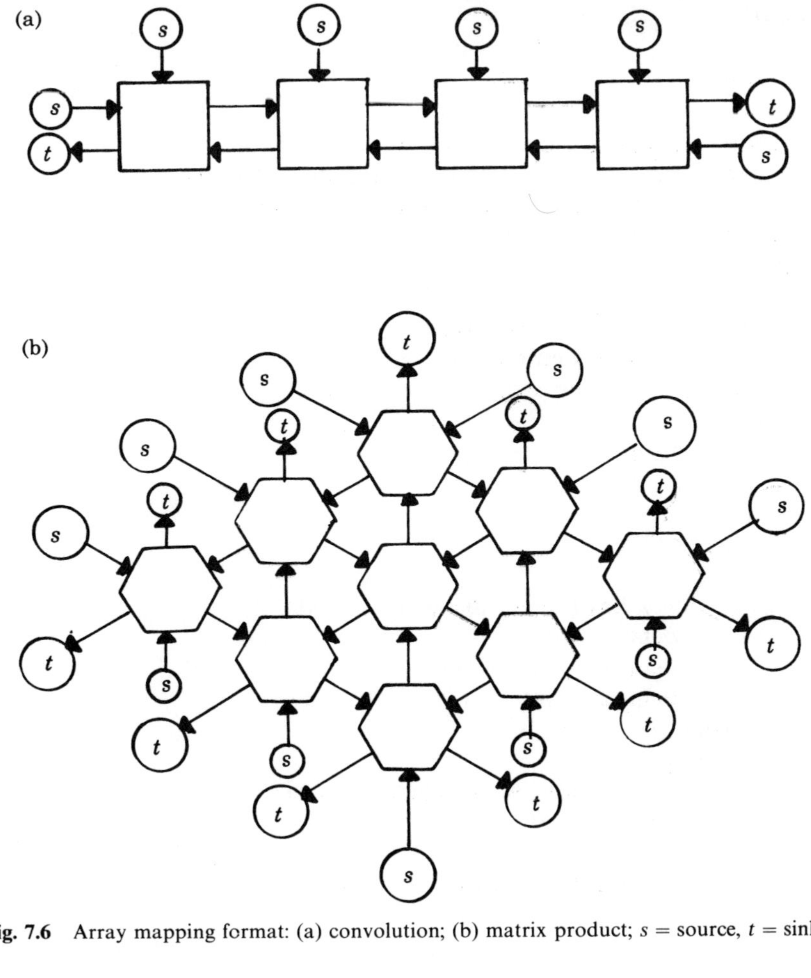

Fig. 7.6 Array mapping format: (a) convolution; (b) matrix product; s = source, t = sink

```
-- program 1
--
-- Band matrix-vector multiplication
--
-- Systolic array to multiply an n by n band matrix with an
-- n component vector, the matrix has bandwidth w=p+q-1.

-- problem dependent constants and channels

def n=4=p=2,q=3, w=(p+q)-1 :
def total.time = (2*n)+w :

var xval[n], yval[n], aval[n*n] :
var delay.a, delay.x, delay.y :

chan x[w+1], y[w+1], a[w] :

proc setup =
  --
  -- setup : calculates the delays of inputs
  -- entering the array. Although p and q are constants
  -- if they are modified to create a larger system,
  -- synchronisation delays change
  var xt,yt :
  seq
    -- delay.a computes time cycles
    -- that matrix elements wait
    -- until entering the array
    seq
      xt := p-1
      yt := q-1
      if
        xt > yt
          seq
            -- x has longest distance to travel
            delay.x := 0
            delay.y := xt - yt
            delay.a := xt
        true
          seq
            -- y has longest distance to travel
            delay.y := 0
```

Fig. 7.7 OCCAM code for matrix–vector array

```
            delay.x := yt - xt
            delay.a := yt :

proc cell( chan xin, xout, yin, yout, ain ) =
  --
  -- inner product cell
  --
  var a[1],x[1],y[1],xtmp,ytmp :
  seq
    -- dummy values for
    -- startup
    seq
      xtmp := 0
      ytmp := 0
      -- run the cell
      seq i = [ 1 for total.time ]
        seq
          par
            -- i/o
            xin?x[0]
            yin?y[0]
            ain?a[0]
            xout!xtmp
            yout!ytmp
          seq
            -- perform inner product
            ytmp := y[0] + (a[0]*x[0])
            xtmp := x[0] :

proc source( chan out, value mem[], delay ) =
  --
  -- generic source.
  --    references area of memory belonging to
  --    host, and pumps required data placed there into
  --    systolic array suitably delayed.
  --
  var j,toggle :
  seq
    -- initialisation
    j := 1
    toggle := true
    -- while running
```

Fig. 7.7 (***cont.***)

```
    seq i = [ 1 for total.time ]
      if
        (i <= delay) or (j>n)
          out!0
        toggle
          seq
            -- fetch memory contents
            -- locate next location
            out!mem[j-1]
            j := j + 1
            toggle := false
        true
          seq
            -- dummy spacers
            out!0
            toggle := true :

proc sink( chan in, var mem[], value delay) =
  --
  -- generic sink :
  --    performs data collection; reading out
  --    garbage elements where necessary and placing
  --    valid data back into host memory in correct
  --    position.
  --
  var j,toggle,tmp :
  seq
    -- initialisation
    j := 1
    toggle := true
    -- while running
    seq i = [ 1 for total.time ]
      if
        ( i <= delay ) or (j > n)
          in?tmp
        toggle
          seq
            -- result to host memory
            in?mem[j-1]
            j := j + 1
            toggle := false
        true
```

Fig. 7.7 (*cont.*)

```
            seq
              -- collect garbage result
              in?tmp
              toggle := true :

proc sourcea( chan outpt, value mem[], z1, z2, delay1 ) =
  --
  -- alternative source :
  --    locates, fetches, and pumps data from band matrix into
  --    the systolic array. Addressing of host memory is more
  --    complex as we need extra delays for matrix inputs
  --
  var delay2,toggle,d1,d2 :
  seq
    -- initialisation
    seq
      toggle := true
      d1 := z1
      d2 := z2
      if
        d1 > d2
          delay2 := d1 - d2
        true
          delay2 := d2 - d1
    -- while running
    seq i = [ 1 for total.time ]
      if
      ( i <= (delay1 + delay2)) or (d1 > n) or (d2 > n)
        -- pad with dummy elements
        -- until data arrives
        outpt!0
      true
        if
          toggle = true
            seq
              -- fetch data, locate next, pump
                outpt!mem[(((d1-1)*n)+d2)-1]
                seq
                  d1 := d1 + 1
                  d2 := d2 + 1
                  toggle := false
            true
```

Fig. 7.8 (*cont.*)

```
                    seq
                      -- dummy spacer
                      toggle := true
                      outpt!0 :

proc alloc.sources.sinks(chan x[], y[], a[], var aval[], yval[], xval[]) =
  --
  -- allocation routine : provides the mapping between cells, communication
  -- channels to host environment and systolic array.
  --
  par
    -- create matrix inputs
    par i = [ 1 for w ]
      if
        i <= p
          sourcea( a[i-1], aval, 1, (p-i)+1, delay.a )
        true
          sourcea( a[i-1], aval, (i-p)+1, 1, delay.a)
    -- x-vector and result y-vector
    -- inputs and outputs
    source(y[w],yval,delay.y)
    source(x[0],xval,delay.x)
    sink(y[0],yval,w+delay.y)
    sink(x[w],xval,w+delay.x) :

proc getdata( var xval[],aval[],yval[] ) =
  --
  -- very primitive input routine : reads in the data from user
  -- terminal inserting it into simulated host memory, in this case
  -- simple arrays
  -- n.b great savings can be made by omitting known zeros
  --    in the matrix structure : this not pursued for simplicity;
  --    the main aim was to test the array; not an exercise in data
  --    structuring.
  --
  var tmp :
  seq
    screen!'b';'a';'n';'d';'=';w+'0'; '*s';'=';p+'0';'*s';'q';'=';q+'0';'*n'
    screen!'b';'a';'n';'d';'=';w+'0';'*s';'p';'=';p+'0';'*s';'q';'=';q+'0';'*n'
    screen!'n';'=';n+'0';'*n'
    -- read the band matrix
    seq i = [1 for n]
```

Fig. 7.7 (*cont.*)

```
        seq
          screen!'*n';'['
          seq j = [1 for n]
            seq
              keyboard!tmp;'*s'
              aval[(((i-1)*n)+j)-1] := tmp - '0'
          screen!']'
      screen!'*n';'x';'*n';'['
      -- read x and clear y vectors
      seq i = [0 for n]
        seq
          keyboard?tmp
          screen!tmp;'*s'
          xval[i] := tmp - '0'
          yval[i] := 0
      screen!']';'*n' :

proc putdata( var yval[]) =
  --
  -- another primitive i/o routine this time to
  -- output data. Note; both input and output deal only
  -- with single digit values; restrictive but adequate
  -- for test purposes.
  seq
    screen!'*n';'y';'*n';'['
    seq i = [0 for n]
      screen!yval[i]+'0';'*s'
    screen!']' :

-- main

-- allocation and setup of the system;

seq
  setup
  getdata(xval,aval,yval)
  -- the array
  par
    alloc.sources.sinks(x,y,a,aval,yval,xval)
    par i = [1 for w]
      cell(x[i-1],x[i],y[i],y[i-1],a[i-1])
    -- computation complete
    putdata(yval)
```

Fig. 7.7 (*cont.*)

and *a* data sequences. These values are used by the sources and sinks to compute the number of dummy values that need to be pumped into the array in front of a sequence so that the first element of each sequence arrives at the start position at the same time. The procedure *cell* implements a basic inner product step. The cell computation has two parts, a pumping part and a computation part. In the pumping part all the input and output is performed in parallel and then in the computation part the current input is used to compute the inner product and set the next output. The pumping and computation parts are iterated for the total number of steps (i.e. $\mathcal{T} = 2n + w$). The *source* procedure accepts a vector of values (*mem*) which contains the data sequence to be pumped into the array together with a delay which indicates the number of steps before the data can start to enter the array. In Fig. 2.8 the data enter the array in an alternating pattern of real and dummy values; the source simulates this behaviour by using a Boolean toggle. A *sink* is implemented in a similar manner to the source except that it strips out the delay and dummy values and stores the resultant sequence in the supplied vector (*mem*). The *alloc.sources.sinks* routine sets up and runs the correct number of sources and sinks and is executed in parallel (see main section) with the cells. *Getdata* and *Putdata* are simple input–output procedures for reading and writing the data from the keyboard and screen.

The above example shows that there is a simple and intuitive mapping of systolic program components into an OCCAM program. Figure 7.8 shows another example, this time for the back-substitution network (Fig. 3.1) which requires two different cells and a feedback loop. The mapping is essentially the same as the previous case except that two procedures are defined, one for each cell type. The feedback in the problem also means that any two processes *P* and *Q* are dependent upon each other's outputs so that if communication is not organized carefully deadlock could occur. For example, suppose that *P* is waiting to send data to *Q* and that likewise *Q* is waiting to send data to *P*. The program will never terminate because neither process will be able to send data and consequently waits for ever. In the abstract definition of a systolic array all communication is synchronous and occurs simultaneously so that deadlock cannot occur. But in an OCCAM program communication is asynchronous and deadlock is a real danger. Organizing communication in the way shown in our example prevents cyclic dependency occurring so the array will not deadlock. If the cell had been arranged so that we performed the sequence input–computation–output extra variables would be required to overcome deadlock problems. In general deadlock arises when cycles of data dependencies arise and special attention should be given to such designs.

Two-dimensional designs are also very simple to implement in OCCAM. Figure 7.9 shows an OCCAM program for the hexagonal matrix product array in Fig. 2.10. In this case the problem is how to map array data paths

```
-- program 2:
--
-- solution of a linear system : occam coding of systolic array.
--
-- The array encoded solves a linear system presented as a lower
-- triangular n by n band matrix with band width q. Total compu-
-- tation time 2n + q; with an extra cycle to close down the
-- system. Unit time is the cost of execution for an ips cell

-- array dependent parameters and communication channels

def n=4, q=3, total.time = (2*n)+(q+1) :
var xval[n], yval[n], aval[n*n], bval(n) :

chan x[q+1], y[q], a[q], b :

proc cell1( chan xin, xout, yin, yout, ain ) =
  -- inner product cell definition.
  var a[1], x[1], y[1], xsave, ysave :
  seq
    -- startup values
    seq
      xsave := 0
      ysave := 0
    -- run the cell
    seq i=[ 1 for total.time]
      seq
        par
          -- perform i/o
          xin?x[0]
          yin?y[0]
          ain?a[0]
          xout!xsave
          yout!ysave
        seq
          -- inner product
          ysave := y[0] + (x[0]*a[0])
          xsave := x[0] :

proc cell2( chan xin, xout, yin, bin, ain ) =
  --
  -- solve for x cell
```

Fig. 7.8 OCCAM code for back-substitution array

```
  --
  var a[1], x[1], y[1], b[1], xsave :
  seq
    xsave := 0
    seq i=[ 1 for total.time ]
      seq
        par
          -- perform i/o
          xin?x[0]
          yin?y[0]
          bin?b[0]
          ain?a[0]
          xout!xsave
        -- compute solution
        xsave := (b[0] / y[0])+a[0] :

proc sourcea( chan outpt, value mem[], z1, z2, delay1 ) =
  --
  -- matrix values pumped into systolic array by this
  -- control mechanism.
  --
  var toggle, d1, d2, delay 2 :
  seq
    -- set starting values;
    seq
      toggle := true          -- dummy or real value switch
      d1 := z1                -- delay of data stream.
      d2 := z2
      if
        d1 > d2
          delay2 := delay1 + (d1 - d2)
        true
          delay2 := delay1 + (d2 - d1)
    -- start pumping
    seq i=[ 1 for total.time ]
      if
        ( i <= delay2 ) or ( d1>n ) or ( d2 > n)
          outpt!0
        true
          if
            toggle
              seq
```

Fig. 7.8 (*cont.*)

```
                  -- pump in next value, and
                  -- locate next item.
                  outpt!mem[(((d1 - 1)*n) + d2) - 1]
                  seq
                    d1 := d1 + 1
                    d2 := d2 + 1
                    toggle := false
              true
                seq
                  -- pump in dummy separator.
                  outpt!0
                  toggle := true :

proc source( chan out, value memout[], delay ) =
  --
  -- generic source definition for b,x,y data streams.
  --
  var toggle, j :
  seq
    -- setup values
    toggle := true
    j := 1
    -- pump data until done
    seq i=[ 1 for total.time ]
      seq
        if
          (i <= delay) or (j > n)
            -- pass dummy values
            -- for synchronisation.
            seq
              out!0
          toggle
            seq
              -- send memory value
              out!memout[j - 1]
              seq
                j := j + 1
                toggle := false
          true
            seq
              -- send dummy separator
              out!0
```

Fig. 7.8 (*cont.*)

```
              toggle := true :

proc sink( chan in, var memin[], value delay ) =
  --
  -- generic sink : collects garbage values
  -- and stores results in memory.
  --
  var toggle, j, tmp :
  seq
    -- setup values
    seq
      j := 1
      toggle := true
    -- start running
    seq i=[ 1 for total.time ]
      seq
        -- decide on type of data received
        -- e.g. garbage or result.
        if
          (i <= delay) or (j > n)
            -- synchronise
            in?tmp
          toggle
            seq
              -- store a result
              -- next vacant area
              in?memin[j-1]
              seq
                j := j + 1
                toggle := false
          true
            seq
              -- garbage throw away
              in?tmp
              toggle := true :

proc system( chan a[], x[], y[], b, var xval[], yval[], aval[], bval[] ) =
  --
  -- systolic system definition in terms of basic ips cell
  -- and sources.
  --
  par
```

Fig. 7.8 (*cont.*)

```
    par i = [ 1 for q-1 ]
      par
        -- matrix sources and ips cells
        sourcea(a[i], aval, i+1, 1, q-1)
        cell1( x[i-1], x[i], y[i], y[i-1], a[i] )
    -- reciprocal cell
    cell2( x[q], x[0], y[0], b, a[0] )
    -- periphery sources and sinks
    sourcea( a[0], aval, 1, 1, q-1 )
    source( x[q], xval, q-1 )
    source( b, bval, q-1 )
    source( y[q-1], yval, 0 )
    sink( x[q-1], xval, (2*q)-1 ) :

proc getdata( var xval[], yval[], bval[], aval[] ) =
  --
  -- primitive routine to read in data from terminal
  --
  var tmp :
  seq
    screen!'1';'s'; '*n'
    -- read in lower triangular matrix
    seq i = [ 1 for n ]
      seq
        screen!'*n';'['
        seq j = [ 1 for n]
          seq
            keyboard?tmp
            screen!tmp;'*s'
            aval[(((i-1)*n)+j)-1] := tmp - '0'
        screen!']'
    screen'*n';'b';'*n';'*n';'['
    -- clear x,y vector for startup
    seq i = [ 0 for n ]
      seq
        keyboard?tmp
        screen!tmp;'*s'
        bval[i] := tmp - '0'
        yval[i] := 0
        xval[i] := 0
    screen!']';'*n';'*n' :
```

Fig. 7.8 (*cont.*)

```
proc putdata( var xval[] ) =
  --
  -- primitive routine to write data to terminal
  --
  seq
    screen!'*n';'x';'['
      seq i = [ 0 for n ]
        screen!xval[i] + '0';'*s'
      screen!']' :

-- main program section

-- performs reading and writing of data to Host computer
-- in this case the user terminal.

-- also creates and starts the system running.
seq
  getdata( xval,yval,bval,aval )
  system( a, x, y, b, xval, yval, aval, bval )
  putdata( xval )
```

Fig. 7.8 (*cont.*)

into a list of channels that can be declared in legal OCCAM source code. The method we adopt is simple. Each cell can be given a coordinate in 2-D space (e.g. (1, 1), (1, 2), etc.), an observation that results trivially from our projection mapping technique. Now suppose each cell has $p > 0$ input connections and each channel has a unique 3-D coordinate (i, j, r), that is the rth connection of the (i, j)th processor. A simple mapping of (i, j, r) of the form

$$f(i, j, r) := (i - 1) * n * p + (j - 1) * p + (r - 1)$$

will produce a unique channel number $f(i, j, r)$ for each connection. In Fig. 7.9 the routine *allocpool* implements this function and grabs channels from a 1-D pool of channels derived from a rectangular $(w1 + 1) \times (w2 + 1)$ region (Fig. 7.6(b) shows the special case of tri-diagonal matrices). The same technique can be used to map any of the designs discussed so far into OCCAM programs that use a simple list of channels.

By compiling and executing the programs produced we can confirm that the data flow is correct and that the timing equations are valid. If the array is to be used in a pipelined mode for a series of different problems the for loops in the program need to be changed into while loops controlled by a simple variable. Cell control is achieved by making this variable non-stationary and attaching (tagging) it to the data already moving through the

```
-- program 3
--
-- band matrix multiplier
--
-- program to multiply two n by n band matrices
-- using a hex connected systolic array.
--
-- matrices have band widths w1 = p1 + q1 - 1 and w2 = p2 + q2 - 1
--

-- problem dependent constants

def n=4, p1=2, q1=3, w1=(p1+q1)-1 :
def p2=3, q2=2, w2=(p2+q2)-1 :
def maxchan = (((w1+1)*(w2+1))*3)+3, w3 = (w1 + w2) - 1 :
def don = true, doff = false :

var delay.a, delay.b, delay.c, total.time, min, strtc :
var a[n*n], b[n*n], c[n*n] :

chan pool[maxchan] :

proc setup( var c[] ) =
  --
  -- setup routine ; calculates delays of input data for
  -- synchronisation inside the array ; and total computation
  -- time.
  -- also sets some variables e.g strtc required to setup the
  -- connection network.
  var ctime :
  seq
    -- computation time
    seq i = [ 1 for n*n ]
      c[i-1] := 0
    if
      w1 < w2
        seq
          total.time := (3*n)+w1
          min := w1
      true
        seq
          total.time := ( 3*n ) + w2
```

Fig. 7.9 OCCAM code for hexagonal array

```
            min := w2
  -- offsets and delays
  strtc := w2 + 1
  ctime := q1 - 1
  if
    q1 > p2
      seq
        strtc := strtc + (q1 - p2)
        ctime := ctime - (q1 - p2)
  -- delays of sources
  if
    (ctime >= (q2 - 1)) and ( ctime >= (p1 - 1))
      seq
        delay.c := 0
        delay.a := ctime - (q2 - 1)
        delay.b := ctime - (p1 - 1)
    ( (q2 - 1) >= ctime ) and (q2 >= p1)
      seq
        delay.a := 0
        delay.c := (q2 - 1) - ctime
        delay.b := q2 - q1
    ( (p1 - 1) >= ctime ) and ((p1 - 1) > (q2 - 1))
      seq
        delay.b := 0
        delay.c := (p1 - 1) - ctime
        delay.a := p1 - q2 :

proc allocpool(value x, y, r, var c ) =
  --
  -- the array is built onto a rectangular grid; with processors
  -- at intersections; channels are connected by indexing
  -- processors by underlying grid points
  --
  seq
    c := (((((x - 1) * (w2 + 1)) + y) * 3) + r) - 1 :

proc cell( chan ain, bin, cin, aout, bout, cout ) =
  --
  -- inner product cell
  -- ( hex in the array )
  --
  var a[1], b[1], c[1], atmp, btmp, ctmp :
```

Fig. 7.9 (*cont.*)

```
  seq
    -- initialisation
    seq
      atmp := 0
      btmp := 0
      ctmp := 0
    -- while running
    seq i = [1 for total.time]
      seq
        par
          -- i/o
          ain?a[0]
          bin?b[0]
          cin?c[0]
          aout!atmp
          bout!btmp
          cout!ctmp
        seq
          -- inner product
          ctmp := c[0] + (a[0]*b[0])
          btmp := b[0]
          atmp := a[0] :

proc source( value mem[], z1, z2, delay, flag, chan outpt ) =
  --
  -- generic source
  --   locates, fetches, and pumps data into the array
  --   for simplicity c is assumed to be a zero array
  --   at start of computation.
  --
  var toggle, toggle1, delay2, d1, d2 :
  seq
    -- initialisation; and computation
    -- of source delays
    toggle := true
    toggle1 := false
    d1 := z1
    d2 := z2
    if
      d1 > d2
        delay2 := (d1 - d2)
      true
```

Fig. 7.9 (*cont.*)

```
      delay2 := (d2 - d1)
  if
    flag
      delay2 := (delay2*2) + delay
    true
      delay2 := delay2 + delay
  -- while running
  seq i = [ 1 for total.time ]
    if
      (i <= delay2) or (d1 > n) or (d2 > n)
        outpt!0
      true
        if
          toggle1
            seq
              -- second dummy value
              outpt!0
              toggle := true
              toggle1 := false
          toggle
            seq
              -- fetch, locate next and pump data
              outpt!mem[(((d1-1)*n)+d2)-1]
              seq
                d1 := d1 + 1
                d2 := d2 + 1
                toggle := false
          true
            seq
              -- first dummy value
              outpt!0
              toggle1 := true :

proc sink( var mem[], value x1, x2, delay, flag, extra, chan inpt ) =
  --
  -- generic sink;
  -- almost identical source except that data is
  -- collected and inserted into memory as results
  -- garbage values are removed from the array
  --
  var toggle, toggle1, delay2, d1, d2 :
  seq
```

Fig. 7.9 (*cont.*)

```
-- initialisation
toggle := true
toggle1 := false
d1 := z1
d2 := z2
if
  d1 > d2
    delay2 := (d1 - d2)
  true
    delay2 := d2 - d1
if
  flag
    delay2 := (delay2 * 2) + (delay + extra)
  true
    delay2 := delay2 + ( delay + extra )
-- while running
seq i = [ 1 for total.time ]
  if
    ( i <= delay2) or (d1 > n) or (d2 > n)
      inpt?any
    true
      if
        toggle1
          seq
            -- dummy value
            inpt?any
            toggle := true
            toggle1 := false
        toggle
          seq
            -- insert result into memory
            inpt?mem[(((d1-1)*n)+d2)-1]
            seq
              d1 := d1 + 1
              d2 := d2 + 1
              toggle := false
        true
          seq
            -- dummy value
            inpt?any
            toggle1 := true :
```

Fig. 7.9 (*cont.*)

```
proc allocsources( chan pool[1], value strtc ) =
  --
  -- allocation of sources to
  -- ends of systolic array
  --
  def xlim = w1 + 1, ylim = w2 + 1 :
  par
    -- allocate a(i,j) sources
    par x = [1 for w1]
      var idx :
      seq
        allocpool(x+1, ylim, 0, idx)
        if
          x <= q1
            source( a, q1 - (x - 1), 1, delay.a, doff, pool[idx])
          true
            source( a, 1, (x - q1) + 1, delay.a, don, pool[idx])
    -- allocate b(i,j) sources
    par y = [ 1 for w2 ]
      var idx :
      seq
        allocpool(xlim, y+1, 2, idx)
        if
          y <= p2
            source( b, 1, p2 - (y - 1), delay.b, doff, pool[idx])
          true
            source( b, (y - p2) + 1, 1, delay.b, don, pool[idx])
    -- allocate c(i,j) sources
    par i = [ 1 for w3 ]
      var idx :
      seq
        if
          i <= (w2 - 1)
            allocpool( 1, (w2 - i) + 1, 1, idx )
          i = w2
            allocpool( 1, 1, 1, idx )
          i > w2
            allocpool((i - w2) + 1, 1, 1, idx )
        if
          ((strtc - i)+1) > 1
            seq
              source( c, strtc - i, 1, delay.c, don, pool[idx])
```

Fig. 7.9 (*cont.*)

```
            true
              seq
                source( c, 1, (i - strtc) + 2, delay.c, don, pool[idx]) :

proc allocsinks( chan pool[], value strtc ) =
  --
  -- allocation of sinks to periphery of array
  -- almost the same as the source allocations
  -- and could make one routine but the lack of clarity
  -- in the latter proved a heavy cost in debugging
  --
  def xlim = w1 + 1, ylim = w2 + 1 :
  par
    -- allocate a(i,j) sinks
    par x = [ 1 for w1 ]
      var idx :
      seq
        allocpool( x+1, 1, 0, idx )
      if
        ( x <= q1 )
          sink( a, q1-(x-1), 1, delay.a, doff, 0, pool[idx])
        true
          sink( a, 1, (x - q1) + 1, delay.a, don, 0, pool[idx] )
    -- allocate b(i,j) sinks
    par y = [ 1 for w2 ]
      var idx :
      seq
        allocpool( 1, y+1, 2, idx )
        if
          ( y <= p2 )
            sink( b, 1, p2 - (y - 1), delay.b, doff, 0, pool[idx] )
          true
            sink( b, (y-p2)+1, 1, delay.b, don, 0, pool[idx] )
    -- allocate c(i,j) sinks
    par i = [ 1 for w3 ]
      var idx, tmp :
      seq
        if
          i <= (w1 - 1)
            allocpool( i+1, ylim, 1, idx )
          i = w1
            allocpool( xlim, ylim, 1, idx )
```

Fig. 7.9 (*cont.*)

```
        i > w1
          allocpool( xlim, ((w3 - i)+2), 1, idx )
      if
        (( strtc - i) + 1) > 1
          seq
            sink( c, strtc - i, 1, delay.c, don, i, pool[idx] )
        true
          seq
            if
              i > w2
                tmp := (w3 - i) + 1
              true
                tmp := min
            sink( c, 1, (i - strtc) + 2, delay.c, don, tmp, pool[idx] ) :

proc alloc.cells( chan pool[] ) =
  --
  -- placement of inner product cells
  -- onto the rectangular grid, and connection with
  -- sources and immediate neighbours
  --
  par i = [ 2 for w1 ]
    par j = [ 2 for w2 ]
      var id1, id2, id3, id4, id5, id6 :
      seq
        allocpool( i, j, 0, id1 )
        allocpool( i, j, 2, id2 )
        allocpool( i, j, 1, id3 )
        allocpool( i, j-1, 0, id4)
        allocpool( i-1, j, 2, id5 )
        allocpool( i-1, j-1, 1, id6 )
        cell( pool[id1], pool[id2], pool[id6], pool[id4], pool[id5], pool[id3] )

proc getdata( var mem[] ) =
  --
  -- primitive input routine to read single digit positive
  -- numbers; restrictive but good enough for test purposes
  --
  var tmp :
  seq
    screen!'*n'
    seq i = [ 1 for n ]
```

Fig. 7.9 (*cont.*)

```
      seq
        screen!'*n';'['
        seq j = [ 1 for n ]
          seq
            keyboard?tmp
            screen!tmp;'*s'
            mem[(((i-1)*n)+j)-1] := tmp - '0'
        screen!']'
    screen!'*n' :

proc putdata( value mem[] ) =
  --
  -- primitive routine to output data
  --
  seq
    seq i = [ 1 for n ]
      seq
        screen!'*n';'['
        seq j = [ 1 for n ]
          screen!mem[(((i-1)*n)+j)-1] + '0';'*s'
        screen!']' :

-- main routine

-- allocates and creates running array

seq
  getdata( a )
  getdata( b )
  setup( c )
  par
    allocsources(pool, strtc)
    alloc.cells(pool)
    allocsinks(pool, strtc)
  putdata( c )
```

Fig. 7.9 (*cont.*)

array. As the control tag moves it resets cells or can be used to destroy cells in a wave-like motion as it propagates across the array at the end of computation.

7.2.3 Simulation versus emulation

Systolic programs implemented as described above are clearly soft systolic. Running a program like Fig. 7.9 only simulates the data flow—it is not intended as a practical implementation. To run the array on a network of transputers requires an additional 'configuration' section telling us how to map the individual parallel process onto a given connection topology. If there are less processors than processes a number of cells in our array will have to share the same processor. Each of the processes will have to time-share the processor resources, which introduces extra overheads for context switching and internal communications. The connections between cells on different processors will also force multiplexing of data and introduce further overheads unless the systolic array topology is almost identical to the processor topology and enough hardware links are available for direct external communication. It is beyond the scope of this text to examine general solutions to the problems of physical mapping such as process partitioning and processor load balancing. Instead we point out that when a physical mapping has been achieved the program is emulating, not simulating, the array. The program can be timed and any speed-ups over a sequential version of the algorithm can be measured. If a speed-up is actually produced we can count the program as a valid implementation of the array. Unfortunately, emulations based on the code given above where the cells implement scalar operations and are mapped one per processor tend to produce little or no speed-up. The reason is that the amount of computation and communication are roughly the same and consequently a high portion of the total run time is wasted on communications. However, recent work on block-structured arrays (see Chapter 6) shows that we can produce significant speed-up making emulation a realistic and viable proposition. To illustrate the argument we will consider the problem of implementing model reduction on an array of transputers (Megson 1990).

Briefly, the problem is to take the coefficients of a transfer function with the form

$$T(s) = [A_{21} + A_{22}s + \cdots + A_{2n}s^{n-1}] \times [A_{11} + A_{12}s + \cdots + A_{1,n+1}s^n]^{-1} \tag{7.1}$$

where the A_{ij} are real and constant $m \times m$ matrices (or scalar when $m = 1$) and to produce a continued fraction. In fact the task reduces to a table-generating problem where the table is produced by assigning boundary conditions

$$\begin{aligned} U_{2j-1} &= A_{1j}, \quad j = 1(1)(n+3-1)/2 \\ U_{2j-1} &= A_{2j}, \quad j = 1(1)(n+3-2)/2 \end{aligned} \tag{7.2}$$

and applying the rules in Exercise 4.3. In control theory eqn (7.1) is usually a high-order model produced by some design process. Lower-order (or reduced models) are produced by expanding (7.1) into a continued fraction, neglecting the least significant terms, and then collapsing the fraction back into a transfer function. Controllers which demand only a single input and a single output result in scalar coefficients whereas (multivariable) controllers with many inputs and outputs produce matrices. From our viewpoint the algorithm allows us to vary the block size and hence the granularity of the basic computations in the cells of a systolic design. A systolic array for generating the continued fraction is very similar to the array for the Routh–Hurvitz computation described in Chapter 6, and has the same topological structure as the back-substitution array.

For completeness the OCCAM code for the scalar cell definitions and array layout is shown in Fig. 7.10. Equivalent definitions for the matrix case are produced by substituting the basic operations inside a cell with calls to sequential procedures for computing the equivalent matrix computation and communicating matrices between cells.

Remark. Scalar division is replaced by matrix inverse and multiplication.

The performance of the array running on five transputers is summarized in Fig. 7.11 by a family of speed-up curves. The c values represent the number of coefficients in the problem so that dividing by 2 gives the approximate order of the polynomials in (7.1). The bottom axis of the diagram represents the order of the matrix coefficients while the vertical axis is the speed-up of the transputer array over the equivalent sequential (for-loop) program written in OCCAM. All the testing was performed on T800 transputers. Notice that it is not until the number of coefficients is greater than four that any real speed-up is observed—the flattening of the curves indicates that this is true irrespective of the matrix size. The reason is that the time taken to synchronize the data sequences before computation starts, and to extract results at the end, introduces an overhead (of communications) which destroys any speed-up. Once more than four coefficients are used the time for starting up and closing down the array become less significant compared with the amount of time that the array can perform real computations. The overhead is still present so we can never reach the maximum possible speed-up (i.e. the number of transputers) and all the curves fall short of the ideal. Also notice the general shape of each speed-up curve. For small matrices we lose speed-up because the ratio of computation to communication is poor (i.e. the matrix product requires $O(m^3)$ steps while a communication

a) Linear array generation:

Boundary cell

```
SEQ
  m := 0.0 (REAL32)
  t1 := 0.0 (REAL32)
  t2 := 0.0 (REAL32)
  t3 := 0.0 (REAL32)
  SEQ i = 0 FOR no.of.steps
    SEQ
      PAR
        SEQ
          t3 := t2
          t2 := t1
          forward.in ? t1
        back.out ! m
        to.host ! m
      IF
        t1 = 0.0 (REAL32)
          m := 0.0 (REAL32)
        TRUE
          m := t3 / t1
```

Square cell

```
SEQ
  m := 0.0 (REAL32)
  t1 := 0.0 (REAL32)
  t2 := 0.0 (REAL32)
  t3 := 0.0 (REAL32)
  SEQ i = 0 FOR no.of.steps
    SEQ
      PAR
        SEQ
          forward.out ! t3
          t3 := t2
          t2 := t1
          forward.in ? t1
        SEQ
          back.out ! m
          back.in ? m
      -- compute
      t3 := t3 - (m*t1)
```

Fig. 7.10 OCCAM code for model reduction array

b) Linear array inversion:

Boundary cell

```
SEQ
  m := 0.0 (REAL32)
  t1 := 0.0 (REAL32)
  t2 := 0.0 (REAL32)
  t3 := 0.0 (REAL32)
  SEQ i = 0 FOR no.of.steps
    SEQ
      PAR
        forward.in ? m
        SEQ
          back.out ! t1
          t1 := t2
          t2 := t3
          to.host ? t3
      IF
        t1 = 0.0 (REAL32)
          SKIP
        TRUE
          t3 := m*t1
```

Square cell

```
SEQ
  m := 0.0 (REAL32)
  t1 := 0.0 (REAL32)
  t2 := 0.0 (REAL32)
  t3 := 0.0 (REAL32)
  SEQ i = 0 FOR no.of.steps
    SEQ
      PAR
        SEQ
          forward.out ! m
          forward.in ? m
        SEQ
          back.out ! t1
          t1 := t2
          t2 := t3
          back.in ? t3

      -- compute
      t3 := t3 + (m*t1)
```

Fig. 7.10 (*cont.*)

c) Array specification

```
PROC model(CHAN OF ANY keyboard, screen)

  -- term.p protocol
  -- include appropriate I/O maths lib

  -- Square cell definition

  PROC Sq.cell(CHAN OF ANY forward.in, forward.out, back.out,
                                                        back.in
               CHAN OF ANY port)

    ... Body
  :
  -- Boundary cell definition

  PROC end.cell(CHAN OF ANY forward.in, back.out, to.host,
                CHAN OF ANY port)

    ... Body
  :
  PROC host(CHAN OF ANY to.array, from.array, junk, VAL INT
                                                     array.size,
            []CHAN OF ANY ports)

    ... Body
  :
  -- main program
  -- ports used for interactive debugging
  -- is removed for running on actual network

  [array.size]CHAN OF ANY forward, back :
  [array.size]CHAN OF ANY ports :
  CHAN OF ANY result :
  PAR
    host(forward[0], result, back[0], array.size, ports)

    end.cell(forward[array.size – 1], back[array.size – 1], result, ports[0])
    PAR i = 0 FOR array.size – 1
      sq.cell(forward[i], forward[i + 1], back[i + 1], back[i],
              ports[(array.size – i) – 1])
```

Fig.7.10 ***(cont.)***

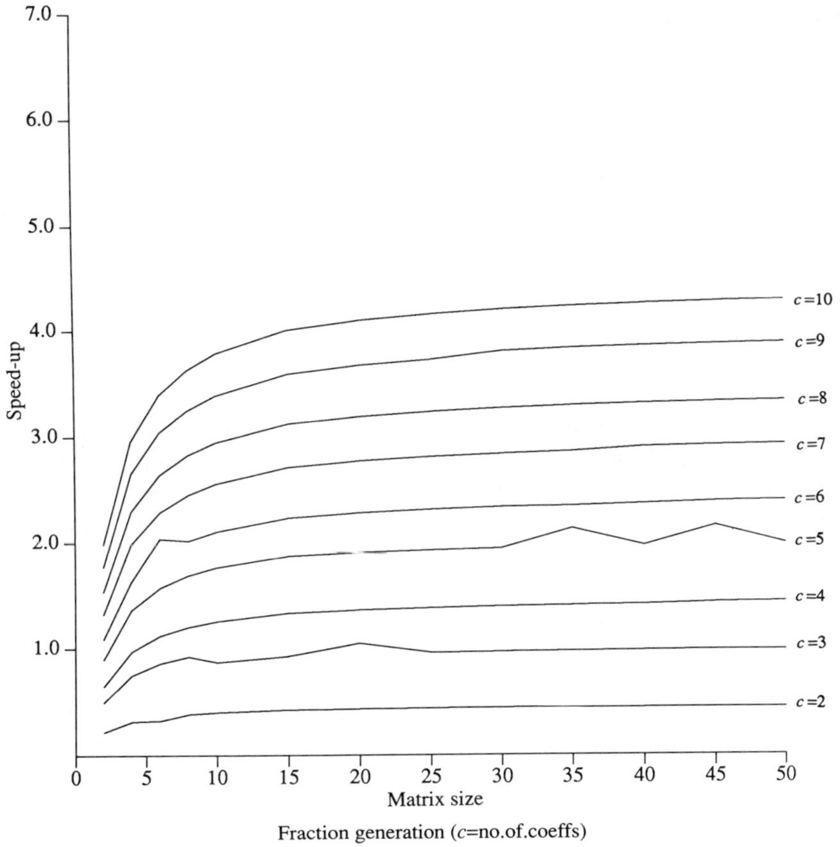

Fig. 7.11 Speed-up graph for model reduction (five transputers)

is $O(m^2)$). As the matrix size increases the computation far outweighs the communication so each cell becomes compute bound. The curve flattens because once the array is full of data the degree of exploitable parallelism is maximized forcing the speed-up to tend to a constant. The constant gives an asymptotic bound on the array speed-up for the number of coefficients. Another interesting point is the starting point of each curve which represents (approximately) scalar operations. In each case we can see that the scalar operations give the poorest speed-up; however, for larger number of coefficients some speed-up is possible. One would expect that provided c is large enough reasonable speed-ups can be produced so that the transputer implementation can be regarded as a practical design—this is true but rather misleading. To explain, notice that as c increases the start of each curve becomes more pronounced. Indeed, the actual starting points begin to get closer and closer together so that the speed-up curves tend to a limiting curve, which indicates when the architecture is saturated with data. Once this point is reached increasing the number of coefficients will not improve performance further (this is the principle of diminishing returns). Even more importantly, the size of the array is related to the number of coefficients so that eventually we will need to add more transputers if we are to avoid a number of cells sharing the same processor. In our example, it is not possible to add many more coefficients before this problem arises.

The above example illustrates the complicated trade-offs that are involved in mapping an algorithm onto an architecture. The problem here is particularly simple in that the structure of the array can be modelled directly in hardware. For more involved structures the analysis is even more complicated. However, one important lesson can be learned. If we want to get the best out of a message-passing-type architecture we need to implement cells which process blocks of information. This is because block computations are compute bound. In many problems such as matrix computations block forms of scalar algorithms can be easily found. Likewise in table-generating problems a block structure can be forced on to the array by choosing a suitable partitioning of the table elements. Finally, a larger array can be mapped onto a fixed number of processors by allocating more than one process per processor. The overheads of this artificial mapping can be reduced by rewriting the (virtual) portion of the array in each processor as a sequential pseudo-block process (the block is formed from the computation of individual processes inhabiting the same processor).

7.3 Other languages and architectures

In principle any language that is capable of representing parallel processes and communication between them can be used to simulate systolic computations. In the above discussion we have used OCCAM because it is based on the so-called message-passing approach to parallelism and is supported by an underlying hardware component. The movement of data between cells in a systolic program is mapped readily onto the idea of messages. Other languages such as ADA also support message-passing constructs and can be used to simulate systolic programs. Transputers also support the execution of multiple processes running on the same processor and implements interprocess links in local memory. As the local memory is shared amongst the processes it is easy to extend the basic principles to simulation of systolic programs on shared-memory machines by reading–writing message strings into the shared memory and controlling access by locking mechanisms (e.g. the tuple-space in LINDA). In recent years a wide range of real parallel architectures have begun to emerge and become available for real programming tasks. Clearly it is beyond the scope of this text to survey all the possible architectural variations. Instead we will briefly consider two contrasting approaches which have received significant attention to date.

7.3.1 Hypercubes

A hypercube consists of 2^n nodes (or processors) connected to form an n-dimensional cube. Each node can be uniquely labelled with a binary integer from 0 to 2^{n-1} and any two nodes whose labels differ by only a single bit are said to be adjacent and connected by a communication link. The number of nodes grows exponentially but the interconnection complexity grows only slowly (i.e. $\log_2 P = n$, where $P = 2^n$). Each processor has its own local memory and communicates along connections using message passing. Control can be synchronous or asynchronous but the interconnection length increases as the cube dimension grows, favouring the latter for large networks. The hypercube architecture has been demonstrated to have several useful properties such as high connectivity, low diameter (i.e. the time to move messages across the network), and fault tolerance. In particular it has been shown that many different interconnection topologies can be mapped easily onto the architecture (including linear and 2-D arrays). Recent work by Ibarra and Sohn (1990) has shown that systolic programs can be mapped onto hypercube architectures. Several commercial and research machines have been built and used for a range of problems (see Mudge and Abdel-Rahman 1987; Chan and Saad 1986; Aykanat *et al.* 1988). Many variations of the basic cube architecture are known, for example the cosmic cube (Seitz 1985), a 64 node machine based on Intel microprocessor chips, and the cube-connected-cycles (CCC) machine (Uhr 1984). Both these variants are suited towards VLSI implementation but the latter has limited connectivity at the nodes which allows better area efficiency.

7.3.2 Neural networks

Like systolic algorithms, neural networks are based on an abstraction of human physiology. Systolic arrays consider the pumping action and circulation of blood around the body and abstract the essential details into data flow and synchronous timing of computations. Neural networks are motivated by the organization of the brain in terms of interconnection networks and distributed computations. Very little is known about how the human brain actually computes different algorithms or how the nervous system operates in general. The human nervous system comprises approximately 10^{11}

neurons with 10^{15} connections between them. Consequently it is thought that human reasoning and thought exploits parallelism on a massive scale.

A neural network in computational terms consists of a set of neurons connected as shown in Fig. 7.12. A 'neuron' is a mathematical abstraction of a physical neuron and operates as follows. A number of outputs from other neurons are connected as inputs and a weight is applied to each input to reflect the relative importance of the connection. The total input is then summed to form a net input and a 'squashing' or activation function is applied to force the output of the neuron to fall into a particular range. In the figure a semi-linear function producing values in the range 0 to 1 is used. Thus by applying a pattern of activation to the input the neurons propagate an activation pattern through the network until a final pattern is set on the outputs. It should be clear that each neuron performs the same computation but produces different outputs dependent on the pattern of activation on its inputs. One of the attractive features of a neural network is that it can learn by experience. A network can be trained by presenting a set of input patterns to it, checking the desired network response against the desired output patterns, and using the error to adjust the weight values (zero weights often imply no connection), a process called training. Training continues until the difference between all output patterns and the network output are below a given tolerance. Many training algorithms are known each with its particular advantages and disadvantages (see Rumelhart and McClelland 1987; Wasserman 1989). Once trained the network can be used for very rapid computation. Furthermore if the input is noisy (i.e. contains some errors) or uses a pattern not in the training set the network will attempt to generalize what it has learned to produce an output. This property is highly useful where noisy input is expected, such as in pattern recognition tasks, and can be used to provide highly fault-tolerant networks. Indeed, this surprisingly simple model has been shown to be quite effective for a wide range of applications including text to speech encoding, battlefield management, data compression, and fetal ECG monitoring.

It should be clear that systolic algorithms and neural networks are not dissimilar. Both are algorithmically specialized, rely on massive parallelism, and exploit a simple basic cell as the processing element. However, neural networks exploit arbitrary interconnection networks which may include long connections while systolic algorithms restrict designs to simple regularly connected topologies. A neural network learns the structure of the connection network and can modify the connection topology in the presence of faults or to incorporate new input patterns (when unsupervised training is permitted). A systolic algorithm defines the connection network directly from the data dependencies of the problem and can only tolerate faults when designed specifically to do so. To design a systolic algorithm the sequential computation must be well defined. A neural network will learn to associate different input/output patterns thus removing the need for a well-defined

(a)

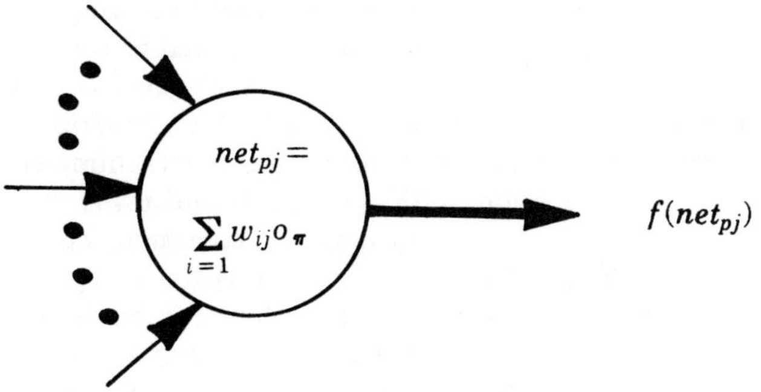

where o_{π} = total output of neuron i for input pattern p

net_{pj} = weighted sum of neron j for pattern p.

$$f(net_{pj}) = \frac{1}{1 + e^{-(net_{pj})}}$$

(b)

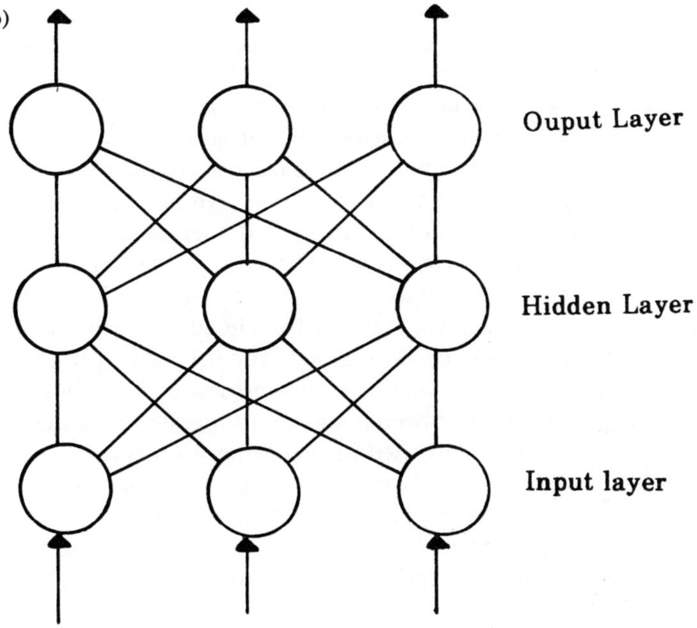

Fig. 7.12 A neural network: (a) neuron; (b) network

algorithm to be known in advance. It should be clear that these attributes are complementary: systolic algorithms are geared to compute-bound number-crunching tasks while neural networks excel at symbolic tasks. Systolic arrays can solve complex numerical problems that humans find cumbersome. Neural networks are fast at recognition, abstraction, and generalization, which are areas of computation where traditionally humans outperform computers. Finally, it is interesting to note that many neural network learning algorithms are often formulated as linear algebra or matrix computations. It follows that systolic algorithms can be designed for simulating neural networks by computing the underlying matrix computations. Where a neural network requires large numbers of neurons such soft-systolic simulation can be promoted as a viable alternative to network construction.

7.4 Design principles

This chapter deals with the idea of systolic programs. The basic theme is that we can map descriptions of systolic algorithms onto general-purpose parallel architectures and generic architectures, or actually construct dedicated VLSI designs. Which type of architecture is adopted depends upon the exact circumstances of the design problem. For example, if the final solution is to be incorporated into an embedded system operating in real time there will be considerable pressure to use a dedicated hardware (possibly silicon chip) implementation. However, simulation and emulation can be important first steps in prototyping a design and checking the timing and data flows. If an emulation or mapping onto a hybrid array architecture meets all the design requirements it may not be necessary to build a truly special-purpose device.

Mapping systolic algorithms into systolic programs can be performed for any parallel language that supports message passing directly or indirectly. The choice of language is left to the designer—we have favoured OCCAM in this chapter because the author has used it successfully to study a wide range of systolic problems. However, handcoding of systolic programs is a laborious task which, once mastered, reduces to specifying the internal computation of sources, sinks, and cells. The generation of a software topology (or harness) can be automated. Indeed some progress towards automatically generating parallel (systolic) programs from both functional and procedural languages has been made. It is suggested here that such tools should be fully integrated and used in the design process.

Finally, the problem of automatically generating efficient parallel code from sequential algorithms remains one of the open questions in parallel processing. The implementation of the design methodology used throughout this book in a software tool together with the automatic generation of systolic programs is an interesting line of current research. It remains to be seen whether the resulting parallel code for systolic programs will run efficiently and compete with equivalent parallel programs designed specifically for different architectures (such as the hypercube, or transputer arrays).

Exercises

1. Write an essay on generic architectures outlining the main features and how they could be used in an existing computing environment.
2. Compare the synchronous model of array operation with the asynchronous model and discuss their effects on systolic systems.
3. Prove that any arbitrary wavefront program can be simulated by an ISA program, and determine complexity bounds for your technique.
4. When a wavefront algorithm involves no backtracking (i.e. no two waves from the same source interfere) show that a WAP can be simulated by a linear array. Comment on the advantages/disadvantages of such a mapping.
5. Encode some algorithms in OCCAM or a suitable parallel language and simulate their behaviour.
6. *Project:* Develop a simulator for systolic algorithms using the ISA concept. Show that your design works by running several examples.
7. Discuss the advantages and disadvantages of emulating systolic algorithms on general-purpose multiprocessors. When would such a practice be beneficial?
8. Demonstrate that a systolic array can simulate a neural network. Comment on the effectiveness of the strategy. When would it be advantageous to simulate a neural network?

8

SYNTHESIS

Synthesis literally means the putting together of parts to make a complex whole. In chemistry synthesis is often taken to mean the artificial production of a desired product from some basic starting materials. Likewise systolic synthesis means deriving a systolic algorithm from a set of recurrence equations. Recently a significant degree of progress towards so-called 'automatic' synthesis of systolic algorithms has been made (Quinton *et al.* 1986; Quinton and Van Dongen 1989; Moldovan 1983; Fortes *et al.* 1988; Li and Wah 1985; Cappello and Steiglitz 1984; Rao 1985). Such developments are promising because they offer to remove many of the tedious technicalities of space–time mappings from the designer leaving him or her free to concentrate on the more intuitive parts of the design process. This final chapter defines the design philosophy of previous chapters more formally and briefly surveys the progress towards software tools for automatic synthesis. It is acknowledged that readers with some knowledge of systolic design will probably skip straight to this chapter and accordingly the author has attempted to make the chapter self-contained.

It is also recognized that synthesis techniques are still relatively new and that the current methods do not provide a completely satisfactory answer. For example, difficulties and restrictions are encountered with:

(1) arrays requiring functionally different cells or multiphase algorithms where the same cell changes function over time;

(2) specification and manipulation of control tags in the design process;

(3) the type of recurrence equation that can be used for the data dependencies;

(4) the structure of the problem domain.

As a result a complete and formal description of every design in this text is somewhat premature, although analysis of some of the simpler matrix problems can be found in the references given above. It is, however, clear that the days of *ad hoc* design are numbered and the promise of such techniques in the future warrants their inclusion.

This material has been left till last for a number of reasons. The first reason is that it requires some additional mathematics. For the uninitiated the first encounter with such details can be a bitter experience which dissuades them from further study. Readers who have troubled themselves to work through the earlier chapters will find that the value of the following mathematical formulation will be readily apparent. Furthermore the intuitive understanding of designs and the design process tends to make the mathematics easier to comprehend. Once a grasp of the basic transformations has been achieved a second pass through the material will provide a much deeper insight into the design process. The ultimate goal of automatic synthesis is to hide away this mathematics in software tools and computer-aided design packages. It follows that a designer needs only to be aware of the general principle of the design process rather than the details of its implementation. The previous chapters have used this general design principle informally and it is hoped that this experience will be an aid to understanding. Indeed, from a historical perspective the recent success in formulating a design principle has resulted mainly from the development of a large pool of clever and practical systolic designs. A concise and informative background to these developments together with a set of excellent references can be found in Rajopadhye and Fujimoto (1990*b*).

8.1 Recurrence equations and data dependencies

In combinatorial mathematics a recurrence equation is an equation that relates a number in a sequence to some of its predecessors. For example

$$x_{i+1} = a_1 x_i + a_2 x_{i-1} + \cdots + a_j x_{n-j} \tag{8.1}$$

is a recurrence equation involving the previous j values in the sequence. When the a_j values are constant the recurrence is said to be *linear*, otherwise it is *non-linear*. A *system* of recurrence equations is simply a set of equations with the form of (8.1) which can be dependent upon each other, or mutually recursive. For example

$$\begin{aligned} x_i &= x_{i-1} + x_{i-2} \\ y_i &= y_{i-1} + x_{i-1} \\ z_i &= z_{i-1} + y_{i-1} \end{aligned} \tag{8.2}$$

and

$$\begin{aligned} x_i &= x_{i-1} + x_{i-2} \\ y_i &= y_{i-1} + x_i \\ z_i &= z_{i-1} + y_i \end{aligned} \tag{8.3}$$

are both systems of recurrence equations in x, y, and z. In the former the values x_i, y_i, and z_i can be computed simultaneously once the preceding values in the sequences are known. In the latter we must compute x_i before y_i, and y_i before z_i. We say that (8.2) depends *strictly* on its predecessors. The set of values that i can take is called the *domain* of the recurrence equation. In the above examples there is no upper and lower bound for the index i so the domain is unbounded or infinite. If we imposed the restriction $i = 1(1)n$ the domain would be bounded or finite for a given value of n. Note that in order to be able to compute the recurrences we require some initial conditions. For eqn (8.2) on the domain $i = 1(1)n$ the values x_0, x_{-1}, y_0, and z_0 must be known. These initial values are not defined as part of the domain and represent inputs to the system of equations.

Equations (8.1), (8.2), and (8.3) have only one index, but there is no reason why recurrences have to be restricted in this way. For example, the following equation is a recurrence with two indices, i and j:

$$x_{i,j} = x_{i-1,j-1} + x_{i-1,j} + x_{i,j-1}. \tag{8.4}$$

It should be clear that each value generated by (8.4) can be located at a particular integer coordinate position in 2-D Euclidean space. Likewise (8.2) and (8.3) can be plotted as points on a line. By extending the notation to express indices as vectors it is clear that (8.4) can be written as

$$f(p) = f(q_1) + f(q_2) + f(q_3) \tag{8.5}$$

where $p = (i, j)$, $q_1 = (i-1, j-1)$, $q_2 = (i-1, j)$, and $q_3 = (i, j-1)$ are vectors belonging to the Euclidean domain of (8.4). Functions are used instead of variables to imply that results are not restricted to simple numerical values but can be functions of the preceding values. A generalization of this idea produces

$$f(p) = g(f(q_1), \ldots, f(q_k)) \tag{8.6}$$

for some $k > 0$. The function g is used to show that $f(p)$ can be an almost arbitrary function of the preceding results. Similarly a system of $r = 1(1)m$ recurrence equations can be expressed as

$$f_r(p) = g_r(f_{r_1}(q_{r_1}), \ldots, f_{r_k}(q_{r_k})) \tag{8.7}$$

and we say that each of the m functions $f_r(p)$ are computed at the point p in Euclidean space.

Next we come to an important definition. A recurrence equation is *uniform* if and only if $q_i = p - w_i$ and the w_i are constant vectors for $i = 1(1)k$. For example, using (8.5), $w_1 = (1, 1)$, $w_2 = (1, 0)$, and $w_3 = (0, 1)$ are constant. It follows that (8.5) is a uniform recurrence equation (URE). The w_i are often called data dependencies because they show which points and hence which functions (or data) the point p depends upon. If we connect points p and q by an edge directed from p to q when q is used on the right-hand side of a recurrence equation and p on the left, the so-called data dependency graph of the URE is produced (reversing the direction of the arcs gives the data flow). For unbounded domains the graph is obviously infinite. Fortunately a finite-sized graph (the reduced data dependency graph (Rao 1985)) can be used to represent the data dependencies. Consider the system of equations in (8.7). To construct a reduced graph, make nodes for each function f_r and then connect the nodes by an edge labelled with the appropriate dependency vector whenever f_j occurs on the right-hand side of the equation defining f_i. In particular suppose we define a single URE as a system of equations (Quinton 1984)

$$\begin{aligned} f_1(p) &= g(f_1(p-w_1), f_2(p-w_2), \ldots, f_k(p-w_k)) \\ f_2(p) &= f_2(p-w_2) \\ f_3(p) &= f_3(p-w_3) \\ &\vdots \\ f_k(p) &= f_m(p-w_k). \end{aligned} \tag{8.8}$$

In this case the reduced dependency graph consists of k nodes and the edges are defined by the data dependency vectors w_i.

UREs are important because it is exactly these kinds of recurrences that allow a direct mapping of computations on to locally connected architectures. In his original work Quinton used only a subset of true UREs which demanded that the parameter k in (8.6) was independent of the problem. The reason for this restriction can be explained as follows. Suppose that (8.6) was to be evaluated on a 2-D domain defined by $i, j = 1(1)n$. If $k = n$ the functions evaluated at each point in space are all different and so intuitively the space is not 'uniform'. The consequences for systolic design are that many different cell types with variable numbers of inputs and data communication (i.e. irregular data flow) across large distances could result. On the other hand restricting k to be independent of the problem (to, say, a small constant) causes the input data for a function at a particular point to be restricted to a localized neighbourhood—thus bounding communication distance and allowing a template of the data dependencies (the reduced data dependency graph) to be replicated across the domain.

8.2 Deriving arrays

We are now in a position to cast the informal design philosophy (used in previous chapters) in a more formal way. The design process derives arrays using three basic steps.

1. *Specification.* This determines a suitable URE for the design process. The derivation is the key to producing novel designs and some manipulation is often necessary to produce a *canonical form* suitable for the rest of the method. In particular more natural (or abstract) representations of the computation can be produced by using linear or affine recurrences which then require the application of a *uniformization* process to produce an equivalent system of UREs.

2. *Determine a timing function.* The timing function defines a partial order

(or *schedule*) on the Euclidean space determining when the points will be evaluated. More formally it is a mapping of the points in the domain to the set of positive integers denoted $t: D \to Z$ where D is the set of points defined by the domain in n-dimensional space. Clearly, two points p and q in D must satisfy $t(p) > t(q)$ if the functions at p depend strictly on functions at q. In particular it is known that if a URE is computable a linear timing function exists. Consequently we assume that t has the form

$$t(p) = \lambda^t p + \alpha \tag{8.9}$$

where λ is an unknown $n \times 1$ vector and α is a scalar. For a single URE (8.9) can be determined by the construction and solution of a linear programming problem derived from the domain and the data dependencies of the problem. A system of UREs leads to an iterative method which requires a solution of a linear program at each stage. In the former case of single UREs the solution of the linear programming problem produces timing functions which are within a constant bound of the optimal result. For the latter it is not known if the timing function is optimal.

3. *Determine an allocation function.* The allocation function maps the computations into a Euclidean space of fewer dimensions. Formally, it is a mapping of the form $a: D \to Z^{n-1}$ where the URE domain is n dimensional. Again (and for purposes of simplicity) allocations will be assumed to be linear functions with the form

$$a(p) = \Gamma p \tag{8.10}$$

where Γ is an $(n-1) \times n$ matrix which has to be determined. Clearly any choice of Γ must ensure that the image of the domain D in $n - 1$ dimensions is bounded, otherwise the resulting array would require unbounded numbers of cells. In addition, for points p and q in the domain $a(p) \neq a(q)$ if $t(p) = t(q)$, otherwise two computations would have to be performed simultaneously on the same processor. For small dimensions (such as $n < 4$) visualization of the Euclidean space gives a good intuitive 'feel' for the type of mapping required. Indeed allocations are simple projections which can be determined by borrowing ideas from computer graphics. Observe that a 3-D space is reduced to 2-D space, and 2-D space to 1-D space, so that practical array topologies are produced. In general a sequence of v projections will map the dependency graph into $(n - v)$-dimensional space providing different scheduling and allocation trade-offs for different designs.

Pairs of timing and allocation functions define different systolic designs. As an illustration consider the following trivial example

$$y_{ij} = y_{i-1,j-1} + a_{i-1,j} \times b_{i,j-1} \tag{8.11}$$

which is to be evaluated in the domain defined by $i, j = 1(1)2$. In this case we can assume that the equation is already in a suitable form so step 1 is not required (we discuss what suitable means later). For $p = (i, j)$ the dependencies are (1, 1), (1, 0), and (0, 1) respectively and a possible partial ordering is evident—point (1, 1) must be computed before points (1, 2) and (2, 1) which can be computed in parallel, etc. Applying this principle across the domain produces the linear system

$$\begin{bmatrix} 1 & 1 & 1 \\ 1 & 2 & 1 \\ 2 & 1 & 1 \\ 2 & 2 & 1 \end{bmatrix} \begin{bmatrix} \lambda_1 \\ \lambda_2 \\ \alpha \end{bmatrix} = \begin{bmatrix} 1 \\ 2 \\ 2 \\ 3 \end{bmatrix} \tag{8.12}$$

which can be solved by Gaussian elimination to produce $\lambda_1 = 1$, $\lambda_2 = 1$, $\alpha = -1$ so that the timing function is

$$t = i + j - 1. \tag{8.13}$$

At this point the reader may be puzzled by one or two facts. For example, the right-hand side of (8.12) is known—hence (8.13) must also be known so why use the linear system at all? The answer is that the problem is so trivial that it is easy to guess a timing function that works. Indeed for small domains one can easily generate a possible right-hand side so the solution of (8.12) just confirms the timing schedule and produces the function (8.13). In general domains may be large and dependencies complicated so such intuitive observations are not easy. Besides, even if we could guess a timing schedule for the domain points, how do we know that the schedule is optimal (i.e. the fastest)? The simple answer is that we do not. The formation of the linear programming (or optimization) problem, which we consider shortly, alleviates the difficulty by constructing a timing function (and hence schedule) which is minimized according to some criteria.

Next consider the allocation function. Because the domain is two dimensional the allocation function demands a 1×2 matrix (or a vector in this case). Again in this case the problem is simple and three projections are immediately obvious:

$$\Gamma_1 = [1 \;\; 0], \quad \Gamma_2 = [0 \;\; 1], \quad \Gamma_3 = [1 \;\; -1]. \tag{8.14}$$

Substituting these values for Γ in (8.10) produces the projections shown in Fig. 8.1. Observe that any other projection direction can be selected provided that it is not parallel to the timing function. If the projection direction is parallel to the timing function it will map computations that need to be performed simultaneously on to the same processor. Intuitively one would expect projection directions perpendicular to the surface defined by the timing function to be most beneficial, because this direction tends to admit the greatest degree of parallelism.

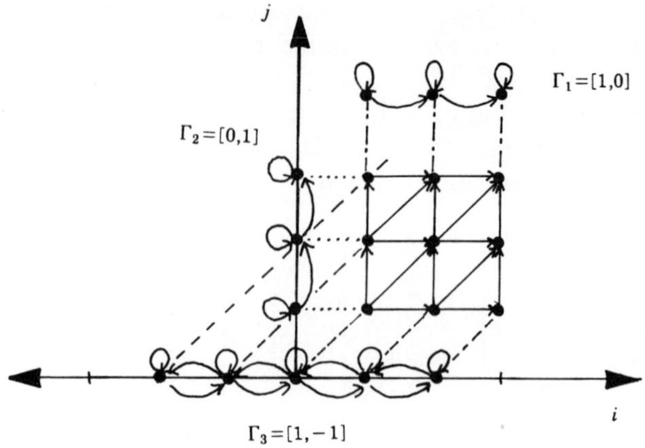

Fig. 8.1 Example projections

Finally a few words about producing the actual systolic array. It is known from the recurrence equations that (2, 2) is the last point of the domain to be calculated. Hence evaluating (8.13) at (2, 2) shows that $t = 3$ steps are required to compute the whole domain. By extrapolating these results to rectangular domains with the form $i = 1(1)n$ and $j = 1(1)m$ and substituting (n, m) into (8.13) the timing equation $\mathcal{T} = n + m - 1$ is produced. Observe that this assumes that computation starts immediately (at time step $t = 1$) and takes no account of any initialization that may be required such as sunchronizing data sequences. A step is, of course, the time to compute all the functions at a point in the domain. The allocation function determines the connection topology and can be used to estimate the design area by counting the number of nodes in the projected graph. Observe also that if the domain is truly 'uniform' the same computations get mapped to every cell of the projected design, so the cell functions are easily determined. If the domain is partitioned into sets of points with different functions the cell actions are more difficult to determine and require some analysis of the projection itself. The only things left to specify are the input and output data sequences, but before we can do this some additional information is required.

8.3 Canonical (or normal) form

Step 1 of the derivation method above asserts that a URE has to be in a suitable form before the rest of the technique can be applied. This standard form is often referred to as the *normal* (Quinton and Van Dongen 1989) or *canonical* form (Cappello and Steiglitz 1984). A canonical form has the following properties:

1. All the UREs have the same index dimension and all the terms are fully indexed.
2. UREs are either input, output, or computation equations.
3. The variables are either input, output, or intermediate variables.

In practice the design method requires only the data dependencies of the computation equations but the input and output equations allow the separation and derivation of the input and output data sequences for the final array design.

To illustrate how to convert a design to canonical form consider the following simple example for evaluating a matrix–vector product. The first step is to write down the problem in recurrence form, that is

$$y_i = y_i + a_{ij}x_j, \quad i = 1(1)n, j = 1(1)n \tag{8.15}$$

where a_{ij} are the elements of an $n \times n$ matrix and x_j are the components of an $n \times 1$ vector. The value y_i accumulates the ith component of the $n \times 1$ vector y and is assumed to be zero at the start. The first thing to observe is that (8.15) is not fully indexed—a_{ij} requires two indices and requires 2-D space, while y_i and x_j have only one index and can be represented in 1-D space. To index the equation fully we simply add zeros to produce

$$y_{i0} = y_{i0} + a_{ij}x_{0j}, \quad i = 1(1)n. \tag{8.16}$$

Now all variables can be mapped into 2-D Euclidean space. For consistency the positioning of the zeros is made so that i indexes stay in the first position and j indexes stay in the second position. Next, notice that (8.16) is not a strict recurrence because y_{i0} depends upon itself. To avoid this problem we will pipeline the y variable to produce

$$\begin{aligned} y_{ij} &= y_{ij-1} + a_{ij}x_{0j}, \quad i = 1(1)n, j = 1(1)n \\ y_{i0} &= 0. \end{aligned} \tag{8.17}$$

The term *pipelining* is appropriate because the partial results of y are pumped in the (0, 1) direction. Unfortunately we still have another problem. The design method (discussed so far) only works for UREs but the equation is non-uniform. Indeed the data dependency vectors are (0, 1), (0, 0), and $(-i, 0)$. The vector $(-i, 0)$ is not constant so (8.17) cannot be uniform. Now jumping ahead of ourselves for a moment, it can be shown that a non-uniform recurrence can be converted into a uniform version by the repeated application of two transformation methods called *pipelining* and *routing*. (The methods are discussed more formally in Section 8.5.) One application of this method produces (8.17) and another can be used to produce

$$\begin{aligned} y_{ij} &= y_{i,j-1} + a_{ij}x_{i-1,j}, \quad i = 1(1)n, j = 1(1)n \\ x_{ij} &= x_{i-1,j} \\ y_{i0} &= 0 \\ x_{0j} &= x_j \end{aligned} \tag{8.18}$$

which change the dependency $(-i, 0)$ into $(1, 0)$, which is constant, making (8.18) a fully indexed system of UREs.

The next step in producing a canonical form is to separate out the input, output, and computation equations using additional variables. It is clear that x_{0j} and y_{i0} are inputs and so is a_{ij}. Likewise we know, from the definition of the computation, that $y_{i,n}$ will be outputs. It follows that (8.18) can be rewritten as follows

$$\left.\begin{aligned} y_{i0}^{(1)} &= y_{i0}, \quad i = 1(1)n \\ x_{0j}^{(1)} &= x_j, \quad j = 1(1)n \\ a_{ij}^{(1)} &= a_{ij}, \quad i, j = 1(1)n \end{aligned}\right\} \tag{8.19a}$$

$$\left.\begin{aligned} y_{ij}^{(1)} &= y_{i,j-1}^{(1)} + a_{ij}^{(1)}x_{i-1,j}^{(1)}, \quad i = 1(1)n, j = 1(1)n \\ x_{ij}^{(1)} &= x_{i-1,j}^{(1)}, \quad i, j = 1(1)n - 1 \end{aligned}\right\} \tag{8.19b}$$

$$y_i = y_{i,n}^{(1)}, \quad i = 1(1)n \tag{8.19c}$$

where (8.19a) are input equations, (8.19c) is an output equation, and (8.19b) are computation equations. Variables with superscripts are intermediate or computation variables, and values with no superscripts are either input or output variables but not both. Equation (8.19) satisfies our three criteria defined above and is in canonical form. Notice that all the data dependency information is contained in (8.19b), the computation equations; (8.19a) and (8.19c) are not required for the determination of timing and allocation functions but can be used to determine the form and direction of input and output data sequences. Figure 8.2 shows the domain of (8.19) together with the data dependencies. Notice that the whole domain can be considered as the union of three separate domains, one each for the input, output, and computation equations. Each domain has its own equations.

8.4 Timing functions and linear programming

Section 8.2 illustrated how to produce the timing function for a design once a schedule for the points in the domain is known. In general the problem of deriving a timing function involves determining the schedule which minimizes the total number of steps to evaluate all the functions at all the

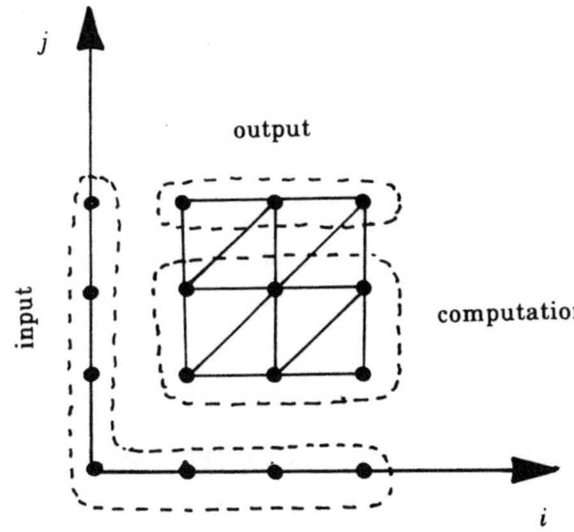

Fig. 8.2 Domains in the canonical form

points in the domain. In this section we show how to solve this scheduling problem for a single URE.

8.4.1 Cones, rays, and vertices

Before we can formulate the problem correctly we require some additional definitions. First, a *convex cone* (S) is a subset of n-dimensional space if and only if any two points p and q in S produce a point $\alpha p + \beta q$ which is also in S for any values $\alpha \geq 0$ and $\beta \geq 0$. Second, the *ray* generated by a point p in n-dimensional space is the set of points defined by $q = \alpha p$ for $\alpha \geq 0$. Now in order to be able to determine whether the URE defined in the domain is computable and has a linear time schedule we need to place certain restrictions on the type of domain allowed. In particular (and for reasons too complex to be discussed here) we must assume that the domain is bounded and can be defined by a set of linear inequalities involving points in the domain. Each inequality defines a half space (i.e. divides the Euclidean space into two disjoint sets of points) and by keeping one-half of the space we can build up a domain that is a convex polyhedron. The corners of this polyhedron are termed *vertices*. Further, it can be shown that the intersection of a finite number of half spaces defines a convex polyhedral cone. Thus the bounded domain of our URE is part of a convex polyhedral cone and reasoning about relationships between points in the domain can be expressed in terms of the properties of convex cones.

8.4.2 The optimization problem

Our task is to determine a timing function with the form (8.9) by defining relationships using the vertices of the domain, the data dependencies of the

URE, and the rays lying inside a convex cone containing the domain. The first two are known from the problem definition, and the latter can be computed.

If we assume that each point in space requires unit time to compute its associated functions it is clear that for two points p and q, $t(p) \geq t(q) + 1$ whenever q is on the right-hand and p is on the left-hand side of the URE. Now let $q = p - w$ where w is the data dependency vector so that the above condition is equivalent to $t(p) \geq t(p - w) + 1$. Because the function t has the form (8.9) we can write

$$\lambda^t p + \alpha \geq \lambda^t(p - w) + \alpha + 1 \rightarrow \lambda^t w \geq 1 \tag{I}$$

which defines the first set of constraints on the schedule. Next, observe that all the vertices v of the problem must satisfy the condition

$$\lambda^t v + \alpha \geq 0 \tag{II}$$

which simply states that all vertices must be computed at some time $t > 0$. Equation (II) produces our second set of constraints. Finally, our third constraint can be written as

$$\lambda^t r > 0 \tag{III}$$

for all the rays r in the convex cone defined by the domain. This last condition is justified as follows. Suppose that the points p and q happen to lie on the same ray r; then $p = \beta r$ and $q = \gamma r$ where $\beta > 0$, $\gamma > 0$, and $\beta > \gamma$ because q precedes p by definition. Now because q precedes p it follows that $t(p) > t(q)$. Thus

$$\lambda^t p > \lambda^t q \rightarrow \beta\lambda^t r > \gamma\lambda^t r$$

and as β and γ are both positive $\lambda^t r > 0$, otherwise we could find a case when $t(q) > t(p)$ which is not allowed.

Conditions (I), (II), (III) allow the formulation of a linear program of the form

$$\text{minimize } \lambda^t g + \alpha = t(g)$$

subject to

$$B\bar{\lambda} \geq d$$

where $\bar{\lambda}$ is an $(n + 1) \times 1$ vector which is just λ augmented with α in the $(n + 1)$th position, d and B are derived from (I), (II), (III), and g is a given point in the domain. If there are k data dependency vectors, e rays, and f vertices, B has dimensions $(k + e + f) \times (n + 1)$. In practice k, e, f, and n are usually small and it is practical to solve the problem using suitable linear programming algorithms (such as the simplex method or an equivalent integer programming method).

To illustrate the technique consider recurrence (8.11). The dependency

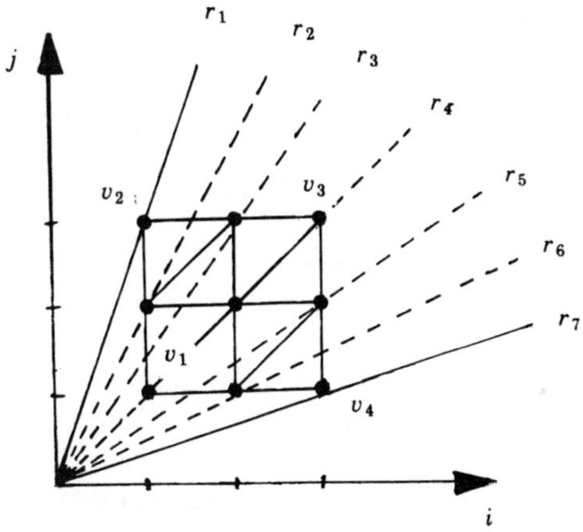

Fig. 8.3 Rays and vertices

graph together with the vertices, rays, and cone are shown in Fig. 8.3. Notice that we choose only the rays which pass through points in the domain. A single ray may pass through many points so the number of rays is usually significantly less than the number of points in the domain. The corresponding set of equations yields

$$B = \begin{bmatrix} 1 & 1 & 0 \\ 1 & 0 & 0 \\ 0 & 1 & 1 \\ 1 & 1 & 1 \\ 1 & 3 & 1 \\ 3 & 1 & 1 \\ 3 & 3 & 0 \\ 1 & 1 & 0 \\ 1 & 3 & 0 \\ 3 & 1 & 0 \\ 1 & 2 & 0 \\ 2 & 1 & 0 \\ 2 & 3 & 0 \\ 3 & 2 & 0 \end{bmatrix}, \qquad d = \begin{bmatrix} 1 \\ 1 \\ 1 \\ 0 \\ 0 \\ 0 \\ 0 \\ 0 \\ 0 \\ 0 \\ 0 \\ 0 \\ 0 \\ 0 \end{bmatrix}$$

Now we want to minimize the time to compute the last point (3, 3) in the domain, so the objective function is

$$\text{minimize } 3\lambda_1 + 3\lambda_2 + \alpha.$$

The solution to this optimization problem is $\lambda_1 = 1$, $\lambda_2 = 1$, and $\alpha = -1$, confirming the result used earlier in Section 8.2. Notice that the timing function is produced without any prior knowledge of the schedule. Indeed it is the URE itself that defines the schedule using parameters independent of the domain size.

For systems of UREs we proceed in a similar manner but first convert the system of equations into a single URE using a process known as *tupling*. Tupling works by noticing that all the functions of a system that are computed at a single point in space can be interpreted as a single function. For example, the system in (8.7) would be written as a single equation with the form $F(p) = \{f_1(p), \ldots, f_m(p)\}$ which is a tuple of the original equations. The $f_i(p)$ occurring on the right-hand sides of the original equations are replaced by $P_i F(p)$ where P_i is a function that produces the ith component of the tuple. Tupling avoids the problems of an iterative solution process but cannot guarantee that the timing function is optimal. Indeed tupling to a single URE is regarded as a conservative method because it is only sufficient to determine a schedule, not necessary.

8.5 Uniformization

A criticism of the design technique described so far is that we need to specify a URE in canonical form for input to the timing and allocation procedures. Further, we saw in Section 8.3 that the form of the initial recurrence may be non-uniform or become non-uniform as we make modifications to produce this canonical form. In particular it was noted that non-uniform equations resulted when a recurrence was fully indexed by adding zero indices. It follows that the success of the design procedure relies on a positive answer to the following question. Can we always rewrite a non-uniform system of recurrence equations as an equivalent set of uniform recurrence equations? For restricted classes of recurrences and domains this question can be answered in the affirmative. In particular, Quinton and Van Dongen (1989) and Rajopadhye and Fujimoto (1990b) show that this mapping exists for linear and affine recurrence equations. The proof of this important result is beyond the scope of this text but leads to the two mechanisms of *pipelining* and *routing* which can be used to produce systems of UREs. The process of rewriting is called *uniformization* and allows the input to the design method to be given in a way that is closer to the original problem specification.

8.5.1 Representing non-uniformity

The first problem to overcome is how to represent a non-uniform recurrence in a way that is amenable to manipulation. One way is to replace the q_i vectors in (8.6) by equations of the form

$$M_i p + b_i \tag{8.20}$$

where M_i is an $n \times n$ matrix and b_i is an $n \times 1$ vector when p is an index vector of dimension n. So, for example, the right-hand-side vectors of the non-uniform recurrence

$$y_{ijk} = y_{i-1,i+k,k} + x_{i-1,j,k-1} \tag{8.21}$$

can be written as

$$\begin{bmatrix} i-1 \\ i+k \\ k \end{bmatrix} = \begin{bmatrix} 1 & 0 & 0 \\ 1 & 0 & 1 \\ 0 & 0 & 1 \end{bmatrix} \begin{bmatrix} i \\ j \\ k \end{bmatrix} + \begin{bmatrix} -1 \\ 0 \\ 0 \end{bmatrix} \tag{8.22a}$$

$$\begin{bmatrix} i-1 \\ j \\ k-1 \end{bmatrix} = \begin{bmatrix} 1 & 0 & 0 \\ 0 & 1 & 0 \\ 0 & 0 & 1 \end{bmatrix} \begin{bmatrix} i \\ j \\ k \end{bmatrix} + \begin{bmatrix} -1 \\ 0 \\ -1 \end{bmatrix} \tag{8.22b}$$

from which it is clear that $M_i = I$ for a uniform index.

8.5.2 Pipelining

The first uniformization mechanism we consider is due to Fortes and Moldovan (1984) and is based on the following observation. Suppose we can choose an arbitrary (non-null) vector v such that $Mv = 0$; then

$$Mp + b = Mp - Mv + b = M(p - v) + b. \tag{8.23}$$

Now suppose our system of equations has the form

$$f(p) = g(\ldots, r_{I(p)}, \ldots) \tag{8.24}$$

where $I(p) = Mp + b$ and r is a variable. Further, denote d_v as the set of points p in the domain of (8.24) for which $p - v$ is not in the domain. We can rewrite the system as follows:

$$f(p) = g(\ldots, R(p), \ldots) \tag{8.25}$$

where

$$R(p) = r_{I(p)} \quad \text{if } p \text{ is in } d_v \tag{8.26a}$$

$$R(p) = R(p - v) \quad \text{otherwise.} \tag{8.26b}$$

The mechanism is best illustrated with an example. Taking (8.22a) we put

$$\begin{bmatrix} 1 & 0 & 0 \\ 1 & 0 & 1 \\ 0 & 0 & 1 \end{bmatrix} \begin{bmatrix} v_1 \\ v_2 \\ v_3 \end{bmatrix} = \begin{bmatrix} 0 \\ 0 \\ 0 \end{bmatrix}$$

from which it is clear that $v = (0, 1, 0)$ is a valid solution. Thus we can rewrite (8.21) as the equivalent system

$$\begin{aligned} y_{ijk} &= Y_{ijk} + x_{i-1,j,k-1} \\ Y_{ijk} &= \begin{cases} y_{i-1,i+k,k} & \text{when } (i,j,k) \text{ is in } d_v \\ Y_{i,j-1,k} & \text{otherwise.} \end{cases} \end{aligned} \tag{8.27}$$

As $y_{i-1,i+k,k}$ occurs only outside the domain it can be treated as an input data item and so (8.27) is uniform.

A more practical example is the problem of convolution discussed in Chapter 1. The recurrence equation is of the form

$$y_{i,j} = y_{i,j-1} + w_j x_{i+j-1}, \quad i = 1(1)n - k + 1, j = 1(1)k \tag{8.28}$$

where the x and w values are known and k is a constant value independent of n. First, fully index the system by adding zero indices to get

$$y_{ij} = y_{i,j-1} + w_{0,j} x_{0,i+j-1} \tag{8.29a}$$

$$y_{io} = 0, \quad i = 1(1)n - k + 1 \tag{8.29b}$$

$$w_{0j} = w_j, \quad j = 1(1)k \tag{8.29c}$$

which is non-uniform. Thus applying (8.20) we express the indices as follows:

$$\begin{bmatrix} 1 & 0 \\ 0 & 1 \end{bmatrix} \begin{bmatrix} i \\ j \end{bmatrix} + \begin{bmatrix} 0 \\ -1 \end{bmatrix} \tag{8.30a}$$

$$\begin{bmatrix} 0 & 0 \\ 0 & 1 \end{bmatrix} \begin{bmatrix} i \\ j \end{bmatrix} + \begin{bmatrix} 0 \\ 0 \end{bmatrix} \tag{8.30b}$$

$$\begin{bmatrix} 0 & 0 \\ 1 & 1 \end{bmatrix} \begin{bmatrix} i \\ j \end{bmatrix} + \begin{bmatrix} 0 \\ -1 \end{bmatrix}. \tag{8.30c}$$

Expression (8.30a) is already uniform and needs no further action. For (8.30b) notice that $v = (1, 0)$ satisfies (8.23) so v is a pipelining vector. Similarly $v = (1, -1)$ satisfies (8.23) for (8.30c). Now applying the pipelining method we can rewrite (8.29) as

$$y_{ij} = y_{i,j-1} + W_{ij} X_{ij}, \quad i = 1(1)n - k + 1, j = 1(1)k \tag{8.31a}$$

$$W_{ij} = \begin{cases} w_{0,j} & i = 1 \\ W_{i-1,j} & i > 1 \end{cases} \tag{8.31b}$$

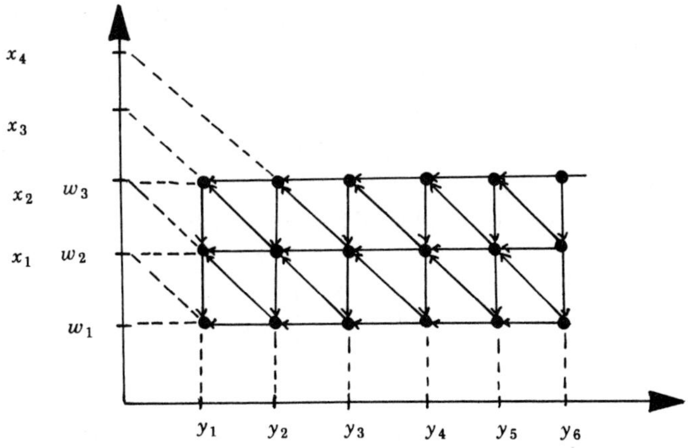

Fig. 8.4 Data dependency graph for convolution

and

$$X_{ij} = \begin{cases} x_{0,j-1} & i = 1 \\ X_{i+1,j-1} & i > 1 \end{cases} \tag{8.31c}$$

$$w_{0,j} = w_j, \quad x_{0,j-1} = x_j, \quad y_{i,0} = 0. \tag{8.31d}$$

Figure 8.4 shows a portion of the data dependency graph for (8.31). A timing function for this graph is $t = 2i + j - 2$ and an allocation function corresponding to the direction $(-1, 0)$ is the vector $(0, 1)$. Other allocations are possible but we choose the one above because $j = 1(1)k$ and k is a small constant independent of n. Projecting out the array produces the design in Fig. 1.1(a). The data sequences can be produced directly by analysing the timing and the projection of the input and output values. It follows that $\mathscr{A} = k$ cells are required and that $\mathscr{T} = 2(n - k + 1) + k - 2 = 2n - k$ steps are necessary. A further $k - 1$ steps must be added to synchronize the data initially.

8.5.3 Routing

Pipelining relies on the fact that we can find a vector v which satisfies (8.23) for a particular index. The set of all v satisfying $Mv = 0$ is called the kernel and it follows that pipelining can only be applied as long as the kernel contains some non-null vectors. Any of the non-null vectors can be used as pipelining vectors provided that they satisfy the conditions for determining a timing function. If the only solution of (8.23) is the null vector pipelining cannot be applied and another method called routing has to be adopted. Routing is based on the idea that all vectors in a given space can be written as a linear combination of vectors that span the space. An n-dimensional space can always be defined by a linear combination of n vectors, that is

$$p = \alpha_1 e_1 + \alpha_2 e_2 + \cdots + \alpha_n e_n \tag{8.32}$$

where α_i are known values and the set of vectors e_i is called the basis. One obvious basis is to choose e_i so that all elements are zero except for the ith value which is one. For example, 3-D space can be represented as

$$p = i\begin{bmatrix}1\\0\\0\end{bmatrix} + j\begin{bmatrix}0\\1\\0\end{bmatrix} + k\begin{bmatrix}0\\0\\1\end{bmatrix}. \tag{8.33}$$

Any point (i, j, k) can be decomposed into i translations in the (1, 0, 0) direction, j translations in the (0, 1, 0) direction, and k translations of the (0, 0, 1) direction. In routing we use linear combinations of vectors but do not demand that a basis is required so in practice a combination with less than n vectors can be used.

To show how to apply the above idea suppose we have the following recurrence

$$y_{ij} = y_{i,j-1} + x_{i-1,j+i-1}. \tag{8.34}$$

The index of x produces a non-uniform equation and can be represented as

$$\begin{bmatrix}1 & 0\\1 & 1\end{bmatrix}\begin{bmatrix}i\\j\end{bmatrix} + \begin{bmatrix}-1\\-1\end{bmatrix}. \tag{8.35}$$

It is easy to show that the components of any vector v in the kernel of the 2×2 matrix must satisfy $v_1 = 0$ and $v_1 + v_2 = 0$. Thus the only vector v available for (8.23) is the null vector preventing the use of pipelining. Equation (8.34) tells us that the data at point $(i-1, j+i-1)$ is required by (i, j) so the linear combination

$$\begin{bmatrix}i\\j\end{bmatrix} - \begin{bmatrix}i-1\\j+i-1\end{bmatrix} = \begin{bmatrix}1\\-i+1\end{bmatrix} = \begin{bmatrix}1\\1\end{bmatrix} + i\begin{bmatrix}0\\-1\end{bmatrix} \tag{8.36}$$

shows how to route data (or results) from $(i-1, j+i-1)$ to (i, j)—simply move one step in the direction (1, 1) and i steps in the $(0, -1)$ direction. Figure 8.5 shows the original and routing vectors. The non-uniformity in (8.34) can be replaced by a linear combination of constant vectors. For each of the directions in the routing path we add an additional variable to the system and control the movement of data using a set of control tags that can be used to change direction at the appropriate points. Thus (8.36) replaces the variables with non-uniform indices by variables with uniform indices but with conditional recurrence equations.

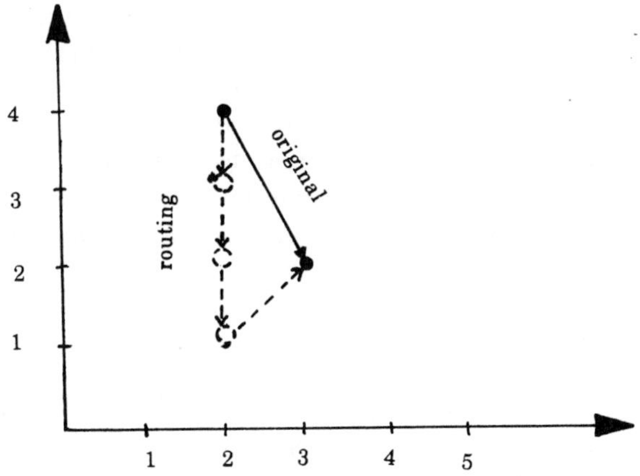

Fig. 8.5 Routing

The idea of routing is to replace non-local movements of data over long distances by sequences of local point-to-point movements. It should be clear that routing can always be applied to a non-uniform equation so why do we need pipelining? The answer is one of efficiency. Routing builds a composite path involving direction changes which in turn lead to additional routing computations and hence extra equations. We must keep track of these changes and build extra control into any cells resulting from a projected design. In pipelining we determine a single vector (v) which is used to replace a particular non-uniformity. This vector yields only a single data dependency and direction of data movement thus simplifying the design.

8.6 Design environments

The preceding sections have defined a design methodology for synthesizing systolic array descriptions by applying various transformations to a system of recurrence equations. However, having worked through the examples the reader is in a position to appreciate that manual application of these transformations is a very tedious and error-prone task, even for simple designs. In particular, derivation of the timing function involves solving the associated linear programming problem which is best left to standard and generally available numerical software packages. The reader can also imagine that the design task would be considerably simplified if facilities for performing pipelining and routing, converting non-uniform recurrences into uniform ones, and generating data sequences were available. Imagine also the possibility of visualizing data dependency graphs on a computer terminal and being able to 'walk' around the domain to view the graph and timing schedules from different perspectives before choosing allocation functions.

An integrated set of software tools for performing these tasks would constitute a systolic algorithm design environment (SADE). Unfortunately (at the time of writing) SADEs are not generally available although some progress towards usable software tools is gaining momentum.

Historically a number of ongoing attempts to develop synthesis software have been made. The most notable among these are ADVIS (Moldovan 1987), DIASTOL (Gachet *et al.* 1986), and SDEF (Engstrom and Cappello 1957). The first is based on a single instance of a system of UREs and uses the tupling approach to produce one URE. ADVIS was also one of the first tools to suggest using an allocation function and recently this idea has been extended to allow the choice of the interconnections to be restricted so that it conforms to a desired topology. In addition it is possible (in certain circumstances) to partition a design so that it produces a multipass algorithm designed for a fixed-size network. DIASTOL and the more recent tool PRESAGE (Van Dongen 1988) are also based on the tupling approach but consider parameterized families of problems and permit the domain to be the union of arbitrary convex polyhedra. Indeed most of this chapter is based on the work of Quinton. The SDEF system is different from the others because it adopts space–time representations of directed acyclic graphs (DAGs). DAGs allow a more intuitive mapping of UREs into space–time and were the basis for the informal discussion in Chapter 2. The original work on DAGs was restricted to completely regular computations. However, it has some advantages in that it allows the user to visualize the design easily and can be augmented to generate code for actual connection topologies. Many other systems exist—some are geared towards generating code for existing architectures while others consider only the determination of timing and allocation functions and leave the rest of the problem to the designer. Synthesis using systems of equations rather than the conservative approach of tupling has also been investigated (cf. Rao 1985).

Systolic synthesis tools are still at early stages of development and a fully integrated system is still some way off. The author hopes to have convinced the reader that continued development is a worthwhile and necessary task. Work is progressing on the use of non-linear timing and allocation functions, the determination of so-called space–time minimal designs, and the generalization of problems in terms of recurrence and domain specification.

8.7 Design principles

Given that primitive SADEs exist and will continue to improve in sophistication, what role is left for the designer? Software tools only aid the design process—they cannot innovate or produce novel designs without guidance. It should be appreciated that, in principle, we could build tools which would take recurrences and search through all the possible design paths and consequently all the timing and allocation functions. Such an approach is not practical because the search space is very large and would consume significant amounts of computer time. Indeed, not all the possible decisons will produce 'good' results. A designer is required to apply intuition and experience to prune the search space and narrow down the possible designs to an acceptably small set for possible implementation. It is hoped that the early chapters in this book will impart some knowledge as to which design decisions seem most profitable.

Another question worth answering is: how can previous design experience be used to guide the synthesis process? To answer this question we need to examine the design method and highlight the areas where choice is important. The first point to note is that the specification of the initial recurrences for a problem is very important. In particular the number and structure of indices leads to the definition of the problem domain and flexibility in the way the problem is converted into canonical form. The computation equations of the canonical form and specification of the domain determine the linear programming problem and hence the timing function. Choose different recurrences and hence different data dependencies, or different ways of fully indexing equations, and different timing functions are produced. Each timing function is only optimal with respect to the defining recurrence equations. Which design produces a globally minimum time schedule is still the subject of research.

Once a problem is in canonical form we have to apply uniformization principles to ensure that the resulting problem is uniform. Recall that for each non-uniformity a set of pipelining vectors corresponding to the kernel of the matrix defined in (8.20) could be used. If we have $n > 0$ non-null vectors there are n different ways of removing the non-uniformity (although not all may lead to valid schedules). For k non-uniformities each with n_i possible pipelining vectors, $i = 1(1)k$, the number of possibilities is $n_1 n_2 \ldots n_k$. The same is true for routing vectors when pipelining cannot be applied. At each stage the choice of pipelining or routing vectors can affect the data dependencies of the problem and hence the timing schedule of the design. We conclude that there is great flexibility in the design process. Once a timing function is known it is necessary to construct connection topologies from projections. In principle we are free to choose virtually any direction for projection provided functions to be evaluated at the same time are mapped to different processors. Many of the projections will provide little or no improvement to the area–time trade-off of a design and must be avoided. Designs in previous chapters have exploited projections that repeatedly prove advantageous. These projections are usually in one of the directions associated with an axis of the index space but directions normal to the surface defined by the timing function are also useful.

Finally, in Chapter 2, we introduced the concepts of array projection, unrolling, and retiming. Let us now take a few moments to relate these intuitive ideas to components of our formal model. It should be clear that an array projection can be represented by a simple many-to-one mapping which we have termed an allocation. That is, many points of the dependency graph are mapped to the same point (or cell) of the array and many arcs are mapped to the same communication link. It can now be appreciated that array unrolling is an 'inverse' mapping which attempts to reconstruct the data dependency graph from the array. We use the quotation marks and say attempts, because in general an unrolling will not produce an exact copy of the data dependency graph and so is not a true inverse. The reason is that an array includes information about routing of the input–output data sequences from the array boundary to the site of the first computation—this information is not explicit in the original data dependency graph. The final concept introduced in this section is that of 'uniformization' which allows non-uniform data dependencies to be converted into uniform ones by use of pipelining and routing. In Chapter 2 we introduced the idea of retiming and cuts. It should be clear that these concepts are applied to an already-projected array to remove non-local connections (i.e. non-uniformities in data flow) and to improve throughput. In contrast pipelining and routing perform much the same task by removing non-uniformities and delay in the unprojected data dependency graph. At which level you choose to apply retiming methods is largely a matter of experience and familiarity with design technique.

In conclusion, this text has been an introduction to the concepts of systolic processing and design. We have concentrated on the intuitive aspects of the design process by introducing a number of designs for different problems. The view has been that the mathematical details of design will (eventually) be hidden away in software packages. The designs presented can be viewed as building blocks and used as a basis for developing more complex algorithms by borrowing concepts of data and control flow, synchronization, and connection topologies to help guide the design process. The design methodology has been used mostly informally so that the technique can be applied and illustrated manually. This final chapter has developed a formal description of the methodology and goes some way to justifying the axioms of systolic computation defined in Chapter 1. It is hoped that designers will graduate to the use of 'automatic' design methods as the software tools become increasingly available.

Exercises

1. Show that any finite computation graph can be represented as a system of UREs.
2. Using the convolution problem in (8.28) experiment with different ways of fully indexing the system. Produce appropriate timing and allocation functions and generate the resultant systolic arrays.

3. The product of two $n \times n$ matrices $C = AB$ can be written as

$$c_{ij} = c_{ij} + a_{ik}b_{kj}$$

for $i = 1(1)n, j = 1(1)n$, and $k = 1(1)n$. Apply the design method to derive timing and allocation functions for the recurrence and compute the maximum computation and the number of cells.
4. Work through Chapters 3, 4 and 5 applying the design principles to each of the problems discussed.
5. Write a program to determine the timing schedule of a given URE using the constraints (I), (II), (III) in Section 8.4.
6. Write a program to compute the projection of a data dependency graph.
7. Develop an algorithm to perform pipelining and routing on a system of recurrence equations.
8. Produce a program to visualize data dependency graphs and their projections. Extend the design to produce snapshots of the computation using a timing function.
9. Consider the design issues associated with the development of a SADE and sketch an outline for the integration of the tools in Exercises 6–8 into your system.
10. Suppose we have m objects which are to be included in a knapsack of capcity c. Let p_j for $j = 1(1)m$ be the value and w_j the weight per unit j. Find the maximum total profit without exceeding the capacity, that is

$$f_k(g) = \max\left(\sum_{j=1}^{m} p_j z_j : \sum_{j=1}^{m} w_j z_j \leq c, z_j \geq 0, j = 1(1)m \right)$$

when z_j is the number of objects of type j and $0 \leq g \leq c$, $1 \leq k \leq m$. The solution can be expressed as

$$f_k(g) = \max(f_{k-1}(g), p_k + f_k(g - w_k)).$$

Apply the design method to this recurrence commenting on any difficulties encountered.

BIBLIOGRAPHY

Ajjanagadde, V. G. and Patnaik, L. M. (1988). Design and performance evaluation of a systolic architecture for hidden surface removal. *Computer and Graphics Journal* **12**(1), 71–4.

Ahmed, H. M., Delsome, J. M., and Morf, M. (1982). Highly concurrent structures for matrix arithmetic and signal processing. *Computer*, **15**, 16–82.

Athale, R. A. and Lee, J. N. (1984). Optical processing using outer product concepts. *Proceedings of the IEEE*, **172**(7), 931–41.

Aykanat, C., Ozguner, F., Ercal, F., and Sadayappan, P. (1988). Iterative algorithms for the solution of large sparse systems of linear equations on hypercubes. *IEEE Transactions Computiny*, **C-37**, 1554–68.

Barada, H. and El-Amawy, A. (1988). Systolic architecture for matrix triangularisation with partial pivoting. *IEEE Proceedings Pt E*, **135**(4), 208–13.

Berzins, M., Buckley, T., and Dew, P. M. (1983). Systolic matrix iterative algorithms. *Parallel Computing 83* (ed. M. Feilmeier, G. Joubert, and U. Schendel), pp. 483–8. North-Holland, Amsterdam.

Bocker, R. P. (1984). Algebraic operations performable with electro-optical engagement processors. *Proceedins of the IEEE*, **72**(1), 212–20.

Bonuccelli, M. A., Lodi, E., Luccio, F., Maestrini, P. and Pagli, L. (1983). A VLSI tree machine for relational databases. *10th Ann. Int. Conf. on Computer Architecture*, 67–3. IEEE Press, New York.

Brenner, K. H. and Lohmann, A. W. (1986). The digital optical computing program at Erlangen. *Conpar86, Proc. Conf. Algorithms and Hardware for Parallel Processing*, Lecture Notes in Computer Science, Vol. 237 (ed. G. Goos and J. Hartmanis), pp. 69–76. Springer, Berlin.

Brent, R. P. and Kung, H. T. (1979). *The area-time complexity of binary multiplication*, Technical Repot CMU-CS-79-05. Department of Computer Science, Carnegie Mellon University.

Brent, R. P. and Kung, H. T. (1984). Systolic VLSI arrays for polynomial GCD computation. *IEEE Transactions. Computing* **C-33**, (8), 731–6.

Brent, R. P. and Luk, F. T. (1984). A systolic Array for the linear time solution of Toeplitz systems of equations. *Journal of VLSI and Computer Systems*, **1**(1), 1–22.

Brent, R. P., Luk, F. T., and Van Loan, C. (1982). Computation of the generalized singular value decomposition using mesh connected processors. *SPIE Real Time Signal Processing*, **341**, 66–76.

Brent, R. P., Kung, H. T., and Luk, F. T. (1983). *Some linear-time algorithms for systolic arrays*, Report CMA-R01-83 (Cornell University) and invited paper *9th World Computer Congress 1983, Paris.*

Brudaru, O. (1985). Systolic algorithms to solve linear systems by iteration methods. *Analele stiintifice ale Universitatii, 'Al.I.Cuza' din Iasi, Tomul XXXI S. Ia Matematica*, pp. 300–6.

Brudaru, O. (1987*a*). Systolic arrays for polynomial quadractic factors computation. *CompEuro'87—VLSI and Computers, Hamburg*, pp. 712–15.

Brudaru, O. (1987*b*). Systolic arrays to solve nonlinear equations by a non-iterative method, *Analele stiintifice ale Universitatii, 'Al.I.Cuza' din Iasi, XXXIII S. Ia Matematica*, f.4, pp. 305–10.

Burden, R. L., Faires, J. D., and Reynolds, A. C. (1981). *Numerical analysis*, 2nd edn, Prindle, Weber, Schmidt, Boston, MA.

Burlisch, R. and Stoer, J. (1966). Numerical treatment of ordinary differential equations by extrapolation methods. *Numerische Mathematik*, **8**, 1–13.

Cappello, P. R. and Laub, A. J. (1988). Systolic computation of multivariable frequency response. *IEEE Translations Automatic Control*, **AC-33** (6), 550–7.

Cappello, P. R. and Steiglitz, K. (1984). Unifying VLSI array design with linear transformations of space-time. *Advances in computing research*, Vol. 2, 23–65. (ed. F. P. Preparatia). JAI Press, Greenwich.

Carré, B. (1979). *Graphs and networks*. Oxford University Press.

Caulfield, H. J., Gruninger, J. H., and Cheng, W. K. (1984). Using optical processors for linear algebra. *SPIE Real Time and Signal Processing*, 190–6.

Caulfield, H. J., Rhodes, W. T., Foster, M. J., and Horvitz, S. (1981). Optical implementation of systolic array processing. *Optics Communications*, **40**, (2), 86–90.

Chan, T. F. and Saad, Y. (1986). Multi-gird algorithms on hypercube multiprocessors. *IEEE Transactions Computing*, **C-35**, 969–77.

Chandy, K. M. and Misra, J. (1986). Systolic algorithms as programs. *Distributed Computing*, **1**, 177–83.

Charlier, J. P. and Van Dooren, P. (1987). *A systolic algorithm for Riccatti and Lyapunov equations*, Research Report, Philips Research Laboratory. An abstract appears in *1st Int. Conf. on Industrial and Applied Mathematics* (*ICIAM 87*), Brussels.

Chen, M.-J. and Yao, K. (1987). On realizations of least-squares estimation and Kalman filtering by systolic arrays. In *Systolic arrays* (ed. W. Moore, A. McCabe, and R. Urquhart), pp. 161–70. Adam Hilger, Bristol.

Choffrut, C. and Culik II, K. (1983). Folding of the plane and the design of systolic arrays. *Information Processing Letters*, **17**, 149–53.

Choffrut, C. and Culik II, K. (1984). On real-time cellular automata and trellis automata. *Acta Informatica*, **21**, 393–407.

Codenotti, B. (1986). The matrix equation $AX + XB = C$ in the VLSI model. *International Journal of Computer Mathematics*, **19**, (1), 93–8.

Corry, A. and Patel, K. (1983). A CMOS/SOS VLSI correlator. *Proc. 1983 Int. Symp. on VLSI Technology: Systems and Applications*.

Culik II, K. and Yu, S. (1985). Translation of systolic algorithms between systems of different topology. *Proc. IEEE-ACM Int. Conf. on Parallel Processing* (ed. D. Degroot), pp. 756–63. IEEE Press.

Deutsch, J., Maulik, P. C., Mosur, R., Printz, H., Ribas, H., Senko, J., Tseng, P. S., Webb, J. A., and Wu, I. C. (1988). Performance of WARP on the DARPA architecture Benchmarks. *Proc. Int. Conf. and Exhibition on Parallel Processing for Computer Vision and Display, Leeds, 1988*.

Dew, P. M. (1984). VLSI architectures for problems in numerical computation. *Workshop on Progress in the Use of Vector and Array Processors* (ed. D. J. Paddon and S. D. Pryce), pp. 1–24. Clarendon Press, Oxford.

Dew, P. M. and McEvoy, K. (1988). The cut theorem—a tool for design of systolic algorithms. *International Journal of Computer Mathematics*, **25**, (3–4), 203–33.

Dew, P. M., Dodsworth, J., and Morris, D. T. (1986). Systolic array architectures for high performance CAD/CAM workstations. *NATO Advanced Study Institute on Fundamental Algorithms for Computer Graphics*, pp. 659–94. Springer, Berlin.

Dew, P. M., Manning, L. J., and McEvoy, K. (1986). A Tutorial on systolic array architectures for high performance processors. *Report 205 Leeds University*, and *2nd Int. Electronic Image Week*, Nice, France.

El-Amawy, A. (1989). A systolic architecture for fast dense matrix inversion. *IEEE Transactions. Computing*, **C-38**, (3), 449–55.

Engstrom, B. R. Engstrom, B. R. and Cappello, P. R. (1987). The SDEF systolic programming system. In *Concurrent Computations* (ed. S. K. Tewksbury, B. W. Dickinson, S. C. Schwartz), Ch. 15, pp. 263–301. Plenum Press, New York.

Evans, D. J. and Hadjidimos, A. (1980). A modification of the Quadrant Interlocking Factorisation parallel method. *International Journal of Computer Mathematics, Section B*, **8**, 149–66.

Evans, D. J. and Megson, G. M. (1986). Romberg integration using systolic arrays. *Parallel Computing*, **3**, 289–304.

Evans, D. J. and Megson, G. M. (1987*a*). Matrix inversion by systolic rank annihilation. *International Journal of Computer Mathematics*, **21**, 319–57.

Evans, D. J. and Megson, G. M. (1987*b*). Construction of extrapolation tables by systolic arrays for solving ordinary differential equations. *Parallel Computing*, **4**, 33–48.

Evans, D. J. and Megson, G. M. (1987*c*). The solution of parabolic partial differential equations by systolic marching techniques. In *Advances in computer methods for partial differential equations* (ed. R. Vichevelsky and R. C. Stepleman) pp. 44–51. IMACS, Lehi.

Evans, D. J. and Megson, G. M. (1988*a*). A systolic array for the quotient difference algorithm *IEEE Proceedings, pt E*, **135**, (1), 60–6.

Evans, D. J. and Megson, G. M. (1988*b*). Compact systolic arrays for incomplete factorisation methods. *International Journal of Computer Mathematics*, **25**, 235–86.

Evans, D. J. and Megson, G. M. (1988*c*). Fast triangularisaton of a symmetric tridiagonal matrix. *Journal of Parallel and Distributed Computing*, **6**, 663–78.

Faddeeva, V. N. and Faddeev, D. K. (1963). *Computational methods of Linear Algebra.* W. H. Freeman & Co.

Feng, T. Y. (1972). Some characteristics of associative parallel processing. *Proc. 1972 Sugamore Computing Conf., Syracuse University*, pp. 5–16.

Feng, T. Y. (1981). A survey of interconnection networks. *IEEE Computer*, Dec. 1981, pp. 12–27.

Fernando, K. V. and Hammarling, S. J. (1986). *Systolic array computation of the SVD of complex matrices*, NAG Technical Report TR4/86, NAG Ltd, Oxford.

Finn, A. M., Luk, F. T. and Pottle, C. (1982). Systolic array computation of the singular value decomposition. *SPIE Real Time Signal Processing V*, **341**, 35–43.

Fisher, A. L. (1984). Implementation issues for algorithmic VLSI processor arrays. Ph.D. thesis. Carnegie Mellon University.

Fisher, A. L., Kung, H. T., Monier, L. M., Walker, H., and Dohi, Y. (1983). Design of the PSC: A programmable systolic chip. *Proc. 3rd Caltech Conf. on VLSI*, (ed. R. Bryant), pp. 287–302. Computer Science Press. Rockville, MD.

Fisher, A. L., Kung, H. T., and Sorocky, K. (1984). *Experience with the CMU programmable systolic chip*, Report CMU-CS-85-161, Carnegie Mellon University. *Proceedings of the SPIE*, **495**, *Real-Time Signal Processing*, **VII**, 1984.

Flynn, M. J. (1972). Some computer organizations and their effectiveness. *IEEE Transactions. Computing*, **C-21**, 948–60.

Fortes, J. A. B. and Moldovan, D. I. (1984). Data Broadcasting in linearly scheduled array processors, *Proc. 2nd Annual Symposium on Computer Architecture*, pp. 224–31. IEEE Press, Silver Springs, MD.

Fortes, J. A. B., Fu, K. S., and Wah, B. W. (1988). Systematic design approaches for algorithmically specified arrays. In *Computer architecture: concepts and systems* (ed. J. M. Milutinovic), pp. 454–94. North-Holland, New York.

Foster, M. J. and Kung, H. T. (1980). The design of special purpose VLSI chips. *IEEE, Computer*, **13**, (1), 26–40.

Frison, P. and Quinton, P. (1985). An integrated systolic machine for speech recognition. In *VLSI: algorithms and architectures* (eds. P. Bertolazzi and F. Luccio), pp. 75–186. North-Holland, Amsterdam.

Fu, K. S., Hwang, K., and Wah, B. W. (1985). VLSI architectures for pattern analysis and image database management. In *VLSI and modern signal processing* (ed. S. Y. Kung, H. J. Whitehouse and T. Kalaith, pp. 434–50. Prentice-Hall, Englewood Cliffs, NJ.

Gachet, P., Joinnault, B., and Quinton, P. (1986). Synthesizing systolic arrays using DIASTOL. In *Systolic arrays*, (ed. W. Moore, A. McCabe, and R. R. Urauhart), pp. 25–36. Adam Hilger, Bristol.

Gentleman, W. M. and Kung, H. T. (1981). Matrix triangularization by systolic arrays. *SPIE Real Time Signal Processing IV*, **298**, 19–26.

Goodman, J. W., Leonberger, F. J., Kung, S. Y., and Athale, R. A. (1984). Optical interconnections for VLSI systems. *Proceedings of the IEEE, Special Issue*, **72**, (7), 850–66.

Guerra, C. (1986). A unifying framework for systolic designs. *Proc. Aegean Workshop on Computing*, Lecture Notes in Computers Science, Vol. 227, (ed. G. Goos and J. Hartmanis), pp. 47–56. Springer, Berlin.

Guerra, C. and Kanade, T. (1985). A systolic algorithm for stereo matching. In *VLSI algorithms and architectures* (ed. P. Bertolazzi and F. Luccio), pp. 103–12. North-Holland, Amsterdam.

Guibas, L. J. and Liang, F. M. (1982). Systolic stacks, queues, and counters. *Proc. 1982 Conf on Advanced Research in VLSI, MIT*, pp. 155–64, MIT Press, Cambridge, MA.

Guibas, L. J., Kung, H. T., and Thompson, C. D. (1979). Direct VLSI implementation of combinatorial algorithms. *Proc. Caltech Conf. on VLSI*, pp. 509–21. California Institute of Technology.

Handler, W. (1977). The impact of classification schemes on computer architectures. *Proc. 1977 Int. Conf. on Parallel Processing*, pp. 7–15. IEEE Press, New York.

Haynes, L. S., Lau, R. L., Siewiorek, D. P., and Mizell, D. W. (1982). A survey of highly parallel computing. *Computer*, Jan. 1982, pp. 9–23.

Hehner, E. C. R. and Hoare, C. A. R. (1983). A more complete model of communicating processes. *Theoretical Computer Science*, **26**, pp. 105–20.

Heller, D. E. (1985). Partitioning bit matrices for small systolic arrays. In *VLSI and modern signal processing* (ed. S. Y. Kung, H. J. Whitehouse, and T. Kalaith), pp. 185–99. Prentice-Hall, Englewood Cliffs, NJ.

Heller, D. E. and Ipsen, I. C. F. (1982). Systolic networks for orthogonal equivalence transformations and their applications. *Proc. Advanced Research in VLSI*, pp. 113–22. MIT Press, Cambridge, MA.

Hoare, C. A. R. (1978). Communicating sequential processes. *Communications of the ACM*, **21**, 666–77.

Hochet, B., Quinton, P., and Robert, Y. (1989). Systolic Gaussian elimination over $G(P)$ with partial pivoting. *IEEE Transactions. Computing*, **638**, (9), pp. 1321–4.

Hockney, R. W. and Jesshope, C. R. (1988). *Parallel Computers 2.* Adam Hilger, Bristol.

Hopcroft, J. E. and Ullman, J. D. (1979). *Introduction to automata theory, formal languages and computation.* Addison-Wesley.

Horowitz, E. and Sahni, S. J. (1978). *Fundamentals of computer algorithms.* Pitman, London.

Householder, A. S. (1980). *The Numerical Treatment of a single non-linear equation.* McGraw-Hill, New York.

Hsu, F. H., Kung, H. T., Nishizawa, T., and Sussman, A. (1982). *LINC: The link and interconnection chip*, Report CMU-CS-84-159, Carnegie Mellon University. *Proc. Conf. on Advanced Research in VLSI*, pp. 113–22. MITT Press, Cambridge, MA.

Huang, A. (1984). Architectural considerations involved in the design of an optical digital computer. *Proceedings of the IEEE*, **72**, (7), 780–6.

Huang, C. H. and Lengauer, C. (1987). The derivaton of systolic implementation of programs. *Acta Informatica*, **24**, (6), 595–632.

Huang, K. H. and Abraham, J. A. (1984). Algorithm based fault tolerance for matrix operations. *IEEE Transactions. Computing*, **C-33**, (6), 518–28.

Hughey, R. P. (1991). Programmable Systolic Arrays. Ph.D. dissertation. Brown University.

Hurley, S. (1986). *Computation of the singular value decomposition using systolic arrays*, NAG Technical Report TR1/86, NAG Ltd, Oxford.

Hwang, K. and Briggs, F. A. (1984). *Computer architecture and parallel processing.* McGraw-Hill, New York.

Hwang, K. and Cheng, Y. H. (1982). Partitioned matrix algorithms for VLSI arithmetic systems. *IEEE Transactions. Computing*, **C-31**, (12), 1215–24.

Ibarra, O. H. and Sohn, S. M. (1990). On mapping systolic algorithms onto the hypercube. *IEEE Parallel and Distributed Computing*, **1**, (1), 48–64.

IEEE special issue on systolic arrays. (1987). *IEEE Computer*, **20**, (7).

Inmos (1984). *OCCAM programming manual*, International Series in Computer Science. Hoare, Prentice-Hall.

Ipsen, I. C. F. (1984). Stable matrix computations in VLSI. Ph.D. thesis. Ann Arbor, MI.

Johnson, L. W. and Reiss, R. D. (1977). *Numerical analysis*, ch. 5. Addison-Wesley, Reading, MA.

Jou, J. J. and Abraham, J. A. (1986). Fault tolerant matrix arithmetic and signal processing on highly concurrent computing structures. *Proceedings of the IEEE*, **74**, (5), 732–41.

Kane, R. and Sahni, S. (1987). A systolic design rule checker. *IEEE Transactions. Computer Aided Design*, **CAD-6**, (1), 22–32.

Katona, E. (1982). String pattern matching algorithms for cellular processors. *Parallel Computing 83* (ed. M. Feilmeier, G. Joubert, U. Schendel), pp. 431–6. North-Holland, Amsterdam.

Katona, E. (1985). A programming language for cellular processor. *Parallel Computing 85* (ed M. Feilmeier, G. Joubert, U. Schendel), pp. 371–6. North-Holland, Amsterdam.

Knuth, D. E. (1973). *Sorting and searching: The art of computer programming*, Vol. 3. Addison-Wesley, Reading, MA.

Koren, I. and Pradhan, D. K. (1986). Yield and performance enhancement through redundancy in VLSI and WSI multiprocessor systems. *Proceedings of the IEEE*, **74**, (5), 699–711.

Krishnan, D. and Patnaik, L. M. (1987). Systolic architecture for boolean operations on polygons and polyhedra. *Eurographics, the European Associaton for Computer Graphics*, July 1987.

Kunde, M., Lang, H. W., Schimmler, H., Schmeck, H., and Schroder, H. (1985). The instruction systolic array and its relation to other models of parallel computers. *Parallel Computing 85* (ed. M. Feilmeier, G. Joubert, U. Schendel), pp. 491–8. North-Holland, Amsterdam.

Kung, H. T. (1980). The structure of parallel algorithms. *Advances in Computers*, **19**, 66–112.

Kung, H. T. (1982*a*). Notes on VLSI computation. In *Parallel processing systems* (ed. D. J. Evans), pp. 339–56. Cambridge University Press.

Kung, H. T. (1982*b*). Why systolic architecture? *Computer*, Jan. 1982, 37–45.

Kung, H. T. (1984*a*). *Systolic algorithms for the CMU WARP processor*, Report CMU-CS-84-158, Carnegie Mellon University. A preliminary version appears in *7th Int. Conf. on Pattern Recognition.*

Kung, H. T. (1984*b*). *Systolic algorithms. Large scale scientific computing*, pp. 127–39, Academic Press, New York.

Kung, H. T. and Lam, M. S. (1984). Wafer-scale integraton and two-level pipelined implementation of systolic arrays. *Journal of Parallel and Distributed Computing*, **1**, 32–63.

Kung, H. T. and Lehman, P. L. (1980). Systolic (VLSI) arrays for relational database operations. *Int. Conf. Management of Data, ACM-SIGMOD*, pp. 105–16.

Kung, H. T. and Lin, W. T. (1983). *An algebra for VLSI algorithm design*, Report CMU-CS-84-100, Carnegie Mellon University.

Kung, H. T. and Menzilciogly, O. (1984). Warp: A programmable systolic array processor. *SPIE Real Time Signal Processing*, **495**.

Kung, H. T. and Song, S. W. (1982). A systolic 2-D convolution chip. Extended abstract in *Proc 1981 IEEE Computer Society Workshops on Computer Architecture for Pattern Analysis and Image Database Management*, pp. 159–60. Also *Multicomputers and image processing, algorithms and programs*, pp. 373–84. Academic Press, New York.

Kung, H. T., Ruane, L. M., and Yen, D. W. L. (1981). *VLSI systems and computations* (ed. H. T. Kung, B. Sproull, and G. Steele), Computer Science Press, Rockville, MD.

Kung, H. T., Ruane, L. M., and Yen, D. W. L. (1983). Two-Level pipelined systolic array for multidimensional convolution. *Image and Vision Computing*, **1**, 30–6.

Kung, S. Y. (1984). On supercomputing with systolic/wavefront array processors. *Proceedings of the IEEE*, **72**, (7), 867–84.

Kung, S. Y. (1985). VLSI array processors. *IEEE ASSP Magazine*, July 1985, 4–22.

Kung, S. Y. (1988). *VLSI Array processors.* Prentice-Hall, Englewood Cliffs, NJ.

Kung, S. Y. and Gal-Ezer, R. J. (1982). Synchronous versus asynchronous computation in very large scale integrated (VLSI) array processors. *SPIE Real Time Signal Processing V*, **341**, 53–65.

Kung, S. Y. and Hu, Y. H. (1983). A highly concurrent algorithm and pipelined architecture for solving Toeplitz systems. *IEEE Transactions. Acoustics, Speech, and Signal Processing*, **ASSP-31**, 66–75.

Kung, S. Y., Arun, K. S., Basher, D. V., and Hu, Y. H. (1981). A matrix dataflow language/architecture for parallel matrix operations based on computational wavefront concepts. *VLSI systems and computations* (ed. H. T. Kung/B. Sproull, and G. Steele), pp. 235–44. Computer Science Press, Rockville, MD.

Kung, S. Y., Arun, K. S., Gal-Ezer, R. J., and Bhashar, D. V. (1982). Wavefront array processor: Language, architecture and applications. *IEEE* Transactions. Computing, Special Issue on Parallel and Distributed Computers, **C-31**, (11), 1054–66.

Kung, S. Y., Whitehouse, H. J., and Kalaith, T. (1985). *VLSI and modern signal processing.* Prentice Hall, Englewood Cliffs, NJ.

Lang, H. W. (1986). The instruction systolic array, a parallel architecture for VLSI. *Integration—the VLSI Journal*, **4**, 65–74.

Legendi, T. and Katona, E. (1988). Micro-programming of cellular processors. *Proc. CONPAR88, Manchester.*

Leighton, F. T. and Leiserson, C. E. (1985). Wafer-scale integration of systolic arrays. *IEEE Transactions. Computing*, **C-34**, (5), 448–61.

Leiserson, C. E. (1981). Area efficent VLSI computation. Ph.D. thesis. Carnegie Mellon University.

Leiserson, C. E. and Saxe, F. (1983). Optimizing synchronous systems. *Journal of VLSI and Computer Systems*, **1**, (1), 41–67.

Lengauer, C. (1988). *On the projection problem in systolic design*, Report CMU-CS-88-102, Carnegie Mellon University.

Li, G. H. and Wah, B. W. (1985). The design of optimal systolic arrays. *IEEE Transactions. Computing*, **C-34**, (1), 66–77.

Lin, F. C. and Wu, I. C. (1985). Area–period tradeoffs for multiplicaton of rectangular matrices. *Journal of Computer and System Sciences*, **30**, 329–42.

Lipschutz, S. (1974). *Linear algebra*, Schaum Outline Series. McGraw-Hill, New York.

Lipton, R. and Lopresti, D. (1986). Comparing long strings on a short systolic array. *Systolic arrays* (ed W. Moore, A. McCabe, and R. Urquhart), pp. 181–90. Adam Hilger, Bristol.

Luk, F. T. and Park, H. (1988). An analysis of algorithm based fault tolerant techniques. *Journal of Parallel and Distributed Computing*, **5**, 172–84.

McCanny, J. V. and McWhirter, J. G. (1982*a*). Completely iterative, pipelined multiplier array suitable for VLSI. *IEEE Proceedings*, **129**, (2)· 40–6.

McCanny, J. V. and McWhirter, J. G. (1982*b*). Implementation of signal processing functions using 1-bit systolic arrays. *Electronics Letters*, **18**, (6), 241–3.

McCanny, J. V. and McWhirter, J. G. (1983). Yield enhancement of bit serial systolic array chips using fault tolerant techniques. *Electronics Letters*, **19**, (14), 525–7.

McKeown, G. P. (1984). *Iterated interpolation using a systolic array*, Report CSA/21/1984, UEA, Norwich.

McKeown, G. P. and Rayward-Smith, V. J. (1984). *A note on the use of systolic arrays for solving network problems*, Report CSA/22/1984, UEA, Norwich.

McKevoy, K. (1986). *A formal model for the hirarchical design of synchronous and systolic algorithms*, Report 7.86, Centre for Theoretical Computer Science, University of Leeds.

McWhirter, J. G., McCanny, J. V., and Wood, K. W. (1982). Novel multi-bit convolver/correlator chip design based on systolic array principles. *SPIE Real Time Signal Processing V*, **341**, 66–73.

Mathias, P. C. and Patnaik, L. M. (1986). A systolic evaluator for linear, quadratic and cubic expressions. *Journal of Parallel and Distributed Computing*, **5**, 729–40.

Mead, C. and Conway, L. (1979). *Introduction to VLSI design*. Addison-Wesley, Reading, MA.

Megson, G. M. (1990*a*). Sorting without exchanges on a bit-serial systolic array. *IEE Proceedings, Pt G*, **137**, (5), 345–52.

Megson, G. M. (1990*b*). Transputer implementationnof systolic arrays for model reduction. *IEE Proceedings, Pt. E*, **137**, (5), 343–52.

Megson, G. M. (1990*c*). A systolic helix for matrix triangularisation with partial pivoting. *Parallel Computing*, **14**, 199–206.

Megson, G. M. (1990*d*). A Fast Faddeev Array. To appear in *IEEE trans on Computers*.

Megson, G. M. and Evans, D. J. (1985). Soft-systolic pipelined matrix algorithms. *Parallel Computing 85* (ed. M. Feilmeier, G. Joubert, and U. Schendel), pp. 171–80. North-Holland, Amsterdam.

Megson, G. M. and Evans, D. J. (1986). The unification of systolic differencing algorithms. *The Computer Journal*, **30**, (3), 83–91.

Megson, G. M. and Evans, D. J. (1987). Matrix power generation using an optical reduced bandwidth systolic array. *IEE Proceedings, Pt J*, **135**, (6), 435–42.

Megson, G. M. and Evans, D. J. (1988*a*). Systolic arrays for group explicit methods for solving parabolic equations. *Proc. Int. Conf. on Systolic and Array Processors, California, USA, 25–27 May 1988.*

Megson, G. M. and Evans, D. J. (1988*b*). Algorithmic fault tolerant matrix operations for triangular arrays. *Parallel Computing*, **10**, 207–19.

Megson, G. M. and Evans, D. J. (1988*c*). A triangular systolic array for matrix product and factorisation. *International Journal of Computer Mathematics*, **24**, 321–43.

Megson, G. M. and Evans, D. J. (1988*d*). Improved matrix product computation using double pipeline systolic arrays. *Computer Journal*, **31**, (6), 567–9.

Megson, G. M. and Evans, D. J. (1989). Systolic algorithms for the iterative solution of sparse linear systems. *Journal of New Generation Computer Systems*, **2**, 111–28.

Megson, G. M. and Evans, D. J. (1990*a*). An orthogonal systolic design for the assignment problem. *Computer Journal*, **33**, 562–9.

Megson, G. M. and Evans, D. J. (1990*b*). The systolic control ring instruction processor (SCRIP). *Integration—the VLSI Journal*, **9**, 287–302.

Megson, G. M. and Evans, D. J. (1990c). On the Suitability of Higher Block matrix forms for systolic LU decomposition. *Journal of New Generation Computer Systems*, **3**, (2), 143–58.

Megson, G. M. and Gaston, F. M. F. (1990). Improved matrix triangularisation using a double pipeline systolic array. *Information Processing Letters*, **36**, 103–9.

Melhem, R. and Rheinboldt, W. C. (1984). A mathematical model for the verification of systolic networks. *SIAM Journal of Computing*, **13**, (3), 541–65.

Minsky, M. (1967). *Computation: finite and infinite machines.* Prentice-Hall, Englewood Cliffs, NJ.

Miranker, W. L. and Winkler, A. (1982). *Space-time representations of computational structures*, IBM Research Report RC9775. (1984) *Computing*, **32**, 93–114.

Moldovan, D. I. (1983). On the design of algorithms for VLSI systolic arrays. *Proceedings of the IEEE*, **71**, (1), 113–20.

Moldovan, D. I. (1987). ADVIS: A software package for the design of systolic arrays. *IEEE Transactions. Computer Aided Design*, **CAD-6**, 33–40.

Moldovan, D. I. and Fortes, J. A. B. (1986). Partitioning and mapping algorithms into fixed sized systolic arrays. *IEEE Transactions. Computing*, **C-35**, (1), 1–12.

Moore, W., McCabe, A., and Urquhart, R. (ed.) (1987). *Systolic arrays.* Adam Hilger, Bristol.

Mudge, T. N. and Abdel-Rahman, T. S. (1987). Vision algorithms for hypercube machines. *Journal of Parallel and Distributed Computing*, **4**, 70–94.

O'Leary, D. P. (1987). Systolic arrays for matrix transpose and other re-orderings. *IEEE Transactions. Computing*, **C-36**, (1), 117–22.

Probst, D. K. and Li, H. F. (1988). Abstract specification of synchronous data types for VLSI and proving the correctness of systolic network implementations. *IEEE Transactions. Computing*, **C-5**, (6), 710–20.

Quinton, P. (1984). Automatic synthesis of systolic arrays from uniform recurrent equations. *Proc. 11th Symp. on Computer Architecture*, pp. 208–14. IEEE, New York.

Quinton, P. and Van Dongen, V. (1989). The mapping of linear recurrence equations on regular arrays. *Journal of VLSI Signal Processing*, **1**, 95–113.

Quinton, P., Joinnault, B., and Gachet, P. (1986). A new matrix multiplication systolic array. In *Parallel algorithms and architectures* (ed. M. Cosnard *et al.*), pp. 259–68. Elsevier, Amsterdam.

Rajopadhye, S. V. (1989). Synthesizing systolic arrays with control signals from recurrence equations. *Distributed Computing*, **3**, 88–105.

Rajopadhye, S. V. and Fujimoto, R. M. (1990*a*). Synthesizing systolic arrays from recurrence equations. *Parallel Computing*, **14**, 163–89.

Rajopadhye, S. V. and Fujimoto, R. M. (1990*b*). Automating systolic array design. *Integration—the VLSI Journal*, **9**, 225–42.

Rao, S. K. (1985). Regular iterative algorithms and their implementation of processor arrays. *Ph.D. thesis.* Stanford University.

Robert, Y. (1985). Block LU decomposition of a band matrix on a systolic array. *International Journal of Computer Mathematics*, **17**, 295–315.

Robert, Y. (1986*a*). Systolic algorithms and architectures. *RR-621I Techniques de Informatique des Mathematiques de la micro electronique et de la microscope quantities, TIM3.*

Robert, Y. (1986*b*). Algorithmique parallele: reseaux d'automates, architectures systoliques, machines SIMD + MIMD. Doctor of Science Thesis. L'Institut National Polytechnique de Grenoble.

Robert, Y. and Tcheunte, M. (1984). Parallel solution of band triangular systems on VLSI arrays with limited fan-out. *Int. Workshop on Modelling and Performance Evaluation of Parallel Systems* (ed. Becker), pp. 209–29.

Robert, Y. and Tchuente, M. (1985). Reseaux systoliques pour des problems de mots. *RAIRO Informatique Theorique/Theoretical Informatics*, **19**, (2), 107–23.

Robert, Y. and Trystram, D. (1985). *An orthogonal systolic array for the algebraic path problem*, Report 553 IMAG 1985, Informatique et Mathematiques Appliquées de Grenoble.

Rosenberg, A. L. (1983). Three dimensional VLSI: A case study. *Journal of the ACM*, **30**, 397–416.

Rote, G. (1985). A systolic array for the algebraic path problem. *Computing*, **34**, 191–219.

Rote, G. (1986). On the connection between hexagonal and uni-directional rectangular systolic arrays. *Proc. Aegean Workshop on Computing (AWOC86), VLSI Algorithms and Architectures—2nd Int. Workshop on Parallel Computing and VLSI, Greece*, Lecture Notes in Computer Science, pp. 70–83. Springer, Berlin.

Rumelhart, D. E. and McClelland, J. L. (1987). *Parallel distributed processing*, Vols I and II. Massachusetts Institute of Technology, MIT Press, Cambridge, MA.

Sameh, A. H. and Kuck, D. J. (1978). On stable parallel linear system solvers. *Journal of the ACM*, **1**, 81–91.

Sami, M. and Stefanelli, R. (1986). R3configurable architectures for VLSI processing arrays. *Proceedings of the IEEE*, **74**, (5), 712–22.

Samwell, P. M. (1986). Experience with occam for simulating systolic and wavefront arrays. *Software Engineering Journal*, Sept., 196–204.

Savage, J. E. (1981). Area-time tradeoffs for matrix multiplication and related problems in VLSI models. *Journal of Computer and System Sciences*, **22**, 230–42.

Schreiber, R. (1982). Systolic arrays for eigenvalue computation. *SPIE Real Time Signal Processing V*, **341**, 27–34.

Schreiber, R. (1983*a*). *Computing generalized inverses and eigenvalues of symmetric matrices using systolic arrays*, Report NA-83-03, Stanford University.

Schreiber, R. (1983*b*). *On systolic array methods for band matrix factorisations*, Report TRITA-NA-8316, The Royal Institute of Technology, Stockholm.

Schreiber, R. (1983*c*). On the systolic arrays of Brent, Luk, and Van Loan. *SPIE Real Time Signal Processing VI*, **431**, 72–7.

Seitz, C. L. (1985). The cosmic cube. Communications of the ACM, **28**, 22–33.

Shapiro, E. (1984). Systolic programming, a paradigm of parallel processing. Extension of the draft paper in *Proc. Fifth Generation Computer Systems (FGCS) 1984*.

Shih, Z. C., Chen, G. H., and Lee, R. C. T. (1987). Systolic algorithms to examine all-pairs of elements. *Communications of the ACM*, **30**, 161–7.

Song, S. W. (1980). A highly concurrent tree machine for database applicatons. *Proc. Int. Conf. on Parallel Processing*, pp. 259–68. IEEE Press, New York.

Sorensen, D. C. (1985). Analysis of pairwise pivoting in Gaussian elimination. *IEEE Transactions. Computing*, **C-34**, (3), 274–8.

Speiser, J. M. and Whitehouse, H. J. (1983). A review of signal processing with systolic arrays. *SPIE Real Time Signal Processing*, **441**.

Swartzlander, E. (1986). Systolic FFT processors. In *Systolic arrays* (ed. W. Moore, A. McCabe, and R. Urquhart), pp. 133–41. Adam Hilger, Bristol.

Thompson, B. C. and Tucker, J. V. (1985). Theoretical consideratons in algorithm design. In *Fundamental algorithms for computer graphics*, (ed. R. A. Earnshaw), pp. 855–78. Springer, Berlin.

Thompson, C. D. (1979). Area–time complexity for VLSI. *Proc. 11the Annual ACM Symp. on Theory of Computing*, pp. 81–8. ACM, New York.

Thompson, C. D. and Kung, H. T. (1977). Sorting on a mesh connected parallel computer. *Communications of the ACM*, **20**, 263–71.

Todd, S. (1978). Algorithm and hardware for mergesort using multiple processors. *IBM Journal of Research and Development*, **22**, (5), 509–17.

Turkedjiev, N. P. (1986). Synthesis of systolic algorithms and processor arrays. *Conpar 86*, Lecture Notes in Computer Science, Vol. 237 (ed. G. Goos and J. Hartmanis), pp. 165–72. Springer, Berlin.

Uhr, L. (1984). *Algorithm structured computer arrays and networks*. Academic Press, New York.

Ullman, J. D. (1984). *Computational aspects of VLSI*. Computer Science press, Rockville, MD.

Umeo, H. (1982). *Two-dimensinal systolic implementation of array algorithms*, Report AL82-32, Osaka University.

Umeo, H. (1985). A class of SIMD machines simulated by systolic VLSI arrays. In *VLSI algorithms and architectures*, (ed. P. Bertolazzi and F. Luccio), pp. 39–48. North-Holland, Amsterdam.

Umeo, H. and Nakatsaka, I. (1987). A design of pipeline interval optimum systolic stack. *Short Communication, Parallel Computing*, **4**, 215–19.

Umeo, H. and Sugata, K. (1982). *Systolic simulation of synchronous SIMD parallel computers*, Report AL82-21, Osaka University.

Umeo, H., Morita, K., and Sugata, K. (1982). Deterministic one-way simulation of two-way real-time cellular automata and its related problems. *Information Processing Letters*, **14**, (4), 158–61.

Van Dongen, V. (1988). Presage, a tool for the design of low-cost systolic arrays. *ISCAC 88*, pp. 2765–8. IEEE Press, New York.

Wah, B. W., Aboelaze, M., and Shang, W. (1988). Systematic designs of buffers in macropipelines of systolic arrays. *Journal of Parallel and Distributed Computing*, **5**, 1–25.

Wasserman, P. D. (1989). Neural computing—Theory and practice. Van Nostrand Reinhold, New York.

Weiser, U. C. and Davis, A. L. (1981). A wavefront notation tool for VLSI array design. In *VLSI systems and computations*, (ed. H. T. Kung, B. Sproull, and G. Steele), pp. 226–34. Computer Science Press, Rockville, MD.

Wirth, N. (1976). Algorithms + data structures = programs. Prentice-Hall, Englewood Cliffs, NJ.

Wynn, P. (1962). Acceleration techniques for iterated vector and matrix problems. *Mathematics and Computing*, **16**, 301–22.

Yaccoby, Y. and Cappello, P. R. (1988). Scheduling a system of affine recurrence equations on regular arrays. In *Int. Conf. on Systolic Arrays* (ed. K. Bromley, S. Y. Kung, and E. Swartzlander), pp. 373–81. IEEE Computer Society, San Diego.

Yang, C. B. and Lee, R. C. T. (1986). The mapping of 2-D array processors to 1-D array processors. *Parallel Computing*, **3**, (3), 231–41.

INDEX